We Dream of
Honour

We Dream of Honour

John Berryman's Letters to His Mother

EDITED BY Richard J. Kelly

W · W · NORTON & COMPANY

NEW YORK · LONDON

FIRST EDITION

The text of this book is composed in Electra, with display type set in Typositor Willow. Composition and manufacturing by Maple-Vail Book Manufacturing Group. Book design by Marjorie J. Flock.

Kathleen Donahue. Previously unpublished poems by John Berryman—as well as published poems not copyrighted—are printed with the permission of Kathleen Donahue.

Faber and Faber, Ltd. From *The Use of Poetry and the Use of Criticism* by T. S. Eliot. Reprinted by permission of the publishers.

Farrar, Straus and Giroux, Inc. Reprinted by permission of Farrar, Straus and Giroux, Inc.: Excerpts from *Short Poems* by John Berryman. Copyright © 1967 by John Berryman. Excerpts from *Delusions, Etc.* by John Berryman. Copyright © 1969, 1971 by John Berryman. Copyright © 1972 by the Estate of John Berryman. Excerpts from *His Toy, His Dream, His Rest* by John Berryman. Copyright © 1964, 1965, 1966, 1967, 1968 by John Berryman. Excerpt from *77 Dream Songs* by John Berryman. Copyright © 1959, 1962, 1963, 1964 by John Berryman. Excerpts from *Recovery* by John Berryman. Copyright © 1973 by the Estate of John Berryman.

Harcourt Brace Jovanovich, Inc. From *Mrs. Dalloway* by Virginia Woolf, copyright 1925 by Harcourt Brace Jovanovich, Inc.; renewed 1953 by Leonard Woolf. Reprinted by permission of the publisher.

Harvard University Press. From *The Use of Poetry* by T. S. Eliot. Reprinted by permission of the publisher.

Louisiana State University Press. Early draft of "Homage to Film" by John Berryman, reprinted from *The Southern Review* (Spring 1940) by permission of Louisiana State University Press.

Macmillan Publishing Co., Inc. "A Prayer for Old Age", four lines from "Parnell's Funeral": reprinted with permission of Macmillan Publishing Company from *The Poems* by W. B. Yeats, edited by Richard J. Finneran. Copyright 1934 by Macmillan Publishing Company, renewed 1962 by Bertha Georgie Yeats. Eight lines from "Coole Park, 1929": reprinted with permission of Macmillan Publishing Company from *The Poems* by W. B. Yeats, edited by Richard J. Finneran. Copyright 1933 by Macmillan Publishing Company, renewed 1961 by Bertha Georgie Yeats. Seven lines from "Michael Robartes and the Dancer": reprinted with permission of Macmillan Publishing Company from *The Poems* by W. B. Yeats, edited by Richard J. Finneran. Copyright 1924 by Macmillan Publishing Company, renewed 1952 by Bertha Georgie Yeats. Excerpts from the following also reprinted with permission of Macmillan Publishing Company: *Autobiography* by W. B. Yeats, copyright 1916, 1936 by Macmillan Publishing Company, renewed 1944, 1964 by Bertha Georgie Yeats; *Per Amica Silentia Lunae* (also included in *Mythologies*) by W. B. Yeats, copyright 1918 by Macmillan Publishing Company, renewed 1946 by Bertha Georgie Yeats; *The Variorum Edition of the Poems of W. B. Yeats*, edited by Russell K. Alspach and Peter Allt (New York: Macmillan, 1957).

New Directions Publishing Corporation. Ezra Pound: *Personae*. Copyright 1926 by Ezra Pound. Reprinted by permission of New Directions Publishing Corporation.

Jean, Jeanne S. and Robert Overstreet. From a letter written by H. A. Overstreet to John Berryman on September 23, 1942. Reprinted by kind permission of Jean, Jeanne S. and Robert Overstreet.

Oxford University Press, Inc. From *The Collected Letters of W. B. Yeats*. Copyright 1987 by Michael Yeats and Anne Yeats.

Random House, Inc. Eight lines from "Look, stranger, on this island now" reprinted from *W. H. Auden: Collected Poems*, edited by Edward Mendelson (copyright 1937 and renewed 1965 by W. H. Auden) by permission of the publishers.

Eileen Simpson. From *Poets in Their Youth* by Eileen Simpson. Reprinted by permission of the author.

A. P. Watt, Ltd. Richard Kelly acknowledges the permission of A. P. Watt Limited on behalf of Michael Yeats and Macmillan (London) Ltd. to quote from the writings of W. B. Yeats.

Library of Congress Cataloging-in-Publication Data
Berryman, John, 1914–1972.
    We dream of honour.
    Includes twenty of Mrs. Berryman's letters to her son
    Includes index.
    1. Berryman, John, 1914–1972—Correspondence.
2. Berryman, Mrs., 1894–1976—Correspondence. 3. Poets,
American—20th century—Correspondence. 4. Mothers—
United States—Correspondence. I. Kelly, Richard J.
II. Berryman, Mrs., 1894–1976. III. Title.
PS3503.E744Z483   1988   811'.54 [B]   87-5678

ISBN 0-393-02477-6

W. W. Norton & Company, Inc., 500 Fifth Avenue, New York, N. Y. 10110
W. W. Norton & Company Ltd., 37 Great Russell Street, London WC1B 3NU

1 2 3 4 5 6 7 8 9 0

To my mother
Constance Livermore
and to the memory of my father
James W. Kelly

Contents

	Illustrations	ix
	Preface	xv
	Acknowledgments	xix
	Introduction	1
	Chronology	10
ONE	Early Years, 1914–1936	13
TWO	Cambridge, 1936–1938	41
THREE	Wayne State and Harvard, 1938–1943	127
FOUR	Princeton, 1943–1954	197
FIVE	Minneapolis, 1954–1959	261
SIX	Last Years, 1959–1972	329
	Index	387

Illustrations

Following page 72

Mrs. Berryman and her grandfather, General Robert Glenn Shaver.

JB with his father, John Allyn Smith, in McAlester, Oklahoma, circa 1915.

JB and Mrs. Berryman, circa 1916.

John Allyn Smith

JB on the day of his graduation from P.S. 69 (Jackson Heights) with his brother Robert Jefferson, 1926.

JB with his graduating class at South Kent School, 1932.

Ernest Milton "Milt" Halliday, in 1934; JB's friend and classmate at Columbia.

Jean Bennett

Mark Van Doren

JB on graduation from Columbia, 1936.

JB with his friend Pedro Donga, on board the *Britannic*.

Pedro Donga's sketch of JB, done on the *Britannic*.

John Angus Berryman, Mrs. Berryman and Robert Jefferson Berryman, September 1937.

Following page 200

JB with Caroline and Allen Tate.

Mrs. Berryman, after she had begun working in the fashion industry.

JB and Bhain Campbell, 1939.

JB, 1940.

JB at Princeton.

Eileen Berryman at Princeton in 1944.

R. P. Blackmur and Nela Walcott on a Princeton picnic.

Mrs. Berryman at Berryman and O'Leary Inc., 1948. Photo taken by Robert Jefferson Berryman.

Robert Jefferson Berryman, cousin Shelby Williams, and JB in Weston, Massachusetts, January 1949.

Martha May Little, JB's maternal grandmother, in 1946.

Mrs. Berryman and client.

JB, circa 1952.

Allen Tate at the University of Minnesota, circa 1960.

JB, Ann and Paul Berryman in Seville, Spain, 1957.

Saul Bellow and his second wife, Alexandra Tschacbasov, in Minneapolis, 1959.

Following page 360

Facsimile of JB's letter dated December 15, 1966, written from Ballsbridge, Dublin.

JB and Kathleen (Kate) Donahue, March 25, 1961, at the Waikiki Room in Minneapolis.

JB and Kate Berryman at the Bread Loaf School of English at Middlebury College, Vermont, summer 1962.

JB receiving the Russell Loines Award for Poetry from Robert Lowell, May 20, 1964.

JB, Adrienne Rich, Mary Jarrell, Peter Taylor, Stanley Kunitz, Richard Eberhart, Robert Lowell, Richard Wilbur, John Hollander, William Meredith and Robert Penn Warren attending a memorial reading for Randall Jarrell at Yale University, February 28, 1966.

Kate and Martha Berryman.

JB and Kate Berryman in front of the house they lived in while in Ballsbridge, Ireland (1966–1967).

JB writing *Dream Songs* at Ryan's Bar in Dublin. *(Also jacket photograph)*

JB at home in Minneapolis, in 1971.

Last photo of JB—New Year's Eve, 1971.

Mrs. Berryman, on day of JB's funeral.

This brief letter, written in early February 1953, marks a breakthrough in JB's long labors on *Homage to Mistress Bradstreet*, which he completed the following month.

Mother

I have always failed;
but I am not failing now.
I have, to read to you,
next week, the induction
(28 ll.) & the first Section
(158 ll.) & a death-grip on
the second. I am holding out
        love,

the Colonial Poem   Tony

Preface

THIS SELECTION of 228 of John Berryman's letters to his mother, from the more than 700 he wrote to her, is the first collection of his letters to be published. Spanning more than four decades, these letters are by far the most extensive and significant he wrote to any one individual. Because his correspondence with Mrs. Berryman was so voluminous and the emotional bond between them was so consequential for his life and work, these letters—together with a few related documents—form a natural unit, deserving of undiluted attention. In making my selection I have attempted to include those letters of the most general biographical and literary interest, as well as those that most illuminate this remarkably intense and complex relationship, while remaining within a reasonable one-volume compass. The major portion of the excluded letters was written during Berryman's early years at South Kent School.

Judging by the scrupulous care the letters were given by Mrs. Berryman throughout her lifetime (she claimed to have saved every one he ever wrote to her, occasionally even typing some out, when, in later years, his handwriting was especially difficult), it is clear that she increasingly realized their value and foresaw their eventual publication. It is largely owing to her that the majority of them remain in remarkably good condition. Nineteen of her most significant and representative letters to him have also been included, but, unfortunately, only a handful of Mrs. Berryman's letters written prior to 1954 have survived. Thus, her letters figure most prominently in the last two sections. The poet's diaries, published and unpublished manuscripts, other letters and papers, and his personal library have been drawn upon for this volume as well.

After Mrs. Berryman's death, in 1976, the collection of her son's letters, along with carbon copies of many of her own, was placed on deposit in the University of Minnesota Libraries' Rare Book Division, by the poet's widow and executor of his estate, Kate Donahue (Berryman). Some forty of Berryman's letters to his mother from the Cambridge years (1936–38)—which he borrowed from her in writing *Love & Fame*—as well as the originals of many of her letters to him, are included in the large collection of Berryman's manuscripts and papers in the University of Minnesota Libraries' Manuscript Division. Most of the letters in this volume were prepared from photocopies made available by the curators of these two collections, after I had consulted the originals.

The majority of Berryman's earlier letters are typed, while most of his later ones are handwritten. Almost all of Mrs. Berryman's surviving letters are typed. Many of their letters contain marginalia which have been inserted in the text at the intended or most appropriate points. Omissions of passages are as few as possible and almost always made to eliminate material of little general or scholarly interest. Other elisions have been made to avoid offense to those still living. Ellipsis points have been used to indicate any substantive deletions of a sentence or more. For Berryman's English fiancée, I have used the initial B., as was his practice, and I have retained his use of "Lise" (a pseudonym used in *Berryman's Sonnets*) for a woman with whom he was involved in 1947. Initials have also been used in reference to a few of Mrs. Berryman's business associates, whose identification could serve no useful purpose.

With the few exceptions in Berryman's early letters from South Kent School, errors in spelling have not been reproduced. Berryman was, in all circumstances, a careful writer and these infrequent lapses, typographical or otherwise, were almost invariably the result of haste or oversight and there is little point in reproducing them. Berryman's own idiosyncratic spelling of words (e.g., "stopt" for "stopped") has of course been retained as has his English spelling—adopted at Cambridge—of most words with American variants. (Since, at different points, he used both "Shakespearean" and "Shakespearian," I have consistently used the former to regularize the spelling of this word.) Berryman's use of abbreviated word forms, increasingly frequent over the years, has been faithfully retained, with occasional editorial interpretations, as has his custom of sometimes repeating words ("boring boring") for emphasis. Similar principles have also been applied to Mrs. Berryman's letters.

Likewise, the punctuation is, in almost all cases, Berryman's—and Mrs. Berryman's—own. Thus, Berryman's preference, beginning in 1931, for modern British practice—such as a more sparing use of commas and the more subtle placement of punctuation in relation to quotation marks— is evidenced thereafter. Since the number of ellipsis points both of them employ often varies arbitrarily, their most common usage, of two dots, has been adopted to avoid confusion with the editorial use of three within a sentence and four at the end. Berryman's occasional use of dashes fol- lowing periods, or in place of periods, has also generally been retained. Punctuation has been added or altered only on those few occasions where the sense of the letter appeared to require clarification.

Son and mother did not always date their letters or specify their places of composition, but in most cases postmarked envelopes, internal refer- ences, or other contextual evidence made it possible to determine this information. Dates and places that I have supplied always appear in brackets. In the few cases where there were discrepancies between the day of the week and the date cited, I have left both references intact and inserted, in brackets, the corresponding date. Datelines have been regularized according to contemporary editorial practice.

In addition to the verse and verse fragments included in the text of the letters, a number of additional poems by Berryman have also been provided. Most of these poems were sent to Mrs. Berryman with the letters. Those selected are generally early versions of subsequently pub- lished poems or represent previously unpublished work. Such poems either further exemplify Berryman's development as a poet, or, most frequently, are of interest here because of their concern with Mrs. Berryman and other family members.

Throughout the text, I have attempted to insert what seemed to me necessary information without detracting from the letters themselves. The introductory materials, explanatory and connecting notes, and bracketed information will, I trust, serve to clarify the content of the letters and provide some context for them in Berryman's life. It is my hope that the letters selected will engage and enlighten the general reader and provide the student of literature with significant documents for the continuing investigation of one of our most important poets.

A brief chronology of Berryman's life, including a listing of his major works, precedes the letters.

Acknowledgments

I WISH TO EXPRESS my gratitude to numerous individuals and organizations without whose help the completion of the book would not have been possible. First and foremost, I am indebted to Kate Donahue (Mrs. John Berryman) for her permission to publish the letters and for her generous cooperation and assistance in all aspects of the preparation of this volume. I am also extremely grateful to Robert Jefferson Berryman, the poet's brother, who graciously spent a day sharing his thoughts and memories with me and on numerous other occasions invaluably responded to my letter and telephone inquiries. A special word of thanks to Eileen Simpson, John Berryman's first wife, for her kindness and helpfulness in answering many questions concerning their years together.

My warmest appreciation, too, to Dr. A. Boyd Thomes and Maris Thomes who spent an evening with me vividly calling up memories of their friendship with Berryman during his Minneapolis years. Also, to Ernest Milton Halliday, Berryman's closest friend at Columbia University, for his hospitality and helpful comments on the poet's early years. I am greatly indebted to Professor Charles Thornbury, editor of the forthcoming *The Collected Poems of John Berryman*, for his assistance in identifying passages from Berryman's unpublished poems, as well as for sharing details of Berryman's life and family history from his biography in progress. My thanks, as well, to John Haffenden, author of *The Life of John Berryman*, for his encouragement and helpfulness.

In preparing the manuscript, my special thanks to Nancy Tufford for her prodigious help in transcribing the letters, for her helpful advice throughout the project, and for her expertise and patience in typing the numerous drafts which these materials went through. I would also like to thank Mollie MacEachern for efficiently typing the introductory materials and making final corrections in the text. And I am extremely grateful to Martha Berryman, John Berryman's eldest daughter, and to Robert Schalinec, for their excellent contributions in proofreading the manuscript.

For doing everything possible to facilitate my work with the manuscripts and related material, I am deeply grateful to Austin McLean, curator of the University of Minnesota Libraries' Rare Book Division, and to his assistant, Tracy Smith, as well as to Alan M. Lathrop, curator of the University of Minnesota Libraries' Manuscript Division, and to his assistant, Vivian Newbold. I am also indebted to the staff of the Rare Book and Manuscript Library of Columbia University's Butler Library—and particularly to Bernard R. Crystal, Assistant Librarian for Manuscripts— for making available their Berryman materials to me.

Valuable contributions to my research were also made by the following persons and institutions: Ann Levine Berryman; Tom Burnett, Reference Department, Harlan Hatcher Graduate Library, University of Michigan; Diane M. Calkins, Librarian, Business, Science and Industry Department, The Free Library of Philadelphia; Mark Day, Associate Librarian, Reference Department, Indiana University Library; P. J. Gautrey, Under-Librarian, Cambridge University Library; Professor Martin E. Gingerich, Department of English, Western Michigan University, Kalamazoo, Michigan; Professor C. Michael Hancher, Department of English, University of Minnesota; Mary Alice Harvey, Library Director, Grand Marais-Cook County Library; Jeanne Berryman Knight, Reisterstown, Maryland; Thomas F. Langley, Cambridge, England; Professor Robert T. Laudon, School of Music, University of Minnesota; Mark McQuiggan, Farmington Heights, Michigan; Professor Edward Mendelson, Department of English, Columbia University; Paul R. Palmer, Curator, Low Memorial Library, Columbia University; Nicholas Pointer, Search Department, Public Record Office, Richmond, England; Earl M.

Rogers, Curator of Archives, University of Iowa Libraries; Thomas Rooney, Ottawa Room, Ottawa Public Library; Charles Schille, Curatorial Assistant, Harvard University Archives; Eric Taylor, Manager, Bowes & Bowes Bookshop, Cambridge, England; Roberta Thomas, Research Assistant, Maritime History Archive, Memorial University of Newfoundland; David E. Turner, Reisterstown Room, Baltimore County Public Library, Reisterstown Branch; Charles P. Whittemore, Senior Master, South Kent School, South Kent, Connecticut; Leah R. Wolf, Employment Administrator, The Catholic University of America.

I would also like to acknowledge a special debt of gratitude to John Haffenden, Eileen Simpson, Ernest Stefanik, Gary Arpin, Joel Conarroe, J. M. Linebarger, Charles Thornbury, and many others, whose work on Berryman has been constantly at my side to inspire and aid me. My debt to John Berryman, as a writer and teacher, is incalculable for all that he taught and continues to teach me.

To my wife, Lois, for all of the help and sustenance that goes unseen but makes the work possible, my boundless love and appreciation. To my family and friends, my gratitude for their forbearance and understanding. I would also like to especially thank my colleagues in the University of Minnesota Libraries for their constant support and assistance throughout this project, as well as the University of Minnesota for providing me with a sabbatical leave in which to complete it.

Finally, and with considerable pleasure, I would like to thank the following people at W. W. Norton & Company: Kathleen M. Anderson, my initial editor, for her belief in the significance of this book from the first one hundred and fifty pages I sent her, and for her resourceful editorial assistance during all but the final stages of its preparation; Hilary Hinzmann, my later editor, for his valuable guidance in seeing it through to completion; and Lelia Ruckenstein, copy editor, and Rose Kernochan, editorial assistant, for their fine and diligent efforts on this volume.

We Dream of Honour

We dream of honour, and we get along.
—John Berryman, *Dream Song 42*

Introduction

I
T IS NOT UNCOMMON for men of literary achievement to have
had strong, willful, adoring and possessive mothers—Thackeray, Proust,
Hart Crane and Thomas Wolfe are among the writers for whom this
was true. But few can have been the object of such lifelong and consuming maternal devotion as was John Berryman. The sheer volume,
intensity, and nature of his letters to Mrs. Berryman manifest that, for
better *and* for worse, theirs was the key relationship of his life.

The letters begin in 1928, when Berryman was fourteen and away at
preparatory school for the first time, and they end in 1971, less than a
year before his death—and just a few months before Mrs. Berryman came
to live near him in Minneapolis. In the intervening years, they provide
both a remarkably candid account of his often chaotic daily existence and
a fascinating record of his thoughts on a wide variety of topics: writing
and writers, friends and enemies, wives and lovers, books, religion, politics, his travels, his poetry readings, his increasingly self-destructive drinking,
and his father's suicide (when Berryman was eleven), which obsessed him
throughout his life. At the same time, they trace, in some detail, his three
careers as poet, scholar and teacher.

The first stirrings of the young Berryman's interest in literature are
voiced in his letters from South Kent School where, at seventeen, he had
already set himself to "develop my own style." His voluminous letters

from Cambridge University, England, provide a fascinating account of his poetic apprenticeship while there; and the lines and stanzas and poems in progress which throng his narrative allow us to chart his developing competence as a poet. The letters themselves clearly served as a means of testing his powers of observation and expression, while providing him with, as he said, a place in which to organize his thoughts.

"Letters can form a style," he had written to Mrs. Berryman from Cambridge and, over the years, it is interesting to note the stylistic changes in the letters and their parallels in his verse. Eventually, the emerging style of the verse has an even more telling impact on that of the letters. Thus the voice in both moves from one which is conventional, abstract, self-conscious and often grand in tone, to one which is increasingly idiosyncratic, direct, assured and tautly forceful. Finally, the letters document Berryman's gradual mastery, most notably expressed in *The Dream Songs*, of a unique poetic style and voice which would earn him recognition as one of the most accomplished poets of his time.

Berryman's scholarly inclinations are also seen to emerge very early. The pages of his youthful letters—especially from Cambridge—bristle with the titles of books just added to what he would, over the years, assemble into an extraordinary personal library. He once remarked that he found scholarship and poetry almost equally interesting, and this is confirmed by the wide range of scholarly enthusiasms expressed throughout the letters. It is further attested to by his lifelong textual and biographical work on Shakespeare, his biographical and critical study of Stephen Crane, and the many excellent critical essays he wrote, most of which were collected in *The Freedom of the Poet*.

Happily, the letters also focus appropriate attention on Berryman's experiences as a teacher. Scintillating and charismatic in the classroom, the force of his mind and personality seemed to exert a sort of gravitational pull on many of his students—as numbers of them have affirmed— drawing them into his orbit, and having a significant influence on their mental and spiritual lives. The letters trace the vicissitudes of Berryman's academic career, from its uncertain beginnings at Wayne State and Harvard, through Princeton and several other universities, to his final sixteen years at the University of Minnesota, where in 1969 he was honored as Regents' Professor of Humanities. They also evidence the unsparingly strenuous way he went about preparing and giving his seemingly impromptu lectures—he used few notes—as well as his impatience with the amount of time and energy they drew from his writing.

Above all, the letters document Berryman's strikingly intense and complex relationship with his mother. Born Martha Shaver Little on July 8, 1894, and raised in St. Louis and Oklahoma, Mrs. Berryman later described her childhood as an unhappy one from which she sought escape by burying herself in books. When she was five her father, Alvin Horton Little, had deserted the family, and it was partly owing to her resemblance to him that Martha believed her mother never loved her. Taught by a tutoress, she also came to feel isolated from other children until, at twelve, she was taken by her mother, Martha May (Shaver) Little, to McAlester, Oklahoma. There, attending a public high school, she graduated before her fifteenth birthday.

The next fall, she entered Christian College, a junior college for young women, in Columbia, Missouri, and two years later, in 1911, graduated as valedictorian and was voted, by a wide margin, the "most brilliant" in her class. She then returned to Oklahoma, where she taught briefly grades four through six in Sasakwa. A year later she married John Allyn Smith, a young bank manager. In 1914 their first son, named John Allyn after his father, was born and in 1919, a second son, Robert Jefferson (called Bob or Jeff in the letters). Following a move to Florida and Mr. Smith's suicide in 1926, Martha married John Angus McAlpin Berryman, a Wall Street bond salesman, and the family settled in New York.

In the years ahead, as her husband's financial situation worsened, Mrs. Berryman took a job in New York as a secretary. Intelligent, energetic, strong-willed and ambitious, she eventually worked her way up to being a highly successful executive in advertising and women's fashions. Having retained her childhood love of books and literature, she successfully infused her sons with these same enthusiasms. She, further, longed to be a writer and, although she never published, found time to write plays and stories. This fragment, from one of her stories, written in August 1931 when John was sixteen, is a revealing meditation on the intensity of thought and emotion, intention and expectation, with which she had, from the beginning, invested their relationship:

. . .They were alone; she pulled her robe aside carefully, bracing the bottle against her left hand, and knew surcease from a life-long ache as his cheek touched her breast. Until he came, there was no beauty: no beauty of slate-gray, remembering eyes, of fine fingers, of clutching toes, of golden fuzz outlining an ear-curve, no beauty, no beauty. She sought the man through the blurred contours of this, the rough model; even now, she reflected tenderly, he was a person, no longer *that baby*, but a small male one to be loved and cared for, comforted and cajoled, companioned and friended. His life should be beyond hers, he need never struggle along the closed-in ways of agony her feet had known so well; he should go warm and wrapped in the safety of love and tenderness.

He pushed at the bottle with his tongue, hunger assuaged, sleep hanging on his lids. Yearning over him, she dribbled milk on her breast and thrust the hardening nipple into his lax mouth; once, twice, he spit it out and then as the flesh-feel aroused him he closed and tugged, drawing long arduous pulls, ceasing only to wail aloud at failure, nuzzling again for the nipple, pulling and drawing, whimpering and crying at the unnatural nothingness. Needle pain was stilled in her by the ecstacy of his need; futility closed iron claws upon her at the anguish of her sterile breast. She had thought suffering had no new mask for her, but this was the bitterest face yet turned upon her—never first, always the second-best was hers. As presently he relaxed, the bitterness of grief grew less keen; his lids closed, opened, half-closed, widened, hovered, opened, shut to, and there was sleep.

It was not possible to lay him down, to let him go from her arms; she would hold him for a little, for just a little space. Perhaps it had been well worth it, to go all these years taking second-best on every hand, and so come to know the glory of the need of this child. He stirred and she looked at the crib, she would put him down in a minute, but not now, not now. It was sweet with a double happiness to hold him so; never in his life would he be more fully hers than now. Now she could know the splendor of close possession, for a little time she would be god; she the all-giver, he the captive of her bounty. For a brief while they would dwell in each other, all-sufficing, content; surely he was hers more than any child had ever been any woman's. The last of the ice-cliffs, sapped by the warming currents of happiness, slid softly into the calm sea, melted, were gone, their months-long dominion forever vanished. Her heart was at rest.

Soon, soon she must give him back to himself, must relinquish the usurped throne; it would be the most difficult of abdications, as it was the most necessary. The violated rights of humankind moaned bitterly at her feet, their bleeding wounds gaping mouths of protest; it would be spending one's life well, to assist him to come to free, full ownership of himself, to insure pleasant days and peaceful nights, kind thoughts, unprejudiced opinions, freedom of thought and emotions . . . and to give him that rarest of all life foundations, the surety of being the most important person in the world to one whose hand lies ever open, a perch of safety for the free bird. It would require the finest of judgement to determine, as his powers waxed, to the exact degree her influence might be withdrawn from the flowing stream, to enable him at last to guide his life in full and able authority. Old age would be a fulfilled time, in which to realize, not that one had made a man, but that one had permitted and given him the tools with which to build a man's proper life. . . .

Mrs. Berryman's ambitions for her firstborn son, John, as expressed in the story fragment, must have been mightily reinforced by the promise he demonstrated from an early age. Beyond her natural maternal fondness and eagerness for his success, she found reason to believe that, with the proper encouragement and support, he might become someone extraordinary—perhaps even realizing her own unfulfilled aspirations to be a writer. And so she redoubled her efforts to be the "all-giver" and to provide him with the "tools with which to build a man's proper life."

In retrospect, the story fragment also suggests how shortsighted was her understanding of their developing relationship and of the ways in which their lives would thereafter unfold and intersect. By continuing to provide unusual support—"financial, spiritual and domestic" for Berryman, well into adulthood—instead of encouraging independence and freedom, she kept him "a captive to her bounty" far too long. Worse, she insisted on being the most important person in his life and, fearing displacement by wives, or other women, grew increasingly possessive, manipulative and demanding. When he wrote her from Cambridge of B., who would eventually become his fiancée, Mrs. Berryman warned him of the dangers that personal happiness might hold for his work.

Such a warning was needless for Berryman, however, who had already embraced the idea of the suffering life as the necessary curse of the artist. More and more, in later years, there was something recklessly brave, or foolhardy, in his courting of suffering—and in his self-destructive behavior—which, at great personal cost, gave his work an unsettling authenticity and force. In a *Paris Review* interview, near the end of his life, Berryman further articulated his credo: "The artist is extremely lucky who is presented with the worst possible ordeal which will not actually kill him. At that point he's in business." It is one of his strengths that, in poem after poem, he was, in fact, able to transform his suffering into art and to universalize it in a way that touches the reader as well.

Still, it is important to understand that, in his letters, as elsewhere, he is sometimes given to extravagant self-pity and to exaggerations of his own plight and that of those around him. Here, this was done largely to extract sympathy from Mrs. Berryman, who was equally capable of such excesses: at times it is as if they are in competition with each other as to who is suffering the most. Typically, however, Berryman knew this about himself, as his comments from his letter of November 24, 1937, demonstrate: "But you must not worry any longer about me. You must assume that I exaggerate or generalize from a moment . . . ." And a few sentences later he skewers his "unhappily persistent capacity for self-pity."

Berryman's youthful letters to his mother from South Kent and later from Cambridge University are unusual not only for their frequency and length, but for their intimacy of tone and feeling. In addition to his exceptional expressions of love and tenderness, he flatters her vanity about her youthful looks and beauty, and reassures her that to no one else has he opened his heart as he has to her. His father's suicide, when Berryman was entering adolescence, surely accounts for some of the obscure but lacerating feelings of guilt he suffered from throughout his life; and Mrs. Berryman's expectations of him as a husband surrogate—even after her remarriage to John Angus Berryman—clearly raised the level of the Oedipal currents swirling around the two of them. In Berryman's novel *Recovery*, the unmistakably autobiographical mother is described as "SEDUCTIVE—'beautiful' forcible, but v. feminine." Whatever the connection between Berryman's early relationship with his mother and his later compulsive womanizing, it is clear that he both sought, and brought out, the maternal instincts in most of the women with whom he became involved.

A persistent thread throughout his letters is a desire to please Mrs. Berryman with his accomplishments. It is as if love manifests itself in achievement and, despite what she says, he cannot be truly loved for what he is, only for what he does. Very early on he evidently came to believe that, in a sense, he was responsible for her health and happiness and well-being. At Cambridge, competing for two scholarships, he noted in his diary entry for October 22, 1937: "I vow to achieve her happiness in all ways open to me. May these prizes give me a start." Throughout his life, even when relations between them were cool, he hastened to let her know of his achievements and honors, seeking her gratification and approval. As she grew older, in a form of emotional blackmail, she often tied her well-being to his writing to her. In her letter of January 3, 1971, when she was ailing, she wrote to Berryman that when her doctor expressed surprise at her improvement, she had informed him "my son's letters were all I needed."

As the years wear on, their letters more frequently reflect a strain between them. On the one hand, Berryman harbors love and gratitude and an excessively grandiose image of her, once even comparing her to St. Teresa of Avila. On the other, he becomes increasingly resentful of her demands, her possessiveness, and her interference in his life. Mrs. Berryman, it appears, had little awareness of when she was overstepping boundaries. Attempting to meet some need of her son's, she would become far too involved and overly helpful and then, having alienated him, withdraw and sulk and resent his lack of appreciation.

Eventually their meetings grew so harrowing that they could hardly bear to be in the same room together. He complained of her nonstop talking and haranguing, a trait confirmed by her second son Robert Jefferson Berryman, who also thought she was at times unaccountably mean to John and did not accord him the respect he deserved. Berryman complained that, often, when they met, she seemed only interested in talking about herself. Some evidence of the swarming, overpowering element of her personality is detectable even in the originals of her letters—where words pour over into the margins and end by crowding the tops and bottoms of pages as though she had to fill all available space—and presumably time.

Given, in addition, Berryman's own extreme intensity, raw-nerved emotional state, and worsening alcoholism (large quantities of alcohol were frequently consumed by both of them when they were together), peaceful meetings between them became nearly impossible for many years. More than ever, letters became their ideal, at times their only, means of communication. In their correspondence, unfettered by tension and drinking, a calm exchange was at least possible—and their more thoughtful selves were able to emerge.

The major turning point in their relationship—a long developing and continuing process—came in the late fifties when Berryman was finally able, with some decisiveness, to break free of his mother's influence and begin to assume more responsibility for his own life. It is no coincidence that thereafter he moved on to the fullest realization of his unique poetic gifts: "Thus his art started, Thus he ran from home / toward home, forsaking too withal his mother / in the almost unbearable smother," he wrote of his protagonist, Henry, in "Dream Song 166." "Dream Song 270," further recalls, in violent terms, Henry's / Berryman's painful process of "halfway" liberating himself from his mother's control over him.

Mrs. Berryman reacted to the gathering force of her son's rebellion by concluding, as seen in her letter of March 26, 1959, that her son was a genius and should not be expected to act as other men. Although there would be continual struggles ahead of them, this professed shift of attitude on her part had the effect of somewhat defusing the situation at a crucial time, of dismissing what she could no longer control, and of preserving what she could of their relationship. But as Berryman knew full well, the only real change had been on his part. In *Recovery*, written in the last year of his life, his alter ego, Alan Severence, speaks of his "unspeakably powerful possessive adoring MOTHER, whose life at 75, is still centered wholly on me."

In the years ahead it was clearly gratifying for Mrs. Berryman to be the mother of a great poet. As in the projected denouement of her short story fragment, old age became, at least on this level, a "fulfilled time," in which to recall how she had provided her son with the opportunities he needed. She had, in a sense, made his achievements possible. Throughout his life, Berryman was also quick to acknowledge how much, amidst the attendant damage, he owed to his mother, as here in *Recovery*: "My debts to her immeasurable: ambition, stamina, resourcefulness, taste . . . , faith (not so clear on that), originality, her sacrifices for my schooling and 1938–39, blind confidence in me."

Then, too, as they grew older, their respective fortunes changed and a role reversal began to occur. After years of struggle and intermittent dependence on her—fame, awards and, prizes and a little money began at last to come to Berryman, while Mrs. Berryman's health and financial situation worsened and she grew increasingly dependent upon his help. In Berryman's last years, he and his third wife, Kate, largely supported her, and eventually brought her to Minneapolis where he attempted, with modest success, to establish a more harmonious relationship with her.

Much earlier Mrs. Berryman had accurately written: "In a tie and relationship as close and long as ours, each has been sadly at fault, each sorely injured." It is remarkable that, despite all of its strain and unravellings, the knot of mutual regard between them held. As Robert Jefferson Berryman noted with some amazement, although it was true they often did not like each other very much, they never stopped loving and admiring one another. That this was true for Berryman is evident in "Dream Song 100," which he wrote on the occasion of his mother's seventy-second birthday in 1966:

> How this woman came by the courage, how she got
> the courage, Henry bemused himself in a frantic hot
> night of the eighth of July,
> where it came from, did once the Lord frown down
> upon her ancient cradle thinking "This one
> will do before she dies
>
> for two and seventy years of chipped indignities
> at least," and with his thunder clapped a promise?
> In that far away town
> who lookt upon my mother with shame & rage
> that any should endure such pilgrimage,
> growled Henry seating, grown
>
> but not grown used to the goodness of this woman
> in her great strength, in her hope superhuman,
> no, no, not used at all.
> I declare a mystery, he mumbled to himself,
> of love, and took the bourbon from the shelf
> and drank her a tall one, tall.

The author of these letters was a serious writer whose reputation must, of course, finally rest upon his art. Like the work, the letters bear within them much of the substance of the man he was—imperfections and all, and yet vividly alive, an undeniable force. Despite an increasingly unmanageable personal life, Berryman never ceased in his efforts to achieve perfection in his art. In this lifelong pursuit he remained, as the British critic Donald Davie once wrote: "not only one of the most gifted and intelligent Americans of his time, but also one of the most honorable and responsible."

Chronology

1914 Born October 25 in McAlester, Oklahoma, the son of John Allyn Smith and Martha (Little) Smith.

1919 Brother, Robert Jefferson, born.

1925 Smith family moves to Tampa, Florida.

1926 JB's father commits suicide. His mother marries John Angus McAlpin Berryman who formally adopts her two sons and gives them his name. Family moves to New York City, where JB attends P.S. 69 in Jackson Heights.

1928–32 Attends South Kent School in Connecticut.

1932 Enters Columbia University. A.B. 1936 (Phi Beta Kappa).

1936 Receives Euretta J. Kellett Fellowship to study in England. Enters Clare College, Cambridge, England. B.A. 1938.

1937 Engaged to B. Wins Oldham Shakespeare Scholarship.

1938 Returns to New York City.

1939 Becomes part-time poetry editor for the *Nation*. Appointed Instructor in English, Wayne State University, Detroit.

1940 Appointed Instructor in English, Harvard University. "Twenty Poems" published in *Five Young American Poets*.

1942 *Poems*, one of a monthly series of poetry pamphlets, published by New Directions. Marries Eileen Patricia Mulligan.

1943 Appointed Instructor in English at Princeton (where he held various positions until 1953).

1944 Awarded Rockefeller Foundation Research Fellowship; works on a critical edition of *King Lear*.

1945 Kenyon-Doubleday Award, first prize, for the short story "The Imaginary Jew."

1947 Affair with "Lise," which is recounted in *Berryman's Sonnets* (1967).

1948 *The Dispossessed*.

1949 Wins Guarantors Prize *(Poetry)* and Shelley Memorial Award (Poetry Society of America).

1950 Publishes critical biography, *Stephen Crane*. Wins Levinson Prize *(Poetry)*.

1952 Appointed Elliston Professor of Poetry, spring semester, University of Cincinnati. Awarded Guggenheim Fellowship for critical study of Shakespeare and for creative writing.

1953 "Homage to Mistress Bradstreet" first published in *Partisan Review*. Spends summer with Eileen in Europe. Separated from Eileen upon their return and spends several months in New York City.

1954 Teaches one semester of creative writing at the University of Iowa and is dismissed for intoxication, profanity and disturbing the peace.

1955 Appointed as lecturer in Humanities Department, University of Minnesota (where he held various positions until his death in 1972).

1956 Divorced from Eileen. Married to Elizabeth Ann Levine. *Homage to Mistress Bradstreet* published as book. Wins Rockefeller Fellowship in poetry from *Partisan Review*.

1957 Awarded Harriet Monroe Poetry Prize, University of Chicago. Son Paul is born. Spends two months lecturing in India for United States Information Service.

1958 *His Thought Made Pockets & The Plane Buckt*.

1959 Divorced from Ann. Receives Brandeis University Creative Arts Award.

1960 *The Arts of Reading*.

1961 Married to Kathleen (Kate) Donahue, his third and last wife.

1962 Visiting Professor at Brown University (1962–63). Daughter Martha born.

1964 *77 Dream Songs*. Receives Russell Loines Award (National Institute of Arts and Letters).

1965   Awarded Pulitzer Prize for *77 Dream Songs*. Receives Guggenheim Fellowship (1966–67).

1966   Lives with family in Dublin (1966–67).

1967   Academy of American Poets Award. National Endowment for the Arts Award. *Berryman's Sonnets* and *Short Poems* published.

1968   *His Toy, His Dream, His Rest.*

1969   Wins National Book Award and Bollingen Prize in Poetry for *His Toy, His Dream, His Rest*. Publishes *The Dream Songs* (complete edition). Appointed Regents' Professor of Humanities at the University of Minnesota.

1970   *Love & Fame.*

1971   Second daughter, Sarah Rebecca, is born. Mrs. Berryman comes to live in Minneapolis. Awarded a Senior Fellowship, National Endowment for the Humanities.

1972   Commits suicide, January 7.

Posthumous Publications

1972   *Delusions, Etc.*

1973   *Recovery.*

1976   *The Freedom of the Poet.*

1977   *Henry's Fate & Other Poems, 1967–1972* (edited by John Haffenden).

PART ONE

Early Years

1914–1936

*J*OHN BERRYMAN *was born John Allyn Smith on October 25, 1914, in McAlester, Oklahoma (population 12,000). Named after his father, he was the first son of John Allyn Smith, a banker, and Martha Little (Smith), a schoolteacher. Shortly after the birth of a second son, Robert Jefferson, on September 1, 1919, the family moved to the even smaller Oklahoma town of Anadarko (population 3,000), where Smith eventually became acting vice president and loan officer of the First State Bank, and where they remained until 1925. Because Smith was a Catholic, Martha had converted when they married and the two boys were raised in the Church. While in Anadarko, JB was an altar boy at Holy Family Church and served mass every morning at six* A.M. *for a Belgian priest named Father Boniface Beri, who, he later wrote, "influenced me as a child only less than my father."*

Owing to personal difficulties with the bank in Anadarko, Smith resigned from his position and worked for a short time as an assistant game and fish warden of Oklahoma. In September of 1925, Smith, his wife, and his mother-in-law, Martha May Little, set out to investigate the possibilities in a then economically booming Florida, where Mrs. Little had long before bought some land, giving her daughter half of it as a wedding present. The boys were temporarily placed in a boarding school, St. Joseph's Academy, in Chickasha, Oklahoma.

After selling half of the property, they jointly bought a restaurant, The Orange

*Blossom, in Tampa and Martha Smith returned briefly to Oklahoma to bring
the boys back with her. She later wrote:*

Mother supervised the kitchen (had 2 cooks), Allyn did the buying and kept the
books, etc. and I learned to make chocolate sodas and all the other drinks behind
the lunch counter, watched over the waitresses during busy times and waited on
the tables in between times, and was cashier. Money rolled in, and luckily such
a good price was offered for the other half of the property, in cash, that against
my mother's wishes, Allyn sold it and he was right.

*Soon, however, things began to go wrong for the family, both economically
and domestically. With the collapse of the Florida land boom in 1926, Smith
was forced to sell the restaurant at a loss, failed in some real estate ventures, and
eventually became estranged from his wife. Before long, he began divorce pro-
ceedings in order to marry a Cuban woman with whom he had been having an
affair.*

*Early in June, the family moved into an apartment in the Kipling Arms, a
building on Clearwater Isle, across the bay from Tampa, owned by a man named
John Angus Berryman. In the ensuing weeks, Smith's behavior became increasingly erratic and threatening both to himself and those around him. Ultimately,
in the early morning of June 26, Martha Smith found her husband's lifeless
body, with a .32 calibre automatic pistol lying next to it, at the rear of the
apartment building.*

*On September 8, 1926, Martha married her landlord, the recently divorced
John Angus Berryman, who, though they called him "Uncle Jack," gave her two
sons his name. About this same time Mrs. Berryman also changed her name
from Martha to Jill Angel. They were married at the Church of the Transfiguration (The Little Church Around the Corner) at 1 East 29th Street in New
York, and soon John Angus began work on Wall Street as a bond salesman. At
the beginning of the school year in 1927, young JB entered eighth grade at
Public School 69 in Jackson Heights, and graduated the following June with an
"A" in both scholastic record and conduct. While there he also won a gold
medal offered by the American Society for the Prevention of Cruelty to Animals.
His composition, "Humane Practices," was selected from those of hundreds of
pupils in the city schools.*

*The next fall he was admitted to the second form at South Kent School, then
beginning its fifth year of existence and situated in the foothills of the Berkshires
in western Connecticut. Molded on the personality of its headmaster and co-
founder Samuel Bartlett, also known as the "Old Man," SKS was an Episcopal
school, and its aged clapboard barracks-like buildings and commitment to devotion and simple tastes made for a largely Spartan existence. It soon became obvious*

that the school, with its further emphases on competitive sports and community spirit, and the not very athletic, withdrawn, intense and intellectual JB were a mismatch.

Thin, bespectacled and openly scornful (a pose most likely assumed in self-defense) of those around him, he was often bullied, once with a nearly tragic result. On March 7, 1931, he recorded in his diary:

Wrote a 500 word, rather informal essay on "The Ideal Way of Living" – the best I've done this year, I think. Did fairly well on the [English] exam. Went for a run in the afternoon. X picked a fight on the tracks and gave me a hell of a beating. I threw myself in front of the train but he, Y and Z dragged me away. Didn't go to the movies, had a long talk with Y and Z. They apologized.

Nonetheless, during his years at SKS he did make a few friends among the other boys, developed some modest athletic ability at tennis, swimming and track, and benefited from sound intellectual guidance from some of the masters—especially Albion Patterson in French and Spanish, Samuel A. Woodward in History, and Father Jasper Kemmis, an Englishman and chaplain who taught Latin and left after JB's second year. As was expected of him, JB distinguished himself academically, consistently ranking at or near the top of his class and, ultimately, becoming the first boy in the school's history to skip the sixth form and go directly on to college. He also wrote articles and editorials for the Pigtail, *the school newspaper, which fostered the habit of writing, and he was increasingly drawn to literature as his major interest.*

Of the more than 300 letters he wrote to Mrs. Berryman from South Kent School, only a few of the most interesting and representative ones have been included here. Most of the letters are concerned with JB's accounts of the academic, athletic and other daily activities of the boys at the school. Many of them draw upon his diaries, which Mrs. Berryman encouraged him to keep, so he could tell her in detail what was happening day by day. A few of them include references to his younger brother Robert Jefferson, who also enrolled at SKS in the fall of 1931. Some of them contain standard boyish complaints about conditions at the school, while others seem to offer a forced cheerfulness for her benefit.

A few of the letters provide insight into JB's strong feelings of anxiety and guilt about being separated from Mrs. Berryman, as seen in the following passage from an otherwise unexceptional letter of January 18, 1929:

I had a most horrible dream last night. . . . I dreamed that you were suddenly taken ill with a fever and died before I could get there. And when I came you were lying on the bed, and you got up and chased me. Then we talked and you said that you were sorry to have to leave me and that it was too bad I'd come too late. Your eyes were glassy and pitiful and you were pale and stiff. I must have cried for hours, even after I woke up and found that it was only a dream. If Jill Angel ever dies, I think I'll kill myself. But De Bebe Dirl isn't going to, is she?

Another letter, written during JB's last year at SKS, attempts to atone for some unspecified but deeply affecting feelings of selfishness, intensified by his perception of his mother's unremitting selflessness and sacrifice:

I was thinking this morning and it came over me how terribly I have acted, both last vacation and for years. I have been terribly and wholly selfish and even my love for you was tinged with it. Here, with the best and sweetest and kindest Mother in the world, I've thought only of myself and made her work harder. . . .

Unfortunately, none of Mrs. Berryman's also numerous letters from these years has survived, but much of their content—from the importance of JB's excelling academically to her desire to be informed about all aspects of his daily life—can be deduced from JB's responses to them. It is also clear that much of his effort—whether academic, athletic or personal—gathered impetus from his desire to please his mother and to meet her high expectations. At the time the letters begin, on JB's fourteenth birthday, he had been at SKS for several weeks.

[South Kent School]
[South Kent, Conn.]

Dear Mother,   Thursday afternoon, 25 October 1928

It seems incredible that I can be fourteen years old, but I am! Neither the cookies nor the stationery have arrived yet, but I expect them this evening. I received both yours and Uncle Jack's letters this morning. I'm glad you were pleased with my grades – I worked pretty hard to get them. Now – not one more word praising myself; I'm afraid that praise has gone to my head.

Mrs. [Clara Christiane] Dulon [the school's house-mother] came back today at noon. Everybody was mighty glad to see her, believe me; everything's become corrupted since she left. I sit at her table now, and it's a good one – she talks most interestingly. She is going to have tea and cake for a few of my friends and me this afternoon later.

I am writing this in study period, but don't be alarmed – all who have over 80 for an average are excused from afternoon study and may do what they wish in that time. That's when I've been writing most of my letters to you lately. You have remarked on the increase in my letters lately, and that's the reason. I have a whole free hour with nothing in particular to do.

Mark how I have advanced in foreign languages: *Ego amo te. Vale, mi mater. Je chéris vous. Au revoir, ma mère.* One of these days I'll be writing letters to you in French or Latin, particularly the latter. I can write, pronounce and translate some *three hundred* Latin words. Isn't that pretty good, considering how long I've taken it?

It is amazing how many French words you can guess the meaning of correctly. I was going through a ten page French vocabulary the other day and found that I knew the meanings of *four hundred* words. Thus, you can easily see that *"arranger"* means "to arrange," by the infinitive ending. And *"chérir"* you could get by remembering "cherish. " It's very interesting.

Must stop now, as study period draws to an end. Lots of love, and a thousand thanks for a happy birthday.

Your devoted fourteen-year-old son,
John Allyn

South Kent School
South Kent, Conn.

Dear Mother,   Monday, 26 November 1928

Day after dafter [sic] tomorrow! Gee! I'll be glad to see you! I'll have been gone three times as long as at camp. And it's only 18 days until I go *home!* Imagine! I don't have an idea as to how the house will look. You're all settled by now, I guess, and I'll be a total stranger. Gee!

And now listen to selfish me – three new *Amazing Stories!* three *Weird Tales* and eleven *Argosies!* Whew! But I'm not going to hibernate like a bookworm. I'll be useful for dishes, windows, cleaning, etc. I've had enough experience! Our whole house couldn't be as bad as Dorm A or Classroom D, New Building (two particularly obnoxious jobs).

We elected a president last night. Pete Merrill, Bill Bagley and John Ward were nominated. As everyone expected, Ward was elected by a large majority and is making a fairly good president.

Maybe it wasn't cold this morning! It was 18 degrees outside and there was ice on the lake – not enough for skating, but we expect that this week. Believe me, it wasn't any fun to pile out at 6:30 with the wind whistling around! And the water for washing was like ice. I shiver to even think of it! It's been freezing all day and heaven help us tonight. I feel like getting under the mattress to keep warm.

We're taking up the Metric System in Math. It is *horrible!* If 1 deka-meter = 4.6293 ft. change 2 yd. 2 ft. 1 in. to dekameters! Whew! O me miserum!

Our history is very interesting. We've finished the Medo-Persian Empire, under Cyrus, Xerxes & Darius, and are taking up the study of ancient Palestine and the Hebrews. It's all about Isiah [sic], Amos, Jere-miah, Solomon and bloody Elijah. My *Bible* is very interesting and help-ful for extra reading. I've read a lot of it – about Abraham and Isaac and Jacob.

A lot of fellows (not lazy me, who was washing windows) were down at the lake today and carried the rink boards down to the shore in prepa-ration for the setting-up of the rink when ice comes. I'm glad I'm out for hockey – manager for hockey is a rotten job.

You'll know this school better than I do before you leave Thanksgiv-ing. I'm going to show you absolutely *everything*. Then in my letters, I can talk South Kent Slang (SKS) like "hours," "called up," etc.

I'm sorry this isn't longer, but the school is very newsless just now. I look forward with pleasure to a letter tonight and more than that to *Thanksgiving* – Love and kisses to all and to the dearest mother on earth

Your loving son,

John Allyn

South Kent School

South Kent, Conn.

Dear Mother,   Sunday, 14 April 1929 – 3:30 P.M.

We got our marks this noon. In one way I was pleased with them, but in another, I wasn't, for they are still below 90, although not so far as before. Here are my marks for this first month:

Subject	First 2 Weeks	Second Weeks	Monthly Average
English	85	91	88
History	83	91	87
French	86	84	85
Latin	90	94	92
Math	92	88	90
Averages	87.2	89.6	88.4

This two weeks' average and the month's average are the highest I've ever had. I don't know how I stand in comparison with [Durand] Echeverria, but I lead the form by 4 points. [H. Dunlop] Dawbarn is 84.1 for the month, [Frank] Forester 81.5, and [John] Ward below 80. I think I have a chance of beating Itch [Echeverria] and leading the school for the year, but that 90 yearly average is – well, I doubt it. By the way, (I'm not working for those prizes or anything, only to please you) but do you remember whether the blazer, etc. were to be for leading S.K.S. or a 90 average?

I received a fine letter from you last night – the first since Tuesday. I gather that you have been busy, and hope you will not be so rushed next week. For some unknown reason my tennis shoes have not yet come: I wonder what could have happened to them. My socks haven't come, either, but I'm not worrying about them. You have sure received them, haven't you?, although you said nothing about them in your letter. I find that several pairs of my socks are too small for me – I can't get my foot into the scout socks and some lighter pairs, although the big heavy woolen ones are large.

How about that laundry case? It's about $1.65 postage prepaid and I can get it in about a week after it is ordered. Then I can use it for the rest of this term.

I haven't been reported on my job or gotten an hour since my last letter, although I had a nasty job yesterday (Dorm B). We've been here almost a month. That's only two reports and no hours in a whole month. But I shouldn't get swell-headed, for it's so easy to get reported.

I didn't go to either poptent or movies last night, but studied and worked on the *Pigtail* [the school paper]. I'm really interested in that and have done more work on it than almost any other "heeler" (a lower former out for the *Pigtail* who hasn't yet made the board). I have thirteen lines in the one that came out Saturday. You'll find my articles on the last page, the one about the new books for the library and the one about Sunday being a hot day. I think my editorial, "The Weather," is going in the next *Pigtail*. Here's hoping. Follows a copy of it:

The Weather

The weather is the most perverse and unstable of all the elements. It is often the exact opposite of what it should be, and is seldom what one expects it to be. If one waits three days for a pleasant one for an outing (during which time it has rained continuously) and decides to give it up and calls the outing off, the next day is sure to be warm and sunshiny and springlike. It is a capricious and playful spirit that controls our weather.

And nowhere is the weather so uncertain as in our own state of Connecticut. Who knows what to expect, when we have an 88 degree temperature in April and snow a week later? We expect everything and are often disappointed.

What do you think of it?

The school and form pictures came the other day and were given out in small, cardboard frames. They are too large to ship conveniently and I think I'll keep them here this term. I have an awful lot of things to show Uncle Jack – do hope he can come up for Father's Weekend. Use your mighty influence, Bebe Dirl, but tell me if you don't think he feels well enough or shouldn't miss the business or anything like that and I'll gladly stop talking about it that moment.

About baseball: When I told you that I could play O.K. without my glasses, all I had done was catch with a fellow from a short distance. I tried outfield practice and find that I can't do a thing – can't see a fly until it's about six feet away and can't judge them. I'm afraid of the ball in batting and can't judge it well enough to hit with any accuracy. I'm not quick enough for the infield. In short, I think baseball is closed to me. I spoke to Mr. [Frank] West, who coaches Kid team baseball, the other day and asked him if I could continue to come down to practice without playing for any special position. He said yes and I'm going to catch every afternoon and try batting until I'm better. Maybe I'll manage baseball next year or play tennis as I don't think I have a chance of ever making any baseball team. But I've tried and I'm going to keep it up all term, although I won't get in any games. Is that all right with you and Uncle Jack?

I may write to Uncle Jack about Fathers' Weekend some time this week and not write to you again until next Sunday. All the love and kisses in the universe to De Bebe Dirl and her fambly from

Your devoted son,
John

[South Kent School]

[South Kent, Conn.]

Dear Mother,   Sunday, 26 May 1929 – 2:00 P.M.

Well, we got our marks this noon (the last until exams) and at last I have 90, but for some reason I can't get enthused over it as I should, probably because with work I could have had it sooner and should be about 93 now. My marks were all the same – I got 90 in every subject. I was certainly royally gypped in Math – had 100 in one test, 95 in another and a 90 average on my daily papers and should have had about 95 on the card, which would have made my average 91. And I had 93 on the History and English exams and only 90 on the card. Two or three guys beat me on the Latin test again. Father [Jasper] Kemmis wrote it on the board, then left, and half the class cheated (Dawbarn, Forester & myself weren't among them). The Second Form is darned rotten in that respect – all but a few cheat. I wish the whole Council would watch us during final exams, but if I said a word, every boy who cheats would be down on me.

I'm working hard for the final exams – they start Friday or Saturday. I think I still have a chance of beating Itch, although he has splendid marks all term. If it's possible, I'm going to get a "96" average on them. Baseball practice is over now and except for an hour or two every afternoon, I study all the time. Didn't go to movies.

About Prize Day – the exercises start at *12:00 Standard Time* – Mr. [Samuel] Bartlett told us yesterday. And if you don't mind, I think I'd much rather go home with you in the car than on the train. After all, only a few fellows will be on it, since the 4th, 5th, & 6th Forms stay over till the 22nd anyway to take Boards (College Entrance Examinations) and a lot of brats are going home in cars. Some parents plan to do the same thing you want to do, so I asked Mr. Bartlett and he said that it would be better for you to write direct to the following address about accommodations:

Kent, Connecticut

We changed tables again this noon, although we changed just last week. I'm at Father Kemmis' table with [James] Braden, [Henry D.] Bixby, [Jr.], [George] Makinson, [William J.] Woodin & [Theodore F.] "Stump" Jones.

Haven't been reported or gotten any hours.

I got out my Chromonica the other day and played it for an hour. It was lots of fun playing the songs I did at P.S. 69. I rarely use it up here.

Have nearly finished [Sir Walter Scott's] *Quentin Durward* – it's an awful long book, isn't it? I haven't started any theme on it yet.

Several days ago, Mr. [Samuel A.] Woodward told us to write a theme entitled "The Race" – he said it could be any kind of a race except the *human* race (what a pun!) Some fellows wrote on airplane races, car races, boat races, footraces, submarine races, but I think mine was the most original: I wrote a 900-word theme about a pilot of a space-flyer in 2763 A.D. who raced to Mars with the only substance that would cure their dying Planet Governor – a race with death! He had to go through a meteor-belt, but escaped and got there in time. Everybody was very interested and I got a darn good mark on it. So yesterday some fellows asked me to tell them a story. I made up a long one about Venus lasting almost two hours and they think I'm the greatest story-teller that ever lived. They've pestered me all day, and I've told one or two more, but it's going too far – Mr. Bartlett asked me to come up and tell him one some time and almost everybody knows about it. But I have a fine stock of tales to tell Bob. By the way, I don't know how I could have forgotten it, but I got a fine letter from him last week and I wish you'd thank him for me and give him my 'special love.

I've had two fine letters from you since Wednesday – more than my usual share. I like the socks and shirts fine – they came Thursday. Thank you for them. The laundry case hasn't come yet, but probably will tomorrow. Mr. [Robert Denzil Bagster-] Collins smokes Lucky Strikes – it seems that all the masters do.

Must stop now & get outside.

All the love ever to the darling Bebe Dirl and her fambly from

Your devoted son,
John

[South Kent School]
[South Kent, Connecticut]

Dear Mother,   Sunday morning, 27 April 1930

It's a magnificent spring day – sunshiny and bright and warm. The kind of a day that poets go into rapsodies (is that the way you spell it?) about and it seems sacreligious to wear anything but a blue coat, white trousers and sport shoes. This is the first real spring that we've had –

yesterday and the day before were nice, but the temperature hovered around fifty. It's a splendid day to play tennis, but unfortunately, I wasn't the only one who thought so, and when I got out to the courts about an hour after breakfast, they were full and the waiting list numbered about twenty. So I hied me in to write a couple of letters and do some studying – I'm sadly behind where I should be in History, but will catch up today, if my nerve doesn't desert me and let[s] me go play a couple of sets of tennis. I'm getting along pretty well – have a decent, part-time serve and a serviceable backhand – you know, my backhand didn't exist last summer. I'm going to have an absolutely divine summer – playing tennis whenever I want and swimming and dancing and driving and just fooling around – boy! I'm going to earn some money too, so I can buy myself a good racquet. . . .

The Marvo came Friday, with samples of cream, powder, perfume and soap and about a million other advertisements. I am following the instructions to the letter and I think it's doing some good – I started using it right away, applying it with cotton four times daily and my skin seems a bit dry and tight already. It says tender skins begin to peel in three days, so mine ought to begin tomorrow or next day. I hope it is completely finished by Friday, because if Uncle Jack does come up, I don't want him to see me with big patches of dry skin hanging off my face. I certainly hope this stuff does work, though I'll admit that it sounds too good to be true. Wonder what it'll look like while it's peeling – so far no one knows I'm using it except my room-mate and if he tells, he knows what he'll get from yours truly. I hate to be kidded, and this would be meat for some Fifth Formers. . . .

Have received two very interesting letters from you this week, Mother. Thanks a lot for the envelopes – you can't imagine how convenient the stamped ones are – we all have to write home Sunday and everybody is rushing around Sunday night trying to borrow a stamp.

I forgot to thank Granny in her letter for fixing my long white ducks, but will you please remind her that the crease is down the front, not on the side, as in sailor pants. When I spoke about some one giving the new nets, it was only as a piece of more or less interesting news – I had absolutely no thought of intimating that you give something. The school has about all it needs anyway, without your spending your hard-earned and easily-spent money on it.

Glad that you liked my marks – [Lowell M.] Clucas [Jr.] is a repeater, but a darned bright one, he is still the smallest in the school and only twelve years old. [Hobson] Brown II gets good marks, but nothing like he did at the beginning of the year, about 75. Echeverria and the three upper forms get marks only once a month, you know. They'll only get two sets of marks this terms, besides the finals; next Sunday and the second of May. Am certainly glad that Bob likes his vacation. Give him my love and say I'll try and write this week.

Must stop now and – – – guess I will, there's the dinner bell. Lots and lots of love and kisses to all from

Your devoted son,
John

[South Kent School,
South Kent, Connecticut]
Dearest Mother,   Wednesday afternoon [April 1931]

This is just a postscript to last night's letter. You see, I thought that lights would be out at half-past nine with the new study period time, but instead they were out at a quarter after and I was caught unprepared. I wrote a note to Bob this morning and will put this in it.

The laundry case just came and I'll ship it back in a day or so. Everything is fine and the eatables are very eatable. Will you thank Granny for me? And I'd appreciate it if you'd ask Uncle Jack to send some razor blades in the case next time. I shave as little as possible, which is pretty often. I wait until five fellows have told me that I need a shave and then I try it – which sets the frequency at about once a week. I dislike it because of the condition of my skin. . . .

I've read three books and seven remarkable short stories this term. Since there's been nothing to do in the afternoon, I'd often go for a short run (my wind is very poor, but I can't seem to do much to improve it because after trotting a half-mile, my side aches so that in a few moments it's impossible for me to go any further. I don't know whether anything can be done for the pain or not, but it's quite a hindrance in sports and will prevent me from ever getting anywhere in track) and then read. The books were: [Charles Yale Harrison's] *Generals Die in Bed*, a very vivid picture of the war, written in the first person by a Canadian soldier. It is in a very clear, graphic style and intensely interesting. It was the first really good war book I'd ever read. It came out about a year ago and had very good reviews, so Father [A. Willoughby] Henzell, who lent it to me, tells me. *Goodbye to All That*, an autobiography of Robert Graves, the English poet. This was also in large part a war story, but was very different from the other. Graves was a junior officer who was very badly wounded by a bursting shell early in the war and went back later. The book is in a very literary style and very interesting reading. The first part is a fine story of life in a large English public school, about which I've read several books this year. Father Henzell lent me this one, too. The third book was *A Connecticut Yankee in King Arthur's Court*, but it wasn't a first reading by any means. We are studying some of Tennyson's *Idylls of the King* in English IV, and I borrowed Twain's book from the school library and perused it for about the fifth time. I'd like very much to see Will Rogers in the talkie version – hope it doesn't come to Great Neck until this summer. It was in New Milford night before last and Bobo [Mr. Collins] went over to see it.

The short stories were all in that Modern Library book, *Great Modern Short Stories*, edited by Grant Overton; they were, "The Three-Day Blow" by Ernest Hemingway, "The Apple-Tree" by John Galsworthy, "Paul's Case" by Willa Cather, "The Prussian Officer" by D. H. Lawrence, "Miss Brill" by Katherine Mansfield, "At Your Age" by F. Scott Fitzgerald, and "The Letter" by W. Somerset Maugham. I won't say anything about them, other than that they were all marvelous and have made me seven new favorite authors, because I hope that you'll read them sometime. The next time that you're in a book shop to buy one of those Modern Library books, will you look at this one? I know you hate to have things recommended, but I'm sure you'd enjoy every one of these.

Bobo read us a very good mystery story in English class the other day – "The Gentleman from America", by Michael Arlen. I thought it far better than the usual run of such stories and don't see how any anthology or representative collection of such stories could help but include it.

And now I'd better be getting out to the courts. There's nothing that I can do out there, because they're being marked, but my presence makes a good impression. Gee, it's cold today. Even if we can play tomorrow, I don't know whether I'll want to, in weather like this – I'm going to wear two sweaters out there. The sun is shining beautifully, bless him, but it'll rain in a day or so, see if it doesn't.

Vos lettres sont toujours agréables.

Il me faut clore.

Lots and lots of love from   Your loving son,

John

[South Kent School]

[South Kent, Connecticut]

Dearest Mother,   Wednesday afternoon [13 April 1932]

This letter will be principally about English. I have other work to do, as always – poor boy, so overworked! – but I consider this more important. As you know, I consider English the only subject I'm taking this year that is really of vital importance, and this term I am doing it justice, the first time I have ever done myself justice in any subject. Mr. [Albion] Patterson has been giving us little themes every day, often just one-paragraph themes. He suggests a subject, such as "Words and Thinking", and tells us to write a short, orderly developed, grammatical paper on it. I think I told you during vacation that a good many fellows in the form couldn't really write English yet. So this is pretty hard for some. I found it fairly difficult at first, but got to work, with good results. Mr. Patterson grades "minus" those papers which he believes wholly unsatisfactory; "check" those from 60% to 80%; "plus" those better than average by quite a bit; and "double plus" extraordinary papers. About three of us usually get plus – [John] Ward, [Theodore] Jones II and myself – though I'm the only one who has had a plus on every paper. Yesterday, we read *Riders to the Sea* by John Synge, and wrote a short paper on it. I spent a great deal of time on the thing – which I enclose – and for the first time was not strictly conventional. I knew that I could get a plus without going below the surface, but I tried to go into the play and see the characters and theme. Patterson read mine and Ward's in class, mine first. I noticed that while Ward's was not as polished as mine (only relatively – mine can be vastly improved and polished, of course) it was more interesting reading because it was more personal and intimate. I have thought several times that my themes were rather cold and calculating; of course, we are writing about impersonal subjects, but still I wondered if I were on the road to becoming an intellect like Francis Bacon. Naturally, I didn't compare myself with him, but he was probably cold and impersonal, if less intellectual, in his youth. So this morning I took a theme that I had re-written, embodying several of Mr. Patterson's suggestions, in to him and we talked for something over an hour. I spoke to him about the detached (I don't know whether I could be detached if I wanted to, but it resembles that) quality of my work of late and asked him about it. We got to talking and I told him how I had read omnivorously when quite young, then had run into this stage of *Amazing Stories* and written several such, as well as part of a book. We talked about my writing; he said that I was practically perfect in the sort of thing that we are doing now. He showed me that last paper we did, on Slang, which he marked double plus, the first he's given this year. He said that in this sort of work, a good man in college English couldn't improve on. I asked what he thought I should do now and he suggested that I merely keep notes (such as on [Willa Cather's] *My Antonia* – that wasn't a polished theme, of course, but it serves the purpose) on books, plays and essays I read, and write. I asked him what kind of writing, and he said that it would be better if I didn't receive any suggestions – just write about whatever I want and not to write for criticism or marks, merely what I feel and think. He said that I could bring it in for criticism occasionally if I wished but it was to be entirely my own. In that way he thinks I can develop my own style and get away from this impersonality. He asked me about what I intended to take up in college, and I said that I expected to major in English and go fairly deeply into Psychology, with advanced French and perhaps German. Asked about what I wanted to do after that, I told him that I hadn't the slightest idea, except that I'd probably go into Wall Street for a year or longer. It's odd, but I really haven't an idea. I am interested mainly in English and literature just at present, but I don't see how I could be an author, because I know absolutely nothing about human nature. I might learn about that in Psychology or by experience, though. Anyway, I don't think I'm practical enough to do well in business, and except for the monetary returns, that doesn't appeal to me at all. I thought for a while – influence of [Sinclair Lewis's] *Arrowsmith* – that I'd like to be a scientific experimenter, but on second thought, I find myself without the patient and unhurried mind that that requires. I have a sound and excellent knowledge of English (for my age, and it will develop), an interest in words and a fairly lucid mind – all inherited from you – and it seems as though I ought to make use of them in my profession. There's time to think about that, though – unless something happens, I'll be able to go to college (Princeton or Columbia – scholarship or working my way).

That's a pretty massive paragraph, but contrary to my boasts, it is neither clear nor orderly and is repetitious. And now that I've written it down, it doesn't seem so important as it did. I seem to have left a lot unsaid – if I think of it, I'll return to it.

I know you are right about *My Antonia* – it is certainly more a novel of the soil than a historical novel. *Only Yesterday* is "an informal history of the nine-teen-twenties", as the sub-title states. It is written in a very clear style and not only gives facts, but also the trends behind the facts. I've learned a great deal from it that I never knew before. I believe it had good reviews and is well-known – it was published in 1931 and the copy [John S.] Fraser has is of the 16th Printing, Ninety First Thousand. I hesitate to recommend books to you, because your reading has been so wide and you may have read many of this type, or perhaps the author – a Frederick Lewis Allen – is not really good, but I think you'd like this.

Hastening to correct a false impression, I asseverate that Fraser's parents do not loom in my eyes at all – none but my own parents do that. And they don't give wisely – these books are beyond Fraser by quite a lot – I don't think I could read them intelligently. You make up a big list of books and if plenitude does not come, on my twentieth birthday, I'll creep into Brentano's and steal them all. We'll have a nice library by hook or crook.

Have just read O'Neill's *The Emperor Jones*. It is in a Modern Library book with his *The Straw*. I enjoyed it very much – would give a great deal to see it acted, though I imagine it would be extremely harrowing. The gradual break-down of the veneer of civilization is grippingly portrayed. Perhaps it cannot be compared to *Mourning Becomes Electra* – though the introduction speaks very highly of it, of course – but I enjoyed it more. It is not nearly so long as the more recent play(s), and the action is more vivid. There was a good deal in the introduction that I didn't fully understand – I believe that O'Neill is quite a bit too mature for me as yet, though I enjoy him.

The weather has been heart-breaking – it rained constantly all day Saturday, Sunday and Monday. Yesterday it was cloudy and drizzled and hailed occasionally, but we went out to the courts and layed out two of them – that is, measured them off from the net-posts and put in nails to attach string to mark by at strategic points. It didn't take but about an hour – after Mr. Cuyler bought the new steel tape, he found the old, so that we could use both at once and get angles. They are perfectly layed out this year, for the first time. We could have done the third court, too, but it was too wet to walk on. Perhaps they'll be dryed enough by tomorrow to brush and roll, but I doubt it. It snowed all morning, but the sun is out now, albeit feebly. Incurable optimist that I am, I'm positive that we'll play Saturday, just as I was quite sure that we would play last Saturday. A baseball game, the first of the season, was scheduled for this afternoon, but was called off on account of snow. Our first tennis match, with Kent Seconds, is on the 23rd, a week from Saturday. How I hope that my game shows some improvement – I'm going to have a grand time this spring, working on my game, and the first thing I'm going to learn is to start the instant the other fellow hits the ball – that way I'll always be in position and have time to prepare my stroke. I have decent strokes, if I can make the places to use them – even my backhand is reliable if unhurried.

I'll try to listen to the opera Saturday, though if the courts are ready and the sun is shining, I can't promise. (Just noticed the "Layed" and "dryed" above – I'll have to be careful of those.) There's no hurry at all about the grey suit – I just wondered if it had been lost in the mail. I'm getting along swell with my blue suit – it's as good as new. And even if Anny should emerge (that doesn't sound very cheerful to me – correction: And when Anny emerges), I wouldn't have another racquet. I've been beaten so often with this racquet in hand that I have to administer just that many beatings with it. Besides, I want it said that I was a one-racquet man – began with his racquet and when he left it, he was on the top (heh, heh!).

My cold prevaricates – in the morning it seems to be better and at night it's worse than ever. Have been going to the Infirmary for treatment. It'll be all right in a day or so. Bob's shoes appeared and are really splendid – so much so that he is going to wear them for dress and his black shoes other times. They came in those convenient little sock-like affairs that you can pack them in. I can wear my white shoes very well, and will wear them for dress this spring and summer, saving my black shoes for next fall – I'll still be able to wear them and perhaps not the

white ones. My Spalding shoes are holding up very well indeed – haven't
even gone through the outer sole yet. They're good for months more.
And my other black shoes are fine – I'm wearing them, too. The shirt
you got me is swell – I've never had one I liked as well. It goes very well
with my brown suit, too. The sneakers I got last summer or spring are as
good as new; the soles have scarcely shown any wear at all and the uppers
are serviceable. Am glad I didn't buy a pair. Would you mind sending
up a few of those steel phonograph needles from home in a letter – I
have a lot of swell records up here that I'd like to play; haven't heard them
for a long time.

Absolutely must stop now and get some work done for tomorrow. I
hope that your work isn't too hard; wish Uncle Jack the best of luck for
me on Anny – the best thing Anny could do for this family would be to
give you and Uncle Jack a long vacation, on a round-the-world trip or in
Bermuda or in Germany or anywhere. I certainly hope that you may get
it. All the love ever,

Most Devotedly,
John

[P.S.] Will you return the themes, please, Mother? No hurry. Love and
kisses.

*JB was accepted at Columbia a year early, but the family had fallen on dif-
ficult times financially and it proved a considerable sacrifice to send him to the
university. His stepfather, John Angus, had experienced various business set-
backs and was by then virtually without income. Mrs. Berryman had taken a job
as a secretary at General Refractories Company to provide for the family. Robert
Jefferson was removed from South Kent School and placed in a public school,
and the family had moved from an apartment on East 60th Street to a less expensive one on 119 East 84th Street. JB lived at home with his family during the
summer of 1932 and for his first year at Columbia.*

*Much more in his element back in New York—and no doubt partly out of
relief at being free of SKS—JB at first concentrated more on extracurricular
activities than on his academic pursuits. The awkward and withdrawn adolescent
began to gradually metamorphose into a vibrant and popular young man—especially among the girls of Smith and Barnard Colleges—admired not only for his
intelligence, but for his social prowess and dancing skills. He had a series of
girlfriends, the most serious relationship being with Jean Bennett who, when
they met in 1935, was just sixteen and in her first year at Hunter College, New
York. As a freshman he also found a friend, Ernest Milton ("Milt") Halliday,
who shared many of JB's literary and social enthusiasms.*

In his sophomore year JB was awarded a scholarship that enabled him to move into a room on the seventh floor of John Jay Hall. Here his social life intensified and he continued to cut classes. In Mark Van Doren's eighteenth century course, he wrote a strong exam but admitted in a note that he had read only 17 of the 42 books for the course. Van Doren had no choice but to flunk him, and as a consequence he lost his scholarship and had to drop out of school for a term.

He returned to Columbia the following semester, having made up the work for English 64, and Van Doren changed his mark for the course. The shock of this experience somewhat chastened him and, combined with his growing admiration for Van Doren, turned him toward more serious application of himself for the next two years. Gradually, largely under Van Doren's influence, JB became increasingly interested in literature and the exercise of his own creative powers.

He began to write seriously and published numerous poems and reviews in the Columbia Review *in 1935 and 1936, and four poems, which appeared in* Columbia Poetry 1935, *won the Mariana Griswold Van Rensselar Prize of fifty dollars. One of this group, "Note on E.A. Robinson," was reprinted in the July 10, 1935, issue of the* Nation. *Robert Giroux, who would later become JB's publisher, was the editor of the* Columbia Review. *In addition to Van Doren, Mrs. Berryman was also a strong influence on JB throughout these years. She continued to prod him to excel academically and encouraged his literary efforts, often making suggestions about his work. Because of JB's proximity to his mother during this period, the only significant written communications between them appear to be the following poems. The first of them, an unpublished sonnet sequence, is interesting for its treatment of love and possessiveness. It was written for Mrs. Berryman's fortieth birthday.*

July 8, 1934

I

I sing a mother's love, too strong to hold
Unto herself her son, though they were two
So near in mind and heart, and eyes controlled
By one strong light, they visioned a single view;
Possessive of naught against the world save her,
She would not see him grow too closely dear,
And, held apart, he waxed in strength under
His own will, on his own life-path, but near
To that wise road she went. And mounting still,
But far below, he strove to build his way
After her quiet, undenying will

To rise unselfish to a self-perfected day.
Beneath her joy in a practised life there moves
A soul that sees and knows and aches – and loves!

II

Full-blown, gently and wise, today she stands
In the hard-won center stretch of an uphill road,
And looks with mingled pleasure down the lands
She's passed intact, unwavering from her code;
Learning from curves and unseen stones in the way,
She climbs by now more carefully than fast,
Though use taught skill and ease replaced dismay;
She found, too, how the winds of men are cast.
Proud, then – a little sad, – she turns to scan
The height ahead, and sees in place of rocks
A long and friendly field, won by the pain
Vanquished below, with roses white and hollyhocks.
Gone the blindness of youth, uncome dim age . .
Clarity and joy her other ills assuage.

III

And she's grown beautiful on the rocky road,
Strengthened a youth lovely–I'm told–until
Today it burns more steadily than rill
Or lake in the shimmering sun, a bright abode
For individual ways and charms that load
Too strong and scales 'gainst any rival's wile.
Hair a whispering, friendly brown to men, and still
But incandescent gold to suns that glowed;
Her waist a slender charming line between
God's twin mysteries in woman, and hands
Unroughened by the rocks, mind quick to glean
The spheres of truth and to record; in bands
Of spangled light her eyes are soft and lean
Inward, for all her kindliness commands.

IV

Paradox, that she should claim her wit
Lies in a trick of speech, a facile word

Struck by the interplay of minds, admit
A verbal brilliance, casual thought transferred;
When from the lyric, veritable wells
Of her mind, her thought as from a cage
Leaps out, and from the wealth which therein dwells
She summons poignant beauty to her page.
The quality that strains behind the words
A poet employs to freeze his soul, nor lose
From a phrase the explosive power of bawling herds–
This tumbles through her lines, though she refuse
An ordered rhyme, like undertones of birds:
Fortunate, to weld prose to verse, nor choose!

A later effort, written to Mrs. Berryman during this time, is this brief Christmas poem:

                                                                    [New York]
Dearest Mum,   Christmas 1934

 The winter's cold and money few,
 But here, my dear, is an IOU
 For tickets (real but not specific)
 To a show that ought to be terrific:
 Thumbs Up. It opens very soon
 And probably will be a boon
 To battered Broadway – Clark & McCullough,
 J. Harold Murray (the singin' fullough),
 Paul Draper, etc. & Hal Le Roy–
 It ought to be a thing of joy!
 Meanwhile, we're merry, mad & "pore"–
 And Thumbs'll be up when money's more!

                                                              All my love,
                                                              John

[*Thumbs Up* was a review which opened at the St. James Theatre on December 27, 1934. It starred Bobby Clark and Paul McCullough, as well as J. Harold Murray, Paul Draper and Hal Le Roy.]

So remarkable was JB's academic turnabout during his last two years at Columbia that he was elected to Phi Beta Kappa and graduated with honors in

English and Comparative Literature. As a senior, he became a candidate for the prestigious Euretta J. Kellett Fellowship, which would provide the winner with an annual minimum stipend of $2,000 for two years to study at Cambridge University in England. Near the end, suffering from strain and fatigue and a serious ear infection, he nearly had to withdraw from school, but prodded by Mrs. Berryman he managed to go on and to win the scholarship. Nonetheless, he had for the first time crossed the threshold of nervous collapse, a condition from which he would suffer recurrently for the rest of his life. After graduation he spent two weeks convalescing at his grandmother's (Martha May Little) home in Roxbury, New York.

[Roxbury, New York]
Dearest Mum,   Thursday [25 June 1936]
   Marvellous letter! – first I've had from you in years; I'd quite forgotten how spirited and able your typewriter is.
   I continue to have a swell time. Have played 14 sets of tennis to date (aie! aie! the willing bones) – none yesterday, but a very nice kid named apparently Gallagher Reed (though Bob my infamous brother seems to have designated him, indelibly, and variously, Gringo, the Gringissimo Kid, Tarzan, etc. etc.) stopped me a few minutes ago and we're gonna play at 5; likewise Dick Ames just (up there at "apparently") came in and wanted to play, so from 4 on the "fun" (also known as the *wheel*) begins. Wonderful time last evening: Sonny or Sunny [Shafer] and I went to a vile & very amusing film here, then strolled, meeting the Admiral, Gringo (who did the victory cry and the war song – Bob will identify all these things for you) etc. and attended a "skimbleton" or "horning": One Edna Lutz just married someone and a great crowd made noise with horns & shotguns around their house about midnight until they got up, came down & let everyone in for beer & cigars. Heigho for the local life! I've some first-rate stories for you. Bob, by the way, is held in vast respect and loving joy by all here – tell him I know, besides those mentioned, a swell chap called Streaky Brandow, Sunny's brother Bob, a superb type rustic appellatus Deke Lutz, etc. etc. I'll write him soon – meanwhile the last letter & this will tell him something of my Roxbury education. They're a fascinating bunch.
   Got nearly up to John Burroughs' place with Mary Ruth [Fanning] yesterday (her almost unspeakable innocence continues to enchant me) when it began to rain, so we took shelter in a most imperfect summer-

house, then in Palen's garage, and ran down the hill through the Shepard place when it let up.

Pride & Prejudice is definitely one of the best – it's so big and strong that the palpable defects don't matter. I've been reading much Whitman (those two lines are wonderful – I remember them as of two years ago but don't know which poem) and some Shakespeare, the *Sonnets* & occasional stuff. Jeez, he could write, dat guy!! . . .

Thanks ever so much for the comment on the poem – will defend my last line in syllabic detail when I return. If you're to move July 1st & I can help, be sure & let me know, Mum, and down I'll come. Otherwise, nobody knows how joyous I'm!!!

Please write again soon-like, kid – all my love & infinite kisses –

John

[JB had sent Mrs. Berryman a poem written, as he said, in the "Yeats manner."]

[Roxbury, New York]
Dearest Mum,   Wednesday [1 July 1936?]

I am beginning to miss all of you vastly, so I'm forsaking this pleasure spot tomorrow – will be home in the evening. "No one to talk to" is getting me down, particularly since I'm having fascinating thoughts – have made some notes for a novel, *The Sky Grew Dark*, and have numerous other plans to discuss with thee. [Virginia Woolf's] *The Waves* is magnificent, by no means even (apparently) but continually brilliant in some way. I'll have been here two weeks and Granny is pleased, I think. So am I – I've had a swell time. My tennis is still no good but it *exists*, which is something. I want a typewriter around, too. And this is only a kind of mild taste of what solitude will be mine abroad! Heigh-ho, I do not relish the prospect of sailing. I wish infinitely that you were going with me, and if I have to loot the Bank of England you have got to come over next summer or the year after. – Awfully glad you're not to move till the end of the month – damn all these separations, anyway.

Well, we will talk mightily tomorrow – goodbye for now and thank you for the well-timed and shamefully apt warning about the Roxbury children –

All my love to all, especially thee,

John

[*The Sky Grew Dark* never progressed beyond the note-making stage.]

After returning home briefly, JB, at Mrs. Berryman's suggestion, took a train
up to Williamsburg, Ontario, in an attempt to further his recovery by means of
the unorthodox ministrations of Dr. Mahlon William Locke, a Canadian phy-
sician and surgeon. Famous throughout North America for his treatment of
maladies ranging from arthritis to nervous disorders by means of foot manipula-
tion, Dr. Locke sometimes saw as many as 1,500 to 2,000 patients a day in his
one-man outdoor clinic. (With his patients lined up by the hundreds, Dr. Locke
would administer as many as five such treatments a minute.)

Stony Craft
Williamsburg, Ont.

Dearest Mum,   Thursday [27 August 1936?]

Thanks cheerily for thy letter – I dropped in just for fun and was
amazed, some ten minutes since. Down with S. [Sinclair] Lewis and up
with J. Anger! [evidently a play of words on Jill Angel] Thanks for looking
after the draft, and for enclosures.

Excellent trip up; Albany first stop, then Schenectady, then Utica
where I had coffee & changed trains; whence, in interrupted fashion, to
Watertown, change, to Philadelphia, change, and along the St. Lawrence – lovely river, especially at sunset (cf. poem on p. 736 of my collected works) – to Ogdensburg. Horrible town, Ogdensburg, misinformation
to left and right (as, and to wit, only one, a six-thirty A.M. bus from
Prescott to the object of my desire). So I spent a very cold night in the
[Hotel] McConville, was paid much deference which was bad for me
and excited my omnipresent urge to lord it. Very much New Yorker in
sticks, etc. Economic: 12,000, very few on relief, soap factory, paper
factory, two garment factories, surrounded (except on North) by small
farms – butter, milk, cheese, vegetables; much [Alfred] Landon; "longest night club in the world", and the Brass Rail – cheapness everywhere,
imitation, but Vat 69; how much immediate content has this symbol:

> "That burlap tree will concentrate my horror".
> [Unpublished verse fragment by JB]

I left, misguided, a call for 5:15 and was duly awakened but, being
cold, went back to sleep ("Hell with it" idea) and so got my ten hours.
Ambled about on arising and learned at the ferry of a 3:15 bus (the only

other one being 5 A.M., which I'd have missed, cursing). Crossed easily
for 25 cents and was properly surprised by the general familiarity of the
Canadian scene and by the unfamiliarity of detail – French, currency
(2% discount on Amer. money), signs. Was stopped for questioning by
the Immigration officer, with another chap – who, *hight* one Paul Stackpole, lives on 114th St, had work[ed] at Columbia & knows people I do,
now composes. Astonishing. Reached here in due time, taking car at
Morrisburg.

An amazing town; I'll reconstruct it in detail when I return, but let
me suggest that the infinite wheel-chairs, erratic nervousness and continual discussion of disease, all recall strongly the atmosphere in which *The
Magic Mountain* operates. Mostly old people, countless accommodations, so I shopped and about the tenth room I saw was this: a huge, very
clean room, 18′ by 20′, with two beautiful double beds, dressing table &
long mirror, closet, three recessed windows, all scrupulously neat (lino-
leum & little rugs), high ceiling, on second floor front of one of the nicest
looking buildings in town, on the main street a block from [Dr.] Locke's
place – oh yes, and excellent blankets, linen, curtains, and two very fine
chairs and a writing table. Perfect, no? Guess the price, mi luv. One
dollar a day! *C'est magnifique.* So I'm very comfortably installed and
expect to stay forever. Dinner last evening at Paul's rooming house, but
the invalids drive me mad – will eat alone, out, hereafter. Tiny theatre
here, saw Chas. Ruggles in *Charley's Aunt* of six years ago – wonderfully
funny, and bed early.

Up at ten, breakfast, and I've had my first treatment by the Ontario
myth, Herr [Mahlon William] Locke. It took approximately 25 seconds,
he merely cracked each foot without saying a word or looking at me – I
felt practically nothing and am somewhat skeptical but will try tomorrow
to ask a question or so. A girl collects the dollars, cracking each of the
bewildered patient's hands in turn, and out you go. Not many today – I
waited less than five minutes – sometimes two hours, I hear.

Heigh-ho, will report progress and events – I'm having a wonderfully
leisurely time. Hope, belatedly, that you and Uncle Jack are bearing up
under the absence of my wit and ever-jovial smile (heh! heh!) and particularly that the moving goes well. Hate to write at length by hand, wherefore my jerkiness. Miss my typewriter, but I'll know next time. Meanwhile,

be happy and worry not & get down to "Bare Iss Hiss Bacque" and find a swell place to stay in Philadelphia –

All my love and several kisses for thy gentle ivory brow –

Cheerily
John

[Alfred Landon was elected by the Republican National Convention in 1936 as the party's presidential candidate to oppose Franklin D. Roosevelt.

Mrs. Berryman was then attempting to write a play called *Bare is His Back*.]

PART TWO

Cambridge
1936-1938

O N SEPTEMBER 18, JB boarded the ocean liner Britannic for England. Seeing him off, at Pier 42 in New York, were Mrs. Berryman and his girlfriend Jean Bennett.* The wide world lay ahead of him and, brimming with enthusiasm and ambition, he set out to make his mark on it as a poet. After a brief stay in London, he moved into his rooms at Memorial Court in Clare College, Cambridge.

Under the tutelage of his supervisor, George Rylands—and with the aid of his own voracious appetite for reading—JB's literary frame of reference and sensibilities expanded enormously. With Ryland's encouragement, he competed for the Oldham Shakespeare Scholarship, which, with its £83 stipend, would help support him in his second year, and he became the second American to win the prize. His fascination with Yeats continued to grow and he gave talks on his master to Clare College's Dilettante Society and to the Nashe Society in St. John's College, and, finally, fulfilled his ambition to meet the great man. During this period he met Dylan Thomas and W. H. Auden, as well.

JB continued his apprenticeship as a poet, encouraged from afar by Mark Van Doren, Allen Tate and Robert Penn Warren. Near the end of his second year at Cambridge, his efforts were rewarded by Warren's acceptance of four poems for the summer 1938 issue of the Southern Review. Influenced by his reading of Shakespeare, he also initiated what would prove to be an intermittent

---

* In "Recovery," in Love & Fame, JB mistakenly recalled his friend "Milt" Halliday being there, too. According to Halliday, he instead met JB upon his return from England.

but almost lifelong fascination with writing plays. With characteristic confidence and high aspirations, he wrote in an early notebook that he considered his chief competitors to be Tennessee Williams and Eugene O'Neill. None of the more than a dozen plays he began (they are in varying states of completion) has so far been performed or published, but the skills he developed in writing them must have contributed to the recurrent and highly accomplished dramatic qualities of his later verse.

Lonely during much of his residence at Cambridge, JB later recalled that he had spent an inordinate amount of his time either reading or writing. He haunted the bookstores—Heffers and Bowes & Bowes and Gordon Fraser's in Portugal Place—and began in earnest the book buying which, over the years, would form his remarkable collection of elegant editions of most of the important English and American poets. His loneliness was greatly diminished one day when, at a party in a friend's rooms in Magdalene College, he met B., a charming young woman studying at nearby Newnham College, who would eventually become his fiancée.

JB's long and frequent letters to Mrs. Berryman from Cambridge, which he asked her to save because they will "make a kind of diary," are indeed remarkably confiding and intimate. They closely document both his intellectual progress and his development as a poet. For letters to his mother, they are unusually candid about personal matters, at one point even discussing the possibility of his having contracted syphilis. The grandness of tone in some of the letters reflect his youthful exuberance and poetic aspirations—perhaps with an eye to future readers, and certainly under the influence of Keats' letters, which he was then avidly reading.

The early Cambridge letters, in particular, manifest how much he respected Mrs. Berryman and sought her advice and approval. And her one surviving letter of the period, written December 15, 1936, shows her capacity for sound counsel and encouragement. Still, while acknowledging his "mania of absolute dependence" on her up to this time, JB providentially voices his need to ultimately rid himself of it.

A recurring element in his Cambridge letters is JB's need to reassure his mother that she is the most important person in his life. The letters continue to flatter Mrs. Berryman's vanity: "Don't take on age dignity until you have given up charm and brightness and vividness of appearance and speech;" and "When I return no one will suppose there is five years between us." When he writes her about being in love, he sounds apologetic—almost as if he were breaking off a romance—and her nonresponse at first is eloquent. Eventually, she does respond, appearing to accept the situation, but later clearly and ominously warns him about the danger of personal happiness affecting his art.

Although JB was later somewhat embarrassed by the intensity of the letters from this period, the autobiographical value he placed on them is underscored by the fact that he eventually borrowed them from Mrs. Berryman to use as source material in writing "Part II" of Love & Fame—*as readers of the poems will unmistakably recognize.*

On Board
Cunard White Star
Britannic
Dearest Mum: Sunday 27 September [1936]
I have such a vast deal to tell you; these are the first words I've written on board, it's been so rough and so fascinating and so continually busy, for me at least. First and fundamental, I've made a real friend, a man so charming and so real that my effort for the next two years will be adequately, and unsuccessfully, to describe him. The merest outline: Pierre Donga, half-Basque half-Spanish, the outstanding political journalist in France and the best caricaturist now working; he has your irrepressible and vivid intelligence, [E.M.] Halliday's ineffable charm and Mark [Van Doren]'s solidity, together with an indescribable manner which is his or French or European. I shall never be able to explain to you what I have learned and thought and felt during this week, particularly now when I am quite incapable of thinking in English: he has eight languages but dislikes English so we have spoken only French since the second day out; we've talked incredibly, at least twelve hours really a day, and now I hear about me only French, translating it unconsciously from English as I listen; my French is better by leaps and we converse with little difficulty now; writing in English is, as it were, a difficult novelty. Let me leave this for a moment and see whether in stereotypes I can regain facility.

I missed you all, specially thee, terribly for a bit, pacing disconsolately up and down the top deck after the pier had rushed finally from sight. Then luncheon and my customary social mask, frigidity, when I anticipate prolonged boredom; three neutral hours in a deck-chair, watching New York and Long Island and America with its numerous tangible and stronger intangible claims receding, while I dedicated myself with the enthusiasm born of isolation to the life of comment, to distance, to in fact art. Then a tall Spanish-looking chap who had been strolling up and down singing with the short, dark fellow who turned out to be Pierre stopped at the rail and began to talk to me in my chair. Very quickly the three of us were engaged in a very complex political discussion of the Spanish rebellion, Pierre saying little however; the other, Arturo Mena, I found to be a Porto Rican returning to Lisbon to finish medical studies; interesting and effervescently animal but without taste or information, I later learned. Donga had said nothing but before dinner asked me to change my seat, which I did delighted and we sat together thereafter. That night we began to talk casually, and for about three days we discussed ideas: economics, anatomy, psychology, sociology, painting, metaphysics, general national attitudes, race make-up, law, and all else; then I began to learn something about him. Fortunately for me, no one else of the some seventy in third class had either French or an interesting mind, and no one else interested me, so we were constantly together. And still are, but he leaves the ship at Le Havre in three hours, so I'm going to write only a little more now. A few more details: he has travelled almost everywhere in Europe, South America, Africa (spent two years there with [Walter Morse] Rummel, the German composer, pianist and metaphysician, doing special reporting while Rummel gathered and recorded native music – the whole north and west coast and far into the interior); knows everyone in Paris who does anything: [Jean] Giraudoux, [André] Malraux, Harry Baur, [Jean] Cocteau, [François] Mauriac, etc.; is thirty-two unbelievably, *très sérieux mais de savoir faire*, sings beautifully, was starred for a season in a Berlin cabaret; he is resourceful and experienced beyond belief, yet still fresh if utterly without naïveté – impossible to describe. Forgive me, I'm going up. . . .

[John]

[Pierre (Pedro) Donga figures in three of JB's poems in *Love & Fame*— "Away," "First Night at Sea," and "London"—and is also remembered as "my loved Basque friend" in "Dream Song 283." In "First Night at Sea," JB identified Walter Morse Rummel, with whom Donga travelled to Africa, as "Memel, the Belgian composer."

JB arrived in London on September 28, 1936.]

London, W.1.
The Seymour Hotel
[No salutation]   30 September 1936

The Poet's First Impressions of London, his First European City – ah historic moment! It's quite an interesting place though (really it is) if you can keep out of the way of the cars and busses which attack from all directions – I simply cannot remember which way to look and my eyes are quite worn out with pivoting, as my legs with dodging. Not an easy thing, Life; you gotta get used to it; America has nearly lost her (unknown) white hope several times in this vicious and unpremeditated traffic. Ah, Sir Thomas Browne! But Beetle is with me.

I encountered vast difficulties, of course, as soon as the detail of existence in our organized insanity was upon me again: the loss of a trunk (which seems since to have turned up and awaits me, I hope, at Cambridge with the other), no rooms at the Cumberland (and a good thing too, inasmuchas said hotel resembles greatly the Waldorf, being however infinitely more expensive, I believe), etc. I am around the corner in Marble Arch at a tiny place *hight* The Seymour, bed and breakfast 9 / 6d. Let us at once, by the way, get British currency straight: unit, the pound, equalling vaguely five dollars; English penny, worth a little over two cents, then the three-penny coin, then the sixpenny coin (very useful, somewhere between a dime and fifteen cents), then the shilling equal to twelve pennies and approximately an American quarter; then the two-shilling piece, then the half-crown (two shillings sixpence), then there may be a crown, I haven't seen any, worth five shillings or about $1.25; then the ten-shilling note; then the pound note (twenty shillings); then the guinea, whether note or coin I haven't discovered, worth 21 shillings, just to make it all fun boys and girls. There it is in a nutshell; nearly everything, roughly speaking, is listed in shillings as units – for instance a book will be "seven and six", seven shillings and sixpence, or somewhere around $1.80. Sixpence is a tanner, the shilling a bob, the pound a quid. Said he fainting definitely.

Numerous things confuse me, but immediately and without reason I love London. For that reason I've *done* almost nothing since getting here about noon on Monday by special train from Tillbury where the *Britannic* docked. The Abbey, of course – and that was where I discovered the mistake all visitors make. I spent a couple of hours there, observed until I was pink with age and emotion, etc. etc. and the whole business was very painful. The point is to know London pretty damn well before you do anything at all; and the only way to find out anything is to go everywhere and simply find out what kind of a city the British live in, before you can understand anything in it. So I've walked vast distances, learned how to use the excellent Underground and the still confusing omnibusses, discovered where the focal points are, etc. I have a superb map of the city showing everything and I've studied it immensely, and everyone one asks is very nice, particularly the policemen (nice sentence, that). So now when I come down for a bit I'll know how to get about. Moreover, I *detest* hotels and all about them, and I'm sure I'll feel far more like really looking at things when (if?) I'm staying with someone in town. It's a little ghastly alone – I do so wish that you were here.

I have of course done several things. Went to a very interesting variety show, the Windmill, Monday night: nothing like the excellence of American individual performances, but a kind of contemporary brightness and cleanness that American shows don't have. And I saw this evening Max Reinhardt's production of *Oedipus Rex* at the Royal Opera House, Covent Garden: Gilbert Murray's impossible fustian, but good speakers in about half the roles and excellent staging – very moving, in fact, which tells me how moving something really decent would be. Everything in London closes at midnight – almost no busses or underground after that and not even many restaurants open; very few people on the streets – what superb and how famous are the names of these streets, incidentally: Oxford, Regent, Charing Cross, Picadilly, Haymarket, the Strand, Trafalgar Square and the thousand other squares and circuses, you know them all and it actually is exciting to walk them. Curiously unlike New York and almost without the air of a city like NY or Chicago – a group of villages, I know, historically and still with those characteristics, but it's something definite and unstateable. And fascinating – and I've only just begun to learn a very few names and places, it's so very large and spreads so in all directions. Those are, besides the Abbey, the only two things I've done, but I've had a wonderful time and eaten in all sorts of curious little places in the West End; I don't really like the food but tea is always first-rate if you get China tea. Have written two poems also, one of them excellent. I went up to Tavistock Square this afternoon to see Virginia Woolf – she and her husband are also the Hogarth Press and I thought, besides wanting to talk to her, that they might be interested in printing "Ritual [at Arlington]" – but unhappily she has not been well and is in the country; I'll write her from Clare. I think they might very well do it.

Thanks ever so much for your letter, it was delightful. Please wish

Bob the best luck in the world at college, and tell him not to dishonour my desk, which has had some noble stuff writ at it, egad. Your instinct about books is quite correct – I'll detail my prizes from Cambridge, it being now quite late and I tired. Dull note from Jean [Bennett] after yours, my only mail. This thing about letter-writing is preposterous, by the way. I want very much to write at some length and with some frequency to you, to Halliday, to Mark, to [George] Marion [O'Donnell], to Jean, to Giroux, and occasionally to at least a dozen others; but palpably it's absurd. I said I'd write twenty letters on board and everyone I knew from London. Well, this is absolutely the only letter I've written, of course, to date, except for a note to [Lewis] Wharton in London thanking him for the book of poems [Songs of Carthage]. I don't understand writing of this sort, anyway – it wears me out, and unless one repeats descriptions it takes years. What advice? Please save all my letters from abroad very carefully, will you, Mum? They'll make a kind of diary, I think. And explain to Bob, Granny and Uncle Jack about my writing – thanks.

I shall go up to Cambridge tomorrow, I think, for want of money and because I want as soon as possible to get settled – I have vast amounts of work to do, particularly Blake, Yeats and Donne, Shakespeare and Milton, as well as my enormous (we hope) occasional reading. Moreover, I have some definite ideas for a play in verse which I should like to get done as soon as possible. How goes it with *Bare Is His Back* (who owns he is a bastard, etc.)? Report progress and send anything that's ready – best of luck with it. Give my dearest love to Bob and Uncle Jack and Granny, inform them what passes with me; I'll try to get off notes in the morning but promise nothing, knowing me. Particularly my love to you – I shall try to do what I most want with my time and strength. This separation is beastly, but the best of us alters not and I shall expect to find you, when I return, more magnificent even than now.

John McAlpin Berryman
Clare College
Cambridge

[Beetle was a household god of the Berrymans', created to watch over and protect them. The name itself was possibly inspired by one of the main characters in Rudyard Kipling's *Stalky & Co.* JB had been awarded a copy of the novel, in 1929, for leading the second form at SKS.]

M 4, Memorial Court
[Cambridge]
Dearest Mum: 5 October 1936
    This place is beautiful beyond imagination – I, even I, am struck
almost dumb before the lawns, the grandeur, the rich historic peace, the
bridges and the Cam, tradition, the fires, the halls. I require a complete
intensity for utterance in any kind:

> And he that digs it, spies
> A bracelet of bright haire about the bone
> [John Donne, "The Relic"]

or

>   O sun,
> Burn the great sphere thou mov'st in;
>   darkling stand
> The varying star o' the world
> [William Shakespeare, *Antony and
> Cleopatra*]

or

> And sang within the bloody wood
> When Agamemnon cried aloud
> [T.S. Eliot, "Sweeney Among the Nightingales"]

    But back to prose and the complacencies of correspondence. I confess
inability to describe Cambridge, you will simply have to come next spring
and see for yourself. The inadequacy of communication is now being
brought home to me in a manner that even I.A. Richards would call
satisfactory; I can tell you how I've wandered about the quadrangles and
the town, and gradually got settled in my magnificent rooms and sit by
the hour fascinated by my coal-fire's incredible and various vitality, how
the sun falls through the elms and burns on the quiet water, the gardens
beat the air with their colour and depth, but it's all quite useless as you
can see. Two more short poems are the only writing I've done here, and
I'm afraid from now on you're going to have to take the atmosphere largely
for granted; hopeless, for example, to try to convey the sensation of rich-
ness I feel reading Keats' letters before the fire tonight or the sudden
appalling vision of majesty and valuable time that struck my brain cross-

ing King's Parade this evening, with the calm buildings on all sides, no one in sight at dusk and the great Chapel looming ahead. *C'est impossible.*

My rooms are really splendid: this, the one I spend all my time in, is about the size of our living-room, with a beautiful and very efficient fireplace, two large recessed windows, well furnished – a chaise longue, a very comfortable deep chair and four other chairs, one large heavy table and two others, etc, rugs and what not; my bedroom is slightly smaller, the bed is first-rate and astonishingly there is a great deal of room – I have got all but about twenty of my books on four deep shelves set in the wall here – high enough for some of my ten-inch books, for a wonder, and capable of holding surprising numbers. Plenty of drawers and cupboard space. The gyp-room, my kitchenette is just outside my door, and I've had a wonderful time outfitting it – tea set, silver, table cloths, tea kettle, cruets, etc – I've never done anything like this before, you know, and I feel a superb bachelor. God forbid I should ever marry. Mrs Mizzen, my bedder, is wonderful and does absolutely everything but shave me – it is amazing having nothing to do but work. By the way, set your mind at rest: I have averaged, during my week in England, something over nine hours a night of sleep and eaten regularly – the meals in hall are excellent, breakfast I have here, find the table set when I come out after she has called me at eight, cold cereal, tea (which I love more than ever now I can have it when I like, which is about five times a day) and two boiled eggs. Then tea with huge bread butter and marmalade in the late afternoon. Term doesn't open officially (that is, Term began Oct 1st but Full Term doesn't begin until Wednesday and no lectures I think till Friday, so the men are returning slowly – neither [Arthur S.] Ramsey nor [Andrew] Chiappe yet back. I've seen [Henry] Thirkill and the Dean, [William] Telfer, who is trying to get Rylands for my advisor. Rylands, George H W, an M A of King's, is a very sound fellow, apparently; I got his book of which I'd heard in the States, in London and after reading it carefully asked Telfer to get me him, if possible. Called *Words and Poetry,* basic assumption (analysis of diction and style will describe poetry) admirable and much good stuff, though silly from time to time; he has read very widely and knows perhaps more about Shakespeare even than Mark. Hope I can get him, ought to know tomorrow. Thirkill has put me in 7:30 Hall instead of in 6:30 with the other Freshmen, which I like –

several I've met are pleasant but *young*. Came up from London with an East Indian who has a degree from Bombay and is following mathematics here, Trinity – have met, in a dozen chaps I've talked to, no one who is reading anything but math, physical or chemical science, and medicine. I shall be quite majestical and lonely in my pursuit of the Muse. The prize I got in London was a copy of Yeats' *A Vision*, numbered and signed, privately printed (600 – mine is No 46) in 1925 and at once withdrawn; to subscribers only for three guineas and I got it for one. The Cambridge bookshops are magnificent, and fortunately for my finances every store in town – it's quite an elaborate town really, eight theatres, superb London shops of all kinds, and dozens of book-shops, esp. Heffers, Bowes and Bowes, and Deighton, Bell – all famous – every store, I say, is anxious to extend credit illimitably. I'm not a fool, of course, but by God I need books so I have got some, principally the *Shorter Oxford [English Dictionary]*, which was only three pounds, and reading just in these several days I've found that a reliable dictionary is essential, particularly since I fancy I'll have to do a good deal of source work this year, change in language, etc. Also [William] Empson's *Seven Types of Ambiguity*, [J.A.K.] Thomson's historical study of Irony [*Irony: An Historical Introduction*], Dryden's *Poems*, Tennyson, Yeats' new book *A Full Moon in March* with two plays & poems, Wm Blake's *Prophetic Books* superbly edited, *The Letters of Keats*, books of poems by [Matthew] Arnold, [Louis] MacNeice, etc., [W.H.] Auden and [Christopher] Isherwood's new play, *The Ascent of F6*, [Samuel] Johnson's *Lives of the Poets*, two books of [I.A.] Richard's, *Oxford Book of 17th Cent. Verse* – nearly all of them reduced, some at ridiculously low prices (as, one shilling for the Johnson). Don't flinch – I'm being damn economical in every other way, and my book-buying hereafter will be intermittent.

I'm in Memorial Court, one of the most recent buildings in the University and Clare's "New Building" – very near the magnificent new University Library with its million and a half books; I'll send Bob a postcard of the Court. What conveniences! There are eight men on each staircase, four on the ground floor, four on the 2nd, each with his apartment; each staircase has two beautiful bathrooms and two beautiful toilets, and each man has hot & cold water in the elaborate basin in his bedroom. I'm amazed. But by God the English don't know when they're cold! Christ, I haven't been warm (except in bed since the God-sent eiderdown came) since I got off the *Britannic*. No heating but these little, if delightful, fires – and it's *freezing* out! Did I say England didn't get cold? Heh heh, croaked the skull. I now understand why the British call America a "hot house". It is, by these standards – unbelievable difference in customary temperatures.

I think I forgot to tell you several things about the trip over, such as that Pierre was robbed. Some one took $230 from his stateroom. He was incredibly calm about it, as he always is except in argument or when playing *be'be'*; we reported the thing and the stupid Master at Arms came and searched *his* room very thoroughly (why, God knows) but of course nothing could be done. Also Pierre inscribed and gave me a magnificent study of Harry Baur he did – it's on the door opposite, yellow and black, I may trace it for you sometime. And he did two drawings of me – one a face caricature, painful but very just, the other a full-length. And tell Bob we had movies every day on board, recent sound-talkies.

Package hasn't come yet but doubtless will – I'll probably write again this weekend if not before. Keep well, Mum – when the novelty wears away, I'm afraid I shall miss thee awfully – these British lads are mild but quite impenetrable – Love to Bob & Uncle Jack & Granny and you always

John

[In addition to George Rylands, whom Berryman describes above, the other Cantabrigians mentioned are:

Arthur S. Ramsey, who was president of Magdalene College, Cambridge.

Andrew Chiappe, who was an assistant supervisor in English at St. John's and Clare College. An American, Chiappe graduated from Columbia in 1933 and was a Kellett Fellow (1934–36) and a winner of the Oldham Shakespeare Scholarship (1935–36).

Henry Thirkill, who was president of Clare College.

Reverend William Telfer, who was dean of Clare College.]

[Cambridge]
Dearest Mother,   Sunday 11 October [1936]
I am at work and for perhaps the first time my mind is expanding enormously and valuably along its line – thoughts, sensations, images come swiftly constantly into the arena of use. Final success in some kind now appears a necessary concomitant to work, and I have a hard joy in the process.

Rylands I have got for my supervisor: very well-read, pleasant, he should be helpful. Two lectures Friday – one on Drama very bad but [T.R.] Henn gave what appears an interesting list of books; the other, by [E.M.W.] Tillyard the Milton authority, on the Romantic Revival was good and the rest of his looks better – Blake, Wordsworth, Coleridge and Keats – Shelley bores me except as infrequent opium – a world of his own as remote as Swinburne's. I'm doing a paper for Rylands, due Wednesday, in refutation of Johnson on Donne and have discovered some things in both texts: Johnson's moral vigilance (my own phrase, I've quit using other men's in so far as I can) is beautiful, however irrelevant to what should have been his account of [Abraham] Cowley & Donne. But theories of criticism interest me decidedly less than heretofore – I want more and more only intensity or the ineluctable authority of precise poetic statement.

In order not to appear rash I'm sending you three poems – one written last night after seeing *The Prisoner of Shark Island,* one on Yeats done night before last, and one written after having Ramsey and Chiappe in for tea on Wednesday. I think they have clarity and form and accuracy; as always, I'd like to know what you really think. Will send next time some more – I've done six others here and in London, all without intent or strain.

Thanks very much for the parcel, Mum – but no more, in faith: it had of course been opened by Customs, and I had – but not of course – to pay three and six (some 90 cents) at this end! Pillow slips, cap, sweater (for which gratitude), nut bar and *Times* – right? And for the letters – the *Safety News* is definitely horrible, the manner of the report, as always, being the horror – not fact but ritual, said he textually and seriously. It's a shame about packages, isn't it – but hardly worth it, and impossible this term, viewing my cash on hand. Incidentally, if each of you were to write me for my birthday – AND *NO MORE* – that would indeed be excellent and more than I wish, really. I've already had a gorgeous birthday dinner, on the 18th last, you know. No, I am a pig; there are two things I should greatly appreciate: if you'd put the two Rembrandts between cardboard & send them over – I don't think postage would be much – and I note that Knopf is to publish this fall [Wallace] Stevens' *Ideas of Order,* with new poems, in a trade edition; if you'd have some bookshop wrap that – when it's out – after you'd written in it, and send it – I'd be completely happy. And think of me somewhat two weeks from today – I shall doubtless be lonely.

The superb camera study of Yeats is over my writing table where I can see it always, looking up, or across from my big chair or the lounge. Mother, what strength and rigorous attention is in that man, what beauty and passion, men five hundred years from now will know as I do now.

And Pedro's ironic, tremendous Baur faces it from the opposite wall, on a panel of the door to my sleeping room. I've done a bad copy of it, to give you some idea – his lines are scrupulous, India ink, black as black, the fringe also, while all the rest of the space inside the borders is brilliant yellow, except the slits in the eyes and the broken triangle of mouth, which are white. A powerful thing. . . .

I hope you read [Allen] Tate's letter – he said some interesting things about "Ritual at Arlington" but condemned it for length & formlessness – neither he nor Mark seem to realize that something damn important is being said. I've tightened it again a bit with minor changes and by God somebody is going to print it or else. I'm going sometime soon to put some short pieces with it and try some publishers – though I hate the sending them off, waiting, mess. Would like a book out, here or there, next fall at the latest.

Met an excellent passage near the end of [Virginia Woolf's] *Mrs. Dalloway* – your copy I seem brazenly to have borrowed:

"A thing there was that mattered; a thing, wreathed about with chatter, defaced, obscured in her own life, let drop every day in corruption, lies, chatter. This he had preserved. Death was defiance. Death was an attempt to communicate; people feeling the impossibility of reaching the centre which, mystically, evaded them; closeness drew apart; rapture faded; one was alone. There was an embrace in death." Wrong, but good mysticism.

I have been in transports over a Second Edition of Shakespeare Rylands has – will tell you what I've found sometime at length. And even I got a 1720 edition of [Matthew] Prior's complete poems, bound in leather, contemporary (he died in 1721), – at Heffers yesterday for – don't faint – *five* shillings! Isn't that gorgeous? And I know you dislike [Ezra] Pound, but look at the remarkable statement I discovered recently in "Homage to Sextus Propertius":

"Standsgeniusadeathless
                    adornment,
            a name not to be worn out with the years."

That is first-rate, Mum, and you know it: the sculptured verse of Dryden
is rarely better. And I've found in Donne's "Love's Dietie" something
corresponding richly and nearly to my use of "ritual" –

                "And that *vice-nature, custome*, lets it be."

Cheerio, my love – back to work. I'm sorry to hear the play isn't
going well – Good luck with it and all health to you – my love to all the
family, and thee –

                                                                John

The three poems JB enclosed were:

[Homage to Film]

This night I have seen a film
That would have startled Henry James
Out of his massive calm
Of disciplines or sent Donne
Into tortuous passion, and all names
Of crafty men flooded with the sun.

The sun of another medium
Comes up the East, mechanical
As any art – slow, but it will come
Faster and finally find
Its noon an Argus brain that shall
Centre all complexities in mind.

Idiom and reference are but
Statistics of catastrophe,
Intensity is the lever that
Releases ecstasy in the bone
Of all men always, in city,
Hills, or in a wilderness of stone.

[Untitled]

A glory there is over Ireland now:
The numerous loud clamor that I hear
Crumbles, pretension falls before that light
Across the water; now I see the night
Scatter, as if enormous wind should blow
Down walls & towers and beat upon my ear
With praise of that great light.

An aged man there is in Ireland now
Alone who is the honour of that praise,
Craftsman intense and disciplined, a man
Who set luxuriance aside and ran,
A creature of bone & heart & rigid brow,
The race that wears the rest, eternal ways,
That solitary man.

Now in another land
Where ceremonies are strange
And on all sides I find
Complexities of change
Casting suspicion even on
The reliable sun,
Where only my past is mine:

What comfortable time
Is this of our afternoon,
Our three idioms the same
In origin, and soon
Talk will have made me a place
For the mind's peace,
A sanctuary for amenities.

Essay upon Love

Antique O uncanny symbol over
Commercial areas will wait
Daylight, declension of lover.

History here erect declares
Darkly the hands settle and
Soothe her excited hair

But manner of arrival knows
And the night remembers, having tongue,
Accent of our time will blow

Even upon her thighs in darkness
(O night has had silence) telling
Mechanical emphasis.

Compensatory symbol over
Commercial areas describes
Daylight, declension of lover.

[Of the three poems above only "Homage to Film" was published (in revised form in the spring 1940 issue of the *Southern Review*). In "Dream Song 7," titled " 'The Prisoner of Shark Island' with Paul Muni," JB again draws upon the same film as a source for the poem. Warner Baxter rather than Paul Muni, however, starred in the film.

"Ritual at Arlington" was a 360-line poem JB had submitted as an entry for the *Southern Review* Poetry Prize, which it failed to win. Allen Tate and Mark Van Doren were judges in the contest.

The Matthew Prior volume is his *Poems on Several Occasions* (London: T. Johnson, 1720). It is autographed and dated 10 October 1936 by JB, and is in his personal library.]

[Cambridge]

Dear Mum,   18 October 1936

Considerations of time and distance are conspiring to make me gloomy – it is more than dull to have been away a month without any intercourse, in the sense of an answer to one of my letters. Alas, how far and long from me thou art! etc.

I don't think I told you of how pleasant was my arrival here; the head porter, Neaves, was expecting me and came out to the cab to carry all my things into the Court and around to my staircase. Then, joyously, there was a huge fire in my room, everything clean and straight, bed made, drawers open and all very welcome. Mrs. Mizzen had lent me linen, and utensils etc. & food in the gyp room. And there were a dozen or fifteen letters on the big table – mostly of course from shops in town (I've had sixty by now, all very formally addressed and endlessly inviting – very different from procedure in the States). I was tired and hungry – got up late in London, packed hurriedly & barely made the noon train; it's three or four hours up, so tea-time and still nothing to eat! I wandered down the huge, secluded avenue of elms that begins opposite the entrance to this court and goes straight some 400 yds. to the other (old) court, crossing the lovely bridge en route. Almost no one back yet (no Chiappe or Ramsey) so I looked about and finally went in Matthew's for tea – a gorgeous Eliz. building (just before 1600), which was in the 18th century a famous Coffee House called "The Turk's Head". Delightful tea and quiet. Then back here to clean up for Hall at 7:30. Saw Thirkill later in the evening and to bed cheerily early. It was an awfully nice introduction.

Had luncheon Thursday at the Union with Chiappe and Gordon Fraser, who owns a splendid book-store here. While at St. John's here, he ran a little press called the Minority & published some twenty books, two by Americans – Mark [Van Doren]'s *John Dryden* & a pamphlet, *Dirty Hands* by [R.P.] Blackmur! Amazing, isn't it? Very interesting fellow. I've met one other interesting bookman – [Thomas F.] Langley, in charge of literature at Bowes & Bowes (the oldest bookshop in England – same building selling books since 1490 something!); had him in for tea Friday. My social record is now complete: Chiappe & Ramsey here for tea; remedy that. Have cut coffee – only one cup since I came up, and that at Ramsey's for luncheon. Still smoking – costs too much in several ways, but I will not stop.

Thanks for the notes on "*that!* disease!" No clinic here, & no University med. staff – must go to one of a dozen recognized physicians in town – all horribly dear, etc. I'm not sure about the "darkfield" – went to a Dr. Wm. R. Walker (I think) somewhere below 42nd St. and West; used the name "J. WARD". If you called them, they might have the record – doubt it, the blood man said the Wasserman was definite proof. At any rate, for Christ his dear sake don't go to work putting M. Walker out of his profession – the whole business is ugly, anyway. And don't say the name was wrong.

I've been trying to make up my mind whether to go again or not – you see, I'd need now both darkfield & Wasserman to be sure. I suppose I have got to, because of the dangers of infecting poor Mrs. Mizzen or someone else who handles my linen. Hate to do it, but I will tomorrow, & let you know.

I wish I had some time to work on a verse play I've been considering,

but I'm so busy (or indisposed) that I can't even get a design out. Mostly
very close work on Donne and Blake – the former under Rylands, who
knows Donne marvellously well thru long study & consultation with [Sir
Herbert J.C.] Grierson (who edited the authoritative text in 2 volumes,
Oxford 1912, [*The Poems of John Donne*] the one I'm using – the first
man to examine the bases in scholastic dogma of Donne's tropes) and
with [John] Hayward, who did the Nonesuch Donne [*Complete Poetry
and Selected Prose*]; incredibly complex poems, really, and magnificent.
Blake I'm doing largely on my own; Tillyard, whose study of Milton I'm
using with [Henry Charles] Beeching's text [*The English Poems of John
Milton*], lectured on Blake in the Romantic Revival last week; he held a
questionnaire also, reading three fragments (from Pope, Yeats & Marvell)
& asking the class for identification & comment – my comment he read
in the next lecture & I had a note asking me to come see him; so we had
a very interesting talk yesterday. Blake, besides being one of the six or
seven best English poets I find in reading, is a heart-breaking example of
a poet who constructed his philosophy rather than accepted one; that's
why his success is even more, in a sense, occasional than Donne's –
whose (if it is) minor place is due to his variety of action. Thus the *Prophetic Books*, in so far as I can now express an opinion, must expound,
not employ, a philosophical and moral system. Cf. Eliot in *The Use of
Poetry:* "A poet may borrow a philosophy or he may do without one. (e.g.
Dante; Chaucer – J.B.) It is when he philosophizes upon his own *poetic*
insight that he is apt to go wrong." (Eliot doesn't mention Blake but I
think he may have had him in mind – Shelley is being condemned, in
fact.) Here is the tortured thinness of "Ritual at Arlington" and the danger. We once discussed this, you remember; I have decided *to* choose but
not *what* to choose. My work in metaphysics & historical thought last
year I regret; I tend to *intellectual* dissatisfaction with what (say, Concept
of Flux, or Yeats' symbology, or dynamic materialism) might, could I
adopt it, prove *poetically* invaluable. – Beetle I reject because of his
uncompromising arrogance.

I'm terribly sorry those sons of bitches haven't done what they ought
about salary, and hope you find something else superb & quick. Glad of
Uncle Jack's sale. Don't worry unless you must, Mum. I, for example,
anticipate horrible difficulties but do they bother me? No Yes No!

Full quart of milk and loaf of bread each day, besides a huge dinner

in hall every evening: as, today: tea, corn flakes, bread butter & marmalade, for breakfast; scrambled eggs, milk, bread & butter, for lunch (here);
tea, with cakes, etc. very soon, and Hall tonight. The only thing is no
green fresh vegetables & no fruit – I'll try to at R.[Ryland]'s for lunch;
Union lunch, C. [Chiappe] & G.F. [Gordon Fraser] (G.F. paid, first-
rate Stilton & a light, excellent Burgundy); Langley here; visit to Tillyard
& 2 visits to Rylands – did 12 pp on Donne, all wrong. Oh yes, and
Ramsey for tea again – he & I are very good friends: much talk on physics
& literature and two charming long walks – came to a funny little town
some three miles away last night.

Back to Donne. My very best to everyone, and I pray that you haven't
sent anything for my birthday – the duties on everything are terrific &
me penniless or thereabouts – think cheerily of me next Sunday, Mum,
and all my love –

John

[Thomas F. Langley was responsible for the English Literature Department
at Bowes & Bowes, where he worked from 1927 to 1940.

Like the Wasserman test, "darkfield microscopy" is a procedure used in
examinations for syphilis. No further mention of this is made in the letters.]

[Cambridge]
Dear Mum,   27 October 1936

Before anything else, let me tell you something about which I have
been thinking for several days and which became crystallized in conversation with Rylands last evening. Unhappily in exposition it will probably
sound mystical or an instance of self-delusion, for it is impalpable as well
as highly concrete in operation. At any rate, here it is: the *tradition* of a
literature is an absolutely existing thing, and its action or inaction is principally a matter of *place*. Platitude, no doubt, but incredibly significant.
It means for example that Rylands, a man with considerable learning and
taste but essentially a dabbler, can in a valuable but intangible sense *know*
Wordsworth as no American scholar can, whatever his equipment. There
is a kind of solid propinquity in an Englishman's study of English poetry
that cannot, I feel, be duplicated. Not that the word "tradition" occurs
here even so often as it does in recent American criticism – but it has a
universal and real, a tacit, meaning. Blackmur is the supreme example
of really magnificent intellect without hieratic base, spending himself on

trivality. Without a tradition of homogeneity in place (Emerson, Whitman, Twain, Dickinson, Melville – individual excellences over a confused babble), Americans must assume that they use the English tradition of letters – so they do, in limitation, but the barriers are immense; moreover, America has never had such learning as the 18th century (Johnson, Addison, Walpole, Swift) had, and the stuff transplanted has been mostly topsoil. Now all this has not to do directly with the contemporary scene; I tend to think British scholarship is still superior in general, but there can be little doubt that American literature has been for thirty years and still is, both generally and individually – with the solitary and definite exception of Yeats – more resourceful, more interesting, more excellent than English literature. Its past is largely fictitious; it lacks, obviously, ultimate vitality – and whether these two observations are related causally, who can say? I am positive that talent, even genius, is but one part of greatness. So I suspect there is a chain. What is to happen, no one of course knows; my real point is that the task of the American writer is infinitely more difficult than anyone has assumed, and that a definite severance in the tradition has taken place. Both now lose – the English by their neglect of isolated splendid writers in America in the 19th century and by their appalling ignorance of a contemporary literature which is analogous to, and more vital than, their own.

The temptation is very great to attempt to identify one's self with the rich valid history of English literature – Eliot could not resist it, and Pound has gone further in taking European culture for his personal tradition. But you never get there, I think: what you write is pastiche in the last analysis: cf. the [St. Thomas á] Becket play [Eliot's *Murder in the Cathedral*] and the *Cantos*. My entire [idea] in fact applies only to a great writer or the possibility of one. The problem is not incorrigibly remote: I wrote Thursday the prologue to a play – again, the temptation is great, nor is it despicable, to use an English milieu or an abstract milieu instead of a local American one, which is all I know – but how can I? Unless Eliot's 40 years in London. So the creation of the action is halted while I decide a problem which it is horrible to think must arise. The real difficulty being this: American standards, a few men aside, are so thin or pedantic (result of adoption of letter not energy) that one hates to be judged directly by them (thus: [Archibald] MacLeish's *Panic* & [Maxwell] Anderson's *Winterset* are called excellent); moreover, since I must use, verbally and ideologically, the English tradition in so far as I can, I dislike raising barriers between my work and the real standards, which are still largely British. Impasse. Continuance of lyrics agonizing in their minor-ness; and perplexity.

I'm sorry to have run into such a damn essay, but I was sure you'd be interested and I was working the thing out as I wrote. Letter-writing, as you suggest and as I've said in some previous letter, is a hell of a problem. Your suggestion of typing with carbons (exactly what Ramsey *did*, curiously) is a good one, but impossible – something to be read by a dozen people would have definitely to be a composition and I shrink from it. More and more I hate any studied appearance of literature except in formal, definite literature – letters should be careless more than set, and personal. You'll have noticed I've taken to penning letters – and I do to everyone – not typing – not by any means affectation, but desire to avoid a literary, mechanical appearance. I'm glad, of course, that Keats' letters are preserved because they're so damn interesting; but fortunately my opinion of my own ability as a letter-writer has descended to nil, so far as general interest goes; and in the event that I become well-known, I should detest having any of my personal letters printed.

There are routine difficulties, of course: now that I've written those priceless words on English and American literary tradition, I should like, despite the overstatement in them, for Mark, Halliday, Blackmur, Tate, Giroux and [George Marion] O'Donnell to see them. But it's palpably hopeless. More than ever, I abhor copying, so that I won't even sit down now and type them off for my own use. Last winter and spring, I copied a few letters before sending them, but never again – what arrogance! So I just write to one person after another, sometimes telling a good deal, sometimes little – only to you have I tried to tell anything like the ALL of my "impressions" (horrible word!). And spacing them over this month (I've written about a dozen besides five to you, and still owe three), it hasn't been too dull. When I see them again, we can talk; if not, it doesn't matter.

In line with this separation of formal literary "personality", by the way, I've practically decided to use simply JOHN BERRYMAN for all verse or dramatic publications, and J.A.M. BERRYMAN for everything else. What think you?

Can't get more in one envelope. Will resume this tonight.

All my love
John

Dearest Mum,   Midnight, 27 October [1936]

The circumstantial letter can wait – I want to speak of what's very nearest the centre of my brain. But there's nothing to say – it's just that great, incredibly great plays *can* be written, and I'm positive – I must be positive for I hope so greatly, so intolerably – that I can write them. I want time and all strength – I've been reading *Lear* over and over in a kind of frenzy – perhaps not for ten years and I've so little to go on and so much to get over – I'm consumed with inessentials, I *want things* and *attitudes* which are of no value, I want love and the apparatus of love but I can feel energy pouring out of me for this, for everything – I've just made some verses that will tell you better than I can:

What absolute horizon calls them there?
I saw the white-haired men go one by one
Up a great stair: the whiteness of the sun
Showed crimson blood pounding beneath the hair.

Yet agony has outline, the flesh bone,
Christ cried a formal anguish on the cross:
Leaving the time and power, he saw the loss
Cancelled with white hair and white hair alone.

Last monuments and crystal, those undone
And those the fierce blood in the vein desires,
Dried white with time, fallen their many fires,
I saw the white-haired men ascend the sun.

[Draft of unpublished poem by JB entitled "Symbol"]

I must have an inexorable discipline, but I will not take it – and even would I, how is it possible? Money, I have to live, and chance energies always – what certainty finally?

– Flowers, flowers

and we'll wear out
In a wall'd prison, packs and sects of great ones
that ebb and flow by the moon.
[William Shakespeare, *King Lear*]

The strict majesty of a ritual, if one can endure it – men, save some fools, were not made for art – it breaks them and breaks them – but I must be willing, for I've no choice.

John

[Cambridge]

Dearest Mum: 28 October 1936

How we gulp over the things we've just said, and attempt to swallow our confusion? No more typewriters, he cried dramatically; but this morning letters came from you and Mark, so temperately and delightfully written and unliterary, albeit typewritten, that I am back at my damn first-love. And a good thing for my correspondents in as much as my dear horrible script is ugly and quite illegible, and a good thing for me in saving time. While I am on letters; I heard the other day from [Robert Penn] Warren of *The Southern Review*. He accuses me [in "Ritual at Arlington"] of imitation of Tate's ode ["Ode to the Confederate Dead"], lack of form, and general crabbedness, concluding: (damn sheet keeps turning in the machine)

Please take these remarks in the spirit in which they are meant. (heh heh) We simply feel that because your work is so good we owe you an explanation for not publishing it as it stands. We are positive that in the near future we shall be able to arrange a large display for you in *THE SOUTHERN REVIEW*, if your present poem can be taken as a fair sample of your general performance. We beg you to keep us in mind and to let us see as soon as possible anything else you may have on hand.

The worst of it being that he is quite correct. There are only two things to do: discard the poem and forget it, or take it to pieces and rewrite. Neither, unhappily, am I disposed to do; but I hate to throw away all my work and some of those lines, so I'm going to see about going over it. Rylands being the only decent person available (unfortunate that I couldn't see Mark or Tate or Warren for detailed criticism), I've given it to him; he says much the same thing (failure to secure emphasis by alternation of intensity, relaxation, etc.) and wants to go over it line by line with me, which we'll do; then I'll see. Glad to have it back: only my occasional spasms for publication want poor or imperfect stuff printed. Meanwhile, as you know, I keep in a frightful state of nervous excitation, writing more poems than is good for me and unable to keep at anything for very long. This climate is very unsettling, I still have a miserable cold, etc. I hope you are all keeping well.

Your offer to type out the letters is very generous, but frankly I don't think I could bear looking at my effusions typed out by some one else in a formal record, and I should think it would kill you to type out some of the idiocy, so heigh ho and thanks awfully much for the offer. I enclose the first and only two pages of my most recent attempt at a journal – the first is largely silly but I want you to note the quotations, and the second it's easier to send than incorporate the material here. If I feel inspired some day writing to someone I shall put a carbon in and send you it. Wrote Granny and Bob – hooray for Bob's blisters, Christ did I have them.

Thanks very much for the memoranda on phone calls; I'll send you a cheque for thirty-five dollars as soon as the charming Registrar communicates with me in the form of two hundred – and if he doesn't, little John will have to take to the heath and be a-cold, pursued by the foul fiend in a whirlwind. Very very glad that you returned half of Granny's gift, very thankful for the gift from all of you and especially pleased that it wasn't more. For God his noble sake don't send, now or in the future, [Wallace] Stevens's book or any other books – even if one end could afford it (being you), the other (being me) couldn't. But general information, anything under a dollar in value can be sent by letter-post duty-free, a good thing to know. All else costs like hell. And things sent from here cost much more – for example, the duty on books entering the United States is a cool *third!* So we shall have to be sufficient unto the day, etc.

The note about borrowing is correct; in fact, members of the University are absolute forbidden to have anything to do with money-lenders. I have got two pounds from Ramsey and expect to get through on that and this. Have contracted of course gorgeous debts in town, for tea things and a little bookcase and coat-slacks-shoes and especially books, but I shall pay them off directly I have my cheque. Think that with strict economy (heh heh, that from me) I can get through till January 1938 and emerge even, in which case the last thousand dollars would have some three hundred dollars left at the end. Can't tell; my vacations must be damned inexpensive, and I've got several ideas on them from Ramsey. Ireland especially. About next summer I don't know; might be home, might not – the only certainty appears to be hunger. The very elaborate set-up and superb service here amuses me greatly in view of my poverty. But please don't worry because I'm not. I have of course bought a hell of a lot of books and I'm reading them not looking at them: they are mostly very inexpensive and books that I will always use; many of them cannot be got in the States and all of them would be more expensive by a great deal there. Your advice is just, except that it's impossible to tell the difference between a book I need and a book I want; for in a sense I don't *need* any books but my Shakespeare and Blake and Donne and Yeats' collected poems and a few others. *But* Montaigne and [A.C.] Bradley's *Shakespearean Tragedy* and Tillyard's *Milton* and Auden's new poems [*Look, Stranger!*] & play [*The Ascent of F6*, co-written with Christopher Isherwood] and Yeats' autobiographies and Cowley and Marvell and King and the Oxford French verse [*The Oxford Book of French Verse, XIIIth Century – XXth Century*] and decent texts of *Hamlet* and *Winter's Tale* and *Lear* – there I merely *want*, if you like; but I need them too. Wherefore, no rule except sanity and buying as damn little hereafter as possible; but I don't regret any I've already got – and I may tell you in confidence, honey, that they are about five hundred million. In any case I can always return them or flee the country or perhaps Beetle will pay. Only one thing is sure: that I shall not ask nor expect anything at all further from you, whatever occurs – only, should I be destitute, I shall demand a loaf of bread to be paid punctually on the nineteenth of each month, and woe betide thee if it fail! I'm awfully glad to hear that something may happen through H. and wish you the absolute best of all luck – let me know directly anything turns up; and should the horrible incredibly occur and things fall short, let me know if I can send you some money. Not, however, my love, until December, unless farthings can help, and few of them. Enough of vile finance. And if you haven't been roaring with laughter through your disapproval I disown you, woman, and all your infamous works.

Can't understand why Jean hasn't heard; I wrote her a day or so after coming up (and again several days ago) and she should have had it by the time you wrote. I've heard nothing but a letter from her in London. Curse the woman for not writing and give her my love.

You are wrong. Ripeness *is* all; and what a superb phrase that is in context, isn't it? By god your writing is difficult, worse than mine I do believe; I have just spent an even eight minutes trying to decode two curious combinations of private symbols. What I always say is I'll bet this is a damn good letter because the scrawl at the end infers that it may be from my mother, but it would be damn nice if I could read it too. Never mind, our writing has a certain careless look which I like, as if it didn't really care whether or not it could be read and as if to say to the puzzled reader Well I'm not going to help you. ——— I have various thoughts on your moral reflections, but am not in a mood to work them out; sometime later. I am curious *re* your accusations about "States"; listen: I heard America called nothing else on the boat coming over, and it is not often called anything else here; America is too general a term and the United States is, as you know, too unwieldly for use, so everyone, from no matter what nation, says "States" and it is a purely descriptive term like Germany or the British Isles, my love. As for the accent: there is of course no such thing as an English accent, I have heard forty accents here and in London; two or three people have seemed to speak more clearly and more pleasantly than anyone I've heard at home, so I suppose it is correct to say that I prefer their accent to the "American" accent – not that there is an American accent either; but my own speech has not changed in the slightest particle, except that I must use certain university expressions and I'm dropping words which are not used here. I don't think it will change, either; Ramsey's has not, and I see no reason why it should. My French improves steadily, by the way, thru Montaigne, Baudelaire, Rimbaud and general reading in French poetry. Have readily learned to eat in the untiring English manner and in some ways it is certainly more efficient, in others (with most vegetables and especially peas) less. My coat is a violent light grey check-tweed, the trousers indiscriminate light flannel; very light colors worn here and no suits at the university; shoes black and excellent; they were all very cheap, and from a good tailor.

The [probably Donald Culross] Peattie article is interesting – too damn "poetic" for my enjoyment but he said some valuable things. Heavens the autumn is gorgeous here, as I think I've hinted: it's a huge joy to go down the avenue between here and the Old Court each time. Have played some tennis with Ramsey, thought of rowing but I don't know; I continue thin and not very energetic except mentally, where I am in a furor, he cried proudly. Must stop this and get to Hall, the bell is about to ring meaning five minutes to get over to the other court, and if you're late, which I always am, you miss the first course or the first two courses or the first three courses and all my punctuality has faded quite, leaving only a mass of instincts, one of which is to eat, so fare thee well, inasmuch as I really must do some Dryden when I come back. All and all my love always,

John

[JB had revised "Ritual at Arlington" and sent it to Robert Penn Warren, then an editor at the *Southern Review*. The poem was rejected and it has never been published.]

Memorial Court
[Cambridge]
Dearest Mum,   11 November 1936
I am still so excited that I want to rush in various contradictory directions. Coming in for breakfast yesterday, I found on my table a letter from Ireland and lo – you are correct – it was from Yeats. Without telling anyone, you see, I swallowed my scruples a month ago and wrote him; a brief letter saying merely that, speaking almost anonymously, I wanted to tell him what I and many other people quite unknown to him thought of his work. I probably never should have come to it except that sitting thinking over one of his books I wrote the verses I've sent you, then it seemed a shame that, whether they were good or not, he should never see them, so I immediately wrote, sending them with the prose praise. In a postscript I said that I hoped to be able to see him when I got to Ireland if that was possible, but that he was very mistaken if he thought I expected an answer to my letter (which was true). So I was all the more astonished and delighted to have this.
The man writes a quite illegible and characterless scrawl – in fact the worst I've ever seen – and it took me an hour to make the few lines out. They are written on a single sheet of white notepaper with an engraved address thus: Riversdale,
Willbrook,
Rathfarnham,
Dublin.
The letter goes:

Dear Mr. Berryman   Nov 9
    I found your letter Oct 9 on
my return home a few days ago.
I thank you for it and the more because

the poems you select for praise
are those that I most approve.
I thank you too for the eloquent
compliment of your verse

Yours
W B Yeats

The "Yours", characteristically, is nothing but two marks (**ℑↄ**), "home" is written over a scratched-out "here" and "it" in the third line and "the" in the sixth are inserted afterwards with under-marks; the "and" is an indiscriminate swirl. Amazing hand. But God the thing is beautifully phrased and how courteous! If only I can see him and talk with him and see the tower and the winding stair and Coole Park, my joy will be complete. I read him constantly and have dozens of the poems by heart, which is good because I needn't have a book to be able to say them anywhere, on the bicycle or in bed. New things strike me all the time, listen to the rich simplicity of this

I meditate upon a swallow's flight,
Upon an aged woman and her house,
A sycamore and lime tree lost in night
Although that western cloud is luminous;
Great works constructed there in nature's spite
For scholars and for poets after us;
Thoughts long knitted into a single thought,
A dance-like glory that those walls begot.
[William Butler Yeats, "Coole Park, 1929"]

I hope the punctuation is right, though often it doesn't matter with Yeats (his first drafts are usually almost without it), but I shan't be pedantic enough to look.

Discouraging perfection in our time
Breaks infinite bright anvils, breeds despair
Over my casual coals; but where has been
Flood will go also brook; may find the sea.
[Unpublished fragment by JB]

Well! Those lines are unique in being composed directly, without premeditation or echo, in a letter, and in being composed on the typewriter; curious, after writing the first line I noted the pentameter and the thing went easily on. Fatal facility. I have written only four lines (and of them really only the second) that I would consider by (or in the same realm with) Yeats:

> Yet agony has outline, the flesh bone,
> Christ cried a formal anguish on the cross;
> Leaving the twelve and time he saw the loss
> Balanced with white hair but white hair alone.
>
> [Revision of middle stanza of "Symbol," page 64]

"Yet" should be strongly emphasized and held, as signifying "still", "even now". I went over five poems with Rylands Monday, and was amazed to find him a brilliant technical and ideological critic – Blackmur could have said no more about them; all need working on, but it is so difficult, I'm not willing to submit to what R P B would call "The discipline of craft". Whereas Yeats writes in his autobiographies: ". . . I had surrendered myself to the chief temptation of the artist, creation without toil. Metrical composition is always very difficult to me, nothing is done upon the first day, not one rhyme is in its place; and when at last the rhymes begin to come, the first rough draft of a six-line stanza takes the whole day." While I am on this, I want to give you another passage from the autobiographies which is absolutely basic – attend very closely:

"I am persuaded that our intellects at twenty contain all the truths we shall ever find, but as yet we do not know truths that belong to us from opinions caught up in casual irritation or momentary fantasy. As life goes on we discover that certain thoughts sustain us in defeat, or give us victory, whether over ourselves or others" (compare here, Mum, the famous statement in [Yeats'] *Per Amica Silentia Lunae*: "We make out of the quarrel with others, rhetoric, but of the quarrel with ourselves, poetry."), "and it is these thoughts, tested by passion, that we call convictions. Among subjective men (in all those, that is, who must spin a web out of their own bowels) the victory is an intellectual daily recreation of all that exterior fate snatches away, and so that fate's antithesis; while what I have called 'the Mask' is an emotional antithesis to all that comes out of their internal nature. We begin to live when we have conceived life as tragedy."

No comment is necessary save that I entirely concur. I am getting farther and farther into Yeats' metaphysics and symbolology; they are engrossing. You will be interested, by the way, to know that Yeats apparently agrees with a statement you made to me: "Perhaps it is safest to have one's life in airtight compartments, with love and affection at home, and mental stimulation & companionship abroad. . . . " In "Michael Robartes and the Dancer", she asks: "May I not put myself to college?"

He:

> Go pluck Athena by the hair;
> For what mere book can grant a knowledge
> With an impassioned gravity
> Appropriate to that beating breast,
> That vigorous thigh, that dreaming eye
> And may the devil take the rest.

I am certain that I should prefer ignorance in a lover to pretension when there is neither taste nor knowledge in her, but beyond that I don't know. The fact remains that, intelligence aside, I get something – a vivacity, a quickened interest – from conversation with women that I get in another way with men. (They must obviously, at the minimum, be attractive or interesting women.) And I miss it sadly here; the girls on the boat were inconceivably stupid, but I had but left home and was in any case sufficiently interested in Donga; but during my first month in England I think I spoke to no women, Mrs. Mizzen excepted. In Cambridge there are the college girls of Newnham and Girton, difficult to meet and all that I have seen in lectures are hopeless, and the town girls, who by a curious and rigid etiquette are looked down upon if they associate with undergraduates; the seduction motif is not, I find, referred to but it is *present*, and the custom is of ancient standing; anyway, only one or two town girls I've seen would matter. The English woman is healthy in the worst and dullest sense: thick, uninteresting, not delicate or charming, so far as I can see from my non-existent experience. Complete celibacy bores me ineffably. There are many dances in the town, some with and some without proctorial permission, but cutting is unknown, there are few men alone and I suspect the dancing is unspeakably poor. If I don't soon hear from Jean I'll tear the place apart. What in the devil is the girl up to? Tell Bob to beat her. For exactly ten days, before the first of these last two letters of yours (the second came this morning), I received no letter from Amer-

Mrs. Berryman and her grandfather, General Robert Glenn Shaver.

JB with his father, John Allyn Smith, in McAlester, Oklahoma, circa 1915.

JB and Mrs. Berryman, circa 1916.

John Allyn Smith

JB on the day of his graduation from P.S. 69 (Jackson Heights) with his brother, Robert Jefferson, 1926.

JB, far left, front row, with his graduating class at South Kent School, 1932.

Above left, Ernest Milton "Milt" Halliday, in 1934; JB's friend and classmate at Columbia. Above right, Jean Bennett, to whom JB became engaged while attending Columbia.

Below left, Mark Van Doren, JB's most influential teacher at Columbia. Below right, JB on graduation from Columbia, 1936.

JB with his friend Pedro Donga, on board the *Britannic*.

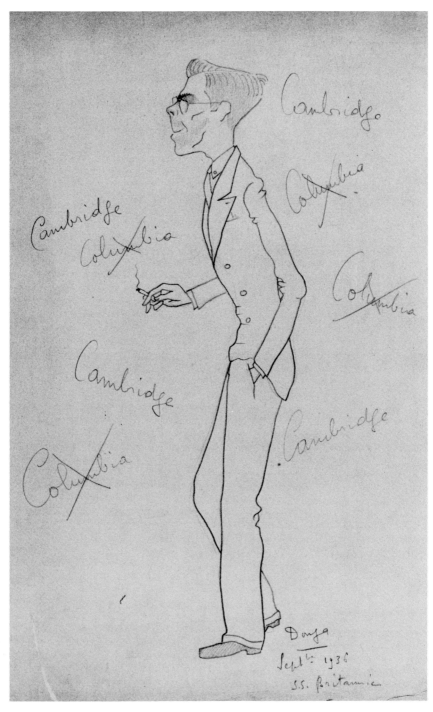

Pedro Donga's sketch of JB, done on the *Britannic*.

John Angus Berryman, Mrs. Berryman, and Robert Jefferson Berryman, September 1937.

ica – several from London and France and many from Cambridge here, but none from New York, none from Mississippi, none from Maine, none from Michigan; it was infuriating. And especially Jean – will you tell her that from [Jane] Atherton, whom I've written once, I've had two letters, while from *her*, who is supposed to be somewhat closer and whom I've written four times, I've had only *one*, and that six weeks ago??? I gnash teeth. Shake the woman soundly and pinch her into correspondence, alack alack, and are the horns sprouting?

I can see that I'm going to have to finish this and answer your delightfully full letters in another envelope, so I'll close this in sending one of Yeats's latest poems, something beyond even that magnificent symphonic line in "Among School Children":

> World-famous golden-thighed Pythagoras

(and you should know that Yeats pronounces the "y" like the I in thigh)
It is called "A Prayer for Old Age"

> God guard me from those thoughts men think
> In the mind alone;
> He that sings a lasting song
> Thinks in a marrow-bone;
>
> From all that makes a wise old man
> That can be praised of all;
> O what am I that I should not seem
> For the song's sake a fool?
>
> I pray – for fashion's word is out
> And prayer comes round again –
> That I may seem, though I die old,
> A foolish, passionate man.

And like most of his poems it should be read aloud a hundred times – sometimes only after weeks of reading have I understood an intonation, as in the seventh line here, with its heavily stressed O and lesser but equal stresses on the two I's. And there's still room for the very recent lines on O'Duffy that apply rather to Yeats himself:

> Had even O'Duffy – but I name no more –
> Their school a crowd, his master solitude;

Through Jonathan Swift's dark grove he passed, and there
Plucked bitter wisdom that enriched his blood.
[William Butler Yeats, "Parnell's Funeral"]

My love to all of you and thee,
John,

[P.S.] Wish I had copied my letter to Yeats; am sure I mentioned "The
Second Coming", the poems in "Words for Music Perhaps", "Sailing to
Byzantium", "The Fisherman", and, I think, "Among School Children", "In Memory of Major Robert Gregory" and several others. But
which ones out of so many splendid?

[Cambridge]
Dearest Mum,   Saturday 28 November 1936

Great congratulations on your early success with the Neva-Wets, and
I hope extremely that the very best has come out of it. Spent several hours
last evening making some stanzas out of my emotion of the circumstances
and you, but nothing much to show; if it gets into tolerable shape, I'll
send it. I verily believe your son's romantic sentimentality is becoming
diffused through his mind: things that never moved me now affect me
strongly and I find heroic possibilities and tragic dimensions everywhere.
But the craft is no better and as I get farther into the seventeenth century
I really despair – the amazing amazing strength and beauty that even the
least of them had. Vaughan especially for the last few days; I'm afraid my
letters have been much too much literary tirades, so I shan't quote or
expostulate any, but when I return we're going to read a lot of them
aloud. I've found myself all fall, since the fine weather wore off, in an
astounding state – all tangents and excitation; have spent many hours
pondering eternity and deity and the short light between darknesses, minute thesis and huge antithesis, and various other things that were best left
alone. Isolation and fragmentary contact work curiously on me; but my
forte is not introspection, and besides in this letter I've resolved to tell
you the things I've neglected to before, external condition etc.

Several weeks ago, for instance, we had the most exciting time dear
Cambridge sees, Guy Fawkes' night (Nov 5, I think). The University
(some 5555) and the entire town (some 55,555) gathered in Market Square,
a large central open place bordered by shops, theatres, and centred with
a fountain, and pandemonium reigned for four hours – immense and
dangerous fireworks, dozens of bobbies, wars of town and gown, vast

noise, fog and general chaos. Enterprising undergraduates scaled the lampposts and put out all the lights on the square but two, with eleven policemen finally guarding one and nineteen the other; one chap was clubbed to insensibility, two others and I carried him out and got a doctor who brought him to; great rushing about & the unpredictable mass movements that always enchant me, taunting of the abstract in the particular "Robert", solidarity and flares and sudden explosions at your heel and leaping. All delightful but it's a source of astonishment to me that many aren't killed; everything shut off about ten minutes of twelve (all undergraduates have, under penalty of expulsion – being sent down – rustication or suspension, to be in their colleges by midnight, and none can leave those precincts after ten, a tedious ruling) and a littered silence prevailed, save for the protests of those students who were arrested for light-putting-out and sent down by their Tutors. The classic imperturbability all over England goes mad on this one night. . . .

I've been following two courses of reading which are peculiarly interesting in my present status. Mencken's *American Language* is really an extraordinary job, and a very good thing to be reading when I hear the island varieties of English so continually, and even the American speech I hear (my own, Ramsey, Kay's) I find I hear more acutely by contrast. Contrary to the usual rule of shortening, I've heard here irrepar'able, agile, futile gar'age, labor'atory (emphases on syllable before accent mark) and of course various oddnesses such as the silence of c in *sche*dule, etc. The rhythms of speech are very different also; unless I attend closely, I sometimes fail to understand several sentences at a time. The other reading is Henry James. I began a month or so ago with *The American,* an early novel I once read for Mark but hastily; then several long stories, esp. *The Aspern Papers & The Turn of the Screw,* then the 900-page *Portrait of a Lady,* which I immensely recommend as one of the finest novels in the language, close in fact to the masters of fiction (all give you different names, when I say masters I mean Dostoievsky, Balzac, Defoe, Fielding, Melville and one or two others); it can be got complete in the Modern Library now, I strongly advise you to read it if you've a chance; am now in the middle of *The Sense of the Past,* a novel he left unfinished, like *The Ivory Tower,* at his death – the famous late style is surely extraordinary, little statement and continual qualification by clause and phrase, amazingly involved, terribly difficult, ambiguous in the extreme, though James is never in the least simple. Particularly interesting to read him here because his themes as you know involve frequently (in every case I've thus far read) Americans abroad, and the various and subtle impacts are superbly rendered. *The Sense of the Past*, incidentally, must be the unacknowledged father of *Berkeley Square* – remarkable similarity. I am theoretically in Chaucer and the seventeenth century exclusively, but this term I've allowed myself much leeway into French and contemporary literature; what the hell is the day to day point of being here if I'm to follow American graduate school grind-teeth curricula? But next term I'll do six hours a day on set work.

Sunday, [29 November 1936]

. . . I may as well say that I am thoroughly convinced of the value of residence abroad for a time, there is no question but that it alters perspectives and shifts emphasis, but the process is bound for me at least to be somewhat painful; what you mainly lose is the defensive attitude which has its dogmatic virtues if narrow and incomplete; what you gain I'm not yet sure, in detail; this is a hell of a good thing for me, always hoping I can emerge fairly even financially, but my fantastic incompetence and at present nerve-edge sensibility make it difficult. If I could make one decent poem, I should feel infinitely better, justified, calm, etc; but I can't or in any case haven't. And at my back I always hear . . I daresay I've wasted this term but it couldn't be helped, and much more to the same effect – you know the tune, my dear. The only thing I'm at the moment certain of is that I wish you and Bob and Uncle Jack and Granny the merriest holiday ever, and you the quintessence of material appreciation of the various genius I have occasion to know so damn well. Please please send practically nothing for Christmas; I should like a small American something that I can keep from each of you, but beyond that nothing; I shall be furious if you spend money. Set me a place at Christmas dinner, said he sentimentally – no, don't, the table isn't big enough. But would you have Jean over on that day sometime and kiss her for me and let her kiss you for me – much, much, love, Mum

John

[Mrs. Berryman had applied for a position with the Neva-Wet Corporation.]

The following letter from Mrs. Berryman is the only one of hers from the Cambridge period that has survived. In it she responds both to JB's November 28 letter and to a "second letter" of his which appears to have been lost:

[Philadelphia]
Tuesday, 15 December 1936
and if not (which it certainly
isn't) the night before Christmas,
still the last day before the
sailing of the last mail to
England before Christmas said she
Dearest John, dear son: on one long breath.

You are a lamb, I love you with practically all crannies of my heart,
but are you definite? no no a *thous*and times no (that is the raging fury
in the old red brick church building on the east side that I made feeble
efforts to drag us to all last summer – I am so glad you saw and from the
musician's flying elbows almost participated in its perpetration) – are you
sure? are you certain? do you know? do you tell? Sadly she shook her
head. I was delighted to learn that you would relish a small something
from America, although at that late last Friday on which I learned it there
was no possibility except by the Queen Mary which means letter mail
only, but you left me completely ignorant of where that s.s. should be
addressed: you 'lowed that you'd probably move out to the Frasers' (poor
addressless folk; no doubt, worthy and perhaps kind, but my dear after all
without address?) the next week, Paris was still unheard from but not
entirely out of the picture, and you just might dash off to Ireland! I can
quite understand that you are or were in a state of some and no doubt
natural or necessary indecision, but should you again attain that state, it
would be well to give your correspondents or at least this one some address
to use for fun boys and girls. As it is, I sent the large envelope to college,
gave that address to John Angus and to Bob who are both writing via Her
Majesty, advised Mother to write there with perhaps copy [to] Paris as I
had done last time, and am sending this in triplicate to college, the Fraser[s']
and Paris: if you do not jaunt continentward this vac, best write the American Express to forward your mail, as you have a collection there by now,
all of mine having been marked "please hold for arrival" and the earliest
dating back to November 26th or so. Life is intricate, complex, and complicated by guys like youse, said she with sombre not simple fervor. . . .

Your November 28th letter, full of information and detail, was happily welcomed and enjoyed – for myself, I find that a certain amount of
leisure or peace of mind, preferably both, is necessary for immersion in

literature or critical analysis, and at this time I have neither. It is inconceivable to me that your study of the amazing strength and genius of the
seventeenth century should make you despair – one can be dazzled by
the light or use it to see the way, in the first it blinds one to despair, in
the second . . there I go again, rubbing the bloom off with stupid reiter-
ation. It is to be expected that you should be very lonely, having had
close contact for so long a time with those to whom you are most dear
and most valued; I am never without a sense of loss in your absence and
it has been intensified by my time spent here in Philadelphia alone [on
business] and by my inability to come to close terms with Bob – and how
much more lonely have you been. But the strength to be gained by the
standing alone should be worth more than all the pangs to you, if you
will forego self-dramatization about them. You really, you know, John,
aren't the worst-off fellow in the world, offhand, I can think of two or
three people in a slightly worse position. Of course, if you want to suffer,
shut my mouth, as the old nigger said – go ahead and wrap yourself in
sable gloom and wear yourself out in moans. If you don't write a good
poem now, you will next month or week or year or tomorrow – after all,
son, you aren't precisely aged yet. And the statement "And at my back I
always hear . ." – I don't know what you think you hear, but it is possible
that it might be the following love and thoughts of any number of people,
or the echo of your own advancing feet. I lived through years of anguish
because I refused to recognize the accomplished fact, I contemplated it
always as something susceptible to change under thought, will or action –
just so is your attitude toward man, time and life: you carry your attitude
of magic into them, grieving as if over a son who could be other if he
would, and that is false premise. They can be no other if he would, and
that is false premise. They can be no other than they seem to you and by
no amount of taking thought can they be other. You are so deeply a
believer in magic, that there is no cause and effect (health is NOT the
result of sound habits of food, sleep and exercise – no, illness does *not*
invade successfully the body weakened by bad habits, it just comes and
then just goes away, causeless and reasonless – I could multiply them by
the millions, these instances), and you contemplate the known things of
existence as if under that contemplation they could make lions into asps.
But no, my son: man can not live without breathing or eating or sleeping,
no amount of thought can make it other, and just as these are true, so

are your own concepts of man, of time, of life – you can accept or ignore your own beliefs on those subjects, but it is the height of stupidity to fight them.

As for your second letter, I am not wrong, there is compensation here albeit nothing beyond. I am of the earth earthy and the compensation here is all I need. For you, I am wrong, but not for myself – this is what I have made with the sweat of my soul and it is good. By its light I live as well as I can, and no light that allows such living is bad, it is good. I am not godlike, I did not say, let there be light and there was light, no – I struggled and fought my taught faith and my faulty reasoning and my slack will, and gradually, not having seen the invading gray of dawn, there was light for my feet. How can you say that the disinterested, passionate intellect of Swift, of Vaughan, is vanished, spent irretrievable: while *you* live and breathe, are they dead? Man has two immortalities: the flesh and the spirit, and the second is often the gift of the artist to one whom he perpetuates. The first is common, the second properly rare, or how crowded would be the mind's inheritance. You writhe as if never before had there been greed, starvation, oblivion – always there have been these, as always have been laziness, weakness, cruelty, indifference, hate – but one need not live on them. Man is what he feeds on, or why should he feed there? You're wrong, I don't wait, except on the small and unimportant details that matter not, I live as well as I can. I believe that I shall live only in the flesh, that the mind will leave nothing tangible behind it in my case, but I have no regrets, the flesh in which I shall live is dear to me, dearer than the plaudits of the knowing. For myself, I am content – for your anguish, I grieve.

I love you so dearly, son.

Your devoted mother,
Jill Angel Berryman

4, Rue Cadet
Paris
Dearest Mum,   Christmas Day [1936]
It's eleven-thirty now, I came in an hour ago and have written Mark – had a long, marvellous letter from him. Good walk: wandered for a time, found myself in the Rue des Martyrs, and systematically followed streets,

watching shops, cafés, theatres and people; got an excellent map of Paris
the first night, but can only generally trace my progress on it – terribly
complex city; one tiny square or ⟨⟨place⟩⟩ will have half a dozen streets,
all different names, going from it at as many angles (and many hills,
streets crossing above streets, etc. Also, I hear, many bridges, none of
which I've yet seen – will begin tomorrow). Roughly, this evening I followed the Bd. de Rochechouart, the Bd. de Clichy (further complication
results from the fact there are also, and at angles, a Rue Rochechouart
and a Rue Clichy, etc., just as there is a section *Montmartre*, a Bd.
Montmartre, and a Rue du Faubourg Montmartre), the Bd. des Batig-
nolles, the Bd. de Courcelles, the Rue du Rocher, passing variously through
the Place Pigalle, the Place Blanche (where I broke down and had "un
chocolat" for 80 centimes; – 100 centimes = 1 franc = (4 cents about),
then to the Gare St. Lazare, passing the superb stone-steel-glass, *très
moderne* building of La Compagnie de Distribution Parisienne d'Électricité;
thence along the Bd. Haussmann and its magnificent stores, the opera,
the Bd. des Italiane[s], the Bd. Montmartre, then stopped at the Café
Brébant, seeing that it's Christmas and me alone, and extravagantly had
another *chocolat* – marvellous chocolate here; curious that in New York
I drink nothing but coffee morning, noon & night & in between, and
love it; in England, never anything but tea; while here I am content
always with chocolate. Thence thru the Faubourg Montmartre here. Lovely
night it is, and the city enchanting. Want to see the river & the Bois &
the Louvre and everything else – begin tomorrow, the holiday extra –
loneliness over.

About yesterday: but it's late and my pencils are all dulled and I feel
like hell and after all Christmas is a poor day to pass without seeing a
single person you know or speaking to anyone but the Concierge and not
even Beetle or writing cheers me and I've a poem going in my head that
I can't get on paper and in fact DAMN and damn again. Good night,
Mum – I suppose all this is excellent for me, but it's difficult to see how –
I'm going to bed before I dissolve in tears of self-pity the most detestable.
Christ & hell, I've not even a decent pain, merely boredom and nothing.
Nothing.

Noon Saturday, 26 December 1936

Well, I do feel much more cheerful, it being a joyous day and I
having finally slept well (my faculty for gloom the European air seems
abnormally to develop—e.g. last night), though I've just had another

disappointment: walked through the happy throngs of the Rue Laffayette and Place de l'Opéra to the American Express in the Rue Auber, but nothing there; I hoped spiritually for a letter from Jean, and financially for a checkbook. You see, I'd paid some bills before coming and didn't bring much (so I lost no staggering amount that famous night), having instructed Lloyds to send me a checkbook when they heard, at long last, from my N.Y. check – bet it hasn't come. Aiai!

Joy joy, I am marvellously ecstatic – since "Aiai" I've been lying on the bed for a half-hour and suddenly scenes began to come & I watched & planned and lo, a whole damn play is in shape in my head and I've just written two short speeches for one of the characters; it wants a lot of thought, but the outline & some detail & the four main people are almost clear – it ought to be magnificent & I swear to God I'll write it – I've been thinking again, it would take hours to write what I've already planned, so will say nothing except that the thing has superb dramatic possibility & might be *huge* – it will be *done*, anyway, & *honest* & powerful. Would give God's teeth for a typewriter here – not even sharp pencils & no knife. But probably it's a good thing there's no one to talk to – my inclination is to rush back to Cambridge & get to work on it, but I'll stay here a bit anyway & think & make notes – Can't write anymore now, have to think. Fury of excitement. ———

3:30 – all excellent: have two pages of class notes and three more speeches; I'm hardly sure I can do it, knowing so little of the theatre, but I intend to go straight thru as far as I can, then you and Mark and Halliday (knows a good deal about the technical stages, pause, what will do & what won't, etc.) and Jean (one of the characters is modelled, roughly, for her) can help me – to hell with being "contemporary", but I'm going to keep it from being "pseudo-Elizabethan" if I can – want a nervous, mechanical accent, giving way only infrequently to full passion. I want to pack a theatre with it for months, but so far as I now see, that involves no pandering – it must simply be good in several ways. The little I've written is verse but it is notation for very important moments – there'll be a lot of prose. My great difficulty will be, as with "Ritual", in keeping the general tempo & emphasis down, in order to get power when it's needed. Curious, the situations, scenes, came first (from nowhere), then people for them, then the scenes faded and I'm already left mainly with the people, to do with as I will, or, rather, *can*. Going for a walk now, to fix pencils & get air. More later or tomorrow. ——

9:30 p.m.

Have just finished a soliloquy – 16 lines – for one of the women, and it seems really to be good; difficult to tell, because I must say the lines aloud and I've never done any acting – would give a lot to have some experience. Using blank verse, but the metre is terribly broken, the tempo slow – and I think I've got enough concentration & tension to justify using verse – if, to anyone who has read *Lear*, justification's needed for verse in drama. And it doesn't seem to be Eliz. pastel either: It's wonderful, Mum, to be writing for other people and for a realizable situation – God, what a splendor of satisfaction it must be really to have mastered dramatic poetry & construction. I pray to what gods there be that I may learn to write great plays. The putting-together & sequence are very difficult – the whole action is by no means clear yet, some invention is necessary; but the outline, the people, the scenes (in general), and about 40 lines of actual verse, are all done – and at noon I hadn't the faintest idea or intention of a play. It's marvellous! I'm going to bed now with paper & pencil (all sharpened) on one side, and [Thomas] Dekker on the other – to read or write drama, or simply to think about it – as my little brain wills. Good night – it's fun, this chronicle-letter, esp. at such an epoch-making time as this, heh heh – I wish you identical (if I indeed can write it) luck with Bare his back & I'll beat the bastard. Sleep tight, Mum. But one more note: I realize now the monstrous ambiguity in all verse & *most* in dramatic verse – punctuation is inadequate and stage-directions must be kept at minimum. Amazing, this.

Midnight

I've got Act I (in 2 scenes) thoroughly plotted, on paper, and everything seems to be taken care of – had to introduce one character beyond my original six, but all else invented itself marvellously – it is very exciting to watch things go, isn't it? The last thing on earth I'd have given myself credit for was a talent for invention and construction such as a novelist, & esp. a dramatist, needs, but I may yet surprise us – I already may, amaze surprise me. The play is incredibly interesting, particularly since I myself have only general tragic notions about what is to happen in the next two acts. I hope to keep it all within a time limit of 6 or 7 hours, from 5:30 to midnight of one evening, and it's all in New York – both of which restrictions make for intensity; the action also is fairly single – in fact, I am writing a classical tragedy, my dear. I am overjoyed to have got so much done – and in 12 hours! Now really for rest, & bless you.

1:15 a.m.

Still thinking and began the first scene, have done four speeches, some 20 lines. But now, finally, to bed – I hope something comes from this astonishing day. ———

God save us, it's 2:45 and I'm still thinking, in bed & all lights out for an hour & a half – have been afraid I'd forget it, so got up & have just written the Second Act in rough detail & made notes for the third – it's uncanny how all my people want to get together from time to time, and how everything helps in at least two ways –

And now – GOOD NIGHT!!!

Noon Sunday 27 December 1936

Have just had breakfast in bed, where I still am and shall stay all day – it's gloomy out. I have only 30 centimes anyway, and my head is going like a race-course – didn't sleep well; I still think I got really a vast deal done yesterday (it sounds incredible; but not having much paper I put it all on 4 double sheets which I've numbered and shall write no more on, thus you can one day see verily the result of my frenzy – not even in July while writing "Ritual at Arlington" was my brain at such a valuable heat); have written nothing today so far, but think & think & shall soon begin. Good thing I've no money and can see no one, or I wouldn't work – I know me – great & enchanting fun as it is. But this is too much of a good thing – can't post this till I get money (costs 1 fr. 50 here, 3 times the English rate), haven't been able to send the letter I wrote Mark Christmas Day – Heigh-ho, mortality – I'm still very excited. This is all of this kind of paper I brought & enough to fill an envelope in any case – will begin directly another letter – hope you have my check by the time you get this – write me at Clare – all my love, Mum –

John

[The play JB had begun, *The Architect*, was never completed.]

4, Rue Cadet
Paris

Dearest Mum, 6 January 1937

When I take a vacation from writing, it's a healthy one, isn't it? My little brain was apparently not designed for consistent performance. A good deal has happened, but as usual I'll begin with the present moment. Which is rather a grim one. I got last week sufficiently interested in physical Paris to prevent my doing any more work on the play; but now I am completely bored and very anxious to get back to Cambridge – not particularly Cambridge, God knows, but somewhere *else*. The simple fact is that I am, and have been for three months, about as lonely as I can be – which is roughly nineteen times as lonely as anyone else you've ever seen. I will not use the word "miss" (it's a ridiculous, meaningless little monosyllable, and in practical use nearly always sentimental, in that the feeling stated is either false or not understood – I hate such words anyway, rarely use them and have invariably a feeling of insincerity and pretension when I do – "hunger" is another: I have often wanted something to eat, but I have never been "hungry" – such words have no right to exist, because people who try to be honest with language are betrayed into using them) but I want like the very God-damned most intense hell to see and talk to you – or Halliday or *someone* (and my list of possible *someones* is, as you know, damn small).

Pedro I have not seen much of. Ah, I feel excellently more agreeable: between the "of" and the "Ah", invisible though it be, lies a lovely dinner; I like very much Parisian food, particularly the wines and the cheeses (have been drinking mostly white Bordeaux – Haut-Sauterne, Barac, etc. – and eating mostly Bleu d'Auverque, Roquefort, etc; an occasional Cointreau, the which you know I love, afterward) – very cheap, too. But this brings me to the thing I most detest here (and I can see this is going to be an even more than usually "by-ways" letter, with infinite parentheses, bespeaking a disordered mind – I hope you're used by now to going after each one back to pick up the thread again – I always have to – my correspondents must hate me – I thought to mark my letters, as some menus here are marked, "Pain à Discretion"; but once I'm settled, I much love writing, even by hand, and especially to you, who know(s) more about me than anyone even God – it's curious, when I want in general so little known about me, that I am passionately anxious that a few friends know as much as possible – underdeveloped exhibitionism, I daresay). . . .

Before I forget this – it may not occur to me again: do you remember speaking to me last year of *The Asiatics*, by Fritz [Frederic] Prokosch which you'd just read? It's much discussed here, so I finally read [Edward Tenney Casswell] Spooner's [Fellow of Clare College] copy – entirely incredible, but quite interesting. Here's the point: Chiappe & the Frasers know him well and Kay was in Majorca when Prokosch was there, writing the novel. At the time, he had never been *East* of *Italy!* God knows where he got his dope – the novel was of course chiefly praised for its travel-descriptions and *knowledge* of the Asiatic mind & environment. He is obviously (from the novel) batty on sex, but what an excellent imagination. The fellow is a fair-to-warm poet, by the way – one book out. . . .

On one of my interminable walks around Paris (I really have acquired in two weeks a remarkable knowledge of the city, by simply walking and looking – it's not too large, and is continually fascinating) last week, I stopped in a Salon de Thé in the Place Victor Hugo for tea – a little place, but perfect: all chromium and glass and wood and mirror – and marvellous tea, and a tart from Heaven. The pastries here are the only ones I've tasted outside our home that were pastries. We'll find that place again when we come together. – Pedro & I separated about five, he to an appointment & I to walk. The all-kinds-of-streets are marvellous, especially now, in holiday time, with construction for the [Paris] Exposition going on everywhere, anti-Franco (child-butcher ideas) propaganda on huge boards, the Seine with its thirty & more bridges, the dirty little ways opening suddenly into immense squares, abbés scurrying along, the lovely shops along the boulevards, the Champs-Élysées (a way for at least ten cars bordered by fantastic sidewalks, on each of which six cars could drive abreast (have cars breasts? – a delicate industrial question), monuments on all sides, and the marvellously-named streets (I am coming to hate the mechanical numbering in New York & most American cities – names have a value numbers will never get).

But my hand is giving me the deuce – ten pages at a stretch is enough, and it's past midnight anyway. Not that I'll sleep – I'm on the sixth floor, but I can hear the people in the cars passing my window, whispering to each other – only they don't whisper, they shout (an old French custom – and every car north of the Nile goes by twice daily – next time, a *quiet* place. – I do hope, *if* you've time, that you'll run these letters off on a typewriter, kid – otherwise my invaluable maundering will be speedily unavailable: I don't believe in fountain pens, as you know, and there is always someone *about* downstairs, which I can't abide when recording my priceless comment. It has only just occurred to me, by the way, (but note again how "priceless" destroys whatever there was to "invaluable", thereby proving my "maundering" was well-chosen: a lesson in irony directed at self) that there must be a good deal strictly personal to you in my letters of these three months, and I'm awfully sorry I asked, carte blanche, you to let Halliday see them. Especially, Mum, if I've seemed to make you a Happy-hunting ground for information about me. It isn't so. The letters are written directly and only to you, as you must know. But in order to let you, who are of course most important by 1000 odds, know nearly everything that goes on with me, it's necessary to write to other people practically not at all. I know that Bob and Granny and Uncle Jack are kept aware through you, and I simply hoped that Jean and Halliday could, to some extent, also. This recount is merely to let you know that the matter is finally all in your hands. And I do thank you extremely for telling Mark and the Dean [Herbert E. Hawkes] what you did. And now my hand really *is* in a state – sleep thee tight, Mum, I love you dearly across many too many miles.

                                                          1 a.m. [11 January 1937]

Nothing at the theatre; *La Jeunesse* was excellent, but too much talking, a rare fault in the Russian film – the trouble with all the American (also English & French) films worth discussing is not that "the dialogue is bad" but that there is any dialogue at all; I'm not at all sure that talking was a valuable discovery – at least they had to make *films* before; now screened plays are not merely possible but prevalent; technical efficiency makes all films more or less attractive, but on a dead level of misdirection. Skillful, meaningless trifles, like the Venus de Milo, which, as I have long thought, is very pretty – just that – the insipid product of the most adroit, the most debased, the least interesting period of Greek sculpture, the Hellenistic, when the sculptors knew so much that they had forgotten what in hell they were about. Its regal position at the Louvre, while Titian's incomparable *Man with a Glove* is huddled among a hundred anonymous canvases on a nondescript wall, so enraged me that my first visit was a total failure – only Botticelli's beautiful frescoes of the Femme Villa, the Nike of Samathrace (well placed, uniquely – the museum is hideously arranged and very badly lighted – overcrowded with great masses of junk, rooms of Rubens – all the frames are blatant & detestable, and the Mona Lisa, or La Gioconda, is *glassed* – even the galleries of the Metropolitan are better done – it's really incredible, and of the French!), some Byzantine mosaic, and a few other things, struck me. I spent the afternoon there again today and in spite of the crowds (*gratuit dimanche*), had a great deal of pleasure in the El Greco *Crucifixion*, da Vinci, Rembrandt (a dozen superb canvases), Vecello, Hals, some exquisite portraits of Velasquez', etc. But I'm apparently in no museum mood – it seemed, both times, dead and long dead and well dead, why not bury it?

It's getting on & I've to be up early, and in any case I feel that there is practically nothing left to tell you about Paris, except one most important thing which I've not mentioned – but that from Cambridge. There's been, or so it seemed to me, so damn much to *say* in these letters that I've had no time for comment, to be amusing, and all that sort of thing – you know, the soul of wit, etc. But for once, if you've borne up under the double strain of my handwriting and my continual irrelevance, it's probably interesting to be told at all but endless length *ce qui se passe*. At least I've kept it in English – not very easy, since I think mostly French. Ignore all gallicisms and all aboard for England, grim and dull. Get in about 6 tomorrow evening & plan to see the celebrated *Hamlet* (absolutely complete, first time in 130 years or something – Lawrence Olivier) at the Old Vic – spend the night & go up Wednesday morning – and there had better, my loves, be mail there! Now, finally, a note to Jean, an end to Halliday, and to bed – Happy New Year, and all the luck you've never had, Mum – from M4[JB's rooms in Memorial Court, Cambridge] next –

all, but *all* my love,
John

[Cambridge]
Memorial Court
Monday evening
[18 January 1937]

Dearest Mum,

Your letter of the 7th has just come, and I feel a damned apoplectic worm for putting you through the horrible details of my first few days in Paris. The experience was detestable at the time, I believe, but it's all sugared over now, for me, by countless "Yes, very pleasant vac, such lovely weather in Paris, so vile here, isn't it?" I'm frightfully sorry to have written you so about it, my grimmer experiences will henceforth be sealed in the Grecian bosom, ample are the chambers of their hearts. I can't think what can be wrong with me, that I sail blithely on from despair to despair – will really try after this to keep my cursed articulate mouth shut.

The cold has settled in about my toes and has a permanent air; was in bed most of today, but nothing to worry about. Hope I don't lose this tooth, at my advanced age we don't get any more, I hear – marvellously capricious, it's loose in the evenings and tightens up by the morning: I give it two days to calm down, then I'll see a dentist (a very low order of being, dentists, contemptible in every respect and they have no sense of *fair play*).

Went to see Rylands this evening, he has a poisoned toe and hardly hobbles; wants to help me with the play and can be a great one, I think. Nothing done on it since I got back, I've been reading perfect reams of plays, [John Millington] Synge, [Noel] Coward, eighteenth century comedy (have found in a very obscure but excellent play *[The Dramatist: Or Stop Him Who Can]* by [Frederick] Reynolds a gorgeous exit speech by Lord Scratch: "Gad I must go and investigate the matter immediately, and if she has wronged me, by the blood of the Scratches, I'll bring the whole business before parliament, make a speech ten hours long, reduce the price of opium, and set the nation in a lethargy." – isn't it wizard?) and various scattered plays, in the hopes of imbibing, so to speak, the business of dramatic construction etc. I think no matter what it looks like I'll write it, because I obviously want practise, and I have a dazzling scheme for my second play. I'm quite serious about this, really: for one thing, it's just possible that I might make a living writing plays, while nothing else I'm adept at pays anything at all. The work can't hurt me, anyway, and my time is not very valuable.

A faffing Australian ass from Jesus [College] came in to tea, one John Manifold a poet, extremely dull, I can't think why I asked him, it must have been a north wind. Dislikes Blake, pretends to know Yeats, laughs much too long at his own quips, will discuss nothing less than Dante (whom he quite fails to understand, knowing only the *Inferno*) and Euripides and Manifold. A tedious variety of half-informed bore, there are many like him in Cambridge – I am beginning to respect Columbia because it was frankly nothing intellectually, for the most part. I heard more pretentious nonsense last term than in all my previous twentyodd years. Rylands strongly advises me to talk on Yeats, I think probably I will; the undergraduates can grin and like it. . . .

I think you're getting into the habit of thinking of yourself as actually your age, which is palpably absurd and must be stopped; it's a pity, but you don't take on age-dignity until you give up charm and brightness and vividness in appearance and speech – and since it'll be a good many years before you give them up, you mustn't go about clad in years. You are distinctly, for example, my contemporary, and you can't get away from it: when I return, no one will suppose there is five years between us, much less more; so you must resign yourself to being the age you look and act and talk and *are* – and no more nonsense out of you, young lady. And you should know me well enough by now to know this ain't no flattery: we're agreed that it's horrible for an old person to pretend to be young, but this is a case of a young person pretending to be old – but not getting away with it, Mrs. Grundy, not getting away with it. A slight confession now: for some long time I've thought of you occasionally as Jill, reserving Mother or Mum for more tender moments, and I've considered taking up "Jill" for all bantering, usual intercourse; would that disconcert you, you ancient tottering one-eyed one, you? R S V P A W O L Q W E R T Y U I O. . . .

I do so hope that something splendid works out of your interviews, kid, it will be fantastic if something doesn't; please let me know when things happen, and what things happen. I probably shan't write again for some time, must gradually do something about this mass of letters when I'm better, and there are lectures, the play, and incidental time-eaters. Please keep well, Mum, God bless you, I love you dearly, think of you constantly and miss you frightfully

John

[Judging by the salutations on later letters JB's idea of his calling Mrs. Berryman "Jill" was not endorsed. However, a few of his letters from the forties and fifties begin "Dearest Jill."]

[Cambridge]
Memorial Court
Dearest Mother: Sunday 14 February 1937
The talk on Yeats [given February 11 at the Dilettante Society, a literary society at Clare College] went reasonably well, and I am glad for many reasons that I accepted [Andrew Chiappe's] invitation to give it. Wanting always ability to speak effectively, I contemplated this, as the Readings in New York, with terror; but, for the first time, my early nervousness passed, I spoke and read easily, with something of assurance

and eloquence, which come only, I think, to men speaking before crowds. I indeed lost count of time; when finally two men rose and came to the door thanking me, saying they must go, I thought it must have been dull, then stricken looked at my watch – the talk was to have lasted an hour from eight-thirty – it was ten-fifteen. I stopped in some confusion, but at their insistence, went on through what I had planned. Discussion and more coffee in other rooms and so goodnight.

I spent rather too much time on Yeats' life and various activities, reading occasionally from the *Autobiographies* and essays and philosophy, and read only some twenty poems, of which I discussed only a half-dozen. There is no compromise possible in these things; not knowing that, I tried to entertain irrelevantly, besides giving information, for a half-hour or so; then, looking up one time when they were laughing at some incident I read, I saw among the inane faces one sharp intelligent face, and thereafter talked to him, as concisely and ably as I could. It was, I learned during the late coffee, Brian Boydell, whom I have wanted for some time to meet, as he told me of wanting to meet me; Irish, an able pianist with a fine voice (I heard him at a Clare recital last term), entirely unlike these others. His mother is a close friend of Yeats, they live in Dublin, he is reading natural sciences here because he wants information beyond the music which will be his work, a member also of the Psychical Research Society here, which I shall join. I think we may be close friends. When the others were borrowing books (a good sign – my central intent was to get Yeats read), he took my volume of music for the dance plays, and will play it for me next week. [Geoffrey] Kitchin [Clare choirmaster] recently played me a song from "At the Hawk's Well" – simple, abstract music it is, what I expected – but although he plays well, his taste is curious and limited and he can be of no use in this.

I learned many things during the preparation. I slept little, broke all engagements, read and wrote nothing but Yeats, working for five or six days as I have not worked before. The rhythms in prose and verse of that strange mind still fill my head, odd passionate insistent things. I have not previously been able to read his writings with any conception of their mass and purposes already in mind, and I was now able to refer constantly to what I remembered elsewhere in him, as relevant or stated in another form or incongruous; I marked a great deal and took many notes. No biography of Yeats has been published, and as I collected and set down a skeleton life with quotations and inference, the possibility of writing one appeared. Tremendous work would be necessary, but now is the time, before material has vanished and the man has died (although in no circumstances would I publish during his lifetime, for many and strong reasons). The Irish trip is settled; I shall be there about a month, returning in the summer perhaps, cycling from Dublin across Ireland to Galway, up to Sligo and Connaught, down into Clare and probably other southern counties. I think certainly to see him, and I hope to talk to people who have known him, even, it may be, to spend time in his library; the places named are where his life has been spent. I don't wish to appear to overestimate the importance of his *life*; if I speak again on him, and another invitation has come in casual form, I shall say almost nothing of it, confining my attention to the poetry; but all obtainable information may be valuable to me as critic, and particularly in Yeats' case, for many of the symbols in his poems are personal symbols, to be understood in terms of his history, and only when understood can they be appraised. The major part of this projected book would be thorough critical study of his achievement in the drama, in various kinds of prose, in moral philosophy, and in poetry. Amazingly little of value has been written on the work; Blackmur's paper I seem to remember as fragmentary, limited, and [Edmund] Wilson's account in *Axel's Castle* is contemptible. I read Wednesday a 1915 "critical study" [*W.B. Yeats: A Critical Study*] by Forrest Reid, entirely negligible, and I shall be surprised if the masses of journalism on him spread over fifty years contain anything more useful than dates.

You will see my notes of course; I cannot send them now because I am still working and may need them. Much of what I discovered is not yet down, particularly the account of influences (mainly, in the development from Spenser, Shelley and Rossetti, French Symbolist and English Metaphysical influences, the hard vigor of Pound's versification, and tightening his stanza forms by comparison with good speech), and random details. For instance, the meaning "revolve" is so clear for "perne" in "Sailing to Byzantium" that I had never examined it; I find that Yeats has apparently coined the verb: the *Oxford [English] Dictionary*, an authority, if there is one, gives no "perne", but lists "pern" in two senses: meaning a honey-buzzard, erroneously derived from a Greek word for Hawk (Yeats' use I take to be derived from this origin); and in the six-

teenth century, Peterhouse, the oldest Cambridge college, had a Master,
Dr [Andrew] Perne, who was noted for changing his mind adroitly, whence
a rare verb "pern", to be unstable for unscrupulous ends. As you like it.
The Library I have at last begun to use; it is at my door and has a magnificent collection, but it has taken thus long to get over my distaste for
libraries. Using the fine collection of Yeats there, I have begun to look at
the earliest versions of the poems in his first few volumes, and have found
that the business of revision is far more drastic than I supposed; twenty
years after its publication, he will take a poem out and tear it to pieces
working toward uniformity of style. The 1935 *Collected Poems* can give
you no idea of what has happened to his style – not that that is important
strictly, I grant, but it's fascinating to know that the first version of even
["The Lake Isle of] Innisfree" began

"I will arise and go now and go to the island of Innisfree" and the
whole poem was in the same metre as that weird line.

Reading continuously, too, his personal symbols came to have tremendous emotional significance, [Yeats' uncle George] Pollexfen and
[John F.] Taylor and Synge and Lady Gregory, and particularly the two
figures who are, I am certain, most important to him: Parnell, as tragic
hero, and Swift, as tragic ironist, both lonely, passionate, ambitious, proud
and bitter men. Do you know the superb epitaph Swift made for himself,
from which Yeats took his poem? It is over his tomb at St Patrick's in
Dublin; someone has taken my Swift, I quote from memory:

> Hic depositum est corpus
> Jonathan Swift
> hujus ecclesiae cathredalis decani.
> Ubi saeva indignatio
> ulterius cor lacerere nequit.
> Abi, viator,
> et imitare, si poteris,
> strenum pro virili libertatis vindicem.

The moment, in a very recent poem "Parnell's Funeral", when he
unites these figures, is a great moment indeed:

> Through Jonathan Swift's dark grove he passed, and there
> Plucked bitter wisdom that enriched his blood.

Wednesday evening while I was reading here, suddenly my attention wandered, as if forcibly; I shut my eyes and an image rose before them, not clear but strong: I saw that it was the figure of Yeats, white-haired and tall, struggling laboriously to lift something dark which was on his right side and below the level on which he stood; as it came into my view, he lifting it with difficulty, I saw that it was a great piece of coal, irregular, black. He raised it high above his head, hair flying and with a set expression, brilliant eyes, dashed it to the ground at his feet, a polished ground that might have been a floor: the pieces rolled away silver.

I have learned that the absolute aesthetic emotion is not pure, as I have thought, but conditional. It cannot be summoned, and its experience depends on many things. Most persons, I think, even cultivated persons, have it infrequently or never. No poem can always summon it even in a person who has been sensitive to that poem. I had it in varying intensity several times this week, but once with blinding force: from a poem which I have read many times and each time admired, but never known. It is "That the Night Come" in *Responsibilities*, now, I see, Yeats' first great poem, and one of the perfect, austere poems of the language. Each word fabulously at work, the metaphor so simple and so astonishing, the balance beautiful and dynamic. I shall never be a scholar, although I may after years have gathered some learning, for my mind is neither systematic nor patient, and two stanzas from [Richard] Crashaw satisfy my hunger for days; but I have something from those two stanzas, and I may make something from them, that most perhaps cannot.

My enemies are extravagance of speech, irrelevant interests and sympathies I find within myself, and the current time, the world, the Body of Fate. Yeats considers that in its gyre the world has now passed the Breaking of Strength and is sweeping outward toward objectivity, a time in which no man can see in his mind images of the actual world; a time poised between action and contemplation, and characterized by abstraction, Shaw and indiscriminate fanaticism. How the analysis is come by does not matter, it is correct. I have been looking at the new *London Mercury*; many recent books are mentioned, many praised, some condemned, nearly all are considered competent and interesting in some way; the reviews are well-written, this is a magazine which reviews perhaps one-tenth of the books sent it and employs competent men and women to judge them; clearly this is a time of great creative and critical power, persons who two centuries ago would have been illiterate now write excellent novels, the level of literature has advanced. The outcome in my head is a kind of insanity, a consuming rage.

> Fantastic yellows assault my eyes,
> Rhetoric and argument cannot abide
> The subtle pattern of a formal dance;
> My ears by easy melody are made mad
> And all my brain rings with this competence:
> The frenzied or dead level defies
> All passion for magnificence,
> All peace that nourishes surprise.
> [Unpublished fragment by JB]

What we require is armor. Not irony; as a consistent method, that is self-destructive. But an uncomplaining recognition of fantasia and a population of clods. If patience and oblivion are impossible, then an uncompromising deliberate hatred for cant and all journalism and faked emotion and popular mediocrity, but never expressed: a waste of strength and time to combat the age. Pound's great talent has gone that way, producing but fragments and an example, where he should have made great poems. To read no reviews, to avoid rather than taunt stupidity, to keep free from any struggle for an "American literature" or a "new state", such as that which exhausted Yeats for twenty years, never to borrow the opinion of an inferior, and to recognize no superior, to work. Never to be competent, never to be satisfied. To form a style which will present what is actual and passionate. To tolerate no compromise with this unfortunate time.

Auden has gone to the Spanish War. God bless him for his generous delusion, and preserve him from Fascist bullets. Consider those in their fanatic pity and their indignation, and that grass will be over them. There are few enough living men who can write poetry.

> Starving through the leafless wood
> Trolls run scolding for their food;
> And the nightingale is dumb,
> And the angel will not come.
>
> Cold, impossible, ahead
> Lifts the mountain's lovely head

> Whose white waterfall could bless
> Travellers in their last distress.
> [W.H. Auden, *Look Stranger!* "VIII"]

                                                                their sorrow
exerts on the rigid dome of the unpierced sky its enormous pressures.
                                                                (much later)
I used carbon with the preceding sheets and will send copies to Halliday and Mark. You are right in believing that a great deal of my energy
goes in letters to you, but it is somehow important that I set down what I
think; I flinch from the discipline of verse (I wrote several weeks ago a
poem in three eight-line stanzas, of which the third is magnificent, the
others poor, and I fight daily from going back to it to rewrite the first
stanzas) and your suggestion of a journal is impossible, I find: I cannot
write into blank air, I must address some near sensibility. Obviously it is
you whom I must, with rare exceptions, address; and I resent implacably
the making of copies. But today, as for several days, I felt in some degree –
I don't know what to say – exalted; and although I had no definite idea
of what I would write, I was sure that it would be of interest, so I put
carbon in as I wrote. This letter is, in fact, of great importance, as this
week has been; I have found in the doing of these pages that if I write
carefully, I can write well, and although there will be faults in style which
could be corrected in a second draft, the whole will be right enough, and
re-writing is not really necessary – which, since I will not re-write (the
letter to Warren is the first I have re-done since coming abroad), is good
to know. And I shall no longer be afraid of "mannered" writing, in the
effort to form a style; nor shall I any more restrict my prose to the kitchen
logic of the news-column. There will be tone and shift and subtlety, and
honesty, and a solid, I hope, individual texture. The point of prose is to
get things said, and my assumption that they can be said as well in a
casual, "un-literary" fashion as in any other, is ridiculous. Letters can
form a style, while informing to the best advantage of communication,
or they can set one in habits of extravagance and triviality. No more of
this.

The enclosed masterpieces [photographs] have words behind them;
the one of me is an unexpected triumph. Ramsey coming in one morning
last term, we decided to try it, neither knowing anything of time expo-
sures and the light bad: I sat like an uncomfortable stone for ninety sec-

onds, Ramsey perched on the edge of the table by the camera, not daring
to get up for fear the camera would move with release of weight. I hope
it's a shabby job of me, but the couch is *too* clear and I could match the
material of my coat. Fireplace to left and doors behind to bedroom.

I approve strongly your plans for writing, particularly the morning
writing and the changing hours, and wish you every luck with it, and that
your typewriter may return to you (a bit of self-thought in that, though I
am palpably stunned by the legibility of this long letter). Let me know of
your success. I have begun something of the same order: the *New Testament* each night before retiring (sorry about retiring—the t's in Testament
and night drove me into it), and [Samuel] Pepys each morning with
breakfast. Both are great fun, and I expect the translators to cure me of
baldness and journalism, as Pepys of lushness and overstatement. The
New Testament I have never read, appalling admission, I was bred on the
rhythms of E.R. [Edgar Rice] Burroughs, and the *Diary* I know only
heretofore in pieces. Did you realize that he was but twenty-seven when
he began it and thirty-six when it stopped, and that his wife was but
fifteen when he married her in 1655, five years before the commence-
ment of the *Diary?* The catholicity of Pepys' interests are a rebuke, his
Johnsonian absorption in fact is a delight. [Richard] Lord Braybrooke
[editor of the two-volume 1825 diary] in his notes quotes [Anthony]
Wood as calling [Sir George] Downing, master of Pepys' first office (rather
complex this), "a sider of times and changes, skilled in the common
cant"; I am struck by its application to [Stephen] Aylward. Dramatization
does not account for that strange move. I am astonished at how different
are the characters the narrators of the Gospels reveal. Matthew the historian, man of fact; Mark the impressionist, fascinated almost equally by
John; Luke the justifier, with a taste for chronology; John the ecstatic
incarnation, a mental case but eloquent beyond the expectation of flesh.

    . . . [Elisabeth] Bergner is desperately bad in *As You Like It* & the
screen is no place for blank verse. I envy you *Faustus* & Wycherley, two
of my favorite plays, very glad you went, hope they were marvellous; write
in detail. Much theatre next week: Abbey Players at Arts, *Playboy of the
Western World & Juno and the Paycock*; Sheridan's *Critic* at the ADC;
Thunder Over Mexico, etc. Very excited, particularly about the Synge.
My play stagnates, too much else, perhaps after full term, shan't go down
till the 25th. Don't be cold, Mum, and keep thee well, and land lovely

positions, and come beaming transatlantically – my dearest luck and love, and to Bob if he is working and to Uncle Jack and to Jean and again and again and again to the Mum one,

John Berryman

25 Harcourt Street
Dublin
Dearest Mum,   6 April 1937

Decisiveness was never one of my virtues, and in any case, once arrived at a place, I tend not to want to leave it (always excepting Cambridge, delicious rabble). Item, I am unwell, bad cold, uncanny weakness, head throbbing, etc. Item, weather in the west continues vile, steady rain, cold – worse than here. Item, God knows, but will in no circumstances tell, when Yeats will be back. Item, time runs on, runs on. I don't know what to do – it looks merely insane to go to Galway and set out walking when there'll be no pleasure in it.

Meanwhile I am delightedly exploring Dublin, which I like better each hour, and talking for hours to entire strangers (when I can get a word in). Not so much rain yesterday and now, but grey and chilly – bad for camera, though I've taken some snapshots. Much to tell you. I went last evening to the Peacock, the Abbey Experimental Theatre, an odd little room seating 90 uncomfortably. First performances of *The Phoenix*, a play about [Oliver] Goldsmith by N. O. B., and a bad play [*Alarm Among the Clerks*] by Mervyn Wall, who afterward appeared in crumpled and ecstatic white tie and made a long, enthusiastic speech – tall, silly man. *The Phoenix* was interesting. Synge still generally disliked here and the whole "Anglo-"Irish Revival discredited by Gaelic fanatics. Strange people.

Dates on letters to you and Jean were a day too late. Let that be a lesson to you, or something. I wish, by the by, that you'd take up *answering* letters again – I wrote last term three or four fascinating letters, and not a word of direct reply. – Those three lines I liked I've put into "Last Days [of the City]" – after "Thoroughfares found the v. & the lost":

'And marvellous coincidences cry
Mad are abroad with moving lips & tongue

> Not the deep grave will order. Ecstasy
> Is before death, but it will not be long?

What do you think of the poem?

The program says Miss Anne Yeats did the costumes & scene-painting at the Peacock – W.B.'s daughter, 18, Miss Yeats (his sister) told me. I own a passionate desire to see her – my God what lines he wrote for her and she in the cradle!

I read Yeats with more immediacy here than ever before and understand things I'd not seen – and, as with Shakespeare anywhere, the more you know (an emotional term, too), the greater the difficulties, the central ambiguities. Yeats knows more about the moral techniques of violence and passion than any other man now living. The tragedies and *Henry IV* I have been reading, too – read and marvel at the language of even a "filling" scene like 2 of Act IV in *Lear*. Nearly all pitch and accent of poetry is in Shakespeare somewhere, the body of language not revealing but creating passion.

> This bodiless creation ecstasy
> Is very coming in.

It's relatively excellent today, I want to get out. If I don't soon see Yeats, I shall be consumed. All my dearest wishes for your success, Mum – *please* let me know directly anything shows. Keep thee well – all my love to all of you –

John

["Last Days of the City" has not been published.]

Memorial Court
[Cambridge]

Dearest Mum,   Sunday 18 April 1937

I am extremely glad about the Neva-Wet position, but damn sorry about your colds and long hours; for God's sake, keep yourself well. Believe me, that I did not enquire every time was not due to thoughtlessness: whenever I think of you, which is hourly, I have prayed for the health of all of you and the establishment of financial security. I do earnestly hope that this will turn quickly into a more responsible, less wearing, and more remunerative thing, and am delighted for the interim. Wrongly, I didn't keep asking because the questions seemed mechanical. Please take as good care of yourself as you can, don't tire yourself with anything else, write me only notes until your time is more free. God bless Bob for helping you, and for his letter to me – no explanation needed for either of you for it, I was grateful without suspicion of resentment. I wish you all the best of luck in it all, getting rid of the farm in [Reisterstown] Maryland, health and lack of worry, together-going happiness and eventual ease.

I disclaim entirely your picture of me insofar as it shows me discontented with, or ashamed of, what you call your "failure" – the attribution is neither well-founded nor correct. I resent being taxed with direct hypocrisy – if you will examine my letters to Granny and to you, you will find no lie, and the nuts, each time and of all kinds, were excellent. While accusing me of complete and vicious inactivity, you in the same letter ignored the long poem ["Last Days of the City"?] I had but sent you – a poem which, I suggest, is absolutely first-rate and of considerable dimension. These items out, the substance of the indictment is right and welcome, though its terms are at times so unwarrantedly harsh that I doubt my acceptance of it had I not come during the past week in London to similar conclusions and already begun relentless work, which I do not intend shall be interrupted until June. You will get no more hogwash from me if study can burn it out; save original work and possibly an essay or two, I shall be in Shakespeare, with occasional excursions into Swift, Yeats, and the seventeenth century. Your invective is stringent, brilliant, I thank you for it though I am terribly sorry for the anguish that called it to being; I wish intensely that you were free to turn it into play-form. I found in this letter the angular passion of [J.M.] Synge's words for Deirdre at Naisi's grave: "Draw a little back with the squabbling of fools when I am broken up with misery" [Deirdre of the Sorrows].

The main objective of my trip has been strangely accomplished. I had tea with Yeats at the Athenaeum Friday and we talked for something over an hour. Many things: Swift, Indian thought and what he calls "artistic pessimism", Spengler, "Demon and Beast", the dance plays and a new one he has written, Parnell, music and poetry, various aspects of his philosophy, and many other things briefly. You'll see his letters and hear in detail when I'm with you again, it can't be told in a letter. The statement I recall most vividly is this: "I never revise now except in the interests of a more passionate syntax, a more natural". He is an utterly strange man. Taller than I thought and large; odd eyes in a great head; very weak now with the heart asthma from which, he told me, he nearly died a year ago. He gives or gave me an impression of tremendous but querulous force, a wandering intensely personal mind which resists natural bent (formal metaphysics by intuition, responsible vision) to its own exhaustion.

"The aesthete" does appreciate fully Ferdinand [a chocolate confection made by Mrs. Berryman] & did mildly roar upon that singular animal last night. Thank you loudly. A lovely and induplicable beast; others we will forget; but not Ferdinand. Thanks very much too for the Synge [*Plays*], what a beautiful and useful volume it is. I'll get a draught in the bank tomorrow and mail it you – cheques take a long time to cash. I am right, by the way, about the *Playboy*; I talked one night to a man at the Abbey who was in the original production, directed by Synge himself: he explained how players through the thirty years since then have inserted comedy, the Irish being always interested in cheap laughs, until the present unrecognizable state was reached. [Arthur] Shields, whom I saw a good deal of, told me much the same thing – he has been the *Playboy* for twenty years.

I came up from London last evening. Full term begins tomorrow, but I might want to get away early in June and I am glad in any case to be back here now. The reading of one book always somehow involves me in the reading of six others, and if the others aren't at hand I feel baffled; for Shakespeare you need reference books and more reference books as soon as you begin seriously to investigate the consequences of his language and imagery and matter. I saw *Henry* V fairly well done at the Old Vic on Friday evening, the first of the histories I've seen; it wasn't too interesting. I wish to hell producers would leave curiosities and the middle comedies alone, and give the tragedies and late comedies and *Henry IV*. Hermione's words in the *Winter's Tale* have haunted me for days; unjustly by her husband accused of adultery, she replies:

> Sir,
> You speak a language that I understand not
> My life stands in the level of your dreams,
> Which I'll lay down.

The third line I have long admired, but alone, until I forgot context and thought Perdita spoke it in love. In the scene these lines have a dignity and beauty (to be found only after long contemplation) that surpasses description or statement. This play and *Lear* and *Cymbeline*, with others, are being given each week now at Stratford-upon-Avon at the Memorial Theatre; I'd dedicate two eye-teeth to the bard to get over for them, but it's more than a hundred miles. Besides, I know they suffer as well as gain in production. We must do a lot of reading aloud when I return; you read beautifully and I am learning; all verse worth looking at wants reading aloud, carefully and rhythmically by someone who has it by heart, and many times, before anything like its entire flavour can be got. I have a poem by Marvell which will stun you with excited joy and jump your heart.

Thank you for the photograph; because your face is dim, the pose and stride are more vivid and make me very lonely. It is a damn frightful pity, my being here and your being there. This letter has taken all afternoon, for I've stopped many times to think; its main point is that I love you and respect you in whatever degree those emotions are capable to me, and that I grieve for your difficulties, nor will I any more increase them. God bless you.

John

[P.S.] Write later this week, no more lapses.

[Cambridge]

Dearest Mum   Tuesday Evening [27 April 1937]
   . . . Delighted to have your letters, and one from Bob, this morning – and a heartbreaking note from Jean, I shall kiss her senseless when I return. I do hope you all keep well – as I am – and that good things happen suddenly at 500 Fifth. Never mind your letters – but it's good to hear under any circumstances. I'm glad Uncle Jack is home.

Extremely busy. Finished the other day a minute study of *Merchant of Venice*, disagreeable play, and will soon be at *Twelfth Night*. I am reading continually now for a play I thought of night before last – spent hours today in the library among the authorities. It's a short, stylized play about Cleopatra, from a most unfamiliar and historically accurate angle. Two songs partly done, some scattered writing, still in research really. I want Brian [Boydell] to do the music and be the Narrator. It's being written mostly for B., her all unwitting: a Newnham (woman's college here, Girton the other) girl who acts very well and does ballet. We were in a group [Andrews] Wanning had for luncheon at the end of term. Ran into her in town Saturday & she came to tea Sunday. Lovely and very able – it helps unbelievably to set a part *for* someone. If it gets done well, we might put it on at the A.D.C. [Cambridge Amateur Dramatic Company] next autumn. Cleopatra is not so vapid as she has come to sound, nor Shakespearean either. Plans are nice anyway, and work on it is very interesting.

I now know what Shakespeare means by "The uncertain glory of an April day" – almost humourous it is. Today indescribable, mild as a perfect avocado – then put forth horns at seven and stormed. Light till nine or so now, I shall take to the river soon. Wish you were here. A certain calm is upon me. God bless you all –

My dearest love
John

[This is the first mention of B., who later became JB's fiancée. The luncheon party, in Andrews Wanning's rooms in Magdalene, and the Sunday tea which followed, were memorialized by JB's poems "Meeting" and "Tea in *Love & Fame*.]

[Cambridge]

Dearest Mum,   4 May 1937

Of course I want desperately to return for the long vac. The reason I've not said anything is that I've not been able to decide.

Money is the question. Granted that I've been foolishly extravagant about books and in Paris, still it's gone & I've got to do with what's left. Now passage is thirty-five pounds. While at home, a pound a week would barely pay for my food, with laundry on top of that – even if I paid nothing towards rent, as I ought. And I have delicious plans for you and Jean and Bob & Uncle Jack, so a good deal more would be spent. Whereas: four pounds (return) to some village in the south of France and less than a pound a week (fact, not hearsay) for everything there.

What I plan for this summer is very simple, and tremendous: Shakespeare. The examination (four detailed three-hour papers) for the Charles Oldham [Shakespeare Scholarship] (literally the highest honor in any English University, and seventy pounds) is held in the first week of October. I have a good chance if, once this play and the Mays [preliminary examinations] are done, I spend four or five hours a day steadily at it –as indeed I can think of nothing more delightful than doing. It might be more difficult to work in New York, but I'd have you and Mark to talk to during the work – a great advantage – and the Columbia Library. The Prize would justify my existence over here and get me through next year – a thing which now looks most complex financially. Full term, by the way, ends June 10th, but I can stay on until the 24th, and will do unless I'm going to America.

There are the facts. I want *frightfully* to see you & the family and Jean – I agonize at the idea of not – but I feel, no, *think* distinctly that I should not return. This mania of spiritual absolute dependence must be got rid of: the summer might do it. But I cannot decide – I have continually counted on being home this vac, and I am paralyzed. I shall write again soon, or directly I determine on anything.

I love you devotedly,
John

[Cambridge]

Dearest Mum Midnight 24 May 1937

The most brilliant thunderstorm I've ever seen fell from the sky a few minutes ago. Mild beautiful weather: suddenly torrents, magnificent lightning & thunder – nearly gone now. This month is a revelation to me the urban.

I appreciate your letter no end, and Jean's also. With them to fortify me, then, I shall definitely not plan to return this summer. It is too true that I'd do no work there, that I can't afford it, and that I'd have next fall all the difficulty I had last. There it rests, and I thank you for being so generous & sympathetic about it. A sorry business, at best.

Busy to some purpose. All the material for a long essay on *Measure for Measure* (to be done next year, perhaps extended to a book-length study of the Unpleasant Plays); *Othello* and *Henry IV* minutely done, and acres of Shakespearean scholarship digested. A draft of *Cleopatra: A Meditation* nearly finished. And I wrote last night the first poem of any moment since one on Swift done in Dublin. Q.E.D.

I have something of importance to tell you, but I shall wait a few days, perhaps longer. Jean I have not written for some time: please ask her to forgive me, say I love her dearly, and that I shall write her when next I write you.

Plans for the summer are mainly clear, but I shall not detail them because probably they'll change. I shall keep my address several weeks ahead. Will be here at least until the fifteenth of June. My exams (which don't matter) are the 3rd & 4th. I hope Bob did extremely well in his.

I am so glad that cleanliness looks to be profitable, Mum – you sound "*une femme d'affaires*" and I'm delighted. Boston & all. I hope things are working out as not even you hoped: let me know when you can.

This brevity is due to my head being full of *Macbeth* and another most perplexing problem.

Goodnight, my dearest love to all of you, and my wish for your continual happiness.

JAM Berryman

34, Bridge Street
[Cambridge]
Dearest Mum,   1 July 1937

I finished the essay yesterday and gave it in at the Registrary at five – total limit. 77 pages in six days. I am very pleased – first, a hell of a job done well and with incredible celerity; next I may win the Prize, to the tune of distinction and money and the personal satisfaction of paying two grudges off; next, it closes this first year in beautiful style; last, it constitutes a lot of knowledge gained and organized and begins very profitably a most busy summer. I am a week, more or less, with forty hours' sleep lost, but it's a small matter compared to the profit. The paper is I think excellent; title-page will interest you:

Preface
I. THE PROBLEM OF CHARACTER
    1. Introductory   5
    2. Historical   8
    3. Analytical   30
II. DRAMATIC SIGNIFICANCE
    General   41
    1. Situation   46
    2. Scolding & Wit   50

3. Complexity   56
4. The "Unpleasant" Heroines   71
5. Suffering & Species   74

Results are published in October or some such time; I shall not waste any speculation or worry.

Your cool letter of the 22nd I found at my court this morning. My reasons for not writing I have explained; there will never be so long again. The feeling I cannot describe: it was like a certainty I should never write *anything* again – for nearly a month I wrote literally nothing except some examinations. One part of it persists strongly and torments me: I do not think I shall write any more poetry. "Verse" I should say – the other I never got to.

The important matter is this: I am definitely and deeply and very happily in love with B. The attachment was immediate, but was not formulated for several weeks and I have since continually examined it. I am not to blame in this. The fact of her being directs, makes full – significant my life as no relationship except yours and mine has ever done before. I will not spin pages in praise, I wish only that you knew her, as I am eager for her to know you. She is 21, physically beautiful and vigorous and graceful, with a strong, direct, skeptical intelligence, no sentimentality, but a powerful emotional nature held rigidly by will and self-examination. She came slowly and profoundly to love me – she is tender and lovely beyond telling, Mum. Neither of us is primarily interested in how long it will last – for each, the present is rich and valuable when we are together and would be intolerable if we were not – that is the point. But we do, in fact, feel married now – without any adventitious strain on "forever."

I have not written Jean because I could not pretend nothing had happened and I wanted before I told her to be sure of my own mind; I now am, so far as possible, and will write her tonight. She has necessarily become less distinct in my mind, after nine months, than she was; but I have not, even now, ceased to love her. I think I love B. more & I scarcely miss Jean now, though I often think of her; but I simply cannot prophesy my feelings, were the three of us to be together now. B. knows all this and insisted on my going home, to find out, but it was financially impossible, and we are not worrying about it any more. I can only tell

Jean all this, ask her to forgive what I cannot help, and let her decide
what to feel or do. I am very fond of her indeed – probably, as I say, I
still love her – but I cannot be sorry for what has saved my utter despair
over not returning (even so, I was indescribably lonely and desperate,
missing you all, last Saturday night, was unable for six hours to do anything on the essay) and gives me in its own right an all but perfect content.

I am very glad you are back in New York since the Southern trip was
so harrowing – not realizing how busy you'd [be], and at what distasteful
work, I hoped really that you'd enjoy the change. Has Uncle Jack been
completely unsuccessful this year? I do hope extremely that the Brophy
connection, or another, works out; it makes me damned unhappy, thinking of your doing work you detest and for which moreover you are not
being well paid. When I do, I feel willing to change my fake-artistic
temperament for a financial shrewdness; which would, a year ago, have
turned into self-pity. I wish you every luck in the world, Mum. . . .

I leave here Saturday. B. is doing Rosaline in *Love's Labour's Lost*
. . . in the south of England & I'll see the last performance. Then London with her parents. We go Monday, she & I, to Germany – Heidelberg. She wants German and I can work anywhere if it's cheap – living
together, it will cost each less. Our rapture now permits working – in
fact, we work marvellously together. Arthur [Vogel] is still there, too.
Plans after August 1st are not settled yet, will say when they are. Write
care of American Express, Heidelberg, and pray for our safety among the
Nazis. Don't mention politics in letters. Bless you, Mum, and Bob &
Uncle Jack & Granny – all my love,

John

Hotel Wagner
bei Frau Bayer
Freiderichstrasse, 10
Heidelberg
Deutschland

Dearest Mum,　　　　　　　　　　　　　　　　　[9 July 1937]
We have just had the most superb dinner imaginable, especially mus-
tard & beer – I feel marvellously casual. Arrived eight last evening after
not too bad a trip: very comfortable crossing from Dover, Ostend at six in

the morning – train, pleasant Belgian fields, Bruges, Ghent, Brussels, Lieges, Aix-la-Chappelle, Cologne. Took off three hours to rest, have some matchless Kaffee filter, and inspect the cathedral, a curious and largely uninteresting job begun in the twelfth & finished in the 19th; fabulous treasury & some good wood-carving, also an anonymous 16th oil I liked. Started at three down the Rhine from Köln – amazing trip: wooded hills, the river lovely in the sun, air fresh just after rain, every inch of ground cultivated, trim rows on terraces practically vertical or miles up across the valley – numberless fascinating castles perched impregnable in ruins on the hills. Lovely ride it was, Mum. Heidelberg at eight, exhausted, straight to bed at the Victoria and "so" for about twenty hours – B. not very well. Found excellent rooms in the Fried-richsstrasse late this afternoon, at a fantastic figure: 60 marks (with *Früh-stück*) for both for a month, which is roughly $7.00 apiece. B's German remarkably good & I'm learning fast – very easy to "get along" in quickly. The orchestra is having waltz fits and every thing is ever so gay – charm-ing town, from what we've seen. Still at the dinner table, each writing its Mum. Arthur's [Vogel] gone down to Vienna, unhappily, but will be back – good man, he left us full instructions & we've had no trouble. Marvellous beer – no Wurzburger Bock here, must try elsewhere. Settle down to work tomorrow, anticipate a perfect month. The Folio & a few odd volumes of modern text are all I've brought – ow, last page! Best of luck with the work, Mum, keep well. Will write each week – my love to Bob & Uncle Jack. B. sends her love – I do hope your birthday was nice, Mum. All my love always

John

34, Bridge Street
Cambridge

Dearest Mum,   13 August 1937

   A good deal of news, none of it important. Mainly I want to congrat-ulate you profoundly for your adaptability and unceasing labour and the success you've had; from what you tell me, luck has entirely been lacking so far, but it can't forever; I do hope the rest of the time in Washington was profitable, not too unpleasant, and that things are breaking marvel-lously in New York; I know so little about it, really, as you must realize, that I have to be vague – I wish I didn't. What delights me most is that you're meeting even in business some people that interest you, and seem in your letters to be definitely hopeful of reward finally. You deserve approximately all the valuable leisure there is, to do what you will for yourself alone and to reflect with complete satisfaction on the section of your life till now spent wholly and magnificently and incredibly in the service of ethical good and of those for whom you care. My praise is moderate; I speak from sound knowledge with what is if anything less than justice. God bless you, Mother.

I have decided, and have permission, to stay this year in these rooms, and shall move tomorrow my extensive belongings over here from Memorial Court. Very comfortable: study on the first floor only slightly smaller than M4, enough bookspace when I've had some shelves put in, excellent light, good desk and large table, more comfortable chairs than before; anonymous little bedroom on the ground floor, but I'm never there; Heidelberg prepared me for no running water; there is however a bathtub thank God; landlady a fat Mrs Young, I shall miss Mrs Mizzen, who is terribly sorry to part with me, lovely little woman. Several strong reasons, principally of course money, fourteen pounds a term instead of over twenty. Also convenience to town, I'm on the main street near Magdalene and Andy's [i.e., Andrews Wanning] old rooms; and Mrs Young, a dishonest soul, has the key hanging so I can reach it through the letter-opening and come & go as I please. Other reasons too. I am not distressed at moving, probably because I wrote that essay in this room and know I can work like hell here.

Spent a heavenly morning in Ghent. St Bavon superb and the carillon in the Beffroi better than I could dream, the [Jan] Van Eyck altarpiece, old houses, Chateau du Girard le Diable, etc. But heat was immense, I was terribly lonely and fled straight to London, more or less ill, that afternoon; stayed that night and saw *The Winter's Tale* at the Open Air Theatre in Regent's Park Saturday afternoon – not too good but it excited me no end, knowing the play by heart and adoring it as I do; wrote for reference what I remembered here the next day, enclose a copy that may possibly interest you. There are few plays better. I've been at work this week largely on *Lear* and criticism, an inconceivably rich and difficult piece of writing, I know it intimately and can't understand dozens of passages & things. The Oldham I consider to be a question of luck, who else is in for it and how much work they've done and how you hit the papers. The slant of the two examiners is important and unpredictable, too. I'm doing all I can, having a brilliant time.

John Ward [a schoolmate at SKS] turned up last evening and we talked till two, very interesting indeed; married & has a small teaching job in a Philadelphia girls' school next year, most unsanguine; going to Holland, then Paris & France, wants me to come but I can't. I don't think I told you, by the way, that I've a full beard; took off the other, after testing goatee & moustache, before I left Cambridge; but didn't shave at all abroad and have only just had it trimmed since returning; delicious not shaving, my sole object; the necessary result I don't mind, scarcely know I have it, and it's generally admired; will have a picture taken and send you one; may keep it permanently or may take it off next week; I look rather like Christ.

Back to verse: four poems, unexpectedly, this week, two of them excellent, and today the first draught of what may be a masterpiece, seven nine-line stanzas. Confidence returns with skill.

I believe I said nothing to Granny about my plans. Gruntled, couth and duplicious are equally ecstatic-making and all yours; mourn not. I wish I could think of one, but I know some fantastically long and funny stories to tell you. *Frühstück* it is, my inimitable penmanship at fault, probably.

I am very sorry that you did not see fit to comment on what is of such extreme importance to me. I of course regret Jean's hurt (if it *was* hurt: I have not heard from her in some two months, which I fail either to understand or pardon; my letter to her, which I hope you have seen, requires answer) but I had absolutely no choice, and managed it as well as I could; I am very fond of her, though I feel far away and do not I think now love her. B. has changed greatly in the last month, is swinging into perfection or all I can believe of it; our happiness is inexhaustible; should she fail, the solid rock will rise as god and strike the earth apart, man go headlong. I never believed such joy and trust could be. This ten days from her has been agony of a special order, as it has been for her; even this is on a plane I have never before attained.

Passionately as I desire not to, I agree with you all but unconditionally about creation and happiness. But I have not a mind that is easily or long satisfied, and I do not expect ever to lack torment. And on my honour, I *cannot* let go by what may be my one chance for a full and rich and permanent (if, necessarily, desperately partial) human happiness. I find capacities I [had] not dreamed of, never admitted the existence of, and derided even in art.

I shall grieve if you say nothing. Of course you do not yet know her, but can you have no confidence at all in me? I am not a fool, nor shall I ever again love easily. B. wanted in Heidelberg to send you her love and could not. Mine you have always and my admiration and such prayers as I can say.

John

34, Bridge Street
Cambridge
[No salutation]   5 October 1937

The Oldham papers are done, they went very well I think. It's been rather difficult. Returning from Stratford ten days ago I picked up somewhere the devil's own cold, and it has raged since, bottling up all my senses, producing galling headaches and general fatigue. Constant work all last week, little sleep and a good deal of nervousness. But several of my special subjects were given: Saturday morning the second essay topic was The Disintegration of Shakespeare, which I've studied in great detail; I looked no further and for three hours hurled analysis and fact on paper; history of the movement, methodology and consensus of results. That afternoon was the general paper, four questions; again one was The Soliloquy, on which I've been for weeks collecting material for an essay – the subject is little known. Yesterday morning was the Tragedies-Poems paper, and in the afternoon the Comedies-Histories. The issue depends entirely on what the rest did; my papers are full, accurate and as nearly exhaustive as it's possible to be in a short time. Writing so little by hand did handicap me somewhat, not greatly. I don't believe there is much chance of my not winning, but I count on nothing. Results out in two weeks or so.

A considerable strain is off, since for several months I've read nothing but Shakespeare and that largely with the examination in mind. But I am full to bursting with masses of information and analogy and criticism that I had no opportunity to use. Intend to do several essays, at least *Measure for Measure* and "The Soliloquy", this year; and want very much to edit

Lear, which Gordon is very interested in: no really good text exists, and I've some new material.

I thank you extremely for writing about B. as you have. It has made her very happy, and me of course also. I am very tired and nervous at the moment; will write again soon; I look forward to another year here without much pleasure, it is all so damned childish. Can't hurt me, but will be very bad for B., I am afraid. She has changed enormously in the last few months, however, and takes my opinion exclusively; it may work out. If I've any prospect for livelihood, we'll marry next year.

Bob's being back at college delights me; I've had several good letters from him, which I'll answer; wish him luck now, tell him to work. I hope you are all well, and that your travels don't exhaust you. All good luck with business; wealth and happiness attend you. My dearest love,

John

The strong influence that Mrs. Berryman continued to have on JB's ambitions at this time is evident from this diary entry for October 22, 1937. JB wrote: "B. came in and got me up about eleven. Found two letters from Mother: one of them birthday, speaking of her own life, caused me the greatest and purest grief I can remember—unable to weep, but long dry sobs tore me to pieces; I vow to achieve her happiness in all ways open to me. Pray these Prizes give me a start."

34, Bridge Street
Cambridge
24 November 1937

Dearest little angel Mum, I have various good news for you, but first I want absolutely to forbid you to worry about me. You have been good to me always beyond measure, my grief is that I have not begun to repay you. I am going to worry about you and think of you continually, and far from considering that you have poured your troubles out to me (as you recently wrote) I implore you to; sharing does really lighten, and no one has a better right than I have to share yours. But you must not worry any longer about me. You must assume that I exaggerate or generalize from a moment, and forgive me. Further financial help is not to be thought of; I am damnably sorry that my past foolish extravagance makes it impossible for me to help you as I ought. Think of me as a cushion who loves you devotedly, will always try to be there for you to sit on, and will endeavour constantly to be as comfortable as possible for you. This is not self-abnegation, despite my unhappily persistent capacity for self-pity; I am perfectly aware of my value; but I know yours.

I've been awarded the Oldham. B. came in to tell me yesterday afternoon when [Theodore] Redpath [a Fellow of Trinity College] and I were still talking after lunch. We thought she might have seen a wish-fulfilment, so we went straight down to the Senate House and lo, there it was. A letter came last night from the University Marshall, begging to inform about the award and telling me it amounted to about eighty-three pounds, which would be given me through my Tutor in three terminal installments; and it was announced in the *Times* this morning, I learned from [James Buckley] Satterthwaite at lunch in Hall. The favourite, a man named [Arnold] Kettle in Pembroke who took a First last year, was named *"proxime accessit"*; I daresay he could rend me cheerfully. This is not a qualification, I am told: had there been any doubt, the Examiners would have divided the Prize (technically it is a scholarship, tenable for one year), as has been done in several recent years. "Came nearest" equals Honourable Mention. I am greatly relieved; I had finally to dam up anxiety but I never got free of a certain tension. It will please you and the family and my friends here and over there, will delight the Dean [Hawkes], and assure my standing here; it justifies my examination-pointing in my work during the summer and prevents a bad taste I might have had hereafter; it saves a lot of my books. You see, it is not "luck" but I might easily not have got it. The Examiners, I discover, were Miss [Enid] Welsford of Newnham and Professor [F.P.] Wilson of London, nonentities both, well-known and ignorant. Moreover, reputations counts for everything here: Kettle has one of sorts and I am a completely unknown "American with a beard". So this is in the nature of a gift, for which let us be thankful.

My dearest love to all of you
John Berryman

[P.S.] I want this to make the *Hamburg*.

34, Bridge Street
Cambridge
7 December 1937

Dearest Mother,

. . . When I wrote you about the Scholarship, I forgot some other good news. Some weeks ago I heard at last from Warren: they plan to print a group "perhaps in the Summer issue", and have accepted five poems, asking to see others since they want to print more than five. They took three of the original mess of twenty-five ("Last Days of the City", "Film", and "Note for a Historian") and two of the four I sent during the summer, "Frequently When the Night" and "Poem in May". The two last I had quite forgotten and read with great pleasure when I discovered copies; they are love poems each in four six-line stanzas and owe their excellence not to isolated phrasing but to composition, which has been my point of weakness until this year; "Poem in May", which begins "An evening faultless interval when", is one of the few symbolist poems I've done, and one of the best in any kind. I think you've seen them all; if not, say so. The "Note", by the way, you may have seen untitled: it goes "Certain men, do you see, died on that day". I am not sure about its value, having since written similar poems that are better. The fifth stanza of the "Last Days [of the City"] I have excised. I've also disturbed the metre in the opening lines of ["Homage to] Film" since you saw it; it seemed too easy.

I am pleased, of course, that after writing steadily in perfect obscurity I shall have a chance of being read; and there is some slight corroboration of my opinion. But I am happily beyond much anxiety on that score. I swear that opinion for which I have no respect shall finally not disturb me. The lack of available other opinion, however, bothers me considerably; for instance, I have here a poem on Blake with alternative three-line endings; what am I to do? Such things as Mark's criticism of "Meditation" must be rare in correspondence. What do you think of my sending that to Warren, incidentally, when I make up a batch for him, as I must do soon? B. advises against it, thinks so personal a poem should appear only in a book, and I am undecided. It wants revision, for one thing. I shall send you soon a number of the most interesting pieces I've done recently, and when you can I want you to read them (I hope with pleasure) and write me if you like. I believe I have never told you how deeply I am grateful for all your relationship with my verse. You neither discouraged nor unduly encouraged, but bore with patience and great wisdom my drivel, directing very quietly indeed my inclinations. Your insistence on the traditional and the plain kept me from sterile obscurity and formlessness. It is certainly most to you, perhaps to you entirely, that I owe what work I have done and shall do. I kiss you with love and gratitude and admiration.

My dearest love
John Berryman

[The summer 1938 issue of the *Southern Review* published four poems of JB's: "Night and the City," "Note for a Historian," "The Apparition" and "Toward Statement."]

[Cambridge]
[14 December 1937]

A proud, a merciless bird
Looked out upon the lake
And saw the wind take
What he held dear.
He shook his comb: 'I hear
Forever what I have heard.'
JAMB

14/12/37

with good wishes
and all the love there is,
Mum – bless you forever.
John

34, Bridge Street
Cambridge

Dearest Mum: Sunday 8 [10] January 1938
     I've only just realized how long it's been since I wrote; here are six excellent December letters from you, unanswered. Two things are responsible: after Christmas letters I felt depleted in an epistolary way and have done since then; and I got into an extraordinary fit of verse-writing. I wrote "The Trial" on Christmas Day and for four or five days thereafter did nothing but remodel poems and write new ones, closing with "At the

Year's End" on the evening of the thirtieth; I'll send you under separate cover the half-dozen or so you've not seen; one is perfect.

. . . I'm so glad you were pleased about the Oldham, Mum; it was a great joy to tell you; and thank you for telling all the rest. If I weren't so far away, I'd be angry about the *Times* picture, but it doesn't matter; only, never again. The problem of name has arisen again, since in the *Southern Review*'s Christmas folder, I'm "John McAlpin Berryman" and it looks all right, though I'd decided on John Berryman (very impressive, by the way, listed with Ransom, Tate, Mark, et al, as attractions during the coming year, I was greatly set up); to complicate, I've now sent some poems to Eliot for *The Criterion* under J. A. M. Berryman. Heigh-ho. [John Howard] Birss I heard from some weeks ago, with two letters by [Hart] Crane he had printed, the most childish productions I have ever seen; wants an autograph[ed] "Elegy [: Hart Crane"] – ha ha. What trash. Crane had probably the most useless mind any poet worth mentioning has had.

Your presents were all marvellous. I never could have got through the vac if it hadn't been for your draft; as it was, little extra joys were possible: *Mourning Becomes Electra*, [Howard] Staunton's *Handbook of Chess* [i.e., *The Chess-Player's Handbook*], which I'm beginning to study seriously, and a ball in town where a gorgeous creature sang two of Auden's new songs. "I'm a bedbug, I'm a pram, I don't know what I am – you've got the spell on me!" The thin cookies may have been responsible for some verse, for I ate them steadily all the time I was working; of the superb nut-cake I've still some left, thank heaven and my self-control; I'm trying vaguely to save some for B. to taste, but don't really expect to be able. It was sweet of you to think of something for her; when I spoke to her of it, she confided that she'd found something for you and then not got it because months ago when she spoke of sending you her love I told her too strongly your view of the foolishness of sending someone you've not met your love. Pretty involved; follow? All cleared up now; I do hope and expect that you two will like each other immensely. The wooden knife and Bob's brilliant cigarette case were total surprises, and delicious. Uncle Jack's tie I wear continually and I've had a very nice letter from him, the only one from home since Christmas, which makes me hope you won't be disappointed at my not writing. I hope you all enjoyed the gifts and the cards; the verses were a last-minute idea as I addressed, some good, some bad, of the six. Mark's was the best, drawing of a baboon looking out, and opposite I wrote:

> The monkey sees behind
> A waste of empty trees,
> Sits down to think it over;
> When he looks up will find
> Ahead the travelled seas,
> Be citizen and lover.

Or something like that. No favoritism, a question of mood, which can apparently change a good deal in five minutes, since all the cards and verses were done in twenty. Tell me if you and Bob are enjoying Kafka, I think him magnificent. Must pop off to bed now, it's one-thirty Wednesday morning. Good night, darling, I hope the best of all years has begun splendidly for you in this one.

                                                             Wednesday afternoon
    I had your letter about Bob just after I'd sent Christmas letters off, thought about it for several hours and decided to wait; a month later, I write exactly what I should have written that afternoon. . . . A few things must be cleared up. First, I am no person to be held up as an example to anyone or quoted by him as a "successful relation". I am sure I have as little acquaintance with that difficult virtue humility as anyone now living; but certain facts are patent: I made an almost total hash of my years at Columbia and at school, and I have done little better over here; my character is a disagreeable compound of arrogance, selfishness and impatience, scarcely relieved by some dashes of courtesy and honesty and a certain amount of industry; I have been, I believe, thoroughly disliked by most of the people whom I have not known intimately. I advise Bob to follow me in no particular; if he is fond of me, good – I am very fond of him; and he can legitimately respect me for a few qualities and abilities; but he must look elsewhere for an idol. I suggest that he look at you, on whose justice and brilliant generosity I have, with little success, endeavoured to model my moral being.
    Next, it is time another legend went the way of all youth. I am very sorry, in a sense, that Bob could not stay at or return to South Kent, but I cannot say I feel he has lost anything. The "cachet" of preparatory

schools is an Anglo-American fiction; it may once have meant something before money-snobbery came in and aristocracy became extinct, it has been useful to Great Britain imperially, and it is probably of vast significance at some third-rate Long Island country-house, but anything more hollow is difficult to conceive. Even here, in the stronghold of "old schools", their value exists only in the lovely crania of rugger blues and Jesus Boat Club toughs. I detested my school, as did everyone here in whom I've the slightest interest; the remembrance of passing the pond above New Milford on my way back for each term is one of my most bitter. Again, I am not by any means sorry I went to South Kent; I am over-stating the case; and I realize that Bob would probably have had a better time of it than I did; but I am strongly opposed to letting him feel (what I think to be false) that his loss is considerable or permanent, or that I, for instance, enjoy thus an advantage of some kind. I hope seriously that this phase of joining (as, the fraternity) will pass, though it is unimportant at the moment; one's human life is finally friends not groups. . . .

Sunday afternoon

I've contracted a devilish cold, otherwise I continue excellent; just finished two excellent games of chess with Geoffrey [Heath], my play is improving. Can't get on with the poem I began last night, the third and fourth stanzas baffle me and the sixth is only begun. But thinking about the verse I've written, I find there are fifteen poems, perhaps others, that are good; and of those a half-dozen are perfectly first-rate, unless I'm mistaken; and I think I judge my own verse as severely as I judge any other. For example, here is "The Trial":

> The oxen gone, the house is fallen where
> Our sons stood and the wine is spilt and skew
> Among the broken walls the servants are
>
> Except who comes across the scorching field
> Historian; but where the wind is from
> That struck the mansion, great storms having failed,
>
> No man can say: What wilderness remains?
> Prosperous generations, scythe in hand,
> Mapped the continents, murdered, built latrines.

Intellectual sores raven among
The faithful organs, striking from within;
To scrape them but the fastidious tongue.

Perforce we sit among the ashes, not
By will, nor have we friends who come to pray,
Nor can discover what disaster brought;

Ignorant who commanded grass to burn
Like Spanish altars, we can scarcely say
Let the day perish wherein we were born.

If there's any difficulty, look again at the opening chapters of *Job*; the system of reference is carefully brought out, contemporary signs being "Our", "Historian" (*Job's* data were "and I only am escaped alone to tell thee", ours is history), the ninth line, "Intellectual" and "fastidious tongue", "Perforce we" and "Spanish altars"; the rest is *Old Testament*, an amazingly close analogy. That the wind is supernatural should be clear, and the assonance-binding of the tercets, but probably not the middle-line knitting: "wine" and "wind" and "hand", "scythe in" and "within", leading to the full rime in the last two. Not that any of this matters if the poem has no effect; but I believe it has, and I thought you'd for once be interested in some technical points.

It's one in the morning and my cold is ghastly, I think I've never before had one so bad. This letter really must end. I'm very contrite, Mum, by the time you have this it will be a month since you last heard from me; do forgive me. I assure you I've not written Halliday for three months or anyone else for a devil of a time; damn correspondence anyway. I hope all of you are well, and especially well you, that a good connection has worked out by now and that you're not working too hard; unlike letters my dearest love for you crosses the Atlantic every day.

                                                                              John

[The Auden song quoted by JB is identified by Professor Edward Mendelson as a paraphrase of a cabaret song composed by Benjamin Britten to an unpublished text by Auden. The "gorgeous creature" whom Berryman heard sing was probably Hedli Anderson, for whom Britten wrote his cabaret songs in the thirties.]

34, Bridge Street
Cambridge
Dearest blessed Mum,   7 March 1938

Please do forgive my not writing, letters have become a perfect mania with me because I owe so many and write none. And other things have interfered: I've had for several weeks the most exhausting cold ever visited on man, I've been writing pretty constantly, and I've been grievously undecided on some important points, finances, the vacation, next year, etc. . . .

The vac is finally arranged, though subject to revision. I shall stay here until the end of next week, about the twentieth, then Paris with B. and [Ben] Brown for ten days or so, then the Lakes for two weeks, probably with John Bateman and perhaps Ben, walking. England is stifling me, I must get out for a bit, and if my health improves I'm anxious to do some walking; I long for vales and cliffs and green. The weather here has been magnificent for some days, I must admit, but it's perfectly unreliable, and beastly cold still now and then. What I should really like is New York or Italy (I've been studying the language, under B., and am getting on well), but they come a little dear. And it's not too long until June. Continue to write me here, it's likely that I'll have mail sent on; or write me at American Express, Paris, if you prefer. Rue Auber it is, I think.

Taking my fortitude in both hands, I went through all my bills and accounts the other day. I shan't go into detail, it's too discouraging, this is merely to let you know that I now know exactly where I stand. I shall be all right, I think; in any case, it is nothing for you to worry or even to think about. You are absolutely correct, I shall never again let debts accumulate, they are a burden. If Columbia acts as any well-behaved university should and offers me a job, the sky will clear; if not, I'll get an instructorship somewhere else, perhaps Louisiana State, though I'd rather, far, be in New York with you. The dear Oldham is a great help this year, but the Dean sent only twenty pounds extra at Christmas, instead of forty as last year, which was a blow. I am spending very little and buying nearly no books; my only extravagance this term has been a suit, which was mere necessity, since I hadn't one I could wear. Gordon [Fraser]'s tailor made it, it is handsome and I hope indestructible.

There's not much news, Cambridge is exceedingly monotonous for me at present. A certain number of sherry parties and teas, some play-reading, a good deal of music and theatre and film, incessant gossip, chess and bridge, darts, drinking, long foolish conversations. My connection with the university is purely arbitrary, since I attend no lectures, am not being supervised (I'll tell you about Rylands and [Herbert Lionel] Elvin [Fellow of Trinity Hall] and the supervision business one day, it's much too complicated to go into on paper), and obey very few rules. Nevertheless it's a vaguely interesting place to be, though I can't say quite why. Next term I shall be working directly and intensively for the Tripos, so I'll be less bored. I've been writing verse and reading Wordsworth, Herrick and Rabelais for the most part. Saw a fair production of [Wycherley's] *The Country Wife* at the Festival last week and a Russian Up-with-the-Czechists in twenty-four scenes last night, was a nervous wreck at the interval, with fifteen to come; *Lear* is being done, badly I hear, at the Arts this week, I'll go along and suffer.

I read some American poetry to the university Poetry Society three weeks ago; Ransom and Stevens only, it went quite well. Under B.'s tutelage, my reading is improving no end, I may soon be bearable. I'm a fanatic on the subject, you'll have to listen to me night and day when I return.

I've written a number of poems recently but nothing else so interesting as the piece I enclose. I hope you like it, I think it brilliant. It takes the place, formally, of a story Kafka didn't write. I'm glad you and Bob like him, by the way; you are right, "The Burrow" is a masterpiece. I had an interesting talk with [Edwin] Muir, his translator, at tea recently, he is at work now on the rendering of *America*, the third long allegorical novel Kafka wrote. I have *The Castle* and *The Trial*, we'll read them together this summer, *The Castle* is one of the finest of all books. Even in translation, I should think Kafka's prose and fictional method would be as good a model as one can find; why don't you and Bob study him, even imitate him for a bit, as you write, which I'm delighted to hear you're doing. I've had several good letters from Bob, will write him this week. Even my odd verse has reached a certain level of competence, I believe, which makes the appearance of good poems more likely to be frequent and assured. I have now between twenty-five and thirty pieces which I hope to continue to respect; after some periodical publication,

I'll be ready for a book. Satan, send a publisher.

I hope business worries aren't as bad as they have been, Mum. What has Uncle Jack been doing since I came away? Wish him good luck for me, and to Bob also. Has Granny come up yet? If not, where can I reach her? I hope you are resting as much as you can, and not worrying, and eating enough; the thought of your Christmas dinner makes me very hungry. If there were nothing attractive in New York but your food, I should still want to return at once. And by my beard which is long and luxuriant I've done practically no drinking since I came over; let us all souse merrily in 408 and whee the rooftops. May this find you all well and everything improving and you happier than even were I an optimist I could think you have been. My dearest dearest love,

John Berryman

[The Kafkaesque poem JB had written might be "Prague," which was published in *New Directions in Prose and Poetry*, 1939.]

Paris
Hotel de l'Univers
30 March [1938]

Dearest Mother,

Forgive me – it's not a city for writing letters, though I think I sent you endless complaints from here a year ago.

Much the same, though I see it from quite another angle now, living here in the centre of the Quartier Latin and in comparative squalor. You remember I luxuriated on the Right Bank last time. Ben [Brown] & B. & I are together most of the time, Ben is staying here and B. with some friends near the Place Victor Hugo. Infinite chess (Parisians do little else, really – Bob would love it), moderate drinking except for six vodkas one evening, some theatre and reading. A bright farce called *Captain Smith* [by Jean Blanchen], [Charles] Dullin's production of the *Plutus* of Aristophanes – very fine – and tonight an intolerable performance of [Corneille's] *Polyeucte* at the Odeon – we fled after ten minutes. Tomorrow [Racine's] *Andromaque* in the afternoon, I pray it will be good; Friday [Louis] Jouvet's new play perhaps & Saturday Cocteau's production of *Oedipus Rex*. Only one film so far, for a wonder: *L'Alibi* with Jouvet, [Erich] von Stroheim, [Albert] Prejean & [Suzy] Prim – excellent. Reading mainly the poems & letters of Jules Laforgue, the extraordinary poet who died at 27 in 1887. A symbolist & a genius. The exchange being so favorable, books can be had for almost nothing & I have all his. Also some Valéry, Stendhal, Racine, Kierkegaard the Danish philosopher who so influenced Kafka, Verlaine, Corneille and the letters of Rimbaud – all of which I've been reading, *comme fou*. My French, I'm glad to report, is much better than I feared.

I've seen this time something of the American side of Paris, which I quite missed before; it is detestable.

Heavenly weather and a gay time altogether – the strain I felt in Cambridge is all but gone. I shall be exceedingly glad to get back there, however, because of mail – which, owing to some obscure mania, I didn't have sent on. I'm very anxious to hear from you and to see if anything happened from Columbia: if they won't take me on, I shall be completely depressed. I largely am, anyway – money, etc, and the fact that nothing seems to come of my verse. And inescapable is what's taking place here on the Continent. I think we shall all very soon be dead – and nothing lost: the just, as you, have already their reward, and the rest of us pass merely from fever. I cannot think I shall attain animal maturity, I have not prepared, the attack will come before my roots are developed. In ill thoughts again, but this is a city of death. Sex is the mask of the fatal rider. The only poem I've written here is one of absolute despair.

I daresay comfortable England will dispel all this – terrible dreams of war I have had cannot continue.

Sorry, Mother, to afflict you – I had the cover on, but it escaped me – no one here knows what I am thinking. I wish we could talk. I am alone day & night. Going back on Sunday, I hope the lakes with John [Bateman] will clear and satisfy my head.

My constant wish is that you are well and happy – my dearest love

John

Far Sawrey
Ambleside
Dearest Mother,   Wednesday 13 April 1938

This is an absolute Paradise – I think I have never in my life so enjoyed a time. Superb, intoxicating air, total peace (there are almost no tourists here this early), beautiful country – especially to me, for I've not been in open country for years, not since I left school really. And we've been marvellously fortunate with the weather: bright, hot sun, clear sky, not a hint of rain as yet – a fabulous circumstance for the Lakes, where it is supposed to, and does, rain continually. I wish passionately that you were here; we must one day come here together.

John [Bateman] and I came up on Saturday – long, tedious train journey from Cambridge to Windermere, where we arrived late in the afternoon; cycled down to Bowness with our bags and took the gay little ferry over; then here, something over a mile down the lake. Excellent landlady, Mrs Atkinson, and a good position: green meadows and odd trees cover the 150 years to the shore. We are about half-way up the western shore of Windermere, which is the largest lake, some ten miles long. Not such wild country as in the north, but more pleasant, and the crags west of Coniston are near enough to be accessible.

High tea that night and a delightful walk in the moonlight into the village of Far Sawrey, just to the west, and up a private road to a house on a height. Sheep everywhere, rabbits, birdsong, wood sounds, and the noise of water always advancing or retreating. We slept wonderfully.

Sunday morning we rode down the Lake, taking sandwiches – a superb day – as every day has been; first to Lakeside, where we sat on a jetty for a long time and watched the bottom – water like crystal. Then to Newby Bridge and up the far shore, slept in the sun several hours and back by the ferry. After tea walked up to Wray Castle, nearly at the head of the Lake: brilliant prospect. We didn't get back til 10:30 or so. The Sunday crowd at Bowness – soft drinks, etc – was the only unpleasantness.

Next morning we went by way of Hawkshead (the most quiet, most charming town I've seen) and Ambleside, to Grasmere, passing Rydal Water and Grasmere itself. The Wordsworth graves are unpretentious – there is little pretension anywhere, nothing like Stratford. Leaving our bikes, we walked up Greenhead Ghyll (it is the scene of [Wordsworth's poem] "Michael") – an excellent, boisterous brook – and got to climbing: like fools, went straight up an exceedingly severe face for seven or eight hundred feet, I judge. At one point, a stone gave just before I put my whole weight on it and my nerves were bad for a bit. Very exciting. We surveyed the valley from the top of it, Rydal Fell, were extremely proud of our little essay, and read a lot of Wordsworth, as we do constantly. Found a path down, staring the sheep off it, and so back. The first climbing I've ever done, I think.

Yesterday we did something rather better and were lucky to get out as well as we did. I'll tell you the story at length in a few months – here's the outline: by Hawkshead to Coniston, then up the Old Man of Conis- ton, one of the highest Southern peaks, 2633 ft. We lost the path as usual and scrambled up a perfect precipice above the last ledge – some ugly moments. It was magnificent up there. Then we spent far too long going along the ridges to other mountains and before we could locate a way down, the sun set. We never found one, but came as best we could down, the valley miles away: ran into cliffs & streams everywhere. At last fell onto the level by sheer persistence and into Coniston just before ten. Dead tired & very cold, back here about two hours later. We've not done anything today, for the first time – John is very stiff & I'm a bit bruised. Some good work yesterday – we thought surely to have to spend the night on the Old Man – and these nights are cold.

I'm sending a sketch-map; we want to get over to Scafell and try it one day, perhaps even Helvellyn, and probably up to Derwentwater. Back to Cambridge next Monday, I fancy – term begins Tuesday.

John is a good companion: a Christian and a writer of verse, 19, serious, charming, honest, in his second year at Sidney. We have excel- lent talks. My mental health has rapidly righted since I had Mark's letter about St John's [College] and my physical is improving here: I'm smok- ing very little, eating & sleeping well and taking hard exercise in the way of cycling, walking & climbing. Some reading, mostly the Lake Sage, whom I enjoy enormously; a poem & several fragments written, but noth- ing finished & good.

I'll write again before I return. I hope Bob has returned to 408 by this, and everything is well there. Particularly may you be happy.

My dearest, dearest love,
John

[P.S.] I have been thinking a great deal about St John's, and my original conviction that nothing could be better has been confirmed at every point. Pray [Scott] Buchanan will think so too.

[When it became clear that a job would not be forthcoming at Columbia, Van Doren had contacted Scott Buchanan, dean of St. John's College, Annap- olis, recommending JB for a teaching position there.]

32, Thompson's Lane
Cambridge
7 June 1938

Dearest Mum

. . . Can't, even now, tell you definitely about dates. But unless I cable to the contrary, expect me on the *Ile de France*, sailing Wednesday week (the 15th) and arriving some six days later. I'll be on it if I can.

Some good news from this madhouse. I had a most encouraging letter from Buchanan, which makes me quite confident that, unless something unforeseen occurs, I shall be at St John's next year. Voilà! Also, James Laughlin IV, the editor of an excellent annual called *New Directions*, turned up the other day and took three of my best poems for this year's issue (October).

Everything else is chaos and I'm suffering from a series of terrible headaches, probably from eye-strain. Bloody packing, arrangements, etc.

I hope you don't find me too much changed, Mum – B. thinks, from what she's seen during the past year, that you may. I think not. If it weren't for all this trouble, I should be ecstatically happy about return-ing – and I am anyway, when I can think of it clearly. I again beg you not to worry. Things are never as bad as they look & sound. Once I'm there and at work, we'll be all right.

Can't write anymore: I feel like the devil and this must get on the *Normandie* – I wish I were coming with it.

I hope you're well, darling, and less worried. B. sends her love; I thank you, but it's impossible for her to come this summer & wouldn't be wise anyway – I've relations to re-establish and new ones to make before she comes. It's sweet of you.

These years have been as much nightmare as anything else, though I suppose I'm glad for them. I think we've marked time long enough now to be allowed to go forward. We've loyalty and intelligence and love. And I think what change there is in me is for better. I shall begin to live again, better equipped, when I get off the boat and kiss you.

My dearest dearest love
always
John

PART THREE

Wayne State and Harvard

1938-1943

ARRIVING back in New York on June 21, 1938, JB at first took up residence in his family's apartment at 408 West 115th Street. During his two years abroad, Mrs. Berryman had become the chief breadwinner in the household. She had worked her way up, through various jobs in advertising and sales promotions, to positions of increasing responsibility and was now an enterprising and successful businesswoman.

JB himself immediately began to meet with a number of job rejections, culminating in a letter from Scott Buchanan, at St. John's College (Annapolis) where he had felt quite certain of a teaching position, saying that they had no place for him. Suffering from strain and nervous exhaustion JB fell ill. Following the St. John's setback, Mark Van Doren invited him for a weekend at his home in Village Falls, Connecticut. Here, Van Doren advised him on his poetry and JB visited Allen and Caroline Tate who were staying nearby.

As the summer wore on and JB's job prospects grew bleaker, Mrs. Berryman sought, unsuccessfully, to help him find employment through her business connections. JB's distaste for those he had interviews with—and implicitly for his mother's occupation—is clear in this diary entry: "The men I have been talking with during these weeks of looking for employment are stupid, but they have a kind of practical shrewdness and self-absorption hideous to see. 'Self-absorption' only if we begin by saying they are without thought, that their occupation . . . is parasitic, vain, they could never be got to understand."

This was a period of great instability and anxiety not only for the world—

*with the war going on—but for JB personally. Although he did eventually find
teaching positions at Wayne State and later at Harvard, his lack of security played
havoc with his increasingly fragile nervous energies. Further, his concern for his
fiancée's safety in England and the gradual dissolution of their engagement,
which, after nearly two years of separation, B. finally broke off in July 1942,
added to the strain. All the while, he was also struggling to establish himself as
a poet and managed to see his first two collections—"Twenty Poems" in* Five
Young American Poets *(1940) and* Poems *(1942), both published by New Directions—into print and to serve a stint as poetry editor for the* Nation.

*Thus the bitter, depressed, resigned-to-the-worst tone of some of the letters
of this period is balanced by his growing confidence as a poet-scholar-teacher.
His growing awareness of his competence as a poet and as an effective reader of
his own work is delightfully recounted in his long and detailed letter of April 8,
1943, describing his first major public performance—the Morris Gray Poetry
Reading at Harvard. Further highlighting these years are his marriage to Eileen
Patricia Mulligan, in 1941, and his friendships with the poets Bhain Campbell
and Delmore Schwartz.*

*Although the letters during this time show some signs of strain between JB
and Mrs. Berryman (usually after they had been together), he continued to rely
heavily on her for support: "domestic and commercial and spiritual," all of which
were eagerly provided. Indeed, Mrs. Berryman's presence is felt everywhere: in
helping him to seek out and retain jobs, in making suggestions on furnishing his
apartments, in lending him money, and in offering him advice and encouragement on his verse and other writing.*

*The section opens with letters he wrote while visiting Allen and Caroline
Tate, who had invited him for a ten-day rest at their home in West Cornwall,
Connecticut.*

Allen Tate's house
West Cornwall, Connecticut

Dearest Mother,   [22 August 1938?]

Thanks very much for the column copies and for sending it off; it
looks excellent. There's only one thing, dear: you don't say anything about
having mailed my letter to her [Jean Rindlaub]. I hope you did so, because
I'm afraid that if the column arrives by itself it will get precisely no attention, especially as there's no address on it.

I wish I could say everything has been quiet, but that would be an
absolute lie. After Allen left on Sunday morning, Caroline [Tate] and I
went over to a birthday party at Sandy [Alexander] Calder's place near

Roxbury; he and Malcolm Cowley were each forty and gave it together. Madhouse affair. Stupid people, the Peter Blumes, the Bob Coates's, the John Chamberlains, the George Soule's (can't remember the rule about these plurals), the Matthew Josephsons, a crowd of Schary's and Zelma Malcy, and a dozen others. Muriel Cowley was very nice altogether, but everyone else behaved abominably. Much too complicated to tell you. I stayed with the Cowleys, Caroline with the Blumes, and we came back yesterday afternoon late, wrecks. Mark has sent pigeons over there to drop poison on them all, and the thing is finished; except that I must have Muriel and Malcolm to luncheon one day in town.

Otherwise it has been and is wonderful. After dinner on Saturday, Mark and Dorothy came over and we talked late. I missed John [Peale] Bishop by one day, it seems; he went South Friday. Allen was very glad I could come, said he'd have asked me a week earlier if he'd known I was free; it's possible that fine Van Doren hand wasn't in this pot. Caroline I like enormously, a most sweet and brilliant woman. Nancy [Tate], who is fourteen, a friend of hers, and a lovely dachschund named Bibi complete the household. Marion Meriwether, a cousin of Caroline's, left this morning. Sorry to bristle with names, darling, but this country absolutely does; I've a lot to tell you.

I hope that the Durlacher terms will be good, and Dupont or Sanforizing much better; and what you find to live in superb. Marvellous here, I hope it's less hot there. Take care of yourself. We're going over to Mark's now; will stop by the Post Office, I pray for a Kirchwey contract. Write again in a day or so. My best love,

John

[Jean Rindlaub was then an advertising executive and friend of Mrs. Berryman's. JB had sent her some examples of his work; writing advertising copy was one of the job possibilities he was then pursuing.]

at the Allen Tates'
West Cornwall, Connecticut

Dearest Mum,   29 August 1938

I was so glad to talk with you last night, and to hear that you'll soon be well settled; I hope 41 Park works out, but if not nothing's lost. Could you let me know our address immediately you settle on it, even before you move? I've a good many letters to write, and I can't do them until I know what New York address to give. If I can help about moving, by the way, let me know and I'll come down. What plans are I don't know, as I told you. Allen will be back on Wednesday, and the present arrangement will hold until Saturday, say. Then I may go North with Allen and Caroline to see the Putnams [Phelps and Ruth] and the Bishops [John Peale and Margaret] at the Cape; or I may stay on here to look after Nancy while they're gone; or I may come back to the city, to which I've several reasons for wanting to return. Edmund Wilson and his wife are probably coming up with Allen, and may complicate things. Mark finishes his *Shakespeare* at the end of this week and will then be free; a decided reason for my staying on. And my health improves, I think, all the time. On the other hand, I'm anxious to see you again. And up here I've written only the piece ["Letter to His Brother"] to Jeff [Robert Jefferson], besides putting "The Trial" into final shape. I'm afraid the long "Meditation II" can be done only in New York. "Herodotus" too is in a doldrum; though Mark and Caroline strongly approve "Survivor".

Not much news. Picnic at the lake with the Van Dorens; the Cowleys over for dinner; [James] Laughlin coming tonight. C. and I read Trollope like mad and shout Yeats. I've learnt a great deal from her about fiction, and have now finished [Allen Tate's] *The Fathers*, an excellent very strange and carefully done novel.

I wanted several times last night to ask about Dupont, Durlacher, etc, but never had a chance. Seven times each hour I send you good wishes and huff and puff at the breach; you'll let me know as soon as you have news, won't you? And tell me if I should see Jean Rindlaub very soon.

The cable clears up nothing, but I should soon hear from B. Fortunately I miss her less here than I did there, though I become daily more convinced of her value as a wife. My birthday love to Jeff, say I'll get him something when I come down. I hope you've been able to rest in the midst of anxiety, Mum, and are well, and that all things good are coming.

My dearest love,
John

[The poem "Letter to His Brother" was published in the summer issue of the *Kenyon Review*. "The Trial" was published in the September-October issue of *Twentieth Century Verse*. Both poems later appeared among JB's "Twenty Poems" in *Five Young American Poets* (1940). "Meditation II," "Herodotus" and "Survivor" have not been published.]

at the Allen Tates'
West Cornwall, Connecticut

Dearest Mum,   1 September 1938

Again thanks for calling. Very glad to know the address, I got three business letters off yesterday. I'm delighted that you all are settled and I hope the decorating process isn't too bad. I said I'd probably be down on Friday because I'm anxious to get back for several reasons, partly to see you and where we live, partly because it's clear I can't do the verse-letter to B. from up here and the material may elude me if I let it go too long. But Allen, who came back Tuesday night, wants me to stay over the weekend to see Edmund Wilson who will probably be up tomorrow or next day, and since I'm reasonably happy here I've decided to do so. They are not going up to the Cape after all, though they may sometime next week spend a night with the Putnams upstate.

Mark and Allen think the letter [poem] to Jeff very good; at Allen's suggestion I've improved the final line and all the detail is now fixed; I've sent it to [John Crowe] Ransom for his new quarterly review [the *Kenyon Review*]. I hope Jeff liked it and is having today "Whatever comfort can be got"; I wished the poem had turned out more cheerful, but I couldn't falsify the evidence. I am beginning to feel in me a kind of authority which I trust and must follow.

Allen also made a suggestion as to "Survivor", and I spent several hours' labour on it last night, altering and writing in another stanza. It is enormously improved, I think faultless, and far richer; Tate says it is a fine poem, perhaps my best.

After tomorrow don't send any more mail up, darling. I shall probably be down on Monday. Bless all your arrangements, domestic and commercial and spiritual. I love you dearly.

John

[The verse letter to B., which was completed on September 27, 1938, has not been published.

"Survivor," which follows, is here published for the first time.]

Survivor

They left under the sun, eager and tall,
Their strongest men, and the armies withdrew.
Half Spartan and half Argive these stood up
And did the only thing there was to do.

And when night came, of the six hundred three
Only saw any change upon the sky;
The ruined others slept magnificent.
Two off to Argos went in victory.

Othryadas, being a patient man
And tireless, on the low Thyrean plain
All night took armour to his empty tents,
Stripping triumphantly the Argive slain.

At dawn he ended and sat down to wait
Surrounded by the vague and splendid dead
Who there made such impression on his mind
That when he loosed his helmet his ear bled.

Arrival of the armies, each to claim
The day and territory; quarrel; fight;
Uncertainty, sun, death; the rout at last
To Argos; tranquillity in twilight.

The Lacedemonians honoured their dead
With fire and anecdote and little praise.
They vowed to let their hair grow long and turned
Their quiet faces from the funeral blaze.

They gathered up their spoils. Othryadas
Was there, his giant shadow with the rest
Turned homeward silent from the long campaign.
They left the lighted circle with their guest,

Who in the dark, thinking it unseemly
That he, of those who stood in the tense air
For Sparta, come alone to Sparta, fell
Behind and hurled his breast upon his spear.

After his visit with the Tates, JB rejoined his family in their new and larger apartment at 41 Park Avenue. Dispirited about his inability to find employment, he sought solace in hard work on his poetry and plays. His English fiancée, B., arrived on October 25 and stayed with them for five months. Although taken with B.'s beauty and charm, Mrs. Berryman disapproved of the extent to which

she dominated JB's attention. Returning to England on April 1, B. was prepared
to wait for JB until he could find a means of supporting them.

On March 20, H. R. Steeves, head of the English Department at Columbia
University, had offered JB a position as assistant in English for the 1939–40
academic year, with a modest salary of $1,000. Although the duties were strictly
journeyman's work—reading papers and conferring with students in their com-
position requirements—JB was relieved to be able to look toward the future with
a definite position secured. In May and June, JB stayed with John Angus—who
was now separated from Mrs. Berryman and living with his sister, Ethel Bird, at
her farm, Fountain Valley, in Reisterstown, Maryland, seventeen miles north-
west of Baltimore.

[Fountain Valley]
[Reisterstown, Maryland]

Dearest Mum,   1 June, 1939

After years of cursing editors, it's just that I should become one myself,
and so I have. I wrote Margaret Marshall an extremely stiff letter last
week, and to my amazement *The Nation* has opened its arms as to a
long-lost son. I am selecting poetry for them. All the details aren't settled
but they don't much matter. Practically no money, but as you know it's
an admirable thing to be doing. I'm extremely busy with that, and revising a broadcast Kurt London is going to give next week for CBS Short
Wave, but I had to write you a note to let you know. Also came yesterday
a fine letter from [Delmore] Schwartz, but still nothing redirected from
41 [Park Avenue] by the Postmaster; I'm rather worried about this, sent
the N.Y.P.O. a card.

I have never worked so hard or had so much good news in my life.
I've done some new poems, but I'm sure you're too busy to read so I
won't send any now. I still owe Irita Van Doren some reviews and *The
Nation* is sending me some other books; the Coleridge will be out in a
week or so; it was sent me today for an addition I refused to make and I
posted it back. I'll have an extremely good group in *Partisan Review* next
month, will have a copy sent you. I am going through *The Nation* verse
sent me, and beginning to write out for some; I don't think any of this
can be printed. And I still owe about ten personal letters, which would
be done by now if all this activity hadn't leapt in the way. My existence
at present is almost entirely epistolary, as you can see, which is as it
should be: if I exist valuably on paper, that does me very well.

Thanks for telling Mark about the [Philip B.] Rice letter, I had a gay letter from him, he says it "shows more sense than I was beginning to believe they had". I think these two groups will have some effect, and while I don't like being watched, it is better than being ignored. I'll show you Delmore [Schwartz]'s letter when I come up: it is the best I've ever had. I'd sent it if I trusted the mails, which I don't.

I hope twenty times a day that things are going well with you. Send me notes when you have time, and do try to come down for your birthday weekend if not before, you badly need some rest. My dearest dearest love,

John

[Margaret Marshall was literary editor of the *Nation*.

Delmore Schwartz was then poetry editor of the *Partisan Review*. His first book, *In Dreams Begin Responsibilities* (1938), had been given a sensational reception by the reviewers. Schwartz had visited JB in April 1939 to discuss some poems JB had sent to the *Review* and a friendship between the two poets ensued.

The "group" of JB's poems that appeared in the summer issue of the *Partisan Review* consisted of: "On the London Train" and "The Statue."

Irita Van Doren was "Books Editor" of the *New York Herald Tribune* and the wife of writer Carl Van Doren, Mark's brother.

JB's review of *Samuel Taylor Coleridge: A Biographical Study*, by E. K. Chambers, appeared in the June 17, 1939, issue of the *Nation*.

Philip B. Rice was editor of the *Kenyon Review*.

Kurt London was a political scientist and writer.]

Fountain Valley
[Reisterstown, Maryland]
Dearest Mum,   10 June 1939
I'm very sorry about all the confusion and the problem of *not* doing copy (contrasting nicely with the problem of doing copy) but I'm delighted to see that you retain your *éclat*: I nominate "disorganized as a dropped egg" for the Nobel Prize in Tropes. When I showed Mark something Tate wrote me ("I have written no letters, and if I continue, as now, to write nothing else, in a few years I may achieve illiteracy") he said, "Well, so long as he can talk about it in that way, no harm is being done."

I hope though that you'll be able to manage better than now appears, and wish I could help. An $8.50 cheque turned up from *Books* [the *New York Herald Tribune*] the other day, but I didn't send it up because I already owed Aunt Ethel three dollars (my correspondence is proving rather expensive but it's necessary) and am using the rest for our day-to-day expenses, largely stamps and tobacco. I'll be glad to see the Columbia [University] salary begin.

I continue busy. Several of my best poems have been written down here, and two long pieces are getting on fairly well, the "Berkeley [, on His Return]" and a meditative piece called "At Chinese Checkers". I am abandoning for the time my formal treatment, and making a consistent effort to adapt *form to substance:* thus, there are nine uses of "ace" in six lines here, to chime the order & grace of the aristocratic ideal set forth, to construct a suitable means as I go. The opening paragraph of a new poem, "Desires of Men and Women", is a good example:

> Exasperated, worn, you conjure a mansion,
> The absolute butlers in the spacious hall,
> Old silver, lace, and privacy, a house
> Where nothing has for years been out of place,
> Neither shoehorn nor affection been out of place,
> Breakfast in summer on the Eastern terrace,
> All justice and all grace.

The ["Doctor] Sapp" poem I sent you shows it too; for me it is a positive advance and my style is handling it well.

Last night, you will be astonished by this, I went in to the High School Senior Dance with the boy and girl of a family out here, the Butlers, with whom I have become friendly. No intention of dancing, but did A LOT and had a very good time really. I'll tell you all about it sometime, it's quite entertaining; I am poor at this sort of thing in a letter.

Some rather interesting verse by a man named [Lindley Williams] Hubbell has turned up; nothing else worth a damn. I've not heard from anyone except Delmore Schwartz, who's going to send . . . [ends here]

["Berkeley, on His Return" and "Doctor Sapp" were never published. "At Chinese Checkers" appeared in the spring 1941 issued of the *Kenyon Review* and then in JB's 1942 collection *Poems.* "Desires of Men and Women" appeared in the spring of 1940 issue of the *Southern Review* and in *Five Young American Poets* (1940).

Ingreet Butler, whom JB took to her Senior Prom, lived on her parents' farm adjacent to Fountain Valley. JB later wrote a poem for her, never published, entitled "For Ingreet Butler."]

[Fountain Valley]
[Reisterstown, Maryland]
Dearest Mum   15 June [1939]

. . . I've written a lot of people, Ransom Stevens Bishop Warren Moses
Auden Tate Putnam etc. but it is too soon to expect to hear. Some more
books have come in for review, I am snowed under. Laughlin wants a
group for *New Directions 1939* and I'm making up one; he pays nothing,
but only the Quarterlies will print me anyway and I shall send him things
they have refused; I have the psychological gain of getting them out of
my hands, a few people will read them, and they'll be reviewed here and
there. Schwartz has begun to recommend my book to him, what will
come of that none can tell. I spend a great deal of time on the book and
am better and better pleased by it; I now have fifty poems in this form,
some of which I shall kill before it goes to press. A few days more of study
and revision and I'll be ready to copy it.

Feel no obligation but send me a line when you can. Luck, and my
dearest love,

John

[*New Directions: 1939* includes a group of poems by Berryman entitled "Six
Poems": "Ceremony and Vision," "On a Portrait in Dublin," "The Second Cactus," "Prague," "The Curse" and "Parting as Descent."]

Fountain Valley
Reisterstown [Maryland]
Dearest Mum,   25 June 1939

Cowley's impudence is really staggering. He took two lines out of
"World-Telegram" and then failed to send me a proof; I was still waiting
for one when *The New Republic* turned up yesterday with the poem in
it. It has taken me some time to learn that magazines and all magazines
and all publishers are unscrupulous, but now that I know it I shall not
forget it. [Philip B.] Rice has betrayed me too: *The Kenyon Review* came
the other day, with only the two poems printed; a letter from [Norman]
Johnson [secretary at K.R.] apologizing and saying Rice will write me
when he gets back from Mexico. The proper refuge for the criminal.

However, for the first time in over a year I have a financial status.
I've opened an account at Glyndon; they charge nothing whatever, not
even a tax on cheques. You and Bob are to get copies of *The Kenyon*

Review (at Brentano's) if you want them, and *New Republics*. The rest of this ten dollars, which you are positively and without murmur to accept, is for stockings or a facial or a dentist or anything at all. It was quite remarkable, cheques came on successive days from K.R. ($30), the *Nation* ($13.50) and the N.R. ($15). If I had not been so depressed generally, I should have been very pleased. I am giving Aunt Ethel twenty dollars, which will at any rate pay for my food.

I hope you and Granny have liked "Ancestor". I have a monstrously bad memory for dates, but curiously enough I had remembered her anniversary and worked to bring the poem about her father in shape for it. Your reminder came after I had sent it off. If you'll give me her address I'll write her. I've written some eighty letters this month, to say nothing of thirty groups of poems which I summoned energy yesterday to reject, all with notes.

My gloom (since it must be apparent, I'll describe it briefly so you won't fancy it worse than it is) began with a series of decidedly unpleasant experiences in Baltimore this week, which I won't bother you with; I came back with a vile neuralgia, and then *The Kenyon Review* appeared. My poems are dead for me when they become public, and I have not published enough to become inured to this, if indeed I ever can. I dread the arrival of *Partisan Review*, which ought to be out shortly; the ["On the] London Train" poem, being two years old, I care nothing about, but "The Statue" is one of my favourites and I shall be sorry to lose it. This feeling is not easy to state but it is quite sickening: you know what I think of the "Letter [to His Brother]" and I have not been able to bring myself even to read it for errors. Why I ever *want* to print anything is a mystery.

My *Nation* collection is getting on, I have a good poem from Auden (he writes on Thomas Mann's stationery and I feel rather as if I had entered Valhalla). The labour of dealing with what comes in in the ordinary way is considerable but now and then I am amused by something. Have I told you about the "Shalom, I smiled the word of peace" poems I get from Miss rebekah ha Levi-Mordski? Just like that; I pronounce it rebekah HA: the small r was difficult at first but you get on to it. Nearly everything is terrible. Some really quite obscene lover poems by a Miss H. of Washington; I wanted to say My dear Miss H.: I am *surprised*. Sincerely. Or John Angus suggests, My dear Miss H.: I enjoyed these

poems very much; send me a photograph. They come from all over the
country, more men than women, more from California than from any
other single state. One is called "Gone With the Wind" and dedicated to
Margaret Mitchell; another is dedicated to "Carl Sandburg, to Franklin
and Eleanor Roosevelt, and to my own father and mother". One writes
a long, painfully confessional letter; one tells me her poem "portrays not
only the skill of an artist and the spirit of summer vacations in out-of-
doors and fishing, but it carries lightly a touch of philosophy concerning
the dreams and wishes of mankind." Actually, it portrays nothing but it
succeeds in suggesting a big and illiterate neurosis. God preserve literature from the poets of the country.

Various other news. Mark's book on Shakespeare has come from his
publisher, and for no evident reason Warren has sent me the beautiful
limited edition of his *Thirty-Six Poems*, published four years ago at $7.50,
with a warmest regards inscription. This is rather puzzling but mainly
delightful, though it means I shan't be able hereafter to curse him with
my usual sincerity; my intermittent anger against that man, for whom
I've the greatest respect and even affection, has become a principle of my
literary existence. But this is enough for one letter. Nothing has pleased
me so much as hearing that you are getting straightened out; I thank God
you'll soon have your first cheque. Send me a note when you can. My
most dear love,

John

["World-Telegram" appeared in the June 28, 1939, issue of the *New Republic*.

"Ancestor" is about JB's maternal great grandfather, Colonel Robert Glenn
Shaver, who was a hero in the Confederate army. His regiment was the last in
the Confederacy to surrender and he was later made a general. Mrs. Berryman
adored her eminent grandfather, who loved and indulged her in return. Shaver
died in 1915. The poem was eventually published in the summer 1943 issue of
the *Sewanee Review* and in *The Dispossessed* (1948).]

*During his earlier months in New York, JB had found a new friend and
kindred spirit in Bhain Campbell. Campbell, a poet and Marxist, was later that
summer offered a position in the English Department at Wayne State University, Detroit. With Campbell's encouragement JB also applied for a position
there, and when Professor Clarence B. Hilberry, chairman of the English
Department, offered one to him, he accepted it on the basis that it would pay
"about twice as much as Columbia now pays me." Before settling at Wayne*

State for the year, JB joined Bhain, his wife, Florence (later Mrs. Morton Miller), and her sister, Annette Johnson, in Grand Marais, Michigan.

Grand Marais, Michigan

Dearest Mum,   1 August 1939

I'm so sorry you've been without news, I thought I wrote shortly after coming up, but either I didn't or the letter went astray. All the uncertainty and moving about upset me rather seriously, and I am just now beginning to settle into work again; also a poem "The Animal Trainer" troubled me for days before I was able to write it. Also nobody writes me and I am gloomy.

What happened in lower Michigan is too complicated to tell now. Briefly, Bhain and Florence [Campbell] were late in coming out, arrived penniless when they did arrive and had to raise money, and Florence's sister, who is with us, turned out to be neurotic, causing us no end of difficulty and elaboration. It was all depressing in the extreme, I was unable to get anything done. We had a pleasant trip North, though, spent the night at Mackinac City, crossed on the ferry next morning and came on to Grand Marais, where without much delay we found an admirable house in town very cheaply and are now settled. Blue Superior, a bay, a spit, dunes, Northern winds and sun; though I've been too busy to enjoy anything yet. Mainly reviewing, with which I'm badly behindhand, and *Nation* stuff; Schwartz hasn't sent a poem, so I'm printing a new, good, longish poem Bhain wrote over this last weekend under my eagle eye; with Stevens, Auden, 2 [Elizabeth] Bishop and 2 [W. R.] Moses, that fills two pages, and the collection will be sent off today or tomorrow. Five more books to review, all for the *Nation*, then I hope some rest.

Did the Pacific [Mills] cheque finally come through, Mum? I gather it must have, and hope this month's will be on time. The best of luck with the spring coatins (can that be right?) and then dress colours; I'm sorry you are going to be so continually busy; you must get away if possible in September if not before. I must run to the Post Office now, just one mail a day out from here, I am really on the outskirts, where granite resists the lake and our type of thinking ends. Bhain and Florence thank you for remembering them and send their best, we speak of you often and I wish you were here. My dearest love to you and Bob,

John

["The Animal Trainer (1)" and "The Animal Trainer (2)" were eventually published in *The Dispossessed* (1948).]

                                                        Grand Marais, Michigan
Dearest Mum,   15 August 1939
    I am very happy about your being settled and so well settled, it is the best news I could have had. The place sounds wonderful, I'm glad you have room and quiet and cool, and it will be good for you to be alone for a bit, while Bob is away (I'll write him). Luxuriate in space and privacy, and rest when you can, my mind is much easier in thinking about you now. You have for years deserved nothing less than this, and a lot more. I hope you'll be happy, Mum, and can enjoy it. . . .
    Finally finished, today, the Coleridge biography (the second one) for *The Nation*, and wrote my review; the only books still to be reviewed are two volumes of criticism and two of verse for them. Nothing for I.V.D. and nothing *from* her, damn the *Herald Tribune*. This journalism is tiresome and perplexing, I think I shall review only for *The Nation* during the next year, and perhaps *The Kenyon Review*, if they send something as they say they will.
    Not a word yet from Rice, and what really infuriates me, nothing from Warren or Tate. For the fiftieth time I am tempted to recall my poems from the *Southern Review* and take up normal life again. And if Tate thinks he can get my book by sitting tight on some grievance, he is quite wrong; I'll burn it or give it to *Harper's* first. I have nearly decided for Laughlin if he'll produce it as I want and without contract for future work. A good letter from Schwartz the other day is my only relief. Also, this will amuse, you, a letter from one Tom Boggs admiring my *Partisan Review* poems, wanting some for an anthology of his, and saying he talks about me in the September *Forum*; look that up if you like. I have been investigating the nature of Irony and have worked up a fairly satisfactory description for an essay on Hardy's poetry in that connection, which I think Warren will do if I can satisfy myself with it. Ordered a Hardy and will be reading, though I can't do the essay until I get to a library. Several new poems, I have a deal of nervous energy to be released and am still writing; one poem of some length. If I weren't so busy, I'd be staggered, lost, without books; for the essay, for example, I have a complete and marked Hardy [*Collected Poems of Thomas Hardy*] in Cambridge, to say nothing of [J.A.K.] Thomson's book on Irony [*Irony: An Historical*

Introduction] and [George] Saintsbury's essay ["Irony"]. To use a phrase of Bob's, remind me to cut off my right hand before I ever again allow my library to be split up across two continents.

Aside from various mental pressures, life goes on easily enough here, though Campbell is my only solace; I have no real sympathy with either of the women, their minds are scientific in a particular way I despise. Bhain I like better and better, and he is developing a remarkable ability at verse; the long poem ["Of Gramatan's Transaction"] I am printing in *The Nation* is really good: sharp and active, here and there brilliant. I help him continually and this exhausts me but it can't be helped, I am glad to. The Lakes and dunes are marvellous, I have seen few things more majestic; I'll send you a poem I wrote the other night after a long tramp across the dunes to the shore at sunset. This is enough for one letter written in pain. Write me when you can, dear. My dearest love,

John

[JB's unsigned review of *The Life of Samuel Taylor Coleridge*, by Lawrence Hanson, appeared in the October 21, 1939, issue of the *Nation*.

Tom Boggs was a writer and anthologist. The anthology referred to was *Lyric Moderns*—but no poems of JB's appeared in it.

JB's proposed essay on Thomas Hardy's poetry was not completed, possibly because Cleanth Brooks (also at the *Southern Review*) had written that they would need it "in a hurry."

George Saintsbury's essay "Irony" first appeared in the March 1927 issue of the *Dial*. It was later reprinted in *George Saintsbury: The Memorial Volume*, edited by John W. Oliver and Augustus Muir (London: Methuen, 1945). In the United States, it was reprinted in *A Saintsbury Miscellany: Selections From His Essays and Scrap Books* (New York: Oxford University Press, 1947).

Bhain Campbell's "Of Gramatan's Transaction" appeared in the September 30, 1939, issue of the *Nation* along with other poems selected by JB.]

Grand Marais [Michigan]
Dearest Mum   Tuesday 29 August [1939]
Bob came Saturday night – arrived like a phantom – and left this morning. He will probably beat this letter to New York – ask him to send me a note, because I shall worry. It is amazing to me, the way he gets about these United but enormous States. I hope he had a good time here, I was extremely glad he could come, and he and Bhain and Florence got on famously. I wish he could have stayed until we go south, as we thought he would; he did rest a bit, but that's all – we talked forever and had a

wonderful tramp across the dunes one night. Bob is maturing very rapidly in every way. I was very proud of him.

I am worn out with writing – re-working a long poem and trying to get some long-due letters off – correspondence is a horror to me now and then, and now is now. No news except from Tate, who has finally written: North Carolina have given up the Series, and he'll try it elsewhere. I'm sorry for Marion's [George Marion O'Donnell] sake, but glad for my own – I don't want to publish yet anyway, and lo! the need for decision is gone. My Columbia [University] cheque hasn't come yet, I'll send you that advance when it does. We are all poor as mice but otherwise well. I hope you are well and still enjoying the apartment and satisfying Pacific with ease, dear. Let me hear when you can. My dearest love,

John

[P.S.] Congratulations and love to Bob for his birthday; I'll send or bring something when I get back to civilization.

[Tate had proposed a poetry series to the University of North Carolina Press, but withdrew the idea when he was informed they would not pay royalties. George Marion O'Donnell was a poet and friend of JB's, who had studied under Tate and John Crowe Ransom. A year later, JB and O'Donnell were anthologized together in *Five Young American Poets*.]

On August 29, as JB said in his letter, Robert Jefferson left for New York in order to apply for a job there. Hitch-hiking and walking, he grew tired and sat on the side of U.S. Highway 27 about five miles south of Indian River, Michigan, to rest. Evidently falling asleep, about one-thirty in the morning he was struck by a car that had swerved off the road, splitting his lip, knocking out four of his upper teeth, breaking his glasses, and badly spraining his left knee. Several days later Berryman and the Campbells picked up Robert Jefferson and brought him back to Grand Marais, and then went on to the Campbell's cabin by Union Lake in Pontiac, Michigan, where he convalesced before returning to New York. JB describes the incident in his poem "Travelling South" (Short Poems).

Route 5, Pontiac, Michigan
Dearest Mum   Sunday 24, September [1939]
I'm sorry I haven't written, dear – impossible. Classes, preparation, settling in here and at Wayne [State University], have taken every minute. Time only, even now, for a money note.

Being not under contract, but on an hourly basis, I shan't have my first cheque until October 13th, and then but $70 odd. So I have borrowed from the Teachers Credit Union $500, as I expected to do anyway, and am sending you $100 to move with. Let me know, now or later, if that is not enough, and I'll send more. $150 (it ought to be $200) to Columbia, $50 to B. (who needs it – her family is financially crippled by the War) – these are the reasons I don't dare send you more until I know you have to have it. Loan fees and immediate expenses have accounted for $50; my Michigan fees must be paid immediately; I must live until the middle of next month. I am sick to think that I can pay no debts, but thus it is.

The teaching itself I find absorbing and like immensely – the labour will be to keep any time free for *The Nation*, my Michigan courses, book-reviewing and correspondence – so far I have had none. It is an exciting and exacting profession. I'll tell you later about my students.

I hope Bob is well, his leg better, and that you've had some rest – I was very worried by your fatigue and illness. Say particularly how you are, dear. Bless both of you.

my dearest love,
John

[The "Michigan fees" were for two courses JB signed up for in the Horace Rackham School for Graduate Studies, an extension division of the University of Michigan in Detroit.]

Detroit

Dearest Mum   Sunday night [1 October 1939?]

Bhain and I have moved into town – we have found a pleasant and very cheap apartment just four squares from the University – and the moving and my trips to Ann Arbor (to register for graduate work) have so consumed time I didn't have that I am now, at midnight, for example, I am faced with what should be eighteen hours' work for tomorrow's classes. I have had not one second free and I am exhausted, paralyzed.

I am as sorry to hear of Bob's difficulties as I am proud, and constantly proud, of the way he has borne the whole accident. His fortitude is a marvel to me. I hope the eye and leg are greatly better, and that the X-rays and extractions will be easier than we think. My dearest love and sympathy to him.

I wish you could have got moved, darling, and hope you have, comfortably, by now – also, that your business strain has let up and you can

rest. Send me a note when you can – to Wayne University, Detroit, simply – I am using no other address. My most dear love,

John

[JB and the Campbells moved into an apartment at 261 East Ferry.]

[Detroit]
Dearest Mother   Sunday 15 October [1939]
    I hope you and Bob are all right, I am a little worried at not hearing.
Did you get moved easily? Let me know where you are and what it's like.
Also, if you can, how much roughly it will cost me to have sent out here
my books in New York, my red leather chair, and my desk. We badly
need furniture, we have been living on the floor for a fortnight – an
arrangement that becomes tedious in the end. If it didn't cost too much,
I might have my bed-couch and the end bookcases out too. I am very
poor just now, and probably shall be all year. One unexpected expense
has just appeared: my topcoat was stolen from my office last week and I
had to buy a new one yesterday in Ann Arbor; the weather here is already
very severe.
    Bhain was very grateful for your remarks on [his poem] "Gramatan"
["Of Gramatan's Transaction"] and I was very interested in them; I'm
delighted that you liked it. Tell me, did your copy come from the *Nation*
office at once, and was it marked? I have had some trouble with them,
not serious, but I am simply checking on their following my instructions.
    My work at Wayne is exhausting and continuous, though I hope to
have it somewhat in order after this week. I have 131 students now and
not a moment for anything else: I began last week an "Elegy for Freud"
that may stand unfinished for weeks or months. This activity paralyzes
my will and imagination, leaves me useless.
    I so hope you and Bob are well, that Bob's mouth and leg are improv-
ing, that you are better and more easy in mind; send me a line when you
can. My dearest love to both of you,

John

["Elegy for Freud" was never completed.]

[Detroit]
[No salutation]   3 December 1939
    A disastrous cold is on me – I am helpless and stupid. Nevertheless I
have corrected four sets of themes over the weekend and written some

vital letters. Laughlin wants to bring out a selection of my poems – with work by [W.R.] Moses, Jarrell, [George Marion] O'Donnell, Elizabeth Bishop – next fall, and I am getting advice. Tate urges me to go in –what do you think? But we'll talk soon. This is nothing but a note to say I am alive – just – and love you & Bob dearly

John

[The anthology referred to is *Five Young American Poets*, which included a selection of "Twenty Poems" by JB and was published November 19, 1940.]

As the fall term progressed, JB began to show signs of being under severe stress. His relations with the Campbells deteriorated seriously. On December 5, JB collapsed just before a faculty meeting, suffering from nervous exhaustion. After a period of recuperation—including a trip to New York—he resumed his teaching activities and within about three weeks collapsed again. Mrs. Berryman briefly visited Detroit and had a talk with Professor Hilberry, evidently helping to smooth out concerns about JB's fitness to continue with his teaching duties.

[Detroit]

Dearest Mum   Saturday 17 February [1940]

Well, I know what it is – or rather we know what it is *if* the electro-encephalogram (brain-wave machine) is right – until [Dr.] McQuiggan accepts the diagnosis I don't like to name it, – but I can tell you that it is a mild form and probably will disappear with fairly simple treatment. This note is to reassure you. [Dr.] Derbyshire, who examined me yesterday, sees no danger in my continuing to teach – and I plan to, unless something extraordinary happens. I sleep badly & have spells of weakness, otherwise I am really better. I will soon be free of the Campbells, who are moving out – without telling me: their whole conduct amazes me. I'll move into better quarters as soon as I can find them. The filth here is more than I can stand. It will all be damned expensive, because physically I am very weak, but it is unavoidable. I still write nothing – this is the first letter in a long time, I had to write it. Don't worry about me, dear. I'll write again when I can. Keep well – it was good to see you even so briefly. Dearest love

John

[P.S.] B. is well, thank God.

[The diagnosis referred to was *petit mal* epilepsy.
The Campbells moved on February 20, leaving JB alone in the apartment.]

5421 3rd Av. [Detroit]
Dearest,   Thursday night [29 February 1940?]

It is very well to say "move, move", and to be sure, this place is sufficiently depressing, filthy and expensive – *but where to move to?* I have very little time or strength to give to looking, and since I *must* live near the University, the field is limited. So far I have found nothing conceivably habitable (except at $60 a month, etc) but a large fine room in a private house on Merrick, which I saw tonight and am tempted to take, though it costs almost the same as this apartment: $40 a month. The people are pleasant and the place well kept; excellent furniture, some of which I would move out; a good bathroom; deep window-ledges, fire-place, etc. About taking meals with them or in my room I forgot to ask, and that is very important: my restaurant diet brought me a terrible diar-rhea this week and absolute disorder; I thought I'd have to discontinue teaching, but [Dr. Eugene M.] Shafarman saved me. Well, what shall I do? Can you write instantly to say what you think?

I am under treatment for my condition, and am generally, I think, better, though not too well tonight. Some of the doctors' bills have appeared, to paralyze me or my bank account. Also, I registered yesterday in Ann Arbor (you'll be amused to hear I have "A" in both the courses I took) and that cost $25. Moving expenses will really "do" me. This is not a plea for money, but news (if I need some ever, I'll ask). I live utterly solitary and have been reading quite a lot – Henry Adams & Haw-thorne – otherwise merely teaching and resting. My *Southern Review* proofs [see note with April 28 letter] came tonight, to no effect – I have little interest in those poems. The portraits are here from [J.A.] Fitzsimmons, and they are excellent, though you won't like them and neither do I.

This is the longest letter I have written this year – You see how inar-ticulate I am. Keep well, dear, and advise me; I live on the edge of perfect despair.

All my love
John

[P.S.] Write me air mail *here*, 5421 Third Avenue.

[JB registered at the University of Michigan in Ann Arbor, at this time, to be eligible to compete for the Hopwood Awards in poetry and drama.

One of the J. A. Fitzsimmons portraits was used, without credit, in *Five Young American Poets.*]

[Detroit]

Dearest Mother   28 April 1940

I am very sorry for my silence. Under continual and paralyzing treatment by Dr. [Marie R.] Salutsky [JB's dentist], I have been in a savage
humour for weeks and probably would not have written even had I had
time. I see her twice a week, and when the end will be the Devil knows;
moreover, the gas I took for the extraction of a molar a week ago affected
me extraordinarily: it was a kind of death. Also, I have been correcting
sixty research papers (two to five thousand words each) and trying to decide
on poems for the collection that finally got sent off this afternoon. O to
be in Shanghai now that Spring is here. War news too has done its bit.
I've not written B. this year. What is happening there I do not like to
imagine. . . .

It is good to hear that you think your business growing more stable,
but I am distressed at the amount of work you do. I hope earnestly that
things are easier now, since the 'line' has opened, and that you have been
able to get up to Windham [N.Y.] and rest somewhat. Bob's account of
your health is very discouraging. Let me hear when you can.

I had not time in the end to put a book of essays together for the
Hopwood [Awards, University of Michigan, Ann Arbor] affair: I turned
in a book called *Twenty-Five Poems* and the play. The results of the
ridiculous competition will be announced I think on June first. I never
spend a moment's thought on it except annoyance at the time it has cost
me and is still costing me. As I told you, I count on nothing, although
the process of becoming eligible has been monstrously expensive in several ways.

Laughlin is still looking for a poetess to fill out his bloody book. I
think it may fall through and I hope it will. I have now a book of about
seventy poems which I want to publish *when* I want to publish it, intact,
and alone. For some months I have had no desire to do anything; I have
not sent a poem anywhere this year. The new *S.R.* [the *Southern Review*]
has some poems of mine, a boring group, and in contemptible company,
but I'll have it sent you.

Where I shall be this summer and what I shall be doing. I think I had
better spend it in a trance, to save the expense of food, rent and travel.
Unless something unusual happens, I shall be as poor as half a mouse. I
want naturally to pass part of it with you and Bob; I want to stay here and

work or go to New York and work and go into the country and work; I want to go to England. By June I may know something. Of even greater importance and perplexity is the question of next year. [H.R.] Steeves has informed me that my precious university [Columbia] does not want me. Whether I can stay here at Wayne, and can bear to, I don't know. Schwartz says Harvard will want me next year, but not this. St John's is a mystery as usual. *Kenyon* is a vague possibility. When I have something definite you'll hear it. Meanwhile take care of yourself, rest as much as possible, don't worry at all about me, and enjoy yourself whenever you can. My dearest love to you and Bob and Granny, bless her,

John

["Homage to Film," "Meditation" and "Song from *Cleopatra*" appeared in the spring 1940 issue of the *Southern Review*.]

[Detroit]

My dear   Friday night [31 May] 1 June 1940

I have nothing from the Hopwood affair. Three awards, of $800, $700 and $500, were given in poetry, and two in drama; but your son was among the casualties. Why I do not yet know, nor have I much interest in inquiring. My state of mind cannot be described. I was well prepared for this, as you know, and I feel little anger or disappointment. But I am more generally bitter than I have ever been in my life.

My students have helped me, or have kept me alive. In the year that ended today I take no pleasure except in thinking of some of them. Error and waste, betrayal, loneliness, disease, war, failure.

Did you cable B. as from me? I have another cablegram from her saying DARLING I THANK YOU BUT FEEL I CANNOT LEAVE NOW, etc. Wanting of course to send for her, I may have done it, I can't tell – it is impossible for me to remember what has happened during the last weeks – but I don't think I did. I have no money, and I was certain she would not come away. God help her, if there were a god, and help us all.

Forgive me this letter, I am really near the end of the miserable rope alloted me by Destiny. Bless you and Bob, I love you,

John

[Detroit]

Dearest Mother   Tuesday afternoon [2 July 1940]

I am just back from four days at the lake with the Campbells – my vacation, I realize now. I wrote two poems, but otherwise I did nothing except talk occasionally with Bhain, whose immediate health is still indifferent, when he felt up to it; badminton, darts, sun: I am better.

The letter from B. was very good and very bad. She is well and her family (the English part of it) are all alive. The Belgian part she has no news of; Gordon [Fraser] is bankrupt; Tony Godwin went to France; Geoffrey Heath went to Norway and did not return. This is the worst. I hesitate to say what I think, but I hope the present troubles in Rumania may involve Russia with Germany, giving England a breathing spell; or in any case the economic league possibly contemplated by Hitler may replace a war on the island. My health is frankly not good: whether I could stand an English trip, even if it turns out to be possible (I am more and more pessimistic on this) I begin to doubt. I will say more about this later.

I do not think I ought to come to New York now, much as I would like to be with you and Bob. First, there are certain things that I must do which can be done better here than there: the revision of my Harcourt, Brace book; the making up of a manuscript for Jay [Laughlin]'s anthology, and writing a preface for it; articles on [Edward] Taylor and [Dylan] Thomas which I have promised the *Nation* and the *Kenyon Review*; I am alone here, my books are here, and my papers are available as I cannot easily make them available elsewhere. Second, I am extremely nervous and am very bad company. Third, I see it my duty to be as useful to Campbell as I can for as long as I can, and I believe he would be very depressed to see me go permanently now, although probably we will see each other for only a few hours each week; also, we have begun work in a volume of translations from Corbière, to be done jointly. This general situation will change as I get things done, but for the present it is thus. Tell me what you think.

My love to Granny! I hope the long weekend will be less gruelling than you think, indeed pleasant. My dearest love to you and Bob,

John

[Bhain Campbell was suffering from cancer.
JB had submitted a group of poems to Harcourt, Brace & Co. where his old

friend Robert Giroux had become an editor. The volume was ultimately rejected.

JB's review of *The Poetical Works of Edward Taylor*, edited by Thomas H. Johnson, was not published.

JB's review of Dylan Thomas' *The World I Breathe* appeared in the autumn 1940 issue of the *Kenyon Review*.]

4827 Second Boulevard
Detroit, Michigan

Dearest Maman   Thursday night, 1 August [1940]

. . . All your letters have come, and I would have written earlier but that I have been under the weather again. After a week at Campbell's, looking after him, I came in town, into the worst of the heat, and was immediately prostrated. Exhaustion, fainting, etc. So I went back out to the lake for a day, but I have not been well since. Although I sleep well, I am constantly tired. I am also afraid, frankly, of the return of my disorder; consequently I do very little, and I have not dared to pack. However, the weather has improved, and I may do so shortly. My books will be worst; but this is very complicated, I'll return to it.

My apologies, dear, for fantastic negligence. I thought of course that I had told you about the Harvard appointment. I received it some weeks ago: a Teaching Fellowship, two classes only, at $1300 odd, with the possibility of a third section which would give me (but [Theodore] Morrison says this is unlikely) $2000. At any rate a position is settled, and your very good and kind plan of my tutoring Bob is fortunately not feasible. Undoubtedly I could have helped and will help him in various ways, but I could not possibly give him the thorough training St John's can: if that can at all be managed, it must be. The year together for the three of us would have been very pleasant; another year we will. How grateful I am for your attempt to save my self respect I needn't say. The "ultimate good", as I once called it, is not in that danger. To be sure, I am penniless and I owe pots of money and I probably shall have to borrow some from you shortly, but I have cheques coming for several articles and poems, advances on two book publications, and in two months I shall have a salary again. I have to be in Cambridge by September 24th, in fact, and indeed very much earlier than that, and this makes my moving problem complex. It is essential that I find a satisfactory place to live this year – I want to find one that will do me for several years if I can – and my needs in the housing way are not simple, so that to have any chance I must settle in Cambridge, I consider, well before the horde arrives, at least by the first week in September. Well! but what am I to do with my possessions, especially my library, during this interesting month of August, which I want to spend scotfree mainly in Windham [N.Y.]? There is my problem, and although I am rather better at managing than I was a year ago, I have not yet solved it. And what has happened to the summer???? For me it has not begun, or not begun in its vacation aspect. I begin to be desperate of peace and leisure; I want to lie on my back and do nothing at all, and as a matter of medical fact I had better do that for a while or I shall be useless. My experience under the heat has taught me the minute quantity of the reserve on which I can call at present. Certainly I anticipate no very hard year in Cambridge, but any continuous rest will be impossible after next month, and I think that is what I need; my nerves are screaming as I sit here.

This is as much as I can write now, and I write so badly that you ought to bless me for stopping. Call me from Chicago if you possibly can: my Detroit number is COlumbia 3439, and I will stay in on Sunday night after eight o'clock. Also, if you have any advice to give me, and I hope you have, write. Sorry for so poor a letter. My dearest love, always,

John

[Theodore Morrison, chairman of the Department of English at Harvard University, had written to JB on June 10 offering him the teaching fellowship.]

4827 Second [Detroit]

[No salutation]   Monday evening [9 September 1940]

I spent most of yesterday & today with [Dr. Eugene M.] Shafarman, and the news is good: he thinks most of my current trouble is due to malnutrition, and under very heavy special feeding all this week he looks for great improvement. Harvard, he says, is certainly feasible, and I agree. The trip was a nightmare, but I slept well last night and have already begun to eat prodigiously. I am of course relieved and in some ways very much better.

Bhain's condition is frightful; he is in a hospital near here & I see him daily. My plans are rearranged, since I will not be going to the Lake. I plan to send the books tomorrow (to Cambridge) and the furniture at the end of the week, staying here until then. Unless it is important for

me to be in New York Saturday, I will come that night. I'll write tomorrow.

dearest love,
John

[P.S.] I hope your ankle has improved.

Bhain Campbell's condition, testicular cancer, continued to worsen and JB wrote to him steadily from Cambridge, Massachusetts. Towards the end of November, he took a train back to Detroit to see Campbell (one last time) and was greatly shaken by how much his friend's condition had deteriorated. A few days after JB's return to Cambridge, Campbell lapsed into a coma and he died on December 3. JB's 1942 collection Poems *was dedicated to Bhain Campbell and concluded with "A Poem for Bhain" and an "Epilogue" which ends "Nouns, verbs do not exist for what I feel."*

10½ Appian Way
[Cambridge, Mass.]

Dearest –   Thursday, 26 September [1940]

I am most sorry to hear of your fatigue – I hope the worst of it is over
or will be over soon. Come up here & rest directly you can.

Many thanks for all you've done. Everything was beautifully packed
and is now unpacked; I marvel at your strength. My suit came also (the
new one as well) – in fact, I have everything now except the watch, and
of course the silver & gramophone have not come. We are getting slowly
settled in, as our landlord paints room after room; he is a madman, but
even madmen come at last to an end. By Monday we expect to be in
reasonable order, ready to cook, ready to work, ready to have you. But if
you can come earlier, do.

My classes began on Wednesday and they go well enough, so far as I
can tell at present. Morrison asked me to take a third section, which I am
now doing, and if the appointment is confirmed (as almost certainly it
will be) I will have $2000 this year. This somewhat relieves the pressure
and will let me loose among my debts. The work I think (and am warned)
will be heavy, but I am sleeping well and eating well and I feel excellent;
and in short I am sure I can do it. If anything suffers, it will be my
writing. We shall see.

Bob has registered at Boston University and begins work; he is writing
a theme at this moment. He has a good schedule and I am certain the

right thing has been done. He is satisfied also. – Except for a few short quarrels, we have got on together admirably. The year looks to be a good one. He likes Delmore & Gertrude [Schwartz], I am glad to say, and they like him.

Forgive the style of this letter – it is the first I have written here, I hate this pen, the house is cold, and I have fifty things in my mind. Bob is a godsend – he has saved me from the greatest part of the paralyzing loneliness that always afflicts me in this situation of novelty. Stop slaving as soon as you can, and come up. My dearest love,

John

[P.S.] How do you like my Woolworth paper? My books & trunks arrived safely from Detroit – they are in the garage, probably forever. I am very worried about B.

JB and his brother Robert Jefferson, who transferred from Columbia College to Boston University, had moved into a house together at 10½ Appian Way in Cambridge. When Robert Jefferson married Barbara [Suter] on October 19, the three of them continued to share the household with equanimity.

In addition to Theodore Morrison, chairman of the English Department, JB's colleagues at Harvard included Harry Levin, Mark Schorer, Andrews Wanning and Wallace Stegner. JB's closest friends, however, were Gertrude and Delmore Schwartz.

[Cambridge, Mass.]

Dearest Mum   Friday [17 January 1941?]

I'm sorry to be so long in writing and thanking you for Christmas: since I came back I have been as busy as anyone can be. I finished my pre-Christmas papers only two days ago, on the last day of classes; yesterday was given to conference; from now, for two weeks, I am free except for three sets of papers and eight books which must be read. This will be a rather more sensibly spent interval than the last was – although I found myself, when I returned from New York, curiously relaxed, and I have not been so tense as I was previously. Probably, in fact, dissipation was my proper pursuit – not that I take credit for foresight (that belongs to you) – on my part it was instinct or luck. I am certain, at least, that going to New York was well-advised, perhaps even necessary. As soon as I have made up some sleep, I expect to be better than I have been for months.

My mind has been greatly relieved by Morrison's decision to give

Howard Baker one of my sections, which Baker is willing to take. I could not prevent this, but I don't think I would have if I could, although it brings about a painful reduction of my income – which we will talk about when next you come up. I feel (notwithstanding my knowledge that I shall still be very busy) wonderfully free: I think I shall be able to sleep enough, to take walks, to read, perhaps to write – and the *constant* strain will certainly vanish. You may see a new man; if you see any man, he will be new. Send me a line to say how you are and what state your problem is in. Come when you can. I'll write again. Dearest love,

John

Robert Jefferson and Barbara left Cambridge in the spring of 1941. He then traveled alone to Los Angeles looking unsuccessfully for a job either as a clerical worker on a defense project at Pearl Harbor, or as a reader at one of the movie studios. He later rejoined Barbara in New York and was admitted to Columbia University for the 1942–43 school year. A daughter, Shelby, was born to them in March 1941.

Beginning September 15, 1941, JB leased an apartment at 49 Grove Street, Boston. While there, he wrote "Second Letter to His Brother," which is here published for the first time:

Second Letter to His Brother

An aimless night: we wandered north and found
We had missed the concert; with nothing to do
We came through Times Square on our way down town
And saw some books we wanted, films we knew,
Couples we had seen before, like images,
Spectaculars and drifting men. We sat
In Childs until the tea was tasteless, then
I took her home. All night I thought of you.

A night for sentiment, casual, real. Tonight
You stand at the door of an imagined year,
Twenty-two years I see accumulate
A scene. Memory makes you dramatic here,
And all the slow change, lines learned, history
Rehearsed in miniature, the make-up man's
Care and deceit, your passion and your fear—
Suddenly a theatre, a shaft of light.

The seasons maunder, but the seasons die,
Forgotten doors, and are another door.
I would say that you are farther on than I,
I would say you came more carefully and more
Kindly, Kindly, from the human island:
A wife, a daughter, and a character
Which brought a whole town to the station once
To wave, wish and forgive and grace you there.

Otherwise on islands where I stay and stare
Down to the waves' rock on the coloured beach,
The absorbing delicate waves, to where
They appear to arise: from an island watch
The face of the coast. From an island, grace
Also, tonight, out of a full heart;
Willing you past your threshold quietly
A sharp and mastered autumn, a new year.

                                                    [Boston]
[No salutation]   Monday 27 [October 1941]
    Many many thanks, Mum, for your gift, and I'm very glad for you
about the bonus. I was as gloomy as usual on the actual day – in spite of
a cable from B. – but tonight I felt fine, with my letters this morning
from you & Bob & Barbara, and I *celebrated!* Never have I enjoyed a gift
more, because it was *free*, you could afford to make it, I could afford to
receive it, and we are so well together now. Here is what I did. When I
came out of staff meeting at five o'clock, I ran to bookshops, and robbed
them, as always I do, of the best books they had; three books I have been
wanting – I do not exaggerate – for years. Katherine Anne Porter's *Flowering Judas*. Then [Ronald Brunless] McKerrow's *Introduction to Bibliography*, which probably sounds dull enough to you but fascinates me;
an Oxford book, never issued in this country, and very expensive: even
in my 1936–7 debauches in Cambridge I refrained; but Phillips has had
a copy since last Spring for 3.50 & I snatched it & made off. Then D.H.
Lawrence's posthumous papers, 800 pp. of them, called *Phoenix* – a fine
collection, with among other things the essay on Hardy and "Pornography & Obscenity"; remaindered at 1.25, how do you like that? I confess

my genius for buying books & records. Well! Then, being half-starved, without a decent meal for four days, I went to the Oxford Grill & had the most superb dinner they could muster. What luxury after my primitive cooking. Shrimp cocktail, a puree, a mixed grill & *vegetables*, a salad, sauterne, a sweet & coffee; it was absolutely delightful. My stomach thanks you. With the meal I devoured Miss Porter's "Maria Concepcion" – very fine.

You may think this would have been enough for me. But no. – asceticism I cultivate through necessity: it ain't natural. Feeling somewhat like a god on a spree I went into a record shop, where I played hordes of good things & bad things & finally bought the Decca recording – the only one, & it is no longer being issued – of William Walton's [First] *Symphony* – very good I think. Walton is a young Englishman; the best composer living [B.H.] Haggin says except for R. Strauss; and it is a nice question whether Strauss is still alive – he wrote his last interesting work in 1909.

So. Happily I came me home, staggering under beautiful things, and I sit down to thank you. The rest of the gift ($13 or so) I am going to call what you suggest, a luxury find for desperate hours. It was a kind & good thought. I hope I shan't need it for a long time.

My boys plague me – I underestimated them, both their quality & their demands. Hurrah for the first, hell to the second. You caught me last week at a specially desperate moment: exhausted, with hours of work to do. I don't expect it to happen again. But then I never do. And I *still* have not worked up a title for the pamphlet. If you see a good shocking title going cheap (VERY cheap) let me know. I am fed up with all the "machinery" of literature.

Come as soon as you can again. We'll have a meal & I'll play you some of my extraordinary records, say the Walton. At two days warning usually I can be quite free. My few ventures into society do not tempt me to others, but probably, in the end, I will entertain a little – don't ask me why – I don't know. All luck with your job, the assistant, bonuses, and life generally. Did you get to the Jooss [Ballet], you slacker? Go to some plays too; and buy a gramophone. When do you move into Heaven? My deepest thanks again, Mum, & dearest love –

John

[P.S.] Thanks for cookbooks; too busy so far.

At a New Year's Day party in 1941, JB met an attractive young woman named Eileen Mulligan, who was a close friend of Jean Bennett's while at Hunter College. The following summer when JB returned to New York and rented a basement room at Lexington and Thirty-Sixth Street, he and Eileen began to see each other almost daily and their relationship intensified. After his return to Harvard in the fall of 1941, Eileen went up to Boston once a month and JB came back to New York for the holidays. Between times they corresponded. That summer, when Eileen met Mrs. Berryman, she found her to be "not beautiful (as John thought she was), but she was attractive and, to my eyes, glamorous because of her youthful appearance, her élan and vitality" (Poets in Their Youth).

The following letter is the first to mention Eileen (also called by JB "Rusty" and "Broom").

[Boston]
Dear Little Mother,   Wednesday night [21 January 1942]

I have just talked with Rusty [Eileen Mulligan] and she says that you sounded quite well on the phone today, for which I am glad. You sounded very weak of course on Monday. I hope that you are staying in, like a sensible woman, and really are much improved. Don't trust the mails between here and New York, by the way; Rusty and I have suffered as a result of our confidence. That's why I rang up finally.

So far as I can make out now, I am coming to New York after all, but when I don't know. It will depend on Delmore. Did I tell you when you were here that the manuscript of his long poem [Genesis] was lost en route to Utah? Well, it was, and for a good part of it he has no copy except a very rough draft. Six months he estimates the reconstruction will take. I put the thing quite calmly because there is no other way to put it; I cannot imagine a worse calamity for him. He is taking it well, I suppose – that is to say, he has not blown his brains out yet – and I am doing everything I can for him, which isn't much. One thing I can do, mysteriously, is to go to New York with him, probably at the end of this week or early next week. He hasn't told me what he wants me to do there, and he hasn't told me why he wants me to go with him, but he is a man who does not act on impulse or whim and I do not concern myself with his reasons.

I need to go to New York anyway. I want to see for myself how you are and how Bob is. It is essential that I have a talk with Rusty. If you can lend me some money, I actively and shamefully need some clothes;

I am uncomfortable every time I go to Cambridge, and the feeling affects
my nerves as well as my teaching. Also, my digestion has gone absolutely
to pieces, owing to my subsisting of late largely on chocolate, which I
can't recommend so heartily as most explorers and soldiers do. The relief
of eating with you and Barbara will be a good good thing. Add to these
some minor reasons, and Delmore's desire, and you get necessity.

For which I am sorry in a way, because I am endlessly tired and fed
up and I HATE the bloody trip, not to sepak of the unsettledness I feel
in the city. I have been working fairly well, too, in spite of the persistence
of college work into this vacation. I finished the manuscript for Jay [James
Laughlin], which entailed a good deal of revision, then I set seriously to
reading. I wrote a very long letter to B.; I hope it will reach her. The last
word I had from her was dated November first. If I hadn't somehow got
used to this by now, it would certainly kill me. Tell me, Mum, did you
get off the box to her that we talked about? I know to what extent you are
occupied, but I think you will want to be reminded of it. And I wrote on
Monday a poem which you may like.

The White Feather

Imagine a crowded wartime street
Down Under. See as little as I:
The woman gives him as they meet
Passing, something – a feather. Try
To make out this man who was going by.
The eye stared at the feather.

He could remember sand and sand,
The punishing sun on their guns; he chose
As the men approached the western end
To move to the left. Who would suppose
A Lieutenant in civilian clothes?
The feather stared back.

He dropped his glass eye in her hand.
Humiliation or fantasy,
He thought; I have seen too much sand
For judgment or anger. It may be I,

> All men deserve the feather's lie.
> *The eye stared at the feather.*

It came directly from a United Press report from Sydney dated January 19th: "Lt. Jack Leslie Perry, who lost an eye in action in Syria and was awarded the military cross for gallantry in action, was handed a white feather today by a young woman as he walked along the street in civilian clothes. Leslie (sic) said nothing but dropped his glass eye in the woman's hand." Perfectly clear, perfectly ambiguous, and very exciting, I thought. I wrote the poem in two minutes. More news (Hotcha Division): An "artist chap" here has written asking me to sit for him. I am giving this important decision the attention it deserves. Love and kisses.

Your son John

[The final version of the above poem, in *The Dispossessed* (1948), was titled simply "White Feather," followed by "(After a News Item)." In the final stanza, "Humiliation" was preceded by two dots and the period after "For judgment or anger" was changed to a semicolon. The poem first appeared in the May 16, 1942, issue of the *New Republic*.]

[Boston]

[No salutation]   Sunday night [25 January 1942]

Ha, what a bright ribbon! I cleaned the keys too. I am in a state of frenzied energy. Inactivity is a thing unknown. Even my power of reading has returned. I am reading *Crime and Punishment*. How shall I tell you how I am reading it? As if I were driving a pack of hounds through a wood, feverishly; only every tree and bush is so unbearably interesting and exciting that I'd like to stop and examine it for a long time, but the hounds are off ahead and won't let me stop. It isn't a good figure because I have never driven a pack of anything anywhere, as you know very well; but my faculties are raging out in front of me. I haven't felt so powerfully in a long time. Even my unhappiness is acute, sharp, engaging. The freedom from the College may be responsible; I have hordes of papers still to do, but really I have forgotten that Harvard exists and I don't give a damn about it. I don't even feel unfriendly. I am writing a story too, and it possesses me; the first serious story I've ever written; it looks now as if it would be a failure, but it keeps pressing and I am going to finish it whatever happens, and then I am going to work on another one which has been developing. My writing is so bad, at present, in this first one, that I think I must have a genuine talent for stories or I wouldn't dare to continue.

I hope you are better. I feel reasonably well in spite of terrible indigestion. I am sleeping excellently. If I can sleep *when I want* I think I can always sleep well; I go to bed at four or five, up at noon. I forgot to tell you: either because the heating has improved, as it certainly has, or because the weather is wonderfully mild, my apartment is comfortable all the time, even at dawn. This is very pleasant. I feel very well, in fact; even this condition of the stomach, which crucifies me when I am low, now simply makes me aware of my well-being. I have done something about my head, for one thing. It has been itching and burning (I don't think I told you) for years, actually, and of late horribly. At last I went to two chain-store specialists in Boston, they wanted a hundred dollars or so, and of course I couldn't do anything. After another week I thought Hell and I went to a man at Harvard Medical, who told me I'd got a longstanding and outstanding case of ecszema (how do you spell that) which was bound to make me bald very quickly and would cause me agony meanwhile. Very cheerful. So I got the prescriptions he gave me filled, and am using them, and for the first time it seems in my life my scalp feels free and comfortable. The scale he says will disappear in a month or so (if I am faithful). But I may be bald anyway, because it has gone on so long that the hair-roots are quite exhausted and my scalp is unreasonably thin. This is not to depress you; I am three-quarters reconciled to it. Of what use is hair? How Rusty and B. will feel about it is my chief worry. I am afraid they will suffer a good deal.

Delmore now tells me that he may not go down this week; he has it seems some preparations to make which he can't make, and he is working desperately on the reconstruction of *Genesis*. He is distraught. But I think I may come even if he doesn't. I explained why in a letter earlier this week which I hope to God you received. [Drew] Pearson and [Robert S.] Allen, by the way, have confirmed in their column my impressions of the mails; one of Rusty's letters is now days late and certainly lost. We had better all use return addresses and acknowledge letters – I had your note of Thursday. If I come alone it will probably be on Wednesday, but I have so much to do that I can't be sure. The thought that I can go at any moment – *now*, if I like – occurs to me ten times a day and it is very pleasant. Of course I can't, having marks to turn in, and the story, and other things, but I like to think it. Indeed I have a general sensation of freedom which delights me.

I must stop this, I could have told it you when I see you. Or perhaps I couldn't. I have thirty hours of College work to do and no doubt I shall feel very differently when I finish it, when I come down three or four days hence. Well! I am glad for you to see me once, or *hear* me, in good spirits, as I undoubtedly am. Have a stiff drink ready for me, Mum; I'm sorry you're not here to have one with me tonight. When I think of how well we understand and sympathize with each other now, I am very happy.

my dearest love,
John

[P.S.] You might show this & my last letter to Rusty & Bob & Barbara; I have written them, but not at such length.

[Boston]

Dearest dearest Mum,   Sunday, 22 February 1942

My heart is sore for you, darling, sorer and warmer than I can say, and at the same time it is so bitter that I hardly know how to console you. The action and the whole circumstance look, at a glance, utterly black. I can scarcely believe it. Of the good and useful people in this lazy fat country of ours you least deserved such injustice; I know what sort of job you have done. . . .

Anger does not appear in your letter – either because you had controlled it, and controlled it finely, before the time when you came to write, or because it was swallowed up in the sickness of grief and loss which is worse to me, in you, than any possible job or any possible other people. I pray that you will be better by the time you read this. I grieve especially for your loss of confidence, which I suppose is unescapable for the moment; but your confidence ought absolutely and quickly to return when you look merely at what has happened and see how irrelevant it is to your proven value. Consider, Mum: it is as if an office boy at the *Southern Review* persuaded the Editors to reject my poems, and thereafter I lost confidence, actually, in my work. . . .

I don't wish to falsify what I know is a terrible situation for you, Mum; but I can't bear that you should make it worse for yourself than it must be. Some aspects even of this situation are plainly good. It can only be good that you are out, completely out, of the strain of enmity and politics in that frightful office; your mental health may show the relief amazingly.

. . . Bob I am sure will have a job shortly (I have heard from him also); he means to send for Barbara; and your responsibilities there will end. I am all right. John Angus and Ethel [Bird] ought to be able to look after themselves; you owe them nothing. There are left your own affairs, and Granny, and Bob and I should be able to help with Granny. Not that I suppose for a moment but that you will be able to make a first-class connection during the next few weeks; may all friendly spirits go with you in the looking, Mum. But I want as little sense of weight to harass you as I think really exists. I am so horribly sorry that this should have come upon you. And yet I am strongly grateful, since the thing must be, that it brings with it the positive good of your escape from that office in which you have suffered such pain and humiliation and fatigue and anxiety and grief. What if we are put to what you call the worst, your not getting a job? (Believe me when I tell you again that I have not the slightest doubt of your finding something magnificent quickly – and I hope that you will be able simply to arrange it, for a month or so ahead, and give yourself a needed needed rest.) You can go South, as you say, or you can come live here, which would give me great joy; and either would be much better for you than either the continuance of your present job or a new job. I see no despair anywhere, and I hope that the man you want to see comes back before the three weeks are out, and I hope that soon, very soon, you will be calm and hopeful again and then will begin to be happy. I love you very dearly, *maman*.

                                                                                         John

[P.S.] I am working at a new long poem – very well.

> [Mrs. Berryman had lost her job at Pacific Mills.
> The long poem JB had begun was "Boston Common."]

                                                                                   [Boston]
Dearest Mum   Saturday night [early March 1942?]

I am tired rather, but I want to write a note now because I may not get to it tomorrow. I shall be busy-busy for days: among fifteen or twenty pieces of mail waiting for me here, most of them insignificant. I found a note from New Directions wanting my ms. at once. Orders from Utah strike me as formidable and I plan to get the collection off as soon as I can make it up. During the week if possible. My college work is getting on; I should finish it tomorrow.

I hope you slept well. Rest as much as you can. Taking the 3:10, I slept some myself, but after breakfast here I went to bed again until two; nine hours now will put me right, I think. The trip was less savage than usual. Porters helped: my bags were like lead. Music, she is heavy. The teapot presented a problem, it wouldn't go *anywhere*. Finally I put it in Granny's pecan-bag & simply carried it. A fine teapot. I made tea as soon as I got here and drank four or five cups without exhausting it. A beautiful teapot. My blue coat I must have left in your closet; if you do come up, and I hope you will, you might bring him.

When I waked about two I called Codman [William C. Codman and Son were agents for JB's landlord] about a servant. He didn't know any, but spoke strongly of an agency called "Little Useful," run by a Mrs. Brigham. Alice in Wonderland, eh? They close apparently on Saturday; I'll try Monday. You see I am keeping my promise. But what a strange feeling, darling: completely impoverished, looking out a servant. I want a man if men don't cost more than women; what would you advise, if anything? Come in at four, you said. But that means three or four hours, doesn't it? Earlier dinner doesn't agree with me. Should I have him (or her) do my marketing? Should he get his dinner here or not? I don't want to trouble you; ignore all this if you like. It seems quite unreal to me. I had servants in Cambridge, and God is aware of me – if he is aware of me at all – as a man who constitutionally requires a servant; but quite unreal. Like [B.H.] Haggin's gramophone. I will write him. Except that that has a disembodied reality the servant-in-this-apartment hasn't got: I think about the damned machine as much as I can think about anything except your physical & nervous condition. I had a fantastic dream this morning in which both you *and* the machine figured, and Brahms' *Variations* (evidently a human being in the dream) was murdered: I felt the cold hand. And how do *you* sleep, Mrs Murgatroyd?

I hope you will sleep well. Nothing has ever astounded me as did your recovery of interest and energy night before last, after our lacerating talk; it was a magnificent sign for me. Please please worry as little as possible about your hospitalization. Let me know how you are during the

next few days if you can – I'll write shortly again. You have all my affection & sympathy & deepest love with you in whatever you do or undergo –

John

[B.H. Haggin, the renowned musicologist, had offered to sell JB his Scott
gramophone. JB had first read Haggin's writings at Clare College, Cambridge,
and had later met him in New York and adopted him as his mentor on music.]

[Boston]

[No salutation]   Tuesday night [7 April 1942]

My fears were vain. Morrison needs me this summer and needs me
next year. So I went to my beautiful bank and pried some money from
them and am buying Haggin's fabulous gramophone. I go to my room,
but I go with a smile, my ears full of exquisite sound.

He hopes to have it ready by this weekend. *Now*, darling, I challenge
you to fulfil your rash promise and drive it up – best, probably, on Saturday (This must not interfere with your work; if it would, we won't do
it. And *sorry* I was a grump at dinner on Sunday.) – just the chassis &
speaker, no cabinets; Mac [Mrs. Berryman's 1941 Ford convertible] will
do it easily. I will come down as soon as I hear from him & from you –
on Thursday or Friday. Send me a card at once, eh?

I hope you went swimmingly in Washington & everywhere. Dearest
luck & love, all you deserve, Mum.

John

49, Grove Street, Boston

Dear Little Mother,   Sunday, 24 May 1942

You travelled person you. I'm glad you have liked Mexico but I'm
glad you're coming back. What business you did there is a complete
mystery to me, and I have opened my 'paper each day trembling lest I
find you committed for large-scale smuggling, espionage or general
induction of chaos.

I am not yet through with the year's work, although classes are over,
and I am writing two long poems; this is a note, simply, to meet you. My
energy and my whole feeling are at a very high point. I never before felt

so keenly the release from my foolish tasks as an instructor. During the two months I am free of Harvard I hope to do a great deal. But this is not my night for letter-writing: I can't put two sentences together properly.

The cabinet is still unfinished, but the machine has been set up temporarily with a pickup & turntable unit from my engineer, and it sounds extraordinary. You must come and hear. It partly is doing what I wanted, in getting me to entertain; at least twenty people have been in during the last fortnight.

I give up. The simple fact is that my attention doesn't take itself away from the unfinished manuscript across the desk. I see

> The crude enactment of his *désespoir*,
> Colossal disappointment, and cold food
> Day after day, coffee and doughnuts block
> The human vision, the human sympathy . .
> [Lines from an unpublished poem entitled "Union Square."]

and that is all I see. As usual I can't write prose when I am writing verse. Forgive, forgive. Happy travelling for the rest of it. I am pleased that Granny is enjoying the trip; my dearest love to her. And her love to Jean [Jeanne Mackey], whom I remember, thinking of her now, with surprising distinctness. If Daughter is there, to her also. To the Dutchers – go to Anadarko if you can without excessive trouble – to anyone who remembers me. How strangely I have come from those years, from the fat and affectioned child of your photographs and my blocked-out memory. None there would know me now at all, and how little sympathy would be in Oklahoma for what I am doing, if it were known. For once, this evening, I feel that loss sharply. Advance would be impossible else, but one gives up much, gives up the home of the human heart. I gave it up, and I go back to work.

My dear love, Mum,
John

["Union Square" was an attempt to put into verse an incident that later became the basis of JB's short story, "The Imaginary Jew."

Jeanne Mackey was a friend and neighbor of the Berrymans in McAlester, Oklahoma.

Richard Dutcher was JB's best friend, as a boy, in Anadarko, Oklahoma.]

49 Grove [Boston]

Chere Maman   Wednesday [3 June 1942?]

Thanks for the p.c. [post card]. The place looks impressive. I hope the trip was better than you expected. Did our horrible relative behave herself?? I have been thinking about Granny, who sent me one also. I can't decide whether or not she is a virtuous woman.

I confess I have been lonely now and then; not very; I haven't had time. Labour, labour. Things have disappeared into drawers and onto shelves, and a marvellous order is imminent. How delightful it is to have a place for everything and not to be plagued with other people's posses- sions; to see about things oneself. I find myself a miracle of competence. Of course I haven't any pepper yet, but what is pepper? It is written, man shall not live by pepper alone. Not even by the daily pepper. Writhe, woman. I bought some McIntosh apples which I have been eating with delight; they have made me witty – much.

Even if you find you can afford them, don't think about bookshelves now, darling. Codman has had shelves put in that closet for me, and with so many books in at Warren House I find myself – astonishingly – adequately shelved. Instead, what I shall need after a bit is a heavy cabi- net for the records and some large books; that can wait. The desperate need *en ce moment* is for rugs. As the floors emerge from chaos they look more barren than I can tell you. My first major investment will be scatter rugs. The bookshelves were a generous and good idea; it's simply fortu- nate that they aren't so badly needed as I supposed they would be. I have the illusion that somebody has stolen a lot of my books. O for those in Cambridge! I must must deal with that debt.

But my sense of present virtue is immense. Will you believe me, I have *still* not spent a penny for anything unessential, and I have taken out of this apartment only one meal, a lunch in Cambridge on Saturday when we were correcting examinations. Praise me! And send me a cook book before I perish of monotony. I don't know how to do the simplest things. Where did you get your excellent orange juicer? I refuse to wrestle with oranges as if they were my equals. Even as a bachelor I have my self-respect.

Your plan for the arrangement is working out extraordinarily well. The couch looks splendid against the desk and shuts this corner off from the social room. Minor adjustments of the plan have been necessary, but in its general features it has been a Godsend, or Mothersend. A good word that. I think you will be pleased when you come. It will be good to see you; when exactly do you plan on coming, next week isn't it? By then all should be orderly as orderly.

I was much pleased and relieved by Bob's news. I may as well say now that I did not expect the Dean to admit him [to Columbia] this fall. He has what looks to be an excellent programme; I am doing what I can to help. The year should be a good one for them.

He gives me bad news about the inverter. A grotesque price and it makes a noise. Damn and hell. I will investigate another possibility he has mentioned, DC motor, and the audio changed to AC-DC, but I am very gloomy about the gramophone and I despair of the radio. And since I can't afford concerts the prospect is depressing.

What a series of items this letter is. Here's another one. I met my sections for the first time this morning, and very young they look. Some surprising names: Fleek (actually), Oppenheimer, Fazio, Reifsnyder, best of all – Ostoposides. Quite a boy, Ostoposides. I mispronounced it, and in his correction I couldn't hear the t. I asked him whether it was silent. "What t?" said Ostoposides. "There's no t in my name." And he advanced to the desk while I prepared to correct a typographical error in the list. But he stared at the name for a long time and finally mumbled, "There is a t, isn't there?" I admitted there was. Some of the Freshmen are said to know what year this is. It's a very large class, by the way, 1100, but so far my sections are close to last year's, 25 in each. Pray for me.

In spite of my brilliant economy it is plain that I am not going to be able to get through until the first, although I have reserved buying whatever I could reserve until after my cheque comes. If you can send me a small amount I'll be grateful. Tell me about your bonus when you have it, I hope for the sake of glasses and tuition that it will be large. And I hope you can get away to Bellport [N.Y.]. Loaf and read something foolish. It doesn't attract me at all: I have quantities of work to do, and my mind is in a healthy, ambitious state. May it remain there. I'll airmail this, so that even if you leave tomorrow morning you'll have it.

Dearest love, John

49, Grove Street [Boston]
Dearest Mum,   Wednesday, 10 June 1942
My dazzled thanks for the Mexican figure, which is wonderful and unpredictable and such a thing as I have wanted for years – a genuine

object in which my eyes can be happy without scruple or motive. I am about to rearrange my room utterly, and the figurine will occupy a place of appropriate honour all alone on the centre of the top of my record cabinet, elevated, single, with enough space behind it, and on dark wood. Good! The glazed base-piece is fine also, and I thank you dearly for remembering me with such kindness and insight.

I am made as happy, as by them, to hear from Rusty how extraordinarily well and cheerful you look, sound, feel, are. Happier! The trip seems to have done all I hoped for from it for you. She says you are a beautiful bronze colour, too, and this intelligence affects me very pleasantly. Even better is the news that you are not worrying at all – and I hope you'll continue not to do – about a job. Good luck withal in everything.

My cold is at its last gasp, I confidently tell myself. I hope soon to be at work again. The two unfinished poems are plaguing me; I have reading to do; I want to try some criticism; I would like to finish and make up and revise and put away my book, the actual first book, which I'll call, probably, *Poems 1936–1942*. When are we to meet? I don't want to leave until the two poems are complete, and I haven't much money anyway. Are you apt to be up here for any purpose? But it is quite possible that – if things arrange themselves, in the indispensable phrase – I'll come down with Rusty in ten days or two weeks. I can't leave with any conscience until I have something done, this year having been an almost complete failure. Summer teaching, by the way, is practically certain, beginning early in August.

Sorry about this typing, I have *ein etwas* headache. I'll write again shortly. It is good to think of you near again, and so spirited, little Mum. Rusty sends her love, and says she is gayer than she was when she saw you in New York. Giroux and [Charles Phillips] Reilly are coming up, it appears; so is Jean [Webster nee Bennett]; we are going to Delmore's tonight; activity right and left. I would like to see you, you brown and travelled woman. My love to Granny, I hope she is well and happy, also to Bob & Barbara (ask Barbara to write me one of her marvellous letters) & Shelby & the fabulous farm. What a stupid letter! Love love love love love,

John

[The "book" or pamphlet was published by New Directions in September and entitled *Poems*.

Charles Phillips Reilly was a civil servant in New Jersey and, more recently, an editor of *Films in Review*.]

[Boston?]

Dearest Mum,   Sunday afternoon [June 1942?]

I am just now at a very difficult point, but for three nights, beginning on Wednesday, and two days, I have been able to work at the poem ["Boston Common"]; and it is progressing at a rate by my present standards astonishing. I can't tell of course what will happen hereafter – the labour so exacting, and my faculties so little at the kind of command I require for this, that each stanza appears a kind of mountain – but I thought you would want to know that I am able to do something. Until yesterday I could work only at night; during the days I read William James and Aristotle and Donne and generally *waited*, in a state best described as frenzy; at midnight I began. Yesterday and today I have worked in the afternoon, but it makes little difference: I could then not work last night, and I am gloomy about tonight. Each session brings more mistakes than the last, as the effort needed increases, as my fatigue increases, and as I approach the unsayable centre. Most of them, so far, I have been able to correct – a poor term, "correct", just as "mistakes" is, but you understand: mistakes, I mean, considered as a deviation from the top of possible intensity and truth.

As soon as I have a complete version, if ever I have, I will copy it for you. Until then, or until I am absolutely stopped, I do not like to speak of the "subject". I read to Rusty when she was here the four stanzas then completed, and that was a very serious mistake. It may be responsible, in ways too complicated to describe, for much of my delay and error. Don't say so of course to her. I was altogether to blame.

Good news and bad news – each in an extreme form – arrived together yesterday, from the *Kenyon Review*. [John Crowe] Ransom has very nearly decided that he wants to print "A Point of Age"; and the *Review* may be suspended for lack of money. The effect on me of this possible loss is greater than you can easily imagine. As probably I have told you, *The Southern Review* ceases publication, for the same reason, next month; and to say nothing of my feeling about the *general* loss, I shall have nowhere to print my work – for instance, the poem I am writing, which will be too long and too complex, I think, for any other magazine in the country, even if there were any other magazine for which I had a grain of respect. This is scarcely the most grievous of my problems, but it is a new and beautiful one.

Forgive the egocentricity of this letter. I hope tomorrow to have encouraging news from you and Bob. Insofar as my thoughts can be free, they are with you.

Love,

John

The following unpublished poem, probably written on the occasion of Mrs. Berryman's forty-eighth birthday, on July 8, 1942, is remarkable for the empathy shown by the son toward the mother's difficulties, as well as for its anticipation of the dialogue, across time and space, between the poet and Ann Bradstreet in Homage to Mistress Bradstreet.

Mother & Son

Counsel me, my son, that I am forty-eight –
The tide is out – I stare, I stare & pace
And cannot find a way to look at it.
Impossible age seems where I must sit down
And wait & wait, like a desperate child
For the curse of sleep. Tell me it is not so.

*   *   *

You have suffered a lifetime in a year, an age
In the time of your mature sorrow:
How tired are you?

*   *   *

        To anything but sleep.
Less & less of me, and yet I am called
Beautiful still.
Counsel me, my son, that I am forty-eight,
Desperate, my love – ill, the hurling years
Have spared me nothing. I stare, I stare & pace
And cannot find a way to look at it.
Impossible age seems where I must sit down,
The dark corner of insatiate desire,
Sit, sit, and wait & wait while time wears
My beauty inconceivably from my face.
Shall I sit there? Tell me it is not so.

*   *   *

You have suffered a lifetime in a year, an age
In the time of your mature & violent sorrow:
How tired are you?

*   *   *

To anything but sleep.

*   *   *

You are not tired to the formal image
I saw in Boston – see him with me now:
The tired & old man resting on the grass,
His forehead loose, as if he had put away
Among the green & the sun & the young who pass
The whole long fever of his passionate day.
Your forehead is taut.

In July of 1942, B. had written to JB breaking off their engagement; it had been nearly two years since they had seen each other. JB and Eileen were engaged shortly thereafter.

On August 24, 1942, a son, Charles Peter McAlpin Berryman, was born to Robert Jefferson and Barbara.

[Boston]

Dearest Mum   Monday afternoon [12 October 1942?]

Here is the certificate – I hope it will, with the passport & adoption proof (I have written Emerson [F. Davis, the family's lawyer]), establish me as a man fit to marry. Many thanks for writing. Will you give it to Rusty? The adoption papers I ordered sent to you also, not here.

Doing fifty things. I can only thank you again for the letter & for the money & for our conversation. If everything goes off decently as I hope it will, they will have a large part of the praise.

Care for yourself, dear. I hope rest & time will do it completely. My most grateful love –

John

JB and Eileen Mulligan were married at 3:00 P.M. on Saturday, October 24, 1942, in the Lady Chapel of St. Patrick's Cathedral in New York. When Robert Giroux, who was then in the Navy, could not get leave to serve as best man, Mark Van Doren graciously took his place. After a brief honeymoon—that night attending the Ballet Theatre at the Metropolitan Opera House, where they saw

Billy the Kid, Pillar of Fire *and* Coppelia, *and a champagne breakfast the next morning at the Murray Hill Hotel to celebrate JB's twenty-eighth birthday—the couple settled into his Beacon Hill apartment.*

                                                              [Boston]
Dearest Mum   Friday night [30 October 1942]
    What a difficult letter to write – Pooh! I won't make it a letter at all, but hello & love & is the lethargy really lifting & are you well? I am well, decidedly, and look to the future with some confidence – an unusual look.
    For Aunt Maude [Prickett]'s death I am sorry; I will write Granny.
    Mark has sent us – miracle – the *whole* of Mozart's *Figaro!* He was extraordinary altogether that day, and this gift ranks almost with yours for imagination & kindness. We got, by the way, out of what you gave us, the overture to *Don Giovanni*, so that we'd have something particular & beautiful to embody for us your generosity & help & love last week.
    Other matters, but I don't feel epistolary yet & they can wait. Do you want the Revelation sent? Anything? All my good wishes for the packing & moving – my sympathy in everything involved there. I am touched, darling – as Rusty is – by your goodness to Marie [Mabry, Eileen's married sister]. We have good friends, dear families, much love. A great deal. Be well & try to be happy –

                                                         my dearest love
                                                              John

    [Maude Prickett was Martha May Little's sister.
    The "Revelation" referred to in this letter and the next is the brand name of a kind of expanding suitcase.]

                                                              [Boston]
[No salutation]   Wednesday [4 November 1942]
    The Revelation has just gone off, Mother mine, and will be at 511 tomorrow or Friday, the expressman told me. I send the notice of prepayment. Many thanks for the long loan of that excellent bag. You must borrow a bag from me some time when I have a bag.
    Bob the Fantastic rang up on Saturday night, late, to tell me that he was giving us *Cosi Fan Tutte:* a gift only slightly more wonderful and incomprehensive than his silence about it heretofore and his choice of a

mystical moment, understood only by himself, in which to tell me. The next time you understand anything he does or does not do, kindly wire me. He also invited us up for this weekend, which is providential because afterwards we won't be able to get away – R has a job in Liberty Mutual [Insurance Company] here, beginning on Monday. We are going tomorrow. What is gloomy is that we won't see you, but we are counting on your expectation of being in Boston shortly, as you wrote, to see a dentist. That will be gay – not the dentist, but seeing you; damn dentists; I must go back to mine when we can afford it. Haha. We can't afford anything, even the trip to Brattleboro [Vermont]. But R continues desperately under her usual weight, is not well otherwise, is lonely, and I hope that the rest & change may do her good: it will be a sort of honeymoon.

I am fairly well, not strikingly, and I have one hundred thousand anxieties, but the news from Africa keeps me up. Certainly it is the best news of our time. I hope it helps you also, and that everything with you goes as well as it can. A very sweet letter has come from Granny, which I am answering. I have a feeling, unusual for me, that all things will turn for the better shortly, as the War has done. Sympathy and love meanwhile, and R sends love to you and Marie.

John

[Boston]

Dearest Mum   15 January 1943

Just a note – I'm exhausted after the hardest day's work of my life – & one of the best: "Boston Common" is quite finished.

But *how are you?* We hope you aren't angry or ill, but have simply got a job. And we hope you are still happy. And did you get the fifty letters or so which I sent on last week? – I am anxious. Dearest love from both. Send a word.

John

["Boston Common" was first published in *New Poems / 1943, An Anthology of British and American Verse*, edited by Oscar Williams.]

[Boston]

[No salutation]   16 February 1943

I was delighted to hear of your job, it raised my spirit for hours, and as glad to hear of the raise in salary; if I didn't write at once, it's because

I have been absorbed without relief and without pleasure in my own affairs, the uncertainty of Harvard, publishing, minor physical complaints, general unhappiness. I am a little better now.

We can't go to Brattleboro this weekend (R has Monday off), as I'd hoped passionately we could. Money is nowhere; we hardly live, debts are heavy, and we must pay about a hundred dollars as first Income Tax installment next month. How? how? The future is worse: Harvard may let me go in June & then I can't see just what we shall do, although it seems likely that I can work up another teaching job somewhere. Your difficulties probably aren't less. Bob has broken his bridge, and can afford now only a rubber one. Marie keeps on decidedly unwell; R worries sick. Charles Tully [Eileen's grand-uncle] died yesterday, the wire came last night & affected R painfully. This is enough wretched news for once.

Counterweight: R & I are happier together, in each other, than we have ever been. She is the top of Wife. We wish you & Jack [Lemon] happiness like ours.

Under Delmore's urging I have put together at last a whole book of my verse which he wants to show to publishers; I think this is a waste of time, but the book is interesting, and you will see it as soon as I can arrange. A Canadian anthologist [George Herbert Clarke] asked me for "1 September 1939" & "The Moon and the Night and the Men" for a war collection, and I am charging him twenty-five dollars, which I believe he will pay. Harvard is giving me the same amount for a public reading of my poems, probably next month; the invitation came disagreeably but in such a way that I couldn't refuse it – just as well, since R & D were very anxious that I should accept. I'm sorry you can't be there: I'll send an account.

Hopscotch & whorehouses. The cold is terrific. Will you draw me out some time a list of my ancestors? I have meant for years to ask this, but I forget. Going as far back as you can. I shall ask Granny also. Something else: do you know where my letters to you from England are? I imagine they are damned stupid, I am no letter-writer, but I want one day to refresh my memory, which is failing me now altogether in my ancient age: there may be verse in them: not verse, I mean, but *subjects*.

We hope you eat & are warm & are well & continue in your fabulous energy & delight in life – you are one of our main & dearest themes of conversation, of hope, of our constant love.

                                                                      John

[Mrs. Berryman had taken a job as an industrial analyst with Associated Manufacturers, Inc., in Washington, D.C. Jack Lemon, the man she was then seeing, was a Lieutenant Colonel in the U.S. Army.

Brattleboro, Vermont, was where Robert Jefferson and Barbara Berryman were then living.

The war collection referred to is *The New Treasury of War Poets*, published by Houghton Mifflin in 1943.

As mentioned in the previous section, JB eventually borrowed and closely drew upon his Cambridge letters in writing *Love & Fame* (1970).]

[Boston]

Dearest Mother,   10 March 1943

I began a letter to you a fortnight ago, when I wrote these poems, but it didn't get finished, and I am afraid this one won't if it tries to be very long. I do not feel very communicative. If I produce one letter a month, all told, I dance. My heart dances – but not with joy, not joy.

Harvard does not look likely. Unfortunately Morrison is a hypocrite, so that I cannot be sure, but I believe that he will not want me again and I am certain that I do not want to stay. I shall try, I suppose, various colleges and schools, in that order, beginning with those in New York. Inquire for me, if you like, about the CSC [Civil Service Commission] jobs – although I have no training, as you know, in economics or in mathematics, and am not willing to undergo any in order to have a *chance* at a job which it is doubtful that I could hold if I got it. The State Department is more remote; Jack's kindness conjures for me skills & opinions & patience which I do not possess.

You are doing famously. I expect every day to hear that you have entered the Cabinet. R & I often ponder for hours your passion & energy and your other virtues: properly set down, they would make something as absorbing as *Twelfth Night*. And I especially had in my head the other night your devotion & kindness at 41 Park, at which I shall never cease to marvel, and be grateful for.

These poems are the first of a cycle I projected last month; but whether I shall be able to continue with it is not clear. Take them with love.

John

[P.S.] Bob & Barbara we very rarely hear from, but so far as we have news I think they are all right. The Draft is serious enough; I have written him also.

[The poems JB refers to are the first of "The Nervous Songs," a cycle which appeared in *The Dispossessed*, published in 1948.]

                                                                    [Boston]
Chere Little Mother,   Sunday 4 April [1943]
    Before I go into anything else let me tell you roughly what our situation is: it is now at last obscurely clear enough to be capable of statement, and all our answers to your proposals, as to Bob's, depend upon it. Harvard is undoubtedly through with me; Morrison although in the ninth hour he has taken to praising me is not going even to give me a summer job. One way this news is not so tart – we are wild as you know to shuffle this geographical blunder Boston-Harvard – but every way else it plunges us into chaos. The apartment-lease ($60 a month until September or October, and four months' rent owing, two of which we are paying today) hold us here over the summer; at the end of the summer we are determined to leave Boston forever. Item, two jobs to get: one for this summer, here, and one for next year, in New York if possible. So I am seeing people and writing letters. R's job, which pays $100 a month, is driving her rapidly to distraction. My salary ceases at the end of June. Besides the rent and living this summer, I should tell you that our payments to the bank ($25 a month) continue until October; income tax, fresh from crushing us last month, will be another $95 or so in June and *another* $95 in September; and moving, which will be expensive, we must prepare for. We have nothing in the bank and live with difficulty from week to week, although neither of us eats enough, we entertain very little, we go nowhere, and we spend on non-essentials practically nothing, on essentials less than we must (clothes for instance both of us need badly)))))
UGH.
    I am a poet.
    In the fifteenth century it was the custom in London to shit out the windows on people one didn't like. A good custom, and worth revival.
    The letter continues. If my attack of grippe earlier this week has left me a little incoherent, please. Not having heard again from you about Brattleboro, we stayed here this weekend, where we can be as depressed as anywhere else. Bob's position I don't understand at all, and we haven't heard since March 14th, perhaps because in my general gloom I haven't written to him. That wretched [Morris Gray Poetry] Reading [at Har-

vard] is fixed for Wednesday – I hope I shall be drunk enough or insensitive enough to stand up and get through it. Did you get some Songs ["The Nervous Songs"] I sent you weeks ago? In France the egg ration is one a month. The point is to lay eggs oneself. I just nervously broke our old & beautiful jigger, Ai! Our love and sympathy to both of you, Mum. We liked the snapshots and we hope Jack is still better. You look well, very well.

John

[Boston]

Dearest Mum,   8 April 1943

I am afraid that if I describe the Reading to you properly, as I am *determined* to do, I shall have to write all day; but I will do what I can – being very bad as you know at descriptions of any sort, and unused to them since I was writing to you from Cambridge five years ago. But I must: I so wanted you there, in some ways (mainly I didn't want anybody there), for the only formal sign of public interest that my verse has had. And my (ridiculous) absorption is still so great that I can think of nothing else. You will hardly believe this, but it is true: on Tuesday I spent nine hours straight – with intermission only for my bowels which were very disorderly – trying to prepare my introductory remarks. The difficulty was to get on paper an approximation of my usual, rather elaborate conversation – in order to have it natural in my voice – and then to *remember* what I had written without the *fact*-of-remembering appearing in the voice. Ugh. And reading poems out here in the room, for duration and stress: all of them boring boring, wooden, stupid – poems which normally in the past I have liked well enough. And my throat was sore. The heterogeneity of the audience made the *pitching* of my remarks very hard to judge. First, R & Delmore & Gertrude, good judges; perhaps a few others; able and *knowing*. Then the members of the Morris Gray Committee (who had invited me – it was under the auspices of the M.G. Foundation-or-whatever-it-is, a fund left for the purpose of inviting to Harvard, and having read their poetry, distinguished poets; most of the best men as well as a good many frauds and jackasses have come – there are five or six readings a year), all three of them bigwigs at Harvard, poets and critics and men whom I despise: Theodore Spencer – big, bland, self-absorbed, wanting-desperately-to-resemble-Yeats, a contemptible poet who writes little ditties (but very pretentious ones) in imitation of Yeats's refrain poems (*marital* imitation); Robert Hillyer – a poetaster (of the "distinguished" smooth New England variety) of Eliot's generation, and Hating Eliot, once (incredibly) in *The Dial* crowd and now ignored, a constant alcoholic, Boylston Professor at Harvard, smug politic & powerful; and Theodore Morrison (*"my Ted"*), undoubtedly the most ear-shocking poet the language has yet had, a very mild handsome disappointed man of forty, a Master bore. Well! I was set, if I did nothing else, on piercing these men not only with my poems, which are ambitious and serious enough to make them uncomfortable, but with comment. And third, the variously literate rest, from other writers down to my students, some of whom I knew would come. How to talk to such a mob, who would hear me on so many levels! And I had resolved to curb my irony, to keep it out of sight; to say nothing savage; because R & Delmore, who much exaggerate anyway my conversational ferocity, were very nervous lest casually I turn in some remark and decapitate someone present. I am through at Harvard – and I don't care about such things in any event – but I wanted them to be comfortable. So I would be *conservative*. And on my own account I decided to say nothing really personal of myself – just as I was not going to read any personal poems: no personal poems, no political poems, no scurrilous poems, and no poems from my damned pamphlet. (In all these aims I succeeded, incidentally, – with an exception which you will see.) In short, I was to be hard and serious, but quiet.

So much for the setting – and if anyone ever asks me again why I don't write novels I will procure from you this miserable account and show it him. Are you interested, Great White Mother? If you aren't, God help you, because I have only just begun. What a pity we can't talk it, so many charming and paralyzing details will get omitted here. And I have even forgotten to tell you one of the main features of my intention: to *entertain* R & Delmore. So I allowed myself some private ironies, in a remark here and there – merely a shifting of tone which only they would hear – and I didn't tell them anything of what I planned to read and say, or very little. Both of them helped me greatly with suggestions, and with their confidence (they were shaking with nervousness however). Delmore was exquisite when we talked on the telephone at noon yesterday; after we had finished, he said, "Now listen John, remember that your poems are *very good*; keep that in mind all the time –" The whole affair, indeed, had charming touches of humour, until about four o'clock Wednesday afternoon, when my stomach dropped out and my throat dried and my kidneys staged a *coup d'état*. The revolt had begun in the morning, and I was resolved, if it persisted into the Reading, to give it its head where I stood, and not at any rate to miss Morrison, who would be sitting in the first row.

But during Monday and Tuesday and Wednesday-until-four, as I don't need to tell you, I experienced every familiar variety, and several new ones, of despair and confidence and dismay, arrogance and fright. At one moment I was convinced that I would be as comfortable and assured as I am with my sections; the next, that I would so tremble that the lectern would shake and that no sound, or worse a mere rasping howl, would issue from what at any other time I should describe as my throat. Ai-y-ai! Still I should say that generally on Wednesday I was easier than I had expected to be: during my sections, during lunch (which R & I had together, she having taken the afternoon from her office for a blessed change – [George Anthony] Palmer [Blackmur's cousin who published poetry under the name George Anthony] came over to our table – but this sort of thing I will have to tell you when we meet), back here for altering my plan *again*. We went out to Cambridge at four, had a hasty sherry in the Square, and I left R on the steps of Widener [Library] (the Reading was held in the Poetry Room at the top of Widener) to meet Gertrude, while I went over to Warren House to sign the "Morris Gray Register", exchange friendly nothings – more nothings than friendly – with Ted [Morrison] and Ted [Spencer] and Robert [Hillyer]; then to the Poetry Room, which to my astonishment was full, and waiting (R tells me I was perfectly white), and then Morrison took the stand and introduced me. Unfortunately, since as you will see I was about to posit an *enemy*, Morrison was verbosely and wildly flattering.

What I said & read I can tell you nearly exactly, from notes & memory; I adlibbed very little, and spoke SLOWLY. (Some impromptu remark to the effect that Mr M [Morrison]'s introduction had badly interfered with mine – mild humour haha – Nevertheless:)

"The occasion of this afternoon, as I understand it, is an *exposition* of my verse, not a *defence* of it, – particularly since no one present, so far as I know, has yet attacked it. I have no wish to defend it anyway. But several of the poems I am going to read are undoubtedly of a kind, in style and subject, which has caused readers, some readers, difficulty; and, desiring very little to send you away perplexed, I planned to devote my introduction to this question.

"Let me begin by reading a letter, which was written to me six months ago by a man in New York – a celebrated and honoured teacher, and author. I read it from the beginning, – although part of the opening paragraph could be construed as complimentary, – because the *temper* of his inquiry is important and unusual. The occasion, I should say, was a publication to which Mr Morrison referred, the volume *Five Young American Poets*, to which I had contributed some poems, and – under duress – a preface; in the preface I had paraphrased one of the poems, 'On the London Train'.

My Dear Mr Berryman: [September 23, 1942]
        May I first thank you for doing an unusually clarifying thing in your ["A] Note on Poetry" in the New Directions volume. It was also a daring thing to do, for you challenged comparison between the experience and the poetic version of it. I am chiefly grateful because I am one of those who is (he means *are*, little Mother) trying desperately to get some sort of clue to much of the poetry that is now being written.
        What I wish you would tell me – if you can take time for the scribble – is what it is in a poem like yours ("On the London Train") that makes a person like myself (fairly intelligent) quite unable to understand it. Is there some idiom I have missed getting? I read your train poem three times – before I read the prose explanation – and could not make head nor tail of it. I caught vague flickers of meaning; but the thing just wouldn't click as a whole. Would you say that I exhibit a pretty reprehensible dumbness; or do other people – a great many of them – find similar difficulty. .
        I am not meaning to be impertinent. I am simply puzzled – have been for a long time. For here is poetry being written and acclaimed that is as inaccessible to me as Einstein's equations.
        Is that perhaps the clue – that you men are writing your kind of Einstein's equations? Are you intending your poetry to be esoteric? Or am I missing some link in your idiomatic chain? How does one get a hang of the new idiom? What can a poor chap like

myself, who is capable of reading E. A. Robinson and Archibald MacLeish, do to learn how to make an intelligent approach to these as yet to me unapproachable types of poetry? For I confess that there isn't much in the New Directions volume that gets even to first base in my thinking.

My deepest reason for perplexity is that I've always hated people who panned the new just because to them it was unfamiliar. I don't want to be that kind of dead-from-the-neck-up person. So I'm hanging on to the hope that I may yet be able to read and understand and appreciate this kind of poetry.

Again, forgive my seeming impertinence. It was this willingness of yours to give the reader a break that made me feel I could put my query to you. Sincerely yours,

(This was from H.A. [Harry Allen] Overstreet, a famous man Delmore told me when the letter came, although I had never heard of him except to see his books, I vaguely remembered, secondhand; I couldn't give his name to the audience because I was reading after all a private letter – which I treated by the way with respect.) He is specifically a psychologist & student of ideas, I think) – all parentheses are to you, Mother; and read my lecture *slowly* or it will sound to you even less satisfactory than it was.)

"Before discussing the letter, I should read the poem and the paraphrase, in order to bring you to something like his position, – although I hope not perfectly his position.

(I read "On the London Train" and the paraphrase & following criticism down to "felt" at the top of p. 48. During the paraphrase two things happened. First, I let my eyes drop once – mainly I looked out over the audience in that low room, set to see no one – & saw Delmore, who had come late, standing just inside the door with some other people; so I asked them to come down to the first row, which was mainly empty, and they did. Second, I became convinced that the whole thing was a hopeless wooden irretrievable failure: once, in the middle of a sentence, I all but decided to say "Look here, this is insufferable ! I'll read some poems & that will be that"; I couldn't feel the audience at all, and I couldn't summon any form of ease or absorption. But I resisted & simply determined to plough on mechanically to the end – dull and cold.)

"To return to the letter. On first consideration it must appear that no answer can be made to this letter I have read you. My correspondent is plainly an intelligent man and a willing reader. If he reads my poems, or some of them, carefully, three times, and is quite unable to understand them – cannot make head or tail of them – the situation seems to be clear: The poems are worthless. (Remarks of this sort – there were many of them – I spoke with some sort of forcing consciousness, some sort of (apparently serious but not at all contemptuous) irony; and I usually heard laughs).

"Now this is not at all times so disagreeable as it may appear – as a conclusion. But it would have the disadvantage of ending our correspondence: of poems which are worthless nothing further could or ought to be said, and I could make him no answer, – although he wants an answer. And on the present occasion, moreover, the assumption is inadmissible, since I am speaking to you under distinguished auspices. Yet the notion of *value* is here inevitably bound up with the notion of *clarity*: if a poem is incomprehensible what value can it have? Obviously none. We can go no further in this direction at present. An impasse.

"Let us look at the other term: the reader – my correspondent. We have granted him intelligence and willingness. Are these qualities all that is needed? They are not enough, it appears, to let him read with comprehension a certain poem, X, which we have agreed not to consider worthless. What is wanting?

"Wordsworth's famous solution will already have occurred to some of you. 'It is supposed,' says Wordsworth, 'that by the act of writing in verse an Author makes a formal engagement that he will gratify certain known habits of association; that he not only thus apprises the Reader that certain classes of ideas and expressions *will be found in his book*, but that others *will be carefully excluded*.' [Preface to *Lyrical Ballads*.] And my correspondent's letter did in fact sound as if (to quote Wordsworth again) it appeared to him that I had not fulfilled the terms of an engagement thus voluntarily contracted.

"It is true that Wordsworth's analysis was directed against misvaluation – the placing low of poems that should have been placed high – and misunderstanding: not *incomprehension*. But I believe that these things are not so easily distinguished as readers imagine. We have seen that value and clarity are not – for our present purpose. And I give you an analogy. One may dislike idiots – actual idiots – in private life; many people do; but a man who took his dislike to idiots with him into Rilke's poem ' The Song of the Idiot', would not get far and would not get much. Afterwards, if someone asked him what he had thought of the poem, he might say one of three things: he might say that he disliked it – letting his hearer imagine, as indeed he might himself imagine, that he had understood it; or he might say – *more* honestly – that he had partly understood it, and disliked it; or he might say that he had not understood it at all *and disliked it* – but the last phrase gives the show away.

(I omitted to make the relation of the analogy clear, as I might have done, by saying that the importation of the wrong attitudes from *other literature* interferes with communication of X exactly as the importation of the wrong attitudes from *life* interfers with *any* communication. Everywhere during the Reading, as a matter of fact, I wanted to be suggestive, not complete.)

"It may be objected, against this explanation of my correspondent's failure in reading, that my poetry – or the piece you have heard – does not resemble Wordsworth's poetry; and I am afraid that this is partly true. But the tradition, as you know – the terms of the engagement, alter. Tradition alters not merely through a century, but in each generation, and alters, as Eliot has shown, with the introduction into its order of each genuine new work. That my correspondent reads, apparently with pleasure, Robinson and MacLeish – writers not of my generation, and writers with whose whole intentions, as I understand them, I believe mine has not much in common – does not argue that he does not look in my work for "classes of ideas and expressions" which are not to be found there.

"Finally, unless the reader's notion of what poetry *can do* bears some close relation to the poet's, he is not likely to read a poem fully or well. It has not been customary recently to state this object, or possibility, in very high terms. I wonder what my correspondent thinks of this statement of Coleridge's – which is for me the most accurate and brilliant in English criticism:

(I read the passage with great calm, deliberation & force.)

> The poet, described in ideal perfection, brings the whole soul of man into activity, with the subordination of its faculties to each other according to their relative worth and dignity. He diffuses a tone and spirit of unity, that blends, and (as it were) *fuses* each into each, by that synthetic and magical power, to which I would

exclusively appropriate the name of Imagination. This power, first
put in action by the will and understanding, and retained under
their irremissive, though gentle and unnoticed, control, reveals
itself in the balance or reconcilement of opposite or discordant
qualities: of sameness, with difference; of the general with the
concrete; the idea with the image; the individual with the representative; the sense of novelty and freshness with old and familiar
objects; a more than usual state of emotion *with more than usual
order*; judgment ever awake and steady self-possession with enthusiasm and feeling profound or vehement; and while it blends and
harmonizes the natural and the artificial, still subordinates art to
nature; the manner to the matter; and our admiration of the poet
to our sympathy with the poetry.
[Coleridge, *Biographia Literaria*, Chapter XIV]

"It may be thought that the claim, or intention, here, is very ambitious. I believe it is. But surely no one will despise *an attempt made*, an
aim set high, in the light of which, – only – what has been done can be
judged.

"This is quite enough prose. I am going to read first a group of poems
which will need little if any commentary. The first is called 'The Statue'.
Its scene may be suggested to those of you who know the place, by my
mentioning the Southeast corner of Central Park in New York, at the
corner of Fifth Avenue and 59th street: on a Sunday evening, early, in
Spring: where the poem was written. [The statue referred to, by Gustave
Blaeser, is of the German explorer and scientist Alexander von Humboldt.]

THE STATUE.

(And in reading it, I did, or thought I did, what I thought I did also
several times later: fell into exaggeratedly emotional reading, sentimentality; – not in an effort to combat the *coldness* in my general talk of
which I was conscious, but in mere repugnance to it. But who can tell
what happens at any time? R afterwards said that she had been affected
to tears, and others said that I had read it well. Who knows?)

"In the next poem, those of you who know Breughel's famous painting, '*Chasseurs dans la neige*', will recognize its presence. It would not
however be correct to say that the painting is the subject of the poem. –

It is useful to bring, in public single reading of this sort, the eye to aid the ear. I am certain that you will be helped in hearing this poem if I tell you that it is written in five five-line stanzas, pentameter, unrhymed; and that it is a single sentence – in two movements: it breaks in the centre of the third stanza.

WINTER LANDSCAPE.
THE BALL POEM.

"The problem presented by this poem in conception, as I see it now, was interesting and unusual. The gain in moral knowledge by the boy, a reconcilement with the external world, was to be symbolized by an identification with that world or with its objects. And the artistic gain or reconciliation, with the boy's problem, could also be represented by an identification of the artist, the poet, the I of the poem, with his object, his subject, the boy. These were to occur simultaneously. It was necessary then to do a very unusual thing: gradually, and at a certain word, completely, *to destroy the point of view.* – Whether it is done successfully I don't know.

"The next poems have in common subjects which were in part events publicly available. The events are handled in various ways. The first is called 'World-Telegram' – which is a pun: a telegram which is to go around the world, and the *New York World-Telegram*, the actual newspaper, – one issue of which is followed closely through part of the poem; that for the eleventh of May, 1939, if this date is correct.

WORLD-TELEGRAM

"The problem was to keep the tone light and yet perfectly steady. – The editor who first printed this poem, in *The New Republic*, wrote that he was rushing me the proof, which he hoped I would rush back, since, he said, "it is a rather perishable poem". So that every few months since then I have inspected the poem carefully for signs of dissolution. So far it seems to be intact.

(I was tempted to tell two other stories. The night I wrote it I took it downtown – on John Angus's and Bob's advice – to try to get the *World-Telegram* to print it! do you remember? And Giroux gave it to [Norman] Corwin at CBS for broadcasting; Corwin explained that it was a fine "script" but that they (radio) had been having trouble with the press, and to broadcast it "just now" would not be politic. But I refrained; if I had begun to adlib I'd never have stopped.)

(And how are you getting on with this "letter". It is now *Saturday afternoon*, and the end is not in sight, and R suggests that I send it in installments, preferably when you take your vacation.)

(I must shorten it, especially since I don't remember just what I said about "The Moon and the Night and the Men" and "The White Feather", which followed "World-Telegram". Of the first, that it was, although deriving from an immediate occasion, properly a meditative poem; and that "Hurt and unhappy" was the extraordinarily moving phrase repeated by some English statesmen on the BBC broadcasts Michael Jacobs and I heard that night – he could say nothing else – British indignation had not yet set in. "The White Feather" I studied in some detail, impromptu – the shifting of attitude & irony, etc., the use of refrain, the attempt (in essence) to write on a subject casually come by a serious and absolutely *honest* poem, which would pretend to no more imagination and particularly to no more knowledge than the poet had; making the subject available (in the news item) as evidence of good faith in the attempt.

(*Eh bien!* and then I read "Boston Common", that long and complex and tough poem – God knows what they made of it – telling them first the story of [Robert Gould] Shaw & his regiment; reading the poem fairly rapidly, since time was getting delightfully *on* towards 5:30. It too, I was sure as I read, hopelessly failed.

And then "The Disciple", which I told them, when I introduced it, would be the last poem; and with the last word I closed the book & gathered my papers & books, and was certain that I had done a bad dull job – not in the argument nor the poems, not *what* I said and read, but *how*: in tone & spontaneity & life.

Then began for me a time of pure fantasy because of pure incredulity. Everyone applauded, Morrison congratulated me very earnestly, [Robert] Hillyer did, Delmore did, Gertrude especially & wonderfully did, R seemed very moved & not in the least – as I expected – disappointed or hurt or on-the-defensive-with-the-others-because-of-my-failure. Now I am very familiar, at these Morris Gray readings, with mechanical congratulations – most of the readings are stupid & tedious; and my suspicion (I frankly thought for ten minutes that everyone was lying) warred with my intense desire (since the damned thing was *over*) to think after all that it *had* gone well although I knew it hadn't, and both warred with my delight to learn at once that even if I had failed everyone was going to ignore it (apparently), and my pleasure simply in hearing such agreeable things, true or not – I was altogether in an extraordinary state, passing very rapidly from absolute & apathetic depression to semi-exaltation & warmth. We all went then to a cocktail party given by [Theodore] Spencer, I suppose for me, and talked and gossiped – all this I will tell you when I see you. I still don't know, actually, what I think about the Reading, and my not knowing kept the thing so on my mind that during dinner (which R & I had with Delmore & Gertrude) I was nearly ill, and all evening and all next day, until a nervous reaction set in towards night of Thursday, I was literally obsessed with remembering the course of the strange hour. I have these facts: R, who is very sensitive and was very nervous, certainly did not think it a failure or find the audience especially bored; Gertrude was delighted; Delmore said that several of the poems were richer & better for him in my reading than they had ever been before – and (a) he has admired & read carefully for a long time all nine except "Boston Common" of the poems I read; (b) he has never liked the way I read verse, especially the way I read my own verse. Also, the members of the Committee, none of them friendly really to me and all of them thoroughly antipathetic to my poetry, were genuinely enthusiastic – although they had nothing whatever to gain by being so; Spencer & Hillyer agreed, even, that it was the best Reading they had had in a long time, and Morrison yesterday deliberately fixed me for an hour's unbearable *tête-à-tête*, beginning "I feel an impulse to try and tell you what I feel about your poems . ." (Ah it was horrible: he is well enough for ten minutes, as with you I remember two or three years ago, but until you have been exposed to that man *properly*, you can form no conception of the abyssal tediousness of his meagre spirit.)

What am I to think in the end?

What does it matter? If I had to do it again – sweet heaven forfend! – I would do it better. No other audience could be so difficult. And I got it done, evidently without disgracing myself or anyone else. I earned twenty-five dollars, which we have been living on, and I learned a number of things – about myself, about audiences, about the impenetrability of men like the Committee members (who ought to have been made speechless by the discrepancy between Coleridge's great statement and their miserable practice), about the unpredicability of all human reactions, and about how much of energy and thought the most trivial occasion (indulged – and the indulging of it does not have to be voluntary) can absorb. If the saw is right, and we really get from anything what we put into it, then I have worked up this week a capital of one hundred thousand dollars. Something even more surprising is about to come to pass, dear small long-suffering and late-reading Mother: *you* owe *me* a letter.

love & a kiss,
John

Boston

Dearest Mum   Sunday [25 April 1943]

  I'm sorry I didn't see you this morning: for one thing, I had a going-off present for you – the decanter poem written out & "dedicated", if so small a thing can be dedicated. I'll send it with this.

  As for your gift! – no gift I think was ever so unexpected & gracious & useful-to-the-point-of-extremity. It lets me go to New York (as I gave up hope of doing) and it has relieved my sense of desperation enough to make me human again. I cannot possibly tell you how grateful, how profoundly grateful R. & I are to you for it – and for *food & stamps &* what not. Unfortunately for the peace of our visit together (the three of us), you came at a time which was (is) for me a nervous crisis; but you have done us great good.

  You needn't tell me you're improved: I saw it & heard it & felt it: unspeakably better. I am very happy for you, Mum. I hope you have a good visit there too. My love to my charming & mad brother – "When shall we meet & sometime spend an hour?" Good luck, good luck.

  But you & I will meet in New York on Friday, *nichts?*

dear love meanwhile, – R's love & thanks too!
John

Enclosed and dated 24 April, 1943, was the following poem:

> Crystal decanter! Long-necked, mirroring!
> When I sit sober why are you so full,
> And why when garrulous imagination
> Whirls & wheels me, are you dry & dull?
> What sort of companion are you?

To mother who gave me the decanter
with love
John

[Boston]

5? 6? [June 1943] I don't

Dearest Mum,   know what damn day it is

Quick note. I am very glad that you have moved, sure that you are right in doing so, and glad about the temporary job; one of the others is certain to open later. Mostly I am glad about the long letter, unhappy as in some ways it is: after talking with you that night, I feared far worse. Our good wishes for Jack's recovery.

I have written to the two universities in Oklahoma, and sent them improved summaries. The Board of Education for various reasons I decided not to bother with at once. I wrote to [Governor Robert S.] Kerr also; here is the letter, which I'd like back when you've read it. I hope it will do. The situation had a sort of poignancy which I found it difficult to control, and then of course I don't know what sort of man he is now. I think I shouldn't have sent it unless R had approved, as she did. Many thanks to you for all this, although to speak truth I expect nothing whatever.

The State Department questionnaire (there was no duplicate) I have filled out, but I can't write the letter at this moment; I will tomorrow or so and send you a copy. That looks better than Oklahoma. Meanwhile, although we have not had anything which could be described as good news, various plans are in the air, and I will write you fully about them within a week or so.

Don't, of course, Jackass, send us "a small cheque to cover the costs" of your affairs. You have done a hundred thousand things for us.

But I am afraid someone else is after you: [some]one from Goodwin Procter & Hoar (a letter from whom I enclose also); I introduced him to the labyrinth of your addresses and he slunk away.

Marie is here for the long weekend and enjoying herself; so is Eileen. We had a wonderful time at Brattleboro, where everything is better than we feared, and it is practically certain (eyes) that Bob will not be drafted; but I cannot go into that now. Good luck, love, from everybody, & most from

John

[Mrs. Berryman had known Robert S. Kerr in Oklahoma in the early twenties. After serving a term as governor (1943–47), he was later a U.S. senator from 1948 until his death on January 1, 1963.]

                                                             Boston
Dearest of Mothers,   13 June 1943

I write to you on this infamous stationery to symbolize my imminent
departure from this whore this Harvard. Boston & the neighbouring slums
I canvassed thoroughly, again, this week: and nothing. Nothing looming,
nothing immediate. Meanwhile R dislike[s] her work every day more,
my leisure is useless to me in uncertainty, and we are doing nothing but
clinging to this wretched apartment.

So we have decided on a plan of prudent desperation. I am going to
New York again on Tuesday: to try to find work at once, work of any sort
in which I can use my experience and training; to be available for the
interviews which should result from some at least of the letters which I
have written to colleges, nearly all of them accessible from there and
none from here. Temporary and permanent work, for me, may come to
the same thing, since under the war programmes many colleges now
begin their years late in June or early in July – another reason why delay
would be idiotic. I will stay with Marie. Ten days later, when R's vacation
begins, she will come down; either I will have something already and she
will look, or we will be looking together. If we get work we stay all summer, coming back only late in August to move. If not, we can try Washington, we can come back here, we can *see*: nothing will be lost, and we
will have tried at least. R's job here, even, will still be hers until July 7th
or so, by which date I will have had almost four weeks of trying and she
two. If we stay there, we are going to sublet the apartment if we can; but
even if we can't, our living will not be more or will be very little more:
we may stay at 511, or we think R's Aunt [Agnes Mulligan], who usually
leaves her apartment in the Bronx empty during July and August while
she is in Bay Park, may let us have that rent-free; at worst, we are sure of
a cheap room where R lived last year, at 109 West 12th.

Meanwhile I have a sharp eye on Washington. I have written to Dr.
J.Q. Adams, Director of the Folger Shakespeare Library, for a research
grant or a job. Delmore has written to Allen Tate, now Curator of American Poetry under MacLeish at the Library of Congress, asking him to
get me something. And of course I have written to Walton Ferris [Divi-
sion of Foreign Service Personnel, Department of State] & sent him the
form; for which very interesting possibility many thanks. I sent the pho-

tograph you suggested, and set the Harvard salary at $2500, the writing at $500 (a handsome ambiguity: I mean 500 in all since I began to publish, they will understand 500 a year); and I exaggerated somewhat my familiarity with certain European languages, to wit French German & Italian. Of the salary I wd accept, I said exactly what you recommended; and a very good recommendation. Directly I hear anything, I'll write.

What do you think of the whole plan? We studied and studied it, and could see nothing else possible. It wd be foolish to give up teaching without another try, and Brattleboro, our going there, wd throw it out. Both of us too want really, in the end, to be in New York for the year if we can; and we have no lodging-expense while we are casting about. Also we are nearly certain that, accidents aside, we can earn much more money, with much more leisure, in New York than elsewhere, and this is the crux.

I have tried to put it all clearly but inevitably much has got left out (most of which however you will understand anyway, old dear) & anyway this is the nineteenth letter, exactly, that I have written today (with seven to go, and it is midnight) & anyway HELL: I feel like a daffodil upended on a polyp. Most of them have been business letters, which may account for the slightly *rigid* air of this one.

We hope your State Dept job comes through shortly, and good luck with the present one, and good luck to Jack [Lemon]. My last letter didn't go astray DID IT? – we have not heard since the worried note of last Sunday. I must stop. Our dearest love. Write me at 511 E 82.

John

[P.S.] Nothing yet from Oklahoma. I forgot to say that I am *dead sick* of trying to sell my bloody services, – but let that pass.

[P.P.S.] *Monday morning:* Your Friday letter has come. We are sorry about Jack's health – good good luck to both of you.

The Berrymans left for New York where they stayed first with Eileen's aunt, Agnes Mulligan, and with her sister, Marie Mabry. The couple endured an increasingly frustrating and difficult summer while JB searched unsuccessfully for a job. One after another, possible teaching positions, magazine and commercial positions, and governmental positions failed. Finally, in desperation, he accepted an offer from a small preparatory school near New York City.

511 East 82nd St [New York]

Dearest Mother   9 September [1943]

The Iona [Preparatory High] School in New Rochelle [New York] increased its offer to $2400 and I took a job there yesterday, teaching English & Latin six hours daily, beginning Monday the thirteenth. This is not a subject for congratulation, but presumably we will be able to live through the year. For the time being – having no alternative – we are continuing at Marie's. Eileen is going to try to get a teaching position also. I am studying Latin.

Your letter of yesterday has just come, and I have just written my overdue thanks to Jack – a handsome note.

Plans for me are now of course at an end (until *next* summer); a million gratitude, Mum, for all your efforts & help & love & confidence. I will probably write soon again –

John

P.S. About your going to Brattleboro [Vermont] I can say nothing useful – I simply don't know

511 East 82nd St. [New York]

Dearest Mum,   Sunday 10 October [1943]

Fortune has suddenly smiled at us. I am being offered a job at Princeton, teaching civilian and Navy, beginning November 1, and I am resigning at Hell-in-New-Rochelle and taking it. If this appears to you incomprehensible, bizarre, touching, and Paradisal, so does it to us, who have been at the end of our minds. The job is less than perfect, paying less than I make now (exactly what, I don't yet know) and being on a term-to-term basis instead of annual, but I won't dwell on these or on any details now. I have a good deal to do and I am exhausted in the eighth day of a heavy cold. This is just to tell you that Life has a new mask on.

I'm very sorry about the delay of your decision in New York. I hope this change of Fortune will become general, for you and for Bob. I am writing to Bob, by the way, but to no one else until I have received & accepted the position officially – tomorrow or Tuesday.

About Iona I have no compunctions, – as to resignation I mean, – having been the victim there of what I am afraid I cannot describe as conscientious treatment, and what I must call inhuman conditions. They

have two-thirds wrecked my health; now the school must find another
goat. Please do not speak to anyone of my having taught there, or in such
a place. It has been grotesque, horrible, from start to end, – the end,
Laus Deo, soon, this week. Then back to the areas of possible Life.

Dearest love,
& hope for all of us,
John

[P.S.] Let us know if or when you come up next – we won't move to
Princeton until the last week of October – maybe we can meet *calmly* –
Hurrah! Hurrah!

Blessing & love–
John

511 East 82nd St. [New York]
Monday, 25 October 1943

Dearest Mum

    I was happy to have your letter this morning, & you're right – there
is no gift I'd have liked better than this, to have you well saved out of
what was destroying you. All my sympathy, Mother, salvation, & luck to
come.

    I've written before but tore the letters up. We have had a ghastly time,
which I hope is nearly ended. I go to Boston tonight to sell what I can of
the furniture & the gramophone – we are shortening our lines of defense –
then down to Princeton, where I begin to teach today week. Some time
next week the one-room apartment we are taking will become vacant:
we'll put in what we can of the remainder sent from Boston, store the rest
again (books etc.), and *have somewhere to live* for the first time in months.
I hope you won't object to, or feel as sorry as I do about, the sale of the
couch, etc. We haven't any choice. If Princeton doesn't reappoint me in
February, off we go again: ETC. The red leather chair & the maple table
& a few other things we are keeping of course; not much else – I just
hope we can get something for the stuff we have to sell. We are poor as
hell, as who (among us) isn't, & we must live until Dec. 1st on what we
have now.

    Our anniversary was a wonderful day, against all expectation. We
wished we could have seen you; but we saw Bob for a magnificent hour
at Sullivan's (remember, on 9th Avenue), saw Mark at his house later

(for the first time in exactly a year), went to the Ballet last night, where was [Anthony Tudor's] *Pillar of Fire* again as on our wedding night. Pleasure exhausts us, in its novelty. I felt at midnight (& feel today) as if I'd spent the day at that School in New Rochelle. In front of us, exactly, at the Metropolitan [Opera], sat, together: Charles [Phillips] Reilly, Andrew Chiappe, Robert Paul Smith & wife. Gad & ugh. Dear Chas. sent you his dear best. Andrew sniped at Delmore & me. R.P. Smith tried to be dignified. But a marvellous day.

I wrote to Granny & to Kansas. Some other university jobs were offered me, including a highly paid one at Duke; certain months too late. I am perfectly content with Princeton, if my nerves hold out & my health improves. Eileen is a little better. Bob's release has not come; I think he is going back to Brattleboro tonight, then returning here – he talks of shipping out on a South American merchant run. And he described to us the plan for a novel, which excited & delighted & impressed me. How he needs some luck.

We all do. But you are free, & Bob has a brilliant work sketched, & Eileen's health improves, & Jim [Mabry] is back from the hospital far better in mind, & I have had an amazing birthday: we went to Silverman today & bought me a *suit* & a superb grey *overcoat*. They will please you greatly. Also Eileen has given me a pair of shorts & *slippers*. I am nearly presentable! And I don't feel so old & desperate as I might, – though old enough –

dearest dearest love,

John

[Robert Paul Smith was an American novelist and dramatist, best known for his book of childhood recollections, *Where Did You Go? Out. What Did You Do? Nothing.*]

PART FOUR

Princeton

1943-1954

*T*HE *"FORTUNE" that had so unexpectedly smiled upon the Berry-mans from Princeton appeared in the form of a letter from R.P. Black-mur, offering JB a four month appointment as an instructor in the English Department. Elated, the couple was soon installed in a small apartment at 36 Vandeventer Avenue, near the university. In spite of the brief nature of the appointment, it was like a reprieve to JB after his long and increas-ingly desperate search for a job.*

As it turned out, Princeton would remain the Berrymans' home for most of the next decade, offering JB a period of relative and much needed economic stability. In addition to Blackmur, whose criticism had captivated JB since his Columbia years, the university boasted such other brilliant intellectuals as Dean Christian Gauss, Erich Kahler, Hermann Broch, Thomas Mann and Albert Einstein. During these years JB also met Robert Lowell, with whom he became close friends, Jean Stafford, Edmund Wilson, Louis MacNeice and Randall Jar-rell.

This was a period in which he began to achieve true distinction as a poet, with The Dispossessed *(1948), and* Homage to Mistress Bradstreet *(1953), which was first published in the* Partisan Review. *After years of labor he completed his flawed but insightful biographical study* Stephen Crane *(1950), and continued to pursue, with the help of a Rockefeller Foundation Research Fellowship, his Shakespeare scholarship, which was then focused on a critical edition of* King Lear. *Several poetry prizes came his way—Poetry's Guarantors Prize, the Shel-*

ley Memorial Award, and the Levinson Prize—and his second published short
story, "The Imaginary Jew," won first prize in the Kenyon Review - Doubleday
Doran contest in 1945. Academically, he was honored by being appointed Alfred
Hodder Fellow at Princeton in 1949, and in 1952 he spent a semester as Elliston
Professor of Poetry at the University of Cincinnatti.

On the darker side, a fourth book, Berryman's Sonnets, was written during
the summer of 1947, but not published until twenty years later. It recounts an
obsessive and short-lived affair he was then having with a married woman called,
in the poem, Lise. The affair and its aftermath jolted JB psychologically and
marked the beginning of the regular heavy drinking that would afflict him for
the rest of his life. Before the end of 1953, JB and Eileen had separated and his
Princeton days were over.

Mrs. Berryman continued to work in Washington, D.C., for a time, and
soon after her return to New York, in 1944, to edit a magazine, Sportswear
Stylist, she had a brief and unhappy third marriage to Nils O. Gustafsson. About
mother and son during these years two factors predominate: she remained heavily involved with his life (usually at his request), though less so than before his
marriage to Eileen, and the cracks in their relationship began to deepen and
spread. Her (unsent) letter of June 9, 1950, and his of July 2, 1951, vividly
document the irritations and difficulties they experienced with more frequency
and severity when together.

Princton, [N.J.]

Dearest Jill   Thursday [28 October 1943]

I got extremely drunk last week while talking with Bob about his novel –
I'm sorry to say – and must apologize most earnestly for my failure to
take leave. It was a miracle that I even got to Princeton at all, much less
whole. I am sending you the wittiest writer I can think of by way of
sorrow: Congreve, whom I read with absolute passion last year for a while.
The Way of the World is greatest, but the four comedies are all astonishing, & ought to be read in his order. The tragedy (*Mourning Bride*) I've
never looked at; Dr Johnson liked it, even calling one description more
perfect than anything in Shakespeare; most improbable, my dear Dr. With
it goes your Kai-Lung book [one of the series of books by Ernest Bramah
Smith], which I find I had, and – though only for loan, because I can't
replace it – James's most superb & last book of stories [*The Finer Grain*].
Read, I implore you, at least "The Velvet Glove" & "The Bench of Des-

A bearded JB, left, with Caroline and Allen Tate.

Mrs. Berryman, after she had begun working in the fashion industry.

JB and Bhain Campbell, 1939.

JB in 1940 in one of the photographs taken prior to the publication of his first collection of poems in *Five Young American Poets*.

JB at Princeton.

Eileen Berryman at Princeton in 1944.
*Photo taken by JB. Reprinted by
permission of Eileen Simpson*

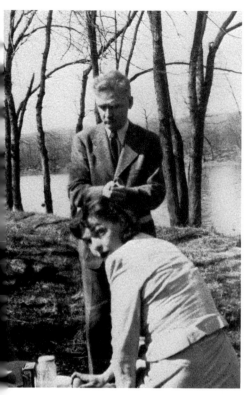

Above left, R.P. Blackmur and Nela Walcott on a Princeton picnic. Above right, Mrs. Berryman at Berryman and O'Leary Inc., working on an advertising layout, 1948. Photo taken surreptitiously by Robert Jefferson Berryman.

Robert Jefferson Berryman, cousin Shelby Williams, and JB. The occasion was Robert Jefferson's marriage to his third wife, Elizabeth Weston, in January 1949.

Above left, Martha May Little, JB's maternal grandmother, in 1946. Above right, JB, circa 1952. © *Rollie McKenna*

ON FACING PAGE: JB, Ann Berryman, and their son, Paul, in Seville, Spain, 1957.

Mrs. Berryman and client.

Allen Tate at the University of Minnesota, circa 1960. *Photo by Peter Marcus.
Courtesy of University Archives, University of Minnesota*

Saul Bellow and his second wife, Alexandra Tschacbasov, in Minneapolis, 1959.

olation", heartbreaking the last; also "A Round of Visits". We are immensely grateful for your hospitality & trouble – many, many thanks –

Love,
John

[P.S.] Not begun teaching yet – very busy with verse – Ragnar Nurske is marrying Saturday & I am best man if the old friend he asked can't come, as I rather hope he can't!

[Ragnar Nurske was an economist and member of the Institute for Advanced Study at Princeton University. Eileen had taken a job at the institute as a researcher for two economists who were working on a book.]

36 Vandeventer Avenue
Princeton, N.J.
Dearest Mum   Tuesday, 2 November 1943

I am very sorry to hear that you are in again. Bless you – I hope you are at least staying in bed & doing everything possible for the condition. If I'd been free last week either in mind or body to do you any good, I think I'd have come down to Washington – I have worried greatly. *Now* I am a hundred times better myself, but I can't get away (classes six days a week, ranging from 7:50 A.M. to 4:50 P.M.). I am *resting* somewhat, & working, & getting to know everybody in the University, and I am really very happy despite our delays in settling & my fatigue & Bob's ill-luck & your illness. I wish I had a place here where you could stay until you're better. No hope – if we ever get our one-room apartment (it is promised for next Tuesday) & move into it, we will be lucky. But what most I hope is that you *are* better. Send me a word to say. At the weekend I'll be less rushed, & Eileen is coming down, & I can write to you properly about this demi-Paradise Princeton & about my own extraordinary & good change of mind. I am *better, better* – I pray you are & will be. Dearest love,

John

[P.S.] I'll try "J.B. [Jill Berryman] at 1133" for this; shd. it be Mrs J.L.[Jill Little] at # 1314? [Mrs. Berryman's addresses in Washington, D.C.]

Princeton
Dear Blessed Mother,   15 January 1944

Bob's news is wonderful, – it lit up the whole horizon for a while. Nothing so astonishing and good has happened to any of us since, since

long since long. As you say, and as he said and as I say, it is the first real
& large chance he has had. After how long! Yet he is very young. Only
at *Time*, where age and statistical education are ignored, would it be
possible. His talent & energy & experience are perfectly suited there for
the moment; I think and I pray, he will do it admirably. Do you remember our old legend, yours and mine? – that Bob would be the successful
one of us? Of course *you* are. And he will be. I crop the grass and stamp
the ground at the edge.

Security (for they are certain to keep him on) and money and experi-
ence-in-writing and an important stage to act on and associates of a quality so much nearer his than he ever had before in any work; and a sense
of compensation at last for so much ill luck and so many missed chances.
I hardly could believe it, I hardly believe it now. How happy I am for
you! And how good, as Eileen said, that he and Barbara were together
when it happened. Is it possible that we behold a human experience
which presents no flash or glow of bitterness, no irony? The Devil and
our devil nodded that day.

Can you come down from New York when you have seen them &
set your own affairs in motion? Even a day would be worth the hour's
trip – Thursdays I have mainly clear, although Eileen of course works
then; a weekend would be much better if you could. But *soon*. We want
to talk to you, and I want you to see Princeton & to see us in our point
of (somewhat) repose. It is more and more unlikely, I'm afraid, that the
University will be able to keep me after next month, and everything in
that event will be vague. The main reason I have not written is that I try
to avoid thinking about this as much as possible. You must come as soon
as you can.

The books you bought in the South sounded very gay. I have bought
only three books in Princeton – Kierkegaard's *The Sickness Unto Death*,
an Aquinas, and Aragon's war poems *Le Crève-coeur*; those emotions I
suppress. But more than half our income each month goes to debts; we
live extraordinarily cheaply; no films, beer once a fortnight, once in two
months a dinner out. Yet we entertain ourselves well enough, and Eileen
particularly is more content than she was in Boston. I have become a
perfect miser: a state of mind I cannot recommend. – Forty dollars is
high for [Sir James G. Frazer's] *The Golden Bough*, but not unreasonably
so; the work is increasingly hard to get. Make sure it is (as it probably is)
the Third Edition, revised. At $25 it would be cheap.

Tate, for reasons of his own imperfectly clear to me, has got the Library of Congress to offer me a post. It paid very badly, but they kept after me, so I set (on Blackmur's & Eileen's advice) a $3000 minimum, and I may have to go down to Washington as soon as I hear – what isn't yet certain – that Princeton will not reappoint me. Nothing is less attractive to me than the Library, but one must live. I will let you know, of course, if I am coming. Did you ever write to [Franklin] D'Olier [a member of the Board of Trustees at Princeton], by the way? I can't think whether I told you, in reply to that thoughtfulness, "no" or "yes" or nothing. Now I think of writing to him myself, a note; would you object to that?

Literary unintelligence. The critic [Arthur Mizener] who attacked my pamphlet *[Poems]* last year for the *Kenyon Review* now says, still in the *Kenyon*, that with Schwartz and me "language tends to be a manifestation of the subject" – whatever it means, this is supposed to be praise – and that "Boston Common" is the best poem I have "ever" written. And then I had a letter recently from an admirer in a CPS [Civilian Public Service] Camp (what is a CPS Camp) who reads my poems aloud while he and a friend are washing socks; I am "poignant and terrifying", or rather my "autobiographical essence" is; I am various things, for it is a long letter, – most of which I couldn't read because of the desperate blinding nervousness which still interferes with my vision when I am so foolish as to try to read anything written about my work. But I don't mean to mock the letter: it was literate, and generous, and it pleased Eileen. The Houghton Mifflin anthology of war poems, with two of mine, finally came; but it was so intolerably stupid that I took it straightway to the University Store and traded it for three Modern Library books – a clear gain. One was Thoreau: if you haven't read *Walden* do some time; I always thought Mark exaggerated its virtues, but he doesn't.

Has your health been better? I hope it has, dear – but don't *say* merely, come and show us. I am glad at least, very glad, that Jack has been less what you feared, more nearly what you hoped. Eileen's throat has troubled her greatly, preventing sleep for weeks, but it is better just now, and her second doctor here (the first was a suburban fool) is helping her with everything else. I am well, or so. Hurrah for Bob! Hurrah for you!

my dearest love

John

[Robert Jefferson Berryman had been hired as a department editor at *Time Magazine* (1943–44).

The CPS (Civilian Public Service) camps, some of which were maintained by the Federal Government and some by the National Service Board for Religious Objectors, employed conscientious objectors in the performance of either noncombatant military duties or other strictly civilian work.

The New Treasury of War Poetry was edited by George Herbert Clark. The two Berryman poems included were "The Moon and the Night and the Men" and "1 September 1939."]

Princeton

Dearest Mother,   6 March 1944

Reading S. Matthew last night I was struck hard by 6.34 – "Take therefore no thought for the morrow: for the morrow shall take thought for the things of itself. Sufficient unto the day is the evil thereof." I hear that voice as One's having authority. What came last summer of all my effort and exacerbation? After five months, a job which nearly destroyed me; and easily, a few weeks later, the job here, for which I need have done nothing. During those five months I earned no money (except my Harvard cheques which continued after my work stopped); I wrote nothing; expensively and in despair we wandered about looking & trying. All I got was experience of Hell – and our marriage nearly tore – and a crude unsatisfying sense of acting responsibly, of "doing my best", – while I violated my responsibility, my friendships and every instinct of humanity.

No more, no more. I went through this last month in prospect; but now I mean to sit tight and wait and work, doing what I can in *what I can do*, not in what I cannot. Sufficient unto the day is the evil thereof.

But lest you worry I will rehearse for you the principal present possibilities and comment quickly on them:

1. Guggenheim Fellowship
2. the League for [of] Amer. Authors, etc.
3. Rockefeller Foundation
4. The Jefferson edition
5. Expansion of the AST [Army Specialized Training] Reservists
6. Oglethorpe University (Atlanta, Ga.)
7. Library of Congress.

I can try nothing – because I can accept nothing – until I hear from the Guggenheim people; probably this month. Then I have been recommended for a $1000 grant from this League of which I cannot remember the name. Then, when Blackmur saw the Rockefeller (Humanities) heads in New York last week, they asked particularly whether he knew me; they saw my *Nation* piece on Shakespeare's text, have looked me up, are interested perhaps in financing the preparation of an edition of *Lear*, etc.; this too I cannot go into until the Guggenheim (which would leave me completely free) has failed. Then Julian Boyd, the Librarian of Princeton and editor-in-chief of the great edition of Jefferson's writings which is soon to get under way, has asked me to come in and talk with him; I know him somewhat, and I read Jefferson, and wait. Then the Army announced on Saturday an expansion of their 17-year-olds training program; later this month, after the examinations, the colleges will know their allotments; I may be rehired here or asked for elsewhere. ([Gerald Hall] Gerould [Chairman of the English Department at Princeton] meanwhile has written to Yale & Cornell for me.) Then Tate is leaving L.C. [Library of Congress, where he had been consultant in poetry] in June or so to edit the *Sewanee Review*; [Archibald] MacLeish & he could give me that job – but don't mention this, or any of this, to anyone, and especially to no Senator, at present.

At least, as you see, the horizon is not bare. Four other possibilities I do not mention because I have told Eileen nothing about them; they are not less definite (or more definite) than the rest, but for special reasons I had rather not speak of them. On *none* of these possibilities, I must tell you, do I count – not, for instance, on a very interesting $4000 job at Oglethorpe which the President [Phillip Weltner] practically offered me last Sunday and which, with several other men, I am investigating. I simply see that they *exist* as possibilities; I try to keep my mind free for judgment; I do not want to become involved, to the exclusion of something firstrate, in anything secondary; I try to avoid anxiety and nervousness, and to recover my health a little, and to write.

Basta! I was for long too low to write to you; now I hope to write regularly; later this week again. I hope you come immensely refreshed back, have every luck, and

all my love,
John

Princeton
Dearest Mother,   17 March 1944
My long letter urging you to come down here last Sunday, sent special delivery to 442 on Friday afternoon, obviously has been lost – Bob tells me other mail has also; we waited in vain all Sunday. I hope the

chance will come soon again. It was a pity, because I felt relatively excellent; more recently I have been low indeed; today a little better. Your letter from Washington of day before yesterday shows your great improvement continued. It makes me very glad. Let us all look *forward*.

Unfortunately my looking forward, as I must do, is like to disintegrate me. Besides the possibilities of which I told you, hanging in the air to destroy me with anxiety, three new ones have come up:

Woman's College, Greensboro, N.C.

Smith College.

Bennington – [Walter] Stewart, an ex-trustee, has asked me to dinner next week to meet its president [Lewis W. Jones].

Still there is no doubt that my situation is better, and my nerves a little better, than last year; and most of my present possibilities are *interesting* – more leisure, better work, more money. I could hardly be described at this moment as sanguine about any one of them, but it does appear to me likely that libraries & high schools & factories will not be necessary even to try: a university or a Foundation will support me. The area into which my friends (Blackmur, Stewart, [Willard] Thorp, etc.) have now thrust me is luckily not affected by the war – all women's colleges.

Meanwhile, since unlike last year most of the casting about is being done by others for me, I have borrowed Helen Blackmur's studio high on the other side of this foolish building where we live, and I am trying to work – waiting for the Guggenheim announcements, until after which I can accept nothing. They will be read with interest in my circle: Stow Persons, a young historian who lives across the court and whose wife Dorothy is Eileen's best friend here, has applied, and David Bowers, in Philosophy, has applied for a renewal of his (he got one at Blackmur's instance last year). My opinion is that David's will not be renewed, that Stow will not get one, and that I will not get one.

We know a spate of people here, really it is astonishing; idly the other day I was thinking of how entertaining it would be to give a big party (in Nela Walcott's house), and I determined that we would have to ask 50 people, including you and a dozen from NY. At lunch some time ago with Blackmur & Julian Boyd & a southern novelist R. P. Harriss, we talked juleps until we were dry, and I described *Printemps* – King's Peg – *mon dieu*, when will the damned invasion begin, and inflation stop, and money flow to us, so that drinks can.

Not that we were dry utterly, although we can rarely have anything in the house and buy nothing ourselves out. In New York as Mark's guests before the Reading, and at a party afterward, we somewhat drank; and Richard & Nela gave parties at one house or another (Helen, war-working from 3 p.m. to 11, rarely can be with us): R. was powerful high last weekend, intense, sweating, muscular, mad, and another evening Eileen! got vague-happy, smiling to herself, and Delmore & I pointed cigars at each other with (I imagine) maniacal expressions of glee. So many people!

We cycled to Kingston with Dorothy [Persons] on Monday (E had a holiday & was ecstatic), and mean to do again tomorrow. They are studying Spanish also – good for you. Camera? Book for me at 442? Idea for book-shelves? Wallace Stevens, did I tell you, makes $85,000 a year – which is too much for any poet. Blessings and love. I am glad about Deac Dunn. Let's meet in New York, soon, and then you came back with us to see Princeton. *Avante!*

John

[Walter Stewart was an economist and member of the Institute for Advanced Study at Princeton.

Willard Thorp was chairman of the English Department at Princeton.

Nela Walcott was a wealthy bohemian painter and friend of the Berrymans' at Princeton. Her portrait of JB was used in some of the Oscar Williams' anthologies (*New Poems, 1944* and *The War Poets*) which included JB's poems.

(Deac) H. L. Dunn was a friend of Mrs. Berryman's who, like her, worked in the fabrics industry.]

[Princeton, N.J.]

Dear Mother,   24 March 1944

My Guggenheim application was not granted. The president of Bennington [Lewis W. Jones] may have a place free in August & wants Eileen & me to come to the college for a long weekend at the end of next month; this being our likeliest & least disagreeable chance – except for the Rockefellers, to whom I will talk next week.

Did you get a longish letter I sent last Friday or so? I hope your spirit & health continue better – luck in all things.

dear love
John

[Princeton]
Dearest Mother   6 May 1944

Good news is a matter so strange to me that I hardly know how to
deliver it. Brace yourself then: the Rockefeller Foundation has given me
a Fellowship for Shakespearean work – to last a year. It is a poor sum
compared for example to Bob's salary, & to my great sorrow Eileen can't
stop working; but it relieves our uncertainty (which has been so horrible
that I couldn't write at all) & lets us stay in Princeton which we like &
will let me do a deal of work. Most of all, it is *something pleasant*. I felt
nothing at the news – last night it came – but I am numb; probably I *will*
feel something, – and Eileen, who has been under ghastly strain, it made
(after the shock) immensely happy. I hope it will you – I am sorry to have
to tell you thus in a letter, & a hasty one, but I have begun to give some
lectures on contemporary literature at Briarcliff (a woman's college near
N.Y.), and having to shuttle back & forth for three weeks. I can't go
anywhere else.

I have been anxious to hear from you, though I hardly deserve to, not
writing. Is your health better? I was shocked by your nervous weakness in
New York & pray you are improving – I pray you may have some good
news of your own.

Heat here has already begun to sear – what can it be like in Washington? You *must rest* as much as you can, no matter what you are doing. I
am terribly grieved – I have felt it constantly – by the news you gave me
here. I wish you all strength & courage

& some relief––
with dearest love
John

[The Rockefeller Fellowship provided JB with a one year grant and a stipend
of $2,500.]

Princeton
Dearest Mother, dearest,   16 June 1944

Yes I have been ill – more than three weeks now of continual half-
prostration, nervous indigestion, constipation, apathy etc etc – but I would
have written anyway if the shock of your letter, following so closely on
Barbara's letter saying that Bob had left her (written May 17), had not

combined with my other terrible anxieties to leave me helpless and mute
with laceration until now. Only your heartbreaking letter of this morning
lets me speak – in spite of its unhappiness it makes me almost happy
because it sounds again like you as I have always known you – your loving note – and for the first time in weeks and months I have a sense that
our family has not utterly disintegrated with affliction & time & grief. . . .

Your trouble hurts my heart. I pray that you will be all right, safe
through it, and as little in agony as you can be. Bob told me part of it,
but I put it away as untrue or so unfortunate that if one did not believe
it, it would pass like a nightmare – my nightmares! In your letter it first
really existed for me, and stunned me for days. Part of my mind went
on – I was writing a long difficult piece, which I had somehow to preserve as I could – but part of it stopped, and has only this morning begun
again. How much relief and how much fresh pain, there is in *feeling*
normally what formerly emotion rejected as impossible! Emotion drives
emotion out: I was trying last month, half-ill, to recover the emotions of
our summer months on Long Island, in Burbury Lane, and when I got
them, or thought I had them, they would not let the present in. They let
in enough to keep me sleepless & unable to eat, but not the flood. – Care
for yourself as well as you can, mother. Have you money? How are you
living, whom are you seeing? I believe the heat there cannot be worse
than here – Princeton is infamous – and I hope it is less weakening. Let
me know how you are.

I thought I had told you while you were here the nature of the Rockefeller project – so far as it *can* be told briefly, being both technical and
complicated; I'm sorry if I didn't. It is to prepare a new full-dress edition
of *King Lear*, a play of which the text in all existing editions is shamefully
unsatisfactory: the establishment of text and commentary on it are the
main labours. I have at last got hold of an office in the Princeton Library –
far from ideal, but a table, book-space and privacy – and will begin steady
work next week. I should have begun a fortnight ago, but I have had
nowhere to work. We are moving, too, today and tomorrow into a slightly
larger apartment (M-1) across the court (same address), I am sending to
Boston for my library, etc etc. Neither of us is at all well but no doubt
the change will help us. Your account of Granny moves me very much –
I wish I could see her – I will write for her birthday.

Worry as little as possible, Mum, and let my dearest warmest love help you if it can. Let us hear constantly. We wish you all strength & safety & love.

Devotedly

John

[Among the calamities referred to in this letter, the most serious was that Robert Jefferson and Barbara Berryman's eighteen-month-old son, Charles Peter, had a few months earlier died after slipping underwater in the bathtub. He had been revived by a police emergency squad, but suffered convulsions and died four hours later.]

Truro [Massachusetts]

Dearest Mother   15 August 1944

I believe that we are enjoying the vacation, although with sunburn & sleepless nights & hellish itching it is not easy to be sure. The Cape at any rate is very pleasant – more varied (hills, woods) than I remembered; Joan [Colebrook, an Australian novelist] is an undemanding hostess: and we are invited here & there to a degree which is exhausting. The hills are full of writers & radicals, to Eileen's delight. I have no more curiosity than I ever had, but I am glad to see Edmund Wilson & Dwight Mac-Donald again, and we spent last night amiably enough with Hart Crane's closest friend, Slater Brown, who was also the "B." of E. E. Cummings' *The Enormous Room.* I lack a taste for all this.

You were very good to remember E's birthday. I did also; I gave her – you can't guess – a book, – and wrote two sonnets on Scott Fitzgerald for her. She is bearing up rather well under her new & extreme age.

I am sorry for the news of Bob; but I think he is well out of *Time.* Where is he staying? I'll ring up from the station as we pass through New York (Saturday, probably) to learn more of both of you. Good luck in the waiting I know so well.

Love,

John

Princeton

Dearest Mother,   3 October [1944]

I wanted to thank you at once for that suggestion, but I got directly to work when I came down to Princeton and have not stopped since even for a letter; a card today from Geo. Boehm asking for Bob's address (saying he knows of a good job for him if he can find him soon enough) recalled me to necessities. It was very difficult to get the Librarian at the Gregg Institute to understand that I do not share her generalized interest in shorthand – that my attention to it stops dead in the year 1608 – but when I succeeded she told me that Mr [John Robert] Gregg has a copy of [Timothy] Bright's 1588 treatise *[Characterie: An Arte of Shorte, Swifte and Secret Writing by Character]*, of which I have seen only facsimiles heretofore, and will bring it into New York from his pastoral mansion whenever I want, on a week's notice. This will be of interest if not of use, and I shall do it later. On Peter Bales and John Willis, who invented the more likely system, she had nothing – like everyone else. It is the devil: the Quarto text, wretched from any other point of view, is unutterably good from the early-stenographic point of view. My new theory is that Shakespeare, disloyal at heart and divided against himself, in a fit of amnesia, "reported" his own play, sold the copy to the printer after carefully destroying all the distinctions in it between prose & verse, and is now merry with wicked joy peeping over Olympus at sorrowful scholars.

You see I can't think of anything else. Wrestling all day with textual situations & graphic principles stops down the brain. When it revives I'll post again. Let me hear what luck you and Bob have had. I send you both good wishes & anxiety & love daily.

John

[George Boehm was a mathematician and friend of Robert Jefferson's.]

Princeton, [N.J.]
Dearest Mother,   25 October 1944
I am thirty years old today and I would feel a hundred and thirty except that I have been writing poems. Also my emotions have been white-haired so long that it is time really for their second youth; and this is what I count on, having wasted my first one. You and I are the characters in Blake's poem ["The Mental Traveller"] (in this point only), that you grow young and I grow old. No more of this sad subject. But to show you that if I quaver in my dotage I have a lively quaver, I send a gay Lament or black Self-portrait I wrote this morning.

Not hearing, and wondering for word of you and Bob, from whom I have not heard either, I would have written before but for a cold worse than any of last year, now in its third week & somewhat clearing. I haven't put down so much as a postcard since last I wrote to you; but this is an old story, not improved by its veracity. How are you both? From Granny a beautiful letter has come saying among other things that her sight has improved. If I could hear that your position or Bob's, or blessedly yours and Bob's, had, the whole darkness would lighten much. But last year, I remember, when I despaired I was impatient or wild with questioning and wishes of "good luck"; and powerless to help, I pray simply that you are not so bad as we then were. No doubt next Spring it begins again for me. Ah, to be indifferent! This happens: what should be normal life comes to have, transient & tolerable, the air of a vacation, unreal interim. The nightmare shows as real. I hope yours is passing.

Dearest love,
John

Enclosed was the following:

> My sins, is it too late to turn around
> And steal a real boat and lie back, downstream
> Descending with a comfortable sound:
>
> Too late for dinner forever, oysters & cream?
> They say we are not hungry, – if we are,
> Should not be, nibble a cloud or munch a dream.
>
> Other indigestibles. Then the swift water.
> Like the cracked exile I was "wrong from the start";
> Ignorant the spring would be so far,
>
> Where we rest. Looking closely in my heart,
> I should have been bred to a blither trade,
> Something less racking, taught a strutting part,
>
> To be a chemist who the great war made,
> A banker be, wearing a bloody hat,
> An operator operating in the shade,
>
> To meet the Devil at his pretty gate
> And have a stiff drink before going on
> Down. Hey derry down. Alas too late:

My breath too short with the current's shock, the sun
Too hot, to turn out of the way of my youth,
Its ordures, ardours. Stroke & stroke again

To crow a wicked note, the old one, truth.

Selbstbildnes aet. 30
[Self-portrait at the Age of 30]

[Paragraph three of the October 26 letter contains some revisions of this unpublished poem.]

                                                        [Princeton, N.J.]
Dearest Mother,   26 October [1944]
    I suppressed my loneliness when I wrote, and my crazy excitement
(of poetry – which continues) partly kept it off, but I knew how sad I had
been by how glad I was when your letter came, towards six o'clock: my
heartfelt thanks. In thirty years I have myself forgotten so many anniver-
saries that if the whole world had forgotten this one I could not have
complained. You have given me the *Oxford [Book of] Sixteenth Century
Verse* [by E. K. Chambers], for which I was anxious & am grateful; also
some more verse when I decide what I can least do without. I am tempted
to use the gift to rush to New York for conversation – of another sort
altogether from the deadly institutional talk which we have been forced
to hear mainly in Princeton of late. Writing constantly, however, I can't;
and then *Lear* we have always with us. The only writer here is R. P.
Blackmur, and I stifle for lack of people of my own kind, *anti- & literate*.
Intellectuals are not intolerable when they are missing; only in excess. If
I could I'd go up every month, but we haven't a cent for such things. For
the first time in ten years, in fact, I find I have stopped carrying my
wallet, – having nothing to put in it; and yet money torments me less
than ever before.
    I wish you every luck with the magazine and am glad for you even of
it; as for Bob's job, which I hope will better. I have stopped payment on
the cheque (which must have been lost – it was dated 31 Aug and I sent
it special delivery, *malheur*, for his quick use), and send herewith another,
which will you give him?
    Revisions of the poem yesterday: 4th from the end, for "down": "in,

down". Last line: "To crow a wicked note, to be a naked mouth". I confess too to having expurgated for you the twelfth line, which ends (indecorous but necessary expression) "sweeter than a fart, – ".

Have you read *The Charterhouse of Parma?* Let me know if not & I'll send it: one of the most strictly *wonderful* European novels.

Granny speaks in her letter to me about distance lenses, but sounds absolutely relieved of anxiety and speaks of the library as if she would continue with it. Like every letter I have had from her for several years it is an extraordinary production, glowing & rich. She is an extraordinary woman; I pray I may see her again. The qualities of joy and selflessness in those who are through age, or long & plainly fatal illness, really upon death, seem to me to redeem us if anything does. William James showed them, and at this moment I don't think of anyone else who did (no large number anywhere), and he did not show them more brilliantly than she does. Of course most men have been knocked on the head by apathy or fear long before.

I have just come on some lines in [Henry] Medwall (15th c.) which represent handsomely and despairingly the current Allied outcry for the destruction, ruralization & c of Germany:

> And men say among, (= "commonly")
> He that throweth stone or stick
> At such a bird he is like
> To sing that bird's song.
> [Henry Medwall, *Fulgens and Lucres*]

As for the national election, I am sorry that I am old enough to vote, i.e., morally required to vote, i.e., have to vote for Roosevelt; and I am sorrier to think, as I do, that there *is* some possibility of the country's electing that impossible scoundrel Dewey to sit on the world's affairs for four mad years. I would vote for – well, who would I vote for otherwise? Thomas Jefferson and Freud are dead, and Freud was not a citizen, and Henry Adams would not play ball with the machines. I would hold my hand.

Kisses for remembering my birthday, my dearest love,

John

[Mrs. Berryman had been hired as an editor of the magazine *Sportswear Stylist*, and returned to live in New York.

Robert Jefferson had taken a job as associate editor with Unicorn Press, an encyclopedia publisher.

Martha Little ("Granny"), JB's maternal grandmother, had returned to Mena, Arkansas, where she had lived, at intervals, for many years. She served as librarian at the public library in Mena from April 1944 to September 1946 when she retired at the age of 83.]

[Princeton, N.J.]
Dearest Mother   Tuesday [16 January 1945]
I was disappointed but the postponement was as well – Eileen & I not only had our colds still, we *have* them still, – but mine is enfeebled & should pass off shortly. We count on you and Bob & Nicky for the same time this Saturday and I hope the weather will be better. Just now it is storming in a lazy way.

Did you see the review of mine in the Sunday [New York] Times? – Yes, I have sunk so low. I'll tell you the story when you come. I have also torn [Russell W.] Davenport's poem [My Country] to pieces for the next Politics. Gnash Gnash: it is the influence of Dante whom I read everyday with wonder & humility. But if they give me stupid books to notice, what can they expect? I was surprised that the Times printed the review; they are changing their colours, no doubt of it.

Say to Bob for me that I hope Nicky's better. I hope you keep well & will work less continuously. Would you bring Mark's World Poetry down if you think of it? I've a particular need. Till Saturday,

Love,

John

[JB's review of The Best Poems of 1943, ed. by Thomas Moult, appeared in the January 14, 1945, issue of the New York Times Book Review.

JB's review of My Country by Russell W. Davenport appeared in the February 1945 issue of Politics.

"Nicky" is Robert Jefferson's second wife, Enid Klauber.]

[Princeton, N.J.]
Dearest Mother   Friday [2 February 1945]
The Henry James piece for Tate has kept me from writing anything else, except a note to a friend of mine wounded in the Bulge – fighting who is being sent back, thank heaven, though in what condition he doesn't

say – otherwise I'd have thanked you at once for so many gifts & for altogether so good an evening. I'd have looked more carefully at your magazine [*Sportswear Stylist*], by the way, if I hadn't supposed you were leaving the copy; I am utterly blank on such subjects, as you know, but I'm curious to see what you've done. I hope it involves less work as you get a staff together.

Your flowers were the first I'd seen in months: we gloated over them. And Bob's cigarettes! I doubt I could have got through the paper on James without them. It turned out both longer (in pages & time) & harder than I expected; but I hope it will have some effect. Unfortunately it involved my bearing down on a *Partisan Review* editor [Phillip Rahv] and a Harvard professor [F. O. Matthiessen] (the latter I like personally). The [*New York*] *Times* has sent me – without my permission, so do they feel their damned writers at their mercy – some more books, and I pray they will be good, or at any rate not so insufferably stupid as these others my treatment of which will cause me to be looked on as Cato, or a hangman. Meanwhile Dante suffers, *Lear* is scanted, my work stops & my health is miserable. But the military news stops every thought like a fog of horror – "good" & "best" as of course I feel it, & hear as it brings the end of the hopeless slaughter as an organized thing. The futility of any attempt for truth or honour (for beauty, less) pierces my breast.

How cold it is! There too? I hope that you & Bob both have heat – we have, we stifle & I am ashamed. Eileen however is coming down with another sore throat & cold. May you not, & be well in all things.

Dearest love,

John

["Henry James," a review of James' *Stories and Artists*, edited by F. O. Matthiessen, *The Great Short Stories of Henry James*, edited by Phillip Rahv, and *Henry James: The Major Phase* by F. O. Matthiessen, appeared in the spring 1945 issue of the *Sewanee Review*.]

[Princeton, N.J.]

Dearest Jill   Monday [26 February 1945]

The book I am sending you is not of course our wedding gift to you & Nils [Gustafsson] – *that* we have racked our brains about so far without success – but simply *a* wedding gift from me to you. It looks to me very satisfactory, in fact much the best thing of the sort I've ever seen;

and gives me, glancing through it, a strong inclination to visit Sweden myself after the War.

We had an admirable time in New York & are most grateful to you & Nils – who I hope *will* be appointed here and stay.

dear love,

John

[Mrs. Berryman and Nils O. Gustafsson, nine years her junior, were married in New York on February 17, 1945. The marriage certificate, curiously, gives her birthdate as July 8, 1912, rather than 1894.

JB's wedding gift was probably *Sweden—Ancient and Modern*, published by the Turisttrafikforbundet in Stockholm.]

Princeton [N.J.]

Dearest Jill,   10 March 1945

I am very sorry to hear – how casually! – about your magazine's [*Sportswear Stylist*] "folding" (is that what is really happening?) – and about the exacerbation of rumours regarding Nils' next assignment: I hope this settles itself soon & very well. I sympathize with his somatic difficulties; part of this week I spent in bed with a grippe, now gone off, and Eileen has been suffering with her back, etc. O health come! We hope you've been well apart from worry.

We should have written to thank you for the weekend, our most pleasant in New York in a long time, breaking I hope our jinx. I do now, and – most gratefully – for the unexpected gift which you ended it with, and which is about to become a pair of trousers for me, I think – or an Italian dictionary and a collection of Provençal verse. This language, I must tell you, ancient Provençal, is the most bewildering I ever studied. Italian is easy easy. Yes the *Sweden* is excellent, *nichts?* I will find you a copy of [probably Marquis William] Childs' book [*Sweden: The Middle Way*] when I come to town next.

A simple honour in which for once I took some pleasure was paid to my work last week, and against custom I tell you of it because I think it will please you. I had a letter "The Library of Congress is much interested in recording for its archives examples of the best work of a limited number of contemporary poets as read by the poets themselves". etc, from Robert Penn Warren, who is in the Chair of Poetry there. There will be no public distribution (possibly after the war) and no payment: "for the present the poet will have for his pains only the consciousness of having rendered a public service and the possession of one set of his own recordings". I may do it, or not, when I go to Washington next month or so, but the request from that source pleased me.

love
John

[P.S.] We hope Nils' brother [Karl] comes. Let us know.

                                                              [Princeton, N.J.]
Dearest Jill,   23 May 1945
    I thought I had better not tell you about the party for Mark until afterward, first because I keep secrets when asked to, second because I had to speak at it and was nervous. But how word gets about! Mark knew, after all, nine days in advance, and as Delmore & Eileen & I were dining, Bob walked into Chumley's, having met either Giroux or you, and then at the Algonquin Giroux reported running into you and telling you. It was the nearest thing to a reunion, in fact, of the people I know that, as Eileen says, I'll ever see: some seventy, of whom I must have known half. We couldn't sit together, unhappily, I was at the small speakers' table with Mark, Carl [Van Doren], [Clifton] Fadiman, [Joseph Wood] Krutch, [Lionel] Trilling, and the Dr [Henry] Rosenthal who arranged the whole thing, – E not far away with Delmore, Haggin & [Stephen] Aylward. Intolerable speeches, most of them – Fadiman would call on people in various parts of the room & read between times messages from those who couldn't come (Tate, MacLeish, [Robert Maynard] Hutchins, Tom Merton etc); since he began with Rex Stout however, I expected them to be even worse than they were and was less bored than Eileen – who did not have either the keying of apprehension to the degree that I did. But the speakers' general philistinism & egotism depressed me very much, so I determined to speak *briefly* and about *Mark* (or rather his poetry) not myself, and *professionally*, i.e. truthfully & to a standard not gossip. This at any rate I did, disposing of three heresies about Mark's poetry, then reading his "Winter Tryst", then attacking his character and reading a poem which I wrote for the party. Next to Carl I think I was the last speaker, I had had a long time for anxiety & felt white as a cat, but E said I sounded well enough. The only speeches I liked were [Jacques] Barzun's and [James] Thurber's (Thurber's very funny, although his

blindness shocked me.). Who else spoke? Scott Buchanan, F. P. A. [Franklin P. Adams], my old enemy Professor [Harrison] Steeves, two pseudo-writers Charles Wagner & John Gassner, [William] Sloane, Mark's publisher, Fr. Aylward (a speech, I'm sorry to say, in as disgusting taste as E tells me his conversation during the evening was), I forget the rest, and of course Fadiman's intermittent drivel. If little was intelligent, however, everything was amiable and nothing was fulsome, and everyone exhibited real respect and love for Mark, which was of the essence. [Raymond] Weaver was there, complaining that apparently we expected him to look decrepit; Giroux, [Charles] Reilly & [Andrew] Chiappe lolled at a table beyond Eileen's; another brother or so of Mark's, one his image, Dorothy and both the boys looking wonderful, Charlie in uniform on leave from his camp in the South, and Johnny dressed like cafe society from St John's, very handsome. Mark, it goes without saying, was superb all evening, neither modest nor vain, with no appearance of embarrassment and endless good humour & self-possession, even when Dr Rosenthal played a recording (by some famous ghastly soprano) of a setting by some hopeless composer, with the Philadelphia Orchestra, of Mark's poem "Let There Be Law", written for the opening of the San Francisco Conference and not used because of the President's death. If you can act perfectly in an impossible situation he did so.

You will probably have been surprised by the courtesy shown me in preference to older & better known friends of Mark's. I was surprised too, and have no explanation for it – Carl particularly, but everyone, was astonishingly kind. Many people asked after you also and wanted news and sent regards. Mrs [Pauline] Fadiman, blonde by profession & unused to competition, watched Eileen with hostility, and Haggin ground his teeth during the music. We felt as if *we* had been teaching for twenty-five years by the time it finally broke up. But Mark was beautiful.

Love, John

By June Mrs. Berryman and Nils Gustafsson had separated.

[Princeton, N.J.]

Dearest Jill   16 August 1945

A sort of lethargy overwhelmed us after the violent emotion of Tuesday evening. We have done nothing but move slowly about household chores during these first two days of Peace, – so that I haven't yet told my own extraordinary news. I found in the mail Monday night the *proofs* of my story that I mentioned to you, and with them a note from [John Crowe] Ransom saying I had won the first prize in their (*Kenyon Review* – Doubleday Doran) contest: $500. I really could not believe it, I sat on the floor & felt like weeping. It is more money than I have earned as a writer in the whole ten years. Of course it is the quality of the story that matters, but I couldn't tell what that was next day when I tried to read & revise it, and I abandon the question to whoever reads it. The money I have wonderful uses for: first, it finishes repaying my old debt to Clare [College, Cambridge] & will bring my books back from England; then some small old debts; and then $100 or so for a coat for Eileen, if you will help us get it. Anything left over goes for Shakespearean books and my Cambridge M.A. I might buy Toynbee and a set of Chekhov too. I feel – or will feel when the cheque comes and for two or three days thereafter – frivolously wealthy: a rather scarce feeling with me: in fact I never (except also in 1936) had it before. Who knows what I will do? I am going to take Eileen dancing also, and I have promised, in a moment of lunacy, to learn the Rumba.

This strange event brings up again for me too the problem of whether I can write stories; I feel as much a fraud as when "The Lovers" was accepted last year. But I take refuge in the adage that (two) swallow(s) do not make a summer. Most of all I am curious to know what you & Bob & several other people will think of the story.

I was glad we had the talk – a very good one – on Monday. Keep well, well.

love,
John

[P.S.] I am having the *Kenyon* sent to you; it should be out shortly.

[Berryman received the *Kenyon Review* – Doubleday Doran prize for his short story "The Imaginary Jew." It appeared in the *Kenyon Review's* autumn 1945 issue. "The Lovers" appeared in the *Kenyon Review's* winter 1945 issue.]

In one of her few surviving letters from this period Mrs. Berryman, who by then had a new advertising position, replied:

Lester Harrison, Inc.
341 Madison Ave., New York
Dearest John,   Monday October 8, 1945
The *Kenyon Review* came this morning. The story is a magnificent piece of work– Pride and affection flooded through me, as I read– It must

be such a satisfactory joy, to produce out of oneself what gives those who love you such real happiness. To be able to make such a gift—

Dear love–
JB

sometime in November 1945
south of the Hoarder

Dearest Jill,   [Princeton, N.J.?]

Eileen took into town with her the beautiful brown sweater and exchanged it for a heavy black one even more beautiful which I like even better and am very grateful to you for. All my youth I wanted nothing better than a heavy black sweater – once I had one but the sleeves wore away – and now my Dream has come true. I don't wear it to bed simply because the weather's not bitter enough yet. Luckily it is very long too and will cover me adequately when all the rest of my clothes shred, as they look to do rather soon. I also feel that it makes me appear mysterious and inaccessible, thus reinforcing my amiable character and collie temperament. It is an excellent gift in short.

Dr. [Erich] Kahler just rang up to say that the *Neue Rundschau* have asked him to translate "The Imaginary Jew"; he wants permission and "How to translate the slang?" It is being translated for a French anthology (or "The Lovers" is – one for an anthology, one for a review, I forget which which) and I feel polyglot. I am not, though: ironically I am just now trying to learn German myself, at the same time studying Elizabethan handwriting and shorthand methods, and juggling the 74 parts of my damned editorial subject. I'd like to rewrite the end of the story, which I haven't liked since I wrote it; but all I can think of is whether it is plausible that the elaborate entry of *King Lear* in the *Stationers' Register* on 26 November 1608 was really intended to differentiate it from the old play *Leir* to which another publisher had copyright.

The woman from whom we rent most of this furniture just rang up from Annapolis to say she wants it at once, and the energy that would have composed the rest of this letter (my first in weeks or months to anyone) has gone into keeping Eileen from despair. I am not cheerful either, in fact. I hope you are and are well and are not overworking. How is Bob? dearest love,

John

[Erich Kahler's translation of "The Imaginary Jew" appeared in the April 1946 issue of *Die Neue Rundshau*. JB later wrote a poem, "The Mysteries," which first appeared in a festschrift for the historian, entitled *Erich Kahler* (1951).]

                                                              Princeton, [N.J.]
Dearest Jill,   Thursday [16 May 1946]
Very sorry about Sunday: I sent a letter to Granny when you called last week, and stopped on my way to the office to find you a book but I couldn't decide on one at that moment and thereafter the matter dropped out of mind: just now I scarcely even try to remember anything uncon-nected with my work, for fear of losing some of the labyrinth I have got to thread. I posted fifty pages of tough close argument to [W. W.] Greg the other day and am now rushing through the text proper; this week so far I've written twelve of text, five of apparatus, eighteen of commentary, and I mean to be done in a month of 15-hour days unless I break up. Needless to say I have given up all pretence to other activities, with the inevitable exception that we got tickets months ago for the Old Vic season and I am combining these with my dentist. Olivier's Hotspur by the way, is one of the major performances of our time; you ought to go. Retro-spective to Sunday I'm sending the *New Directions* [9, which included "The Lovers"] just out, which looks much better than usual and I hope will entertain you.

After talking with the Chancellor [Alexander Guerry] of Sewanee [University of the South], who came to see me, and with Tate, who took the lid off the place, I decided against the *[Sewanee] Review* and have accepted the job Princeton offered me: it means very little work, access to my materials here in the library while seeing *Lear* through the press, access to [Stephen] Crane stuff in Newark, more money far than I ever made before, and not having to move. I despise universities and wish to be free of them as soon as possible, but this will do meanwhile. At any rate I am not any sort of professor, but what is called the Associate in Creative Arts. [Dean Christian] Gauss pushed the President [Howard W. Dobbs] to the invitation, of course – Princeton of itself wouldn't touch me, for I haven't concealed my opinion of the English Department.

Intoxicated by her success with geraniums (which she informs me are fool-proof), Eileen has ventured on petunias and wakes with fear and trembling – not Kierkegaard's sort – each morning of this strange weather.

I'm happy you've got the apartment right. The news of Granny's eyes is the best I have had in a long time. One of my stories ["The Imaginary Jew"] has been seized by the O. *Henry Memorial [Award Prize Stories of 1946]* collection and the other ["The Lovers"] by the O'Brien *Best Stories [The Best American Short Stories of 1946]*. I plan to sign them O'Berryman.

dear love
John

P.S. I always forget health. Well! – Eileen is well, I can't say I am, I hope you are, and I hope Bob is better. Fatigue has put me back just thirty years: I am amazed to report that, for the first time in that period, I wet the bed last night. Is it possible? The brass voice answers: *All things are possible my son my son.*

[Allen Tate had just stepped down as editor of the *Sewanee Review* and JB had been under serious consideration for the position.

JB had contracted with Henry Holt and Company in June 1945 to write a biography of Stephen Crane. *Stephen Crane* was eventually published, however, in 1949, by William Sloan Associates as part of their *The American Men of Letters Series*.

Edward J. O'Brien had been editor of *The Best American Short Stories* from 1914 to 1940.]

Damariseotta Mills, Maine

Dearest Jill,   4 August 1946

I haven't had any news of you because, not dreaming we'd stay on so with the Lowells, I had all mail sent to Delmore's place in Cambridge & haven't seen any in weeks. We go down tomorrow, and I'll write properly by way of reply to whatever's there. I hope Granny has continued to improve & the trip wasn't exhausting for you.

This is the first note I've tried to write to anyone. The month has been lazy, agreeable, interesting & alcoholic; not conducive to correspondence. After a fortnight with the Blackmurs, we stayed briefly with Nela & Jack Mackin in Blue Hill [Maine] (the most alcoholic of all), then here, with Robert Lowell & his wife Jean Stafford. I haven't found anyone so pleasant since Delmore in 1939. They want us to give up going to the Cape altogether, but I have some work to do in Boston & we can't desert Joan Colebrook, so we are only curtailing the stay in Truro and coming back here later in the month. Cal (Lowell) & I are working our way, comparing opinions, through the whole of Western poetry.

Eileen & I are both very fit. My hair is a foot long, though for some reason I haven't stopped shaving & haven't a beard. Of work, very little. I feel free from Shakespeare, more or less.

Will you ask Bob to send me a note at Truro (c/o Joan Colebrook, Truro, Mass.) to say how he is? (I am a slug: I'll write him. Eileen has just come in to strip for a swim & sends love.) I hope much better, & Nicky well, and you *very well*

Dearest love,
John

[After John Walcott's death Nela Walcott had married John Mackin.]

Truro, Mass.

Dearest Jill   19 August [1946]
I woke up this morning thinking of you with such warm affection that it has cast a glow over the first hours even of this wind-&-rainy day. We were very glad to hear, delighted you'd seen Barbara, full of admiration for your settling of Granny (to whom I wrote recently), hopeful that you are as well as you sound, and happy for it.

Despite poor weather and much too much society, the Cape has been pleasant as ever. Just now we are in act of arranging a party to repay the obligations contracted during three years here. Unluckily we lost interest in social life some time ago, and I particularly am finding it difficult even to go through the motions. We are personas gratas to both of the violently opposed political sects in Truro & Wellfleet, so that we suffer periodically the fate of ambassadors: most unjustly, because I am working forward my views & am utterly bored by politics proper. I refuse to quarrel, and impose this refusal where I can. The only serious war I've had was with Dwight [MacDonald] last week when he repeated a canard about Lowell, and this we composed. Worst is the attitude, affable & even ingratiating, of various hacks & has-beens towards me – Ben Ray Redman will do for exemplar – he privately predicted to Eileen that I wd be in Hollywood in five years, ugh. Then there are some Hollywood people around, ugh. Meanwhile I am trying to get on with a story, ugh.

Apparently we are in a hurry to get in town & somebody has dropped in – I'll write later – whether to go back to Maine I haven't decided, but

I think not, & I think down by Labour Day. What I'd like is to make a retreat

dearest love

John

[Ben Ray Redman was an editor, journalist, translator and poet. He also was a vice president in charge of production for Universal Pictures (1936–38), and wrote scenarios for Twentieth Century Fox.]

[Princeton, N.J.]

Dearest Jill,   Friday [14 March 1947?]

Wonderful wonderful about your apartment, and to hear from you altogether: I'd got very worried, though of course it was my own bloody fault as usual for not writing. I can't write anybody. Teaching takes a fantastic time, and what other energy I have I feel I need if I'm to do *anything*. And since my current plan (not a word of this even to Eileen) is to publish three books next year, I must do something. Also I am fed up with teaching, fed up, fed up, and merely snarl if anybody comes near here, which strains further. No more teaching. Part of my design at present is a magazine, firstrate and expensive, to fill the gap left before the War by the death of *The Criterion*; this I'll describe to you when I see you, – on this, silence too. About Easter let me see a little.

When you have time for a novel get Malcolm Lowry's *Under the Volcano*, the first book for years full-sized & new.

I don't even know when Easter is. I live in a daze.

Best is your getting an apartment after so long chaos, but the apartment itself sounds very good, I'm eager to see it. By way of return of this good news I send you finally [John] Davidson's great poem ["Thirty Bob a Week"]. Have wanted you & Bob to brisk down for dinner for a long time, but weekends (which seemed best) have been utterly foxed either for Eileen or me every time – e.g. she is giving psychological tests all this one and next one. Is midweek impossible for you both? Say next Thursday?????? or Wednesday? *say!*

Yes of course put legs on the box-spring if practicable and you want to – whatever you want.

Lowry's novel & Jean [Stafford]'s *[The Mountain Lion?]* (small-scale, brilliant) have lightened my gloom a little. Hardly any *books* are published any more, only anthologies. Actually: one day this week came letters from Scribner's, New Directions, Holt (enclosing a cheque, offering a cheque, trying to get out of offering a cheque) and the next day one from Doubleday with a tupenny fee for German rights to one of the *Best Stories* anthologies. It fills you with contempt & despair. But read Lowry, he is the first man to make real use of the things invented in *Ulysses*, for his own serious purposes.

Love to you, life to your apartment,

John

[JB was at the time seeking support for a new literary review to be modeled on the *Criterion*, which had ceased publication eight years earlier. It was his plan to edit the quarterly review, to be called *The Twentieth Century*. He was, finally, unable to secure the financial backing needed for the venture.

The German rights granted by Doubleday were for Erich Kahler's translation of "The Imaginary Jew," which had been reprinted in *O. Henry Memorial Award Prize Stories of 1946*.]

[Princeton N.J.]

Dearest Jill,   27 September 1947

   I didn't stop in New York even an hour on the way either up to the Cape or back, or I'd have seen you, but my not writing is certainly inexcusable – I think I shall be better about this in future. I am in a better frame of mind, feel a good deal rested, and am able to look ahead more clearly; the summer, in general, may be considered a nightmare from which I have partly waked up.

   Your being out Harrison's [Lester Harrison, Inc.] sounds wonderful, *if* you don't continue to work yourself crazy. Both of us wish you every conceivable luck. Let me say that again more prominently: BOTH OF US WISH YOU EVERY CONCEIVABLE LUCK!!

   A man in the *Politics* office who claims to hear of apartments is going to scout for us, but we haven't any incredible hope. Meanwhile we are going to keep on here, living as cheaply as possible, at least until the *Crane* and *Lear* are finished. Eileen has a part-time job in a statistical survey of the University wh looks to be rather interesting, and besides journalism I hope to get lecturing or something of the sort one night a week somewhere accessible; *Partisan's* sudden wealth will probably help us, since besides publishing verse & whatever stories I write there, I may do a regular verse chronicle for them – at this point on Saturday & Gertrude came by my office to get me out for a walk. But now, Monday morning, I am so savagely nervous that I can't go on. To our immense relief E was accepted finally by the NYU graduate school, but she will tell you about that.

Again all luck to you & Miss O'Leary,

and much love,

John

[P.S.] Under no circumstances, please, speak to *anyone* of *anything* I told you this summer, whether personal or literary. No-one.

[P.P.S.] Did I tell you [Louis] Untermeyer is representing my verse in the new ed. of his anthology [*Modern American Poetry*]? "Canto Amor" & some others.

[In addition to "Canto Amor," *Modern American Poetry* included JB's "Winter Landscape," "Parting as Descent" and "The Ball Poem."

Mrs. Berryman had recently become a co-partner in Berryman and O'Leary, an advertising and public relations firm.]

Although it is not mentioned in the letters, John Angus Berryman died on October 29, 1947, in Reisterstown, Maryland. He was seventy-two. His sister, Ethel Berryman Bird, with whom he had lived for the past decade, died the following year.

[Princeton, N.J.]

[No salutation]   Monday [5 January 1948]

Your party was wonderful, *far* the best New Year's Day party I ever saw, and even with cracking nerves I had a wonderful time. So did Eileen. But since then we have been a state of semi-collapse, especially since we gave a bottle-dance ourselves on Saturday for people here (E designed a rearrangement of the whole apartment, wh. worked beautifully); and I only today got back to work. E's cold is worse, & atrocious, but I hope it's past the peak yesterday & today. I forgot to bring the shirts away: will do. What weather! But two editors have just forgiven me 1947 lapses, and I feel comparatively a new man. Happy new year! I hope you have a very good one, and I hope Bob does, who deserves it extremely. Love to Barba Villim [Mikulicic] too,

& love,

John

[Barba Villim Mikulicic was a mariner and a close friend of Mrs. Berryman's.]

[Princeton, N.J.]

Darling   Friday [2 April 1948]

Back yesterday morning – Grounded two hours by weather in Little Rock, but wonderful luck else. Slept most of the day & am fine – at work – today – luckily, for the deadlines creep on. I was v. grateful to you for letting me come back so fast.

Eileen just fell on her bike at noon, hurting her back, & has had to be strapped again. I hope Monday will see her all right – losing classes costs her trouble. My cold is better, but we'd better not try anything this weekend.

After eighteen months' thought, I came this morning suddenly on the *subject* for the long poem I've been drafting, and am elated; though it will be Fall at least before I can hope to get at it steadily. Meanwhile my second book of short poems is arranged & about ⅔ written. Only these damn prose books hang on me.

I hope you & Bob recover well. Be patient – she is better.

love
John

[P.S.] Have $30 of yours: when I come in.

[JB's maternal grandmother, Martha May Little, died on March 29, 1948. JB and Robert Jefferson flew to Kansas City and took an all night train to Mena to attend the funeral which took place two days later. Mrs. Berryman had been "in a bad state" at the funeral.

Homage to Mistress Bradstreet is the long poem JB had begun to draft.

The Dispossessed is the second book of short poems JB was working on.]

Princeton, [N.J.]

Dearest Jill   Friday 18 June [1948]

Six weeks and reviews; I am fortified with ten years of Patience. Also they are taking it slowly, as I wished. But it will soon begin. Luckily I don't have to read them.

I was in a fog of apprehension until the operation [Eileen's] was decided against, and trying hard since to work, or I'd have written before. The illustrations for *Crane* went to the printers today, having cost me trouble. That's something. Maybe now I will write the text.

Iowa State offered me yesterday $4500 for teaching 3–5 hours a week, and the London *Times* had nodded gravely to "The Imaginary Jew", also an Italian anthologist [Elio Vittorini] offers 9000 Lire for it; my stock is vaguely rising.

I hope you are *really* rather well. I was glad to have a letter. Eileen is very stoical. Can we come to 338 for dinner on Tuesday, and perhaps stay the night? I'll call you that afternoon to see. I am sorry as hell about Bob's sinus.

Love
John

[*The Dispossessed* had been published on May 10. As here, JB always claimed not to read his reviews.

An operation on Eileen's back had been considered following her bicycle accident in April.]

[New York]
For Jill   8 July 1948

No birthday blows but in the elder-bloom
A nameless bird's blue throat rattles & sings:
All spring, all winter-end: we sang our room,
And wring our room for more beautiful & more blue things.

John

Princeton, [N.J.]
Darling   1 November 1948

I've agreed to go to Washington read verse at some Institute or other on Wednesday, but am coming to New York then to see E. in hospital Thursday night & may stay over with you if it's not inconvenient. If a letter turns up for me, will you hold it – there's a poetry conference up the Hudson over the weekend that I may go to or not & I told the man he cd write me at 338. There is a v. favourable review (Delmore says) by a fool in the new *Poetry*. Also *Poetry* just gave me their Guarantors Prize ($100); and *Life* wants me to appear in a group picture of poets to be taken at a party next week for the Sitwells. I think this is all, except that I am back at work again, Eileen is a little better, and we enjoyed indescribably the evening here last week. Soon again.

Love,
John

[P.S.] How odd to transmit news not *bad!*

[The review of *The Dispossessed* in the October issue of *Poetry* was by Richard Eberhardt.

Although JB was present at the Gotham Book Mart party for the Sitwells, he disappeared at the time the group picture was to be taken (see December 1 letter) and is not among those in *Life's* commemorative photograph.]

                                                       [Princeton, N.J.]
Darling   1 December [1948]

I finished the Pound introduction (three times I finished it) & sent it off yesterday. This is a year point. In spite of teaching all day, last night my brain flooded again. Now I have a nightmare month, one month, to finish *Crane* which is absolutely promised for Christmas. Then I am more my own man. This winter I think I will write verse, and the hell with everything. Teaching bores me to the soul but it destroys only two days. What I *can't* stand is this long burden of Pound & Crane.

Thanks for the Yeats photos. Just before, Pound had showed me some similar ones in Washington. Yeats – Ezra said – always had his "Da" standing over him to keep him from writing essays; so he became a *great* poet. Further point – Have you read his father's letters? They are marvellous, you'd adore them.

The Sitwell affair was indescribable. I went, but I couldn't face getting in the photographs – with Wm Rose Benet sitting there like a mummy & Jarrell blazing with ambition down on the right – so I didn't.

I think I told you *Poetry* gave me a prize – the Guarantors, $100; disappeared like butter under Sol. Eliot's Nobel was wonderful was it not? We had him in one day, an odd time I'll tell you about. Eileen is better again I think, though in bed just now. How is Bob's sinus? I have not been very well myself – I only hope not to be worse & unable to work like a dog all month. How have you been? You are coming for Christmas I hope. By then I *will* be exhausted but perhaps in the best frame of mind for years. It depends day-by-day now on Stephen Crane

                                                            Love,
                                                            John

[JB had been commissioned by New Directions to write an introduction for Pound's *Selected Poems*. "The Poetry of Ezra Pound," which appeared in the April 1949 issue of *Partisan Review*, was not, however, used in the volume.

While working on the article, JB had twice visited Pound at St. Elizabeth's Hospital.]

Princeton, [N.J.]

[No salutation]   Monday [28 February 1949]

Just a note to say I have been given something called the Shelley Memorial Award for 1948. It will be in the 'papers in a little, and *in* little if they are following my wishes. About $650, and very useful: I bought a bottle of Scotch, & demolished it, being depressed, bought some books, & the rest goes for doctors & book-bills, Beethoven's *3rd*, & a trip off when we can.

My doctor tells me I am still exhausted from the weeks on *Crane* & forbids me to do anything – even teaching, but this of course I must do – gave me double sedation & slowly I am quieting down. I have been drinking & talking my head off for a month of delirious fatigue. I hope Bob's sinus is better & that you are well. Tell Bob & Liza will you about the award? I don't feel capable of a second account.

Love
John

[P.S.] If I come in late this week I'll call.

["Liza" is Robert Jefferson's third wife, Elizabeth Weston.]

Princeton, [N.J.]

Darling,   Friday, [4 March 1949]

. . . There seem to be four national awards for poetry, at least I know of four: the Pulitzer, the new Bollingen, the National Academy, and the one just tossed at me. The last is evidently much the least important; to tell you the truth I never distinctly heard of it until I opened a letter the other night from the Old Colony Trust Company in Boston and a cheque fell out in good traditional style. It seems to be given, not like the first two awards, for a specific book, but for the body of work in verse done so far, – though of course it must be based in my case on *The Dispossessed*. I learn that Karl Shapiro had it one year, and a man of no importance, another year, and there my curiosity ceases. It is the money that matters, as you said; and this is passionately taxable (we lose about $150 or a quarter, it appears) but extremely useful.

I have just done something worth doing. [Louis] Untermeyer was
having trouble selecting my poems, he wrote, and when our correspondence about this was over, I collected my audacity and with great polite-
ness suggested a total revision of his regular selection from Pound. Now
he writes that he was doing more or less what I suggest anyway, – *although*,
I am told, he has been attacking the Bollingen award to Pound in the
newspapers this last week or so. So: we may get a decent anthology selection of Pound at last, and under the least favourable circumstances possible. I fired at him a final postcard about passages in the *Pisan Cantos*
this afternoon, but I have little hope as to this. His letters by the way are
oddly tentative and defensive. I always used to wonder how these powerful fools felt, and now I am beginning to complete an accurate, depressing idea.

Love,
John

[P.S.] I am a little better, and perhaps E. is. How are you & Bob?

[Princeton, N.J.]

[No salutation]   26 October [1949]

Thank you darling for the letter & gift – the last you shouldn't have
sent but I will buy a hat with it (mine I lost on the Cape) and be grateful.
Yesterday was the usual nightmare only much worse. I had scarcely slept
at all Monday night – very hard work – & was a corpse. All these cele-
brations have to be postponed. Haven't written because no news except
alternations of work & inability to work. Nothing done but very near
Crane-end, a few days I hope. Caught up in a mass protest over the *Sat
Rev of Lit* but am guarding my time. Several periods of depression weath-
ered, and one so intense I can only suppose I will now be all right. I wish
you will have some luck, and Bob. Say I wrote him several weeks ago but
have not had spirit to post it. I keep dreadfully sorry about his birthday.
New York not at all for weeks – no money or time – my teeth still full of
temp'y fillings. Ugh. Yes! Serenity would be it. But resistance swallows
my energy –

Love
John

[The *Saturday Review of Literature* had published two articles by Robert
Hillyer attacking the awarding of the Bollingen Prize in Poetry to Ezra Pound.

A letter, co-signed by 84 writers, Berryman among them, was turned down by the *Review*, but published in the *Nation* on 17 December 1949.

Stephen Crane was published by William Sloan Associates on November 30, 1949.]

During the spring of 1950, JB was a Visiting Lecturer in English at the University of Washington in Seattle.

1856 Shelby St, Seattle 2

Darling,   Sunday night, 23 April 1950

Very many thanks for brownies & letters – I gobble both. So far I have been working like a dog, lecturing, with little energy or time for anything else. I never slept so much in my life. My damned room wd have made any normal life impossible anyway: miles from anything & it has not got a chair in it you can sit in. I am writing in bed. This is the first letter I've written unless to Eileen since I got here except one finally to the Mackies on Friday. I haven't seen much of Seattle and have not been outside the city at all.

But today I located an apartment at last – very close to breakfast, to my office, shops etc. – and move tomorrow; and perhaps life will improve. My fatigue seems gradually to be going off also, and the weather is brightening. It is very beautiful here after all on a good day: water every-where, & green, & heights, & off to East & West the white great moun-tains: everything indeed Princeton has not. But nothing on the other hand that Princeton has. Well, I am almost half through.

Teaching has gone well enough, considering how little practice I've had in recent years and how strange the students are. It is Wayne, & Detroit, all over again. Some are fair: They range too much, however – from juniors & even some sophomores to people (Ph.D.'s) older than I am; – and too many people visit my lectures. Until last week I pressed much too fast & too hard, for them. Now I am slowing down, and many have come to life.

I'm glad you had a pleasant weekend. Don't be silly about the money, whatever Eileen was able to repay; I just wish it were much more. Tell Bob it wd be delightful to hear from him & give his sinus my sympathy. They have not Census'd me yet – I bet they won't catch me. Have agreed, tentatively, to public readings here & in Portland, Oregon, later on. I'd like to do some riding & climbing; no chance yet; students invite me skiing but I need my neck; may go to San Francisco next weekend. What

thing would you like from the Pacific northwest? I hope for luck for you,
mum.

dearest love
John

[P.S.] Love to Bob & Liza, Marie, & all
[P.P.S.] Write me: 1019 E. 43rd St, Seattle 5, Wash.

[Seattle]

Darling,   Sunday afternoon [14 May 1950]

I'm dreadfully sorry about the New Hampshire disappointment. I wish
you, always, such good luck. It'd depressing too to think of your moving
after you've made the place so delightful. This is very gloomy. I *hope*
something will turn. Yes I have been bored and depressed – also very
tired – eight lectures a week is 4 or 5 too many – but I have only three
more weeks, and today feel unusually cheerful anyway: I slept well. You
were sweet to write. Just because the commercial world cashes in on
sentiments mostly not real anyway is no reason to ignore a reasonable
occasion for what almost never gets expressed, and for days I have been
looking for something for you. Without success! But it occurred to me
some time ago that you might like to go to the American Academy Ceremonial on the 25th, though I can't – Eileen does ("You may think I'm
silly but I want very much to go to this. Ain't it impressive?" she wrote) –
and I am having them send you an invitation. It's trash, of course, but
Mark [Van Doren] will be giving [H. L.] Mencken a medal, and so on,
and it might amuse you. I believe I already owe the whole thousand to
my bank, so that this honour is like life's others, somewhat empty. But
let me give you a real gift: look about in the anthologies of verse you have
and find two of Wallace Stevens's early poems, "Sunday Morning" and
"*Le Monocle de Mon Oncle*", and read them; they are very difficult but I
shd be astonished if you weren't delighted with them and we'll talk about
them when I come back. If you do like them, I'll get you *Harmonium*
his first & best book where they are. I think you may like their doctrine,
is the point. I just made a martini, darling, and I drink to you, – the
farthest toast away you've had for years, and the dearest, most admiring
& devoted, imaginable

John

[On May 25, JB was presented with an Arts and Letters Grant for $1,000 from the American Academy of Arts and Letters.]

Upon JB's return to Princeton, he had been appointed Alfred Hodder Fellow for 1950–1951. In the summer of 1950, he and Mrs. Berryman had a falling out, during a telephone conversation, as attested to by the following letter Mrs. Berryman wrote but never sent. At the top of the letter she wrote: "Thought to speak to Dr. [James] Shea [JB's psychiatrist] before sending to be sure it would not be harmful: decided against speech or sending."

[New York?]

Dearest John,   Friday morning, 9 June, 1950

Now, with all force, I punish myself for having failed to work to achieve that mastery of words which would show you my heart and mind in clarity, precision and unmistakable truth. As it is, I can only do my best– a fair epitaph for a failure, that: she did her best.

I have no way of knowing how you feel about honor in connection with me, it may be that your opinion and mine of the value of my word of honor differ. My own opinion is high, since I do not lie consciously about anything of import and, to keep myself conscious, I endeavor to maintain in memory my own exact position as well as that of others without allowing time, desire or ego to shift accents, attitudes or responsibilities. On this basis, I ask you to accept as simple truth what follows.

Knowing how heavy your burdens now, it becomes my duty to relieve you of what may be one of the most painful, now that at last I comprehend the matter. I hope that with the release of this dangling weight dragging at your heels other pressures may ease as your strength is less stretched and strained. With my whole love, which has never failed in my heart however its appearances may have seemed other, I pray that all may go increasingly well with you.

Until shortly before I last spoke with you, on the 'phone, it had never entered my head that you believed I did not, do not love you. Where there is no understanding of the central fact, no proof means anything: your assertions and accusations of last September, for example, grieved me as symptoms of your own suffering. To my Cro-Magnon picture mind, it's as if all of the attributes of red were told and re-told to one born blind – these proofs could mean nothing until he gained sight and then with the knowledge of red, all of the attributes were explicable.

I make this statement now, not to trouble you or to evoke a response but so that you may know the truth and so be set free: I love you. It seems as redundant as that necessitated statement in Andover, so long ago. It is like saying that the sun shines or that living, one bleeds when stabbed.

Only one bolstering accusation will I answer: it is proved that I do not love you by my lack of interest in you and this is proved by not asking questions about or discussing you and your doings. It is or my love for you and belief in your like love for me that led me to talk to you and to hope that you, in turn, would talk to me. When sometimes you did not, I felt as no doubt did the savage who spread his barbaric treasures on the sand in the hope that the traveler would likewise, in trust and affection, spread his.

No more of this. It is your privilege to believe as you like or must, and to behave in like fashion. This privilege is also mine, as it is that of any human being. Having no faintest wish to dictate, or influence, you, so am I therefore necessarily as free in my own person. I can not say to you that this or that should or should not be done or said: I can, and do, say that never again shall I be subjected to such torment and humiliation by anyone, by anyone, that is, who remains on close terms with me. I can not put it beyond your power to howl about me in any restaurant or theatre or office or avenue – I can say that I disassociate myself from this conduct, and refuse utterly to permit it in my presence or to condone it in my absence. Do not mistake me, John – in the terms we discussed Tuesday, I am an exceedingly important person, and no longer may I be treated otherwise. It is in large part my own fault that you have come to treat and regard me as you have done – the groveling must be walked on. But what made me grovel so that you might walk is another matter. I failed you in that I was not what a present, an at-hand, parent should be: powerful, successful, god-like – it is not possible to hate rewardfully the one whose condition, when though one's parent, demands sympathy from the most flint-like.

I regret, so deeply and tenderly as must be inconceivable to you, the pressure put upon you this long while by my failure to understand that all of this is caused by your not loving me. I did not know this, it was no more to be thought of than of how would be the pain of my entrails wound round a windlass. I know it now, and understand everything. The proofs were there for all to read without running, but because the central fact was without the reach and grasp of my comprehension, they meant nothing. It was because you did and do not love me that you accuse me of not loving you, John. I did not know this before. Believe me, it would never have been necessary for you to continue to see me and to put pressure on yourself not to burst out, and – oh well, I mean, if I had known, you would have been released from this necessity which must have been a galling burden to you.

Why it is true does not matter: it may be that to love your father, you must hate me, it may be any of many things. There is no fault in it, nor blame – love is where the heart is and no other love lies at no one's demand. Let this be certain to you, then, John – two things I know, that you believe I do not love you and that you have proved to me at last that you do not love me. In these matters lies no censurable import. You will, no doubt, continue to believe as you have of me, it is impossible that a few words could effect what my life has not done. As for the second, with my knowledge of this fact, you are released in every way. I do not expect you to force yourself to any show of interest or attendance– with this pressure relieved, you may in time come to like me enough to be able to want to see or communicate with me occasionally, or it is of course far more likely that with your not-loving open before you your distaste may grow. That is your affair, not mine.

As for me, I love you and hold you dear, and shall do so always – if my love has not faltered in these past years, there is no reason to suppose that it may now, when all strain is gone. Let my love be no burden to you, but rather a strength – it is not every man who is loved purely and with no self-interest and for himself, his essence, not what he does or says or seems. I know you well, John, and love you. . . .

You will be the better for my discard, of this I am certain – you carry too many burdens to carry this intolerable one farther –

Your loving mother
Jill Berryman

That mother and son experienced further difficulties during this period is evidenced by the nature of this next letter to her—written more than a year after his last one—which alludes to another strained encounter between them. In the interim, JB had continued to teach at Princeton and then, early in the summer, for two weeks at the University of Vermont.

[Manchester, Mass.]

Dearest Mother,   Monday night [2 July 1951]

I am sorry, and have been since a day or so after it, for my stupid outbreak – the cause of which I entirely forgot and am certain does not matter. The only thing to be learnt from it is that it is dangerous for us to try to mix public and private occasions when I am as tired as I was then at the end of the lectures or perhaps at all. I repeat: I am very sorry and I hope that you have forgotten whatever I said; I have, and there was probably not a word of my true opinion but simply nerves in it, as false as drunkenness, – which I expect was involved too.

For weeks or a months after that, I did nothing, as tired perhaps as I have ever been, but (unusually) *able* to do nothing. Then there was as over-social period, end of year, and the last fortnight I have been lecturing at the University of Vermont (a so-called School of Modern Critical Studies) on Crane & Hemingway. Blackmur was there and with an utterly charming character new to me named David Daiches we formed a close corporation until the students moved in during the second week and we were glad when the thing ended. I came back Friday. Yesterday we drove to the shore and toured the bay with Jimmy Worden's new outboard motor and he & I swam in the ocean though Eileen & Betty & Don [Mackie] didn't. At Burlington I had no country except last weekend some people drove me south into the mountains and one man & I climbed a bit, heard thrushes, distinguished pines, found fresh deer-tracks, followed trails through fairy ballrooms, lay philosophically on moss, and enjoyed ourselves very much. Today I began work again and wrote five pages. I would very much like to know how you are and how you feel and what has been happening. I think I will be in town Friday & if so will call.

Love,

John

[Written across the top of the letter by Mrs. Berryman: "Received 11 weeks after the event," and below "4/19."

JB and Eileen were vacationing with the Mackies at their summer house in Manchester.

James Worden was, at this time, a Princetonian and friend of the Mackies.]

For the spring semester of 1952, JB was appointed Elliston Professor of Poetry at the University of Cincinnati—his highest honor thus far. During this period,

he and Eileen formed a close friendship with Van Meter and Elizabeth Ames,
and with J. Alister and Elizabeth Cameron.

256 Greendale Avenue
Cincinnati 20, Ohio
Dearest Mother,   10 February 1952

I have been better in health here than I was all fall or winter in Princeton, but it took me a week to get to work, – for one thing, it rained five days, very depressing, like [William Somerset Maugham's] *Rain* – and till today I haven't been able to think of a letter. No social life yet; just as well, though the change from Pr[inceton] was very sharp for us. This week it starts: press interviews Tues, my first lecture Wed, luncheon for me Thurs, a reading Fri night, a dinner Sunday, etc. We have no real impression of the city or people yet. Were downtown yesterday at a handsome bar, the Terrace Garden, where I invite you to a martini if you come out here, and today to the zoo. Damned good zoo. Everybody treats me with exag't'd respect & mostly yet I've met only men over fifty, deans, heads of departments, etc. The English chairman [William Clark], a stalwart nervous Amherst-man, had us to dinner for the first night & gave us sherry; nothing else since. E has met 20 biddies of this posh neighbourhood at a tea and is v funny about it. Her back has been bothering her, is now better. We have the whole ground floor of the famous (in Cin'ti) Resor Mansion, 14′ ceilings, hundreds of chairs, all incapable of human body; the diningroom has 13, you cd drill troops in it. Two maiden Resors upstairs, one blind & in control of her Ethel Barrymore sister. I got a salary advance from the University and we are making out. Thanks for letting me know abut Bob: I wrote [Marshall A.] Best at Viking instantly, in such strong terms that I think if there is anything whatever he will have called Bob; I haven't heard from either, though. I hope you are having luck, darling. Yr notion of setting down my childhood I'd be very glad of; I forget myself utterly. I'll write again soon.

Love,
John

[P.S.] Clipping from *Enquirer* today from E.
[P.P.S.] Today (Mon.) the enormous citrus assignment came, w. yr Fla. note – many thanks! Also a Viking note: Best has sent on mine to the man in charge.

[Cincinnati]

Dearest Mother,   Wednesday [27] February 1952

The woman [Rollie McKenna] who took that picture you like is sending me a flight of others and of course as soon as I decide on one, you'll
have a print. It is better, certainly, than the orangutang-with-anthrax image
the *N.Y. Times* likes to assault me with; and just in time, because it is
constantly used here, where – clowningly enough – not three days pass
without some story about me in one of the three metropolitan dailies. I
even, once, had a press conference and was duly misquoted, but mostly
they make up things about my lectures or announce them or say who
entertained me. The lectures are a sensation. I always suspected I wd be
good at it, and I am; both series are well started, 2 of each given, and the
2nd [Walt] Whitman tomorrow. Audiences run 175–200, in an excellent new blond just-banked room with *very* good acoustics. The people
who brought me out here were stunned by the initial audiences – the
usual public lecture audience being 75 – and when they did not drop off,
they were stunned again. It is tiring; I sleep eleven hours a night, or try
to sleep – your electric blanket is admirable – and have got nothing done
except Shakespearean work. The public social life is exhausting also, but
most of the worst official part is now over (formal luncheons for the faculty to meet me). Entirely unlike Seattle; everyone very agreeable. I like
best so far the aesthetician Van Meter Ames, a charming guy, who was
actually the only person in Cincinnati I had heard of when I came. He
likes the lectures: this is the chief point. He doesn't say so to me; but he
quotes them, he dismisses his seminars to come, and E said he was all
but in tears at the end of the first Whitman yesterday when he & his wife
came up to her; he also, she says, takes notes all the time. The Shakespeare are better than the Princeton ones, and better delivered. Those of
the other series, so far, have been more effective still, because although
original they are necessarily less ambitious and can seem more perfect. I
was more grateful than I can tell you to you for your sentence in this last
letter about my lecturing. I don't deserve so much praise, but the points
you give me too much credit for are exactly the points in which I would
claim *some* credit; and nobody ever before gave me a general analytical
account, though Eileen is an acute particular critic. She is satisfied with
these also, and thinks I have improved. I'm sorry you don't hear these. A
nervous strain (not in the least of the audience, or of my material – as to

these I have got easy or indifferent) of the *fact* remains, but it is infinitely less than when I was giving the [Alfred] Hodder [Fellowship] series [at Princeton, 1950–51], and I don't suffer such reactions. However, it is no joke, twice a week; the difference from academic lecturing is abysmal; and I wouldn't care to do it forever. Tomorrow I will be nearly a third through – 5 of 17. My poetry workshop so-called is child's play, and entertaining: 13, two good, once a week, late Friday.

Today I strolled around Burnet Wood all afternoon, saw a woodchuck, a racoon, and a big barred owl – these in cages though, in a little museum so-called in the Wood – I'd have liked to let them out, a lovely day. Tomorrow Whitman: the last 3 movements of *Song of Myself* as I've analyzed it, everything from Sect 7 on. Friday, class, to the [Elizabeth and Van Meter] Ames's for dinner and a Modern Art exhibit Mrs. A is sponsoring – she is a witty elegant person 43 not much less bright than her husband. Saturday a big party at some other people's for us. Sunday Shakespeare. Etc. I'll write Bob shortly.

Love,

John

Cincinnati

Dearest Mother,   Wednesday, 16 April 1952

You'll be glad to hear that by great good luck I have at last got a Guggenheim [Fellowship]. It comes to about 3000 after taxes and I have some hope that I can arrange to spend part of the year in England, where I need to work. I applied, as I think you know, simply in Shakespearean biography; but [Henry Allen] Moe has kindly – and very exceptionally – changed the statement of project to read "Creative writing and" Shn studies, in order, as he writes, to give me the greatest possible freedom. This looks like compunction for the four previous rejections (two in poetry, one drama, one fiction) and lends some probability to what I once heard: that an enemy of mine on the board has always blocked appointment – now, presumably, snatched off to hell by perceptive fiends. All this is in confidence, except to Bob, whom I wish you'd tell. I still cannot write letters, this is the first in two months I believe.

In fact I am very deprest. It is true that the lectures are nearly over (they have gone well) and that I have done a good deal of Shakespearean work, but nothing else; and this week, when I stayed here while E went to Nashville, has not yet come to anything. The Guggenheim surprised me intensely, and I feel some relief from the violent hatred I have always felt for them, and the money is useful, but I am not at a point in life when there is much pleasure to be had from this sort of thing, nor from the general acclaim I have experienced here. My poem [*Homage to Mistress Bradstreet*] is not going well. – I am glad for your Easter letter wh has just come, & for yr checks, and will gourmandize with Brownies. Every dear wish & blessing,

love,
John

[P.S] I think the award will be announced next Mon. morning or Tues.

[JB's Guggenheim Fellowship was for the 1952–53 academic year.

Henry Allen Moe was the dean of U.S. foundations and the head of the John Simon Guggenheim Memorial Foundation for thirty-seven years.]

[Cincinnati]

Dearest Mother,   Saturday [May 1952]

I am very very glad about your job, and was, and would have written instantly to say so but that you were in Florida and we had no address (you ought to give us that) – in fact I thought of wiring – but again there was the address. I hope you will be infinitely better in every way for it, though you have sounded wonderful anyway.

Worn out, but nearly through. A trip to Detroit to read my stuff at Wayne, and then an extra public lecture here (making 18) on Eliot, pretty well sank me. I have not got much left to do: one more class (and the kids are clamouring for an extra one, which I'll probably give in to), one address (an elaborate paper on the *Tempest*, not yet finished) to a serious small men's club, a few dinners, 400 farewell parties, and back to Princeton on June 1st, where there will be 400 welcome parties. The president [Raymond Walters] came to the evening Eliot and sent me a letter of congratulation next day; very posh stationery he has. I am in no excellent frame of mind but I have done this job properly.

I have got a very serious favour to ask. I don't like to ask it, but I have to. I have been in love for several months with a young woman here. There is no way for me to write to her, and after I leave we cannot communicate at all unless you are willing to receive letters from her and keep them for me. Will you? If so, throw some affirmative expression inconspicuously into the final sentence of your next letter. What the end of all this will be I can't see yet. It has made life hell. However I can *feel* the possibility of getting to work again. The Colonial poem is stalled but I lately got an interesting short piece started of which I can really see the end with a few days free, & I take heart.

Dear love,
John

Princeton, N.J.
Darling,   [2 November 1952]

I've tried repeatedly for a week to reach you on the 'phone, sometimes the hotel gave me other numbers and when I called them you'd gone, then they said you were away for "two months" etc etc. Immediately after the anniversary business I had to get straight to hard work again but it's not for want of trying that I'm only now thanking you with all my heart for the show tickets (we thought of calling you after the theatre but decided it was too late) and for the stand, which came in the middle of the week. When I unwrapped it, I felt sure it would not do for the folio [a facsimile of Shakespeare's First Folio], but to my astonishment when I got it up here (to the studio) I found it exactly *does*. I am *delighted* with it. The difference it will make I can't describe to you. For years I have been holding that monstrous book on my stomach for hours at a time – it can make you ill, slowly. Now I've only to sit in front of it and read harmlessly; and for reference it is just at my left elbow. Of all the working gifts you've made me it is certainly the most extraordinary. *Mille fois merci.*

We had a v.g. Armenian dinner, enjoyed the show, went to *The Blue Angel* and enjoyed that, then on Saturday saw *Limelight*, which is one of the most extraordinary artworks of this period, and came back to Princeton remarkably broke & tired, but really we had a thoroughly good time – at a lucky moment for E, who had been deprest, and I had been working so hard that the respite was necessary. My work has been going too well to describe yet. I am suddenly deep into a new unpredicted book on Shakespeare that probably Viking will publish in the spring. Thursday I go to Washington for a few days at the Folger. Soon after I get back you must come down here for a dinner & to see the folio-stand & my altogether renovated studio, and I'll tell you the nature of my discovery.

Love,
John

[JB had begun work on a critical study of Shakespeare, which he had contracted with Viking to publish, and continued to labor on *Homage to Mistress Bradstreet.*]

                                                         [Princeton, N.J.]
Mother   [Early February 1953]
    I have always failed; but I am not failing now. I have, to read to you, next week, the induction (28 11.) & the first section (158 11.) & a death-grip on the second. I am folding out

                                                                   love,
                                                                   John

[P.S.] The Colonial Poem

Writing relentlessly while continuing to teach, JB completed Homage to Mistress Bradstreet *in March of 1953. Soon thereafter he suffered a physical collapse.*

                                                          Princeton, N.J.
Dearest Mother,   Sunday 12 April [1953]
    Your caution was a good one, & I thank you for it, but I don't now need it and earlier I doubt I could have attended. Until Friday the doctors here declined to begin my shots, on the score of exhaustion, and Tues & Wed were certainly again dreadful; but I saw nobody all week and *Thursday* I really began to improve: I was less constantly ill, less feeble, and calmer, not sullen, not wild. I have stopt drinking, & can eat. I am still very uncertain and tired, face with distaste the indispensable minimum of preparation for going off, and resentment can throttle me in a moment at any fancied stupidity or imposition; but the movement downward seems to have stopped. I can even bear conversation.
    Where the rage comes from I don't altogether understand, though I know a good deal about it and I think it may be an unavoidable concomitant of a certain kind of intolerably painful, exalted creation. Any artist not a saint, that is, who loves humanity as much, while torturing himself as much, as I did was during parts of the composition of the poem, with that intensity over a protracted time, may be bound to take it out on humanity (any specimens that are unlucky enough to be by) afterward.
    My right arm still trembles continually, that is the worst thing.

Here is a stanza-sheet, which please take care of, showing well enough out of what trash beauty emerges, and nine even of these 20 lines had been already separately composed years before. Do any passages strike you as brainless, strained, or lax? I wd be glad to know Bob's opinion too.

Love

John

[P.S.] It is exactly 4 weeks since I finisht. Another month shd see my imagination well: I hope.

[Princeton, N.J.]

[No salutation]   Sunday [12 April 1953]

Ten minutes after I sealed the letter to you, my nerves jumping, I came on this in Keats:

> The innumerable compositions and decompositions which take place between the intellect and its thousand materials before it arrives at that trembling delicate and snail-like [snail-horn] perception of Beauty.

> [John Keats, "To B. R. Haydon, 8 April 1818," *The Letters of John Keats.*]

John

On April 28, 1953, the Berrymans sailed to Europe. Having stopped briefly in Paris, they drove with J. Alister and Elizabeth Cameron, two of their Cincinnati friends, to Provence, the Côte d'Azur, and on to Florence, and then to Rome where they would stay for several weeks.

Nice

[No salutation]   18 May 1953

I'll write from Rome – I did not like either the boat or Paris and haven't felt like writing – on the drive south my spirits rose – Provence was wonderful, and St Tropez where we stayed the last two nights – tonight we'll be at Rapallo – lunch today we had with us & ate on the beach at Juan-les-Pins after perhaps the most delicious swim I ever had – a blazing day, the blue sea on our right all the way. I hope you & Bob & Liza are well – let me hear at Rome – Love

John

Rome

Dearest Mother   3 June 1953

In the end I decided I had better not leave the ms. of the Bradstreet poem w. you because I found, glancing through as I assembled it, so much other verse-material mixed in; I will have to go over it carefully myself, and then you can see it. I put it in a bundle, with other bundles, in the vault of my bank (Princeton, First National) with instructions on them as to Disposal in the event of my death: two are to be destroyed unopened, the others (I have told Eileen, and had better tell you) may be destroyed unopened if she likes – or you like, shd something happen to both of us – *or* deposited in the Princeton library, not to be opened for a term of years, 50 yrs say, at the end of which time if anyone is interested they may be examined, the copyright being reserved to my heirs if any, or Bob's, or Marie's, in that order.

I have now been here a week, doing v. little, and am I hope getting over travel-fatigue and aesthetic indigestion. But the chief purpose of my movement has insensibly accomplisht itself; I have had scarcely a thought since I left the United States, and feel free of the poem (things [J. Alister] Cameron tells me – told me: he's in Greece – that as lately as St. Tropez I said some of it to a baker at 5 a.m.). I have written nothing & read nothing – except at sea a work on the Aztecs – until yesterday I sat down to [Jacob] Burckhardt. Not that this vacancy can continue: I need money: I have mss. with me and must set about them. You see, however, that I can't yet even write a letter.

5 June

Proofs of the poem came from *Partisan* this morning. Very clean. How long the thing is.

I also began work today: an editorial job on the book of a Princeton friend here, the art historian Geo. Rowley, which will take a fortnight & bring $200 or so, much needed.

Yesterday an astonishing thing happened. It was Corpus Christi and we'd tried to get tribune seats in St. Peter's, for the procession, through the head of the Irish legation, the poet Denis Devlin, who has been uniformly kind. Well, he was told (he's anti-clerical, by the way) there wd be no tribunes & no procession except of canons. But we went to see the church anyway, which we'd seen only at night, and were among the last of thousands to enter, at eleven. There was a voice, and *applause*. I rank as a tall man in Italy and saw, half a mile off against a scarlet cloth, a small figure in white flanked by one in red & one in black. More mysterious applause. At last, men climbing up pillars, children held high to see, people w. backs turning looking in upheld mirrors, slowly the Pope came towards us borne in his chair between aisle-barriers. He waved his palms slowly towards himself, leaning slowly from side to side down over the chair-arms – so Italians wave – while the part of the throng near him shouted. It was all alarmingly informal. A few feet from us he halted to ask who were a contingent of little girls in uniform. Then, a dozen feet off, at the end of the aisle before it turned out of the nave, the chair was swung to face the altar, he rose and solemnly blessed all parts of the congregation. During the few yards out, then, he blessed girls' coifs handed up to him – his outstretched arm was still visible as the chair disappeared. Earlier, we had heard at dinner, he had given his handkerchief down to a man. A very white, kind, beautiful figure. Eileen wept, and I was altogether astonished.

I am tired and must stop. I expect E has described the drive down – I will say something about it when I write soon again. The packet of mail has not come yet: what date, again, did you send it? No, please don't send on magazines, catalogues, etc – but whatever looks like *money*-mail (as from universities etc) please send airmail. Love to Bob & Liza, and always to you

John

[The book by Jacob Burckhardt, the Swiss historian of art and culture, is probably his *The Civilization of the Renaissance in Italy*.

The *Partisan Review* had agreed to publish *Homage to Mistress Bradstreet* in its entirety.

The editorial work JB did for George Rowley was for a book he had written on piazza space that was never published.

The poet Denis Devlin was the Irish minister to Italy.]

Rome
Dearest Mother   25 June 1953

The package and the two packets of mail came. Many thanks. Perhaps you had better send nothing else here, as I think we will leave for London in about ten days – I would like to go even sooner, to see the Oxford production of *Troilus and Cressida* in Paris which closes July

1st – but our plans are quite uncertain – I will talk with E. when she comes back from Naples tomorrow and add a postscript to this. I finisht the editing job and was paid, but still we are very low, and we have no money left in Princeton, and I have no job. We are trying to get on a reduced-rate flight from London to N.Y., Aug. 16th.

E's back was troubling her after so much sightseeing or a defective bed here, so she went south 3 days ago for sun & rest – the Oateses [Whitney J. and Virginia] and Ed[ward] Cone [the composer] being there to look after her if she needed it. I stayed and have begun work again. It looks as if I will not see much of Rome; at first I was too tired, then while working w. [George] Rowley I saw v. little, and since beginning my òwn work I have seen nothing. I have developed a sense of the city however & like it. People have given parties for us and driven us about and been agreeable. I have stopt drinking.

Here are some bills for Shelby, the 1 or 2 lire being rare now since they are worth ⅙ and ⅓ of a cent, respectively. The coins we'll bring. – We met [Milton] Gendel at a party a painter gave for me and have seen him again. We like him. He has offered to get me a discount on a type-writer, which I wish to God I cd take up but I haven't the money. – Your Manchester trip sounds delightful. I wish you could be out of the city more.

28 June 1953

[P.S.] I have several favours to ask. We have got reservations for the 16 Aug. flight but our French Line Passage can't be exchanged in Europe – only there.

1) Will call you Circle 7–7225 (The Cooperative Bureau for Teachers, 1776 Busay) and find out *what* airline their special flight London–NY, Aug. 16th, is on.

2) Will you call the French Line (610 Fifth Ave) and see if they will "endorse" the enclosed passage over to that airline? If they will, it will be for the full amount. If not, it will be – the refund – about 10% less (the agent's fee off).

3) Will you take this passage contract, with the enclosed authoriza-tion, to the French line and a) cancel Eileen's & my passage (space) on the Flandre, Oct 2nd; b) get either the endorsement (but I guess you will have to call the Cooperative Bureau again to see if this is acceptable) or the cash refund.

4) Can you lend me $60 or $80 (whatever is needed to make up the refund to the $440 needed for the flight) till I get back? I am unspeakably short here and can't spare any. Unless England is *very* cheap I don't see how we're to get thro' the 6 wks anyway. If you can't lend it without sacrifice, just cable me so at once.

5) If you can lend it, will you then send $440 for me to the Cooperative Bureau, and let me know by air to Amer. Express, London.

I'm very sorry to put all this on you. It ought to be done at once, too. We will be here a week more; then London.

Love,

John

[Whitney Jennings Oates was then West Professor of Classics at Princeton. Milton Gendel is an art consultant and an old friend of Robert Jefferson's.]

London

Dearest Mother   16 July 1953

E. is better but will be in hospital for abt 3 weeks. The doctors here think it was the May car-trip from Paris to Rome that did it, and the specialist takes a serious view because it is the *other* leg that is now affected by the disc-degeneration. She flew fr. Rome well enough, stayed two days in bed in Paris, and bore the trip here well, but next day (Sun.) was in great pain – we got in a general practitioner Mrs. [Hedli] MacNeice knows, who gave her an opiate & then after 48 hrs. hospitalized her, where she is far more comfortable than she was here at the MacNeices'. The pain is vanishing and the specialist thinks recovery has begun well. At first she was anxious to return but he objects to her moving and now she is content to wait. She is in a room by herself with the BBC to help. The worst of her depression over being incapacitated in London I hope is passing. She has seen Europe a great deal – even here she met many people, for there was a vast party the night we arrived – and I hope she may gain strength fast now she is absolutely flat & in good hands. I am a poor nurse tho' I did my best. Louis & Hedli M[acNeice] have been very kind.

I am intensely sorry for the manifold inconvenience & trouble & distraction you have been to over this trip, and intensely grateful. I don't know how we shd have got on else; and I shd certainly now be in despair, instead of merely very gloomy, but for your wonderful loan-offer which

reached me in Paris, and which I have to accept with all my thanks.
What a chaos our affairs are in, you see. Unfortunately this is not unusual.
In point of dreadful fact, except for the detail that I have not yet got a job
for this fall, we are in some ways even *better* off than usual, hard as this
will be for you to believe. Living is a mystery to me. . . .

The BBC want me to do some programmes for them – a personal
travel talk here, and some recording of poems, then talks on Whitman &
Crane. Of course I am agreeing. Whether *The Times* are printing the
Bradstreet poem I don't yet know. William Empson had read the other
evening my long Shakespeare piece in the *Hudson [Review]*, which I've
not seen, and was by turns aggressive & complimentary about it. I gave
the Princess [Marguerite Caetani] a long story for *Botteghe Oscure* and
have not heard about this either.

I have seen Shakespeare's two earliest histories very well done at the
Old Vic, and this is all the news I have of this dreary time. I'll write again
in 3 or 4 days.

Love,
John

[P.S.] The slacks are delightful, dear – thanks

["Shakespeare at Thirty," based on one of the Elliston lectures JB had given
at the University of Cincinatti, was published in the summer 1953 issue of the
Hudson Review.

JB had given the American-born Princess Marguerite Caetani, founder of
the international literary magazine *Botteghe Oscure*, one of his old stories, in
hopes of her patronage, but to no avail.]

On their return from Europe in August 1953, Eileen informed JB she was
leaving him. To quote Eileen Simpson: "In Recovery *he gives as my reasons 'his*
drinking and bad sex.' Certainly both had made life intolerable off and on during
the second half of our marriage. But it was more his need to live in turbulence—
if it wasn't drinking and women, it was the way he worked on Lear, Crane *and*
Bradstreet—*that finally forced me to make my decision."* [Poets in Their Youth]

With Eileen remaining in Princeton, JB, jobless once more, went to New
York where he lived briefly with his mother in her apartment—and looked for-
ward to the publication of Homage to Mistress Bradstreet, *which appeared in the*
September-October 1953 issue of Partisan Review. *During this time JB, with*
Robert Lowell's help, secured a position—teaching creative writing—at the Uni-
versity of Iowa's Writers' Workshop beginning the following spring semester. By
the beginning of November, JB left Mrs. Berryman's apartment and moved into

the Chelsea Hotel where he renewed his acquaintance, from his Cambridge
days, with Dylan Thomas. After an excess of alcohol and prescription drugs,
Thomas lapsed into a coma there on November 4. He was transferred to St.
Vincent's Hospital where, at 39, he died five days later.

Hotel Chelsea
[New York]
Thanksgiving Day [1953]

Dearest Mother,

I want to tell you how utterly grateful I am to you for all your help to me this year, and especially this fall. I don't know how I cd have got through else, and I certainly cd not have got through comparatively so little damaged. – I feel as you do, too, that it is an extraordinary fact about the development of what was for years a very difficult relation that we have got on so well and are able to love each other with so little reserve.

with love
John

[P.S.] This snapshot is only a loan, but I thought you might like to keep it for a while.

'phone is 3865
606 S. Johnson, Iowa City
Thursday evening [4 February 1954?]

Dearest Mother,

Thank heaven the pneumonia is overset – I wd have been jumping with anxiety if I'd known – you were very considerate not to let me know, though I think you probably ought to have done. I am sorry for the strain of it, but in one way the enforced rest will certainly do you good too. You will have to be careful another week or so.

I haven't written before because of an accident. I got here a week ago tonight, at 6 p.m., tired enough, spent a pleasant evening w. my Princeton friends Stow & Dorothy Persons, came back & unpacked, and, over-estimating my recollection of the dark hall, in returning from the bathroom, pitcht down a flight of bannisterless stairs & thro' a half-glass door, landing surrounded by shattered panes very glad to be alive. Mr. & Mrs. Bristol [JB's landlords] appeared & got me upstairs, where nothing appeared to be wrong except superficial cuts & bruises, and I went to bed. A third sleepless night, that was – in the morning my teeth were still chattering. I felt pretty sure my left wrist was broken – as indeed it was, and my

ankles very bad tho' neither fractured – I was hospitalized for shock &
exhaustion, and very well treated. I was *extremely* lucky to get off so light,
and luckily my workshop & seminar don't meet till next week, because
the slight duties I had the last 3 days left me so tired I spent the whole of
today in bed. The hospital rest did me a great deal of good. But my ankles
are still grossly swollen & sore, and my arm of course almost useless
though the fingers are free of the cast & I use them a little. Cast: another
fortnight.

Of course there is nothing to worry about. It's odd that my landlady
broke *her* left wrist on the same stair a year ago.

The apartment is fine, weather bright & mild, everyone v. pleasant,
& so on. A good library. I am studying Hebrew: my text has a "Conversational Guide" at the back (really, front) of which item 50 is "I shall
become your wife". A party is being given for me tomorrow. I'll write
again as soon as I get easier. I'm glad about the account, though sorry it
wasn't just what you wanted.

שָׁלוֹם = Goodbye

Love,

John

606 S. Johnson, Iowa City

Dearest Mother   Sunday [28 February 1954]

I am seriously to blame, and feel it, for not having let you hear much
sooner than I did & for not writing since. I'm very sorry for your worry.
The accident, after my illness (which of course has raged ever since,
uncheckt) & the trip, besides the strain in such shape of meeting all the
new people one has to on this sort of thing and setting up my courses (at
wh. I've workt v. hard, & I'm teaching beautifully) has not left me much
energy even for Hebrew, wh. I took up partly because I *had* to have
something of my own to do. Wed. was the first day in many weeks I felt
half-way decent, and I spent six hours on Hebrew, by which time I was
also, unhappily & w. intense reluctance, deep into sketches for a new
poem: those 3 days I drafted 60 lines and by Friday night I was desperate.
This weekend I rested, & feel better. They took the cast off yesterday –
arm v. queasy; what was torn in my foot is knitting, but when it buckles,
the town still spins. I am glad to have yr advice abt the wrist. The poem

is abt the deaths of poets & their crazinesses when living and will not be long and ought to be done in a month or so and I hope will be stunning. It begins in Iowa City, part of it is in Hebrew, and it ends (so far) in the Pleiades – with the best passage I ever wrote.

I don't *like* the people here much but have nothing against them. Several of my students are good enough to be worth the trouble. The best is a Princeton girl [Anita Maximilian Phillips] I've known socially there for years without ever knowing she wrote. (You understand that one reason for my busy-ness so far is that every proto-poet I have (20) has given me his collected poetical works as a first assignment.) Studying back over her stuff, I think Cal's admiration for it (she came here to study w. him) has been crucial to her. With luck & health – sick girl – she is going to be first-class. High time some lady was. Miss [Elizabeth] Bishop is my age.

Cal arrived in Rapallo, flying from Cincinnati, an hour after his mother died in the clinic there; so [Robert] Fitzgerald writes me fr. Florence, tho' of course I had heard earlier, falsely, fr. Cincinnati, that she had recovered from the stroke. She was travelling alone. Now he is all alone.

You take care of yourself.

Love,
John

[P.S.] Towels & p. cases came; all thanks. I'll describe my seminar next time: I finally understand Whitman & love him more than ever.
[P.P.S.] We must go see "Roman Holiday" together. I wd love to see it but never wisht to go alone.

[The new poem JB refers to in this letter and the next one was never completed.]

606 S. Johnson, Iowa City

Dearest Mother,   Friday 9 April [1954]

The title of my poem is now changed to "Testament" from "In Here", and it is not getting anywhere. I think if I were well for 3 wks I cd write it, though probably I am wrong abt that. Mind you there is nothing wrong w me, or nothing new. It all just goes on & gets worse. Habit can work against you. But you see I am typing; I began day before yesterday, and it's v easy, and I hope for a good deal from it, since I can now clear off some of the fifty (50) letters I owe. It is next weekend I go to Grinnell College, betw here & Des Moines, to read, & to judge an undergraduate poetry contest, and I mean to treat that & Easter as a watershed, – after which I will be different.

A letter from Bob, wh I was v glad to get today, says you are still rather listless and hope to go to Florida. I hope you will.

Oddly it's not been cold here at all. But there is no Spring either. I am tempted to go to Cincinnati, where there is a Spring, to stay a long weekend w Lowell as he wants, but until I am in better shape I can't go anywhere; anyway I've not the money. He & his wife [Elizabeth Hardwick, whom Lowell had married in 1949] are just separated. She is an old friend of mine too and I'm sorry.

I understand how you feel abt the *Britannica*, because I miss mine like fire in the odd hours when I am reading or working. [John Percival] Postgate's article on "Textual Criticism" will explain to you the sort of thing I was doing w *Lear* and have been doing w emendation ever since. The best translation of Herodotus is by [George] Rawlinson, and there's a one-vol. ed. easy to come by, publ'd perhaps by Tudor. Of Plutarch, hm: the great translation is [Thomas] North's (Eliz'n) which Shakespeare used, but you might like better the 19th c. translation by [Arthur Hugh] Clough (a good poet, friend of Arnold's) which is not antiquated in diction & syntax, and also easy to get, in fact I think there is a one-vol. Mod. Libr. Giant edition. But North is richer & better, though, and unless you have Clough and like him by the time I come back (early June) I'll bring up from Princeton North's five volumes (of six) for you to use. I pickt them up at intervals, odd; the set is expensive. Princeton is making us give up the apartment, and all my books will have to be stored. For that matter, why don't you wait for my Herodotus too? But if you want to read them now, go to it. One of the great points of spiritual life is to read books *when you want to*. Perhaps Eileen wd post them to you at once: tell her they are behind my red leather chair. God knows when I will ever sit in it again. One or two Plutarch vol's are up in my studio, but no matter. The lives are self-sufficient. The other day one of the two men I like best here, Tom Mabry, an old friend of Tate's – a dignified, handsome, self-doubtful Southerner (house in Stockbridge, Mass.) – money out of sight – wife & daughters, years at Museum of Mod. Art. Prizes now for stories; 50 maybe – , was asking me why I was reading Plato through again and said he'd always meant to read Plutarch through. I am delighted that you want to read Plutarch through. I am delighted that you want to read Herodotus and Plutarch. They make most of the authors either ours or transmitted to us look ephemeral & insubstantial.

Aside from anything: I have a Japanese student doing a master's thesis on Japanese poetry from which I have learnt a great deal. I'll show you my notes on it when I get back. Buson's death-poem is this:

Shira-ume ni	Meaning: Things have become like this:
Akuru yo bakari to	There are only such nights (henceforth) (for
Nari ni keri	me) as open from (=end with) the white
	plum-flowers (outside my window). (Final
	weeks, or days precisely, of his life.)

The subject is never exprest in Japanese poetry. And correctively "Maturity is the highest virtue . . is to be obtained by self-effacement." Here is one term: *kokoro-no-furusato*, meaning the native place of the mind (or place) where a soul shd come and be settled finally. I must tell you one other poem, by the greatest master of *waka*, Kakinomoto-no-Hitomaro:

Ashibikino	Now, I'm going to sleep alone a night as long
Yamadori no o no	as the undulating pheasant-tail.
Shidario no	
Naganagashi yo o	
Hitori-kamo nem	

Waka is more lyrical than *haiku* (as Buson); centuries earlier. I am interested in the whole endeavour but particularly this: " 'Ma' is a necessary pause, or a substantial vacancy. How to use '*ma*' effectively is the most important factor in Japanese art. To create reality, Japanese art does not resort to symbols but to '*ma*' ". An analogy to this wd be the notion of imposing a silence *in which* what one has to say can be heard – as, in Buson's poem, the meaningless, emotional particles (called *Joshi*) govern the mood and time of what is revealed. I am thinking of making "Testament" from "In Here" the longest Japanese poem in existence – or the longest since a very few *renga*, or chain-poems, 800 yrs ago.

I know what loneliness is, darling. Strange lives we lead. I have been suffering lately from terrible waking-nightmares and fear of death (a good German wd: *Todesangst*) but my real present opinion is that life is, all, transformation. We must not be glad, or sorry, to be part of it; but we can't help being. And *there* there was some unkindness, somewhere? somewhere? And pity, and kindness.

I saw that beautiful touching woman Miss [Audrey] Hepburn in her Roman film *[Roman Holiday]* several weeks ago – it was here, and after a peculiarly tedious cocktail party in a handsome old house given by the (semi-Shakespearean) head of the English Dept [Baldwin Maxwell] there seemed nothing else for me to do. [Gregory] Peck is a stick and I thought the film poorly written but she is magical. Tell me something detailed abt her *Ondine* performance. It's many years since I saw a new actress. She is very ill, a newspaper columnist informs me. Everybody pays. I wish she wd do a film w Chaplin or I cd write a play for her. Do you remember the low boat-fountain [Pietro Bernini's *Fontana della Barcaccia*] in front of the very high steps, church at top, into wh they come after a shop-window sequence: that's the Piazza di Spagna: E & I stayed at the bottom of the short street striking off down right of the church. The famous English teashop [Babington's Tea Rooms] is just off left there, Piazza del Popolo down the street left, Amer Express right, and so on.

I like clippings from you and I can hardly wait to see [Jacques] Maritain's *[The Living Thoughts of] St. Paul*. May things go on running well w yr new client. I'll tell you next time abt my Workshop & Seminar.

Love,
John

[P.S.] Your tea(s) illuminate my existence

606 South Johnson, Iowa City
Dearest Mother,   Thursday [15 April 1954]
Happy Easter. I'm delighted that you are in Florida, and very pleased about the car. I hope you had my long letter before you left.

The ties charm me; thank you exceedingly. I do sometimes get bored with the ones I have but I don't once a year buy myself one: Eileen used occasionally to insist on my getting one, but now that has stopt I think the last acquisitions were the fine set, which I still wear on state occasions, made from Far Eastern Fabrics, [Inc.]. The one of Persian design, in particular, I never wear to a party but that somebody admires it verbally. The darker of these two is stunning and I will wear it at the various functions I have to attend at Grinnell [College], where I go tonight.

The University insisted on taking some pictures of me, of which one turned out, though it has no artistic quality, to be a better likeness, I think, than any of those in print, so I send you one. In the others I look either comical or haggard. The other day I was trying to look up [Conrad] Aiken's British address in the new American *Who's Who* and lookt over their article on me: it contains about six errors. Daddy's name I remember is given as "John Allen Smith" – so much for the attempted elegance, last century, of that "y". And you appear as "Martha Little B." – I suppose for Berryman. Indeed, in these respects it is more like an assault than an article.

I hope you are resting and will enjoy yourself thoroughly.

Dearest love,
John

[Mrs. Berryman was on vacation at Casa Burr in Titusville, Florida. She had bought a red 1951 Ford convertible, later to be known in the family as "Rudolph."]

606 S. Johnson, Iowa City
Sunday 9 May 1954

Dearest Mother,

Welcome back (as you will be tomorrow): it is good to think of you rested and tanned, and I know you are pleased abt the ten pounds. I am unusually well myself today, though I have been very bad, and I am absolutely delighted with the First Book of [Robert] Fitzgerald's translation of the *Odyssey* which Pound has sent on to me: I urged Robert years ago, before we even met, to do it, and it is wonderful to see how he is going. This is the first pleasure I have had in a long time except for Ransom's visit here to lecture. Lowell is offside again, has had shock, and will be all right they think but will be in hospital there in Cincinnati and then in New York a long time. This news did me no good.

The river-names are marvellous. I've enjoyed all your accounts. Yes I'd love to drive down some time. If I keep up this migratory life I am going to have to buy a car myself and take up driving again.

I don't know what the hell I am going to do abt Eileen or anything else. I am not really looking forward to coming East again, although I detest Iowa City. I'll be back in the first week of June, but what day I don't know because I may go by Cincinnati. (The Rorschach Eileen once did of Cal turned out to be very useful, by the way – you can't test a man in his present state.) Yes I'd like my old room back, if the Chelsea can do it. I go to Cambridge abt July 1st; having meanwhile packt everything in Princeton – in regard to which thanks for your offer and we'll see.

Several v funny things happened, as usual, at Grinnell, of which you'll hear in due course; they're too long for paper. My introduction of Ransom here was short & excellent, I'll tell you it too.

I can't manage the poem yet, though it proliferates.

I have been considering yr suggestion abt the Mayo Clinic. But I was checkt thoroughly just a few months ago. There is nothing wrong w me except a few obvious, stubborn things, and an atrocious state of mind; which I must just try to administrate out of existence, seriatim.

Yes I'll have the *Who's Who [in America]* blunders corrected in the next issue. It hadn't occurred to me – errors abt one being so much a part of life, and very seldom eradicable.

Today is that commercial festival called Mother's Day, which is *not* why I am writing to you and in spite of which I love you v much. But I wish I had been able to get for you by now from England the thing I once spoke of; I haven't been able to because I haven't been able to pay my Blackwell account. I have been clearing up bank loans but precious little else has altered. My Harvard salary will be clearer, and also larger.

I wish this letter were more cheerful. I think very likely my next one will be.

Dearest love,
John

[P.S.] A New Hampshire weekend wd be delightful if my labours allow it, as they ought.

606 S. Johnson, Iowa City
Dearest Mother,   Sunday [30 May 1954]

Forgive a note, I am rushed w graduate papers & other end-of-term matters and a mass of long-overdue correspondence which must absolutely be cleared before I leave.

I'll be in New York either June 2nd or June 3rd, depending on whether I fly or go by train, and that will depend on how I feel then. E is moving on the 5th and I'll have to spend the 4th helping her and packing my own stuff for storage. So I'll be in Princeton very little, and thanks very much for offering to put me up but I'll be working on Shakespeare in New York and had better have my old room [at the Chelsea Hotel] for June, if they can give it to me. This wipes out both Chicago and Cincinnati, where I meant to spend a few days, but it can't be helpt; I have a final seminar on the evening of the 1st.

It is hot here. I *finally* had the denim slacks altered, after carrying them all over Europe & America unwearable, and they are a great help. I will be glad to see that dacron suit, or whatever it is, that I left with you. The slacks had not to be so much altered as they wd have had: I thought I had gained weight and I find I weigh 155, an all-time high – not of course from eating, since I seldom eat, but from the damned 4% ale which is all that Iowa taverns serve. You must see [Edmund] Wilson's magnificent piece in last week's *New Yorker* on *Genesis* ["On First Reading *Genesis*"]. Lowell is going to be all right.

Love,
John

Following a brief stay in New York, at the Chelsea Hotel, JB returned to Harvard, where he taught courses on Shakespeare and writing fiction during summer school (July 6–August 25).

7 Ware St, Cambridge [Mass.]

Dearest Mother,   Wednesday afternoon [7 July 1954?]

Congratulations, darling, and a happy birthday. You are the most amazing woman in the world.

Your real gift will be here next month from England, but I have been so fantastically busy in this ratrace so far that I've not been able to get into Boston to get you a copy of [John] Selden's *Table Talk* (none of the Cambridge shops have one) as I hoped to do either yesterday or today: maybe I can tomorrow. The intolerable Convocation tonight, costing time I need for my *Richard III* lecture, seems to be the final initial demand. I have twenty stories to read by Friday too. They put me at the head table at the luncheon yesterday but I did not have to make a speech. My Shakespeare room is a banked lecture hall like an operating theatre only with two pianos down below in front of me; pity I don't play. My afternoon room is air-conditioned. I am sleeping well and the apt so far is very cool.

Forgive short note, I'm rushed.

You ought to feel very proud of yourself, frankly, on your birthday. I am proud of you. I also think you in many ways staggeringly fortunate. Most people only get one life; you have had about six already, and more are plainly coming. Blessings and my devoted love,

John

[P.S.] I hope the trip down was all well. I can't thank you enough for all yr help.

In September JB returned to Iowa City. Shortly after the beginning of the fall semester, on September 29, occurred what he described to Eileen Simpson as the "Iowa debacle." After a bitter quarrel at a campus bar, he returned late, intoxicated, to the house in which he had rented an apartment and, having mislaid his keys, awakened the landlord. A bitter exchange ensued and the landlord's wife called the police. JB was jailed for intoxication, profanity and disturbing the peace. The incident made news in Iowa and the university administration considered it an embarrassment. Following all day meetings with university officials on October 1, JB was dismissed from his position, placing his hard-won academic reputation in jeopardy.

PART FIVE

Minneapolis
1954 - 1959

*S*OON AFTER the low point of his dismissal from the University of Iowa, JB, in desperation, called Allen Tate who, since their meeting in 1938, had remained something of a father figure to him. Tate was then teaching at the University of Minnesota and, at his urging, JB flew to Minneapolis on October 3. Tate picked him up at the airport and brought him home with him. Within a few days the older poet helped JB find an apartment and, through Ralph Ross of the university's Humanities Program, arranged a teaching position for him beginning winter quarter.

Lecturing on the history of western civilization, as he was now called upon to do, he found both extremely stimulating and demanding, and he later claimed to have learned more in teaching these courses than he had at Cambridge or Columbia. Such classes also provided JB with the scope for pursuing his abiding interest in religious and theological studies. So passionate were many of his lectures on these and other topics in the courses that, as he once remarked, Catholics became Lutherans in them and Lutherans became Catholics.

Coincidentally, Minnesota was the state in which JB's father had been born and, being there, set JB to thinking more about John Allyn's family and early life, his marriage to Mrs. Berryman, and the events leading up to his suicide in 1926. JB also embarked upon a period of intensive dream analysis while, at the same time, beginning to write a new type of poem which would continue to obsess him for the next dozen years. For the Dream Songs, as they came to be known, he invented a fresh stanza form, a diction, a syntax, a relation between *characters (or between different aspects of the same character) and an entire realm of consciousness distinctively his own. Eventually, he could write Mrs. Berryman: "I have a style now pared straight to the bone and can make the reader's nerves jump by moving my little finger."*

Although the Dream Songs would not begin to appear for another five years, during the interim Homage to Mistress Bradstreet was finally published in book form in 1956, winning him a Rockefeller Fellowship in Poetry from Partisan Review and the University of Chicago's Harriet Monroe Poetry Prize. JB also put together a small collection of poems, His Thought Made Pockets & The Plane Buckt (1958), and with his Minnesota colleagues Ralph Ross and Allen Tate worked on essays for an anthology, The Arts of Reading, which was not, however, published until 1960.

Divorced from Eileen in December 1956, he soon thereafter married a bright young graduate student, Elizabeth Ann Levine (called Ann), with whom he had a son, Paul, in 1957. Saul Bellow had come to teach in the University of Minnesota's Humanities Program in the spring of 1956. Here the two of them shared an office and solidified a friendship they had begun at Princeton in 1953. The university awarded JB tenure in 1957, and that same year he visited Japan and then spent two months lecturing in India under the auspices of the U.S. Department of State. In March of 1959, after a troubled two years, JB and Ann were divorced.

For mother and son, separated by half a continent and again forced into a more exclusively epistolary relationship, the period began as one of comparative amity. Still, as early as November 30, 1954, Mrs. Berryman was once again imploring JB to write more often. It is also clear, from many of their exchanges, that when they did see one another, the meetings were becoming increasingly more harrowing for both of them. Luckily, most of Mrs. Berryman's letters after 1954 have survived; a selection of some of the more revealing ones are included in the two remaining sections.

2509 Humboldt Av. S.
Minneapolis 5, Minn.

Dearest Mother,   7 October [1954]

You see I am here, and not there, after adventures too complicated to describe twice in one day: I just wrote a summary account to Eileen, asking her to show you the letter. The upshot is that Iowa and I parted company and I am now living in this extremely agreeable city, where I'll be giving Dante and a Modern seminar in the Humanities division of the Univ. of Minnesota this winter. At present I am just about to get writing.

I only moved yesterday into this apartment, which is a good one, and will be here for at least six weeks. Do please have my mail sent on. I'm sorry not to have written to you from Iowa City but I spent all my time there looking for a possible apartment and did not get a single letter done. . . .

It is curious to be in my father's state. I hope to get out to Stillwater: what were the family names you know of?

Cold, it's cold here suddenly, after the midsummer heat of Iowa last week, and I weirdly seem not to have brought any gloves, though I've a grey pair, black mittens, and very heavy tan lined ones: if any are at yr place wd you send them out? Don't worry about me, dear. I'll write again in a few days. I hope all is extremely well w you.

Love,
John

[JB's father, John Allyn Smith, was born in South Stillwater, Minnesota, on March 21, 1887.]

[New York]

Dearest John,   Wednesday, 13 October [1954]

Your letter to me and yours to Eileen which she sent on arrived Monday morning. I am too numbed to say more than that you are well out of it and to express my relief for you that you like Minneapolis and are in a pleasant, possible apartment. The less said now about such a ghastly experience, the better, I am sure, for you and for anyone who loves you.

I wrote twice to Iowa City, nothing earthshaking in either; I tell you this, in case they were not received. Your mail addressed here is being forwarded today if I can get it done; I am not giving your address to the hotel since, dilatory as pressure of work may make me seem or be, I am more reliable than the hotel employees.

Minnesota is a beautiful state. I think I remember that it was once or may still be called the state of 10,000 lakes – at least, I remember thousands of them!

Your father's family lived in what was South Stillwater when I was there, a bride, in 1912; perhaps it was still called so in 1913 when I was there for some time recuperating from an operation, but in 1926 on my third and last stay I was pretty sure it was changed to Bayport. Your grandfather's name was Leonard Jefferson or Jefferson Leonard (I am fairly

certain of the former) Smith and he had been retired for some years from
the lumber industry when I first knew him. There were ten children and
I will outline, by age as nearly as possible, what I remember through
whatever age-deterioration of memory or blockages set up: Cora (Code),
unmarried, 18 years older, I think, than your father, which would make
her, if alive, 85 – she was postmistress there for years and years, and had
been in 1912, at least I thought it had been a long time then – she was
still living in Bayport in 1926 and, at last hearing, was sure in her own
mind that I had killed your father – her comment, after the funeral, was
what a horrible ordeal it was for her to have to sit there and have people
look at her and say that her brother had killed himself, so I suppose it was
natural that she convince herself this was not true or otherwise she could
not have gone on living there perhaps, one does what one must and I do
not believe that actually she ever really believed me guilty of murder;
Carrie (Cad) [Caroline Genevieve] married a man named [Ranald J.]
McRae (in 1912 they had two daughters and a son ranging, I think, from
10 or 12 down) who was the senior brother in a group owning stores,
banks etc. in the western part of the state and the eastern part of one of
the Dakotas, well-to-do nice man – Cad several years younger than Code;
Will [William James], who died of pneumonia in Holdenville, Oklahoma before Allyn and I met, was older or younger, next in any event,
to Cad – married to an Amy Penney from Iowa – in 1911 they lived in
Holdenville still, she and the three children Allan, [Robert] Hall and the
little girl [Edith Marjorie] aged respectively about 12, 10 and 7 or 8, and
her sister Maude Penney who married Ted Godfrey – all moved to Oregon in 1912 or 13, and Amy et al stayed out there but Ted and Maude
came back to Holdenville but were no longer there in 1926; there were 2
sons next, I think, Ern [George Ernest] I knew, he had prospected in the
Dakotas or Montana before I met him and had been a prison guard at
Leavenworth for some years, was living in Bayport in 1926 – don't recall
the name of the other [Thomas LeRoy], never knew him, he worked in
a bank in Oklahoma (both he and Allyn brought down there by Will,
who owned a bank in Holdenville, but he was already gone when Allyn
came down, I think) and vanished with no trace and while there was a
shortage in the accounts which Will paid up his mother never believed
that he had anything to do with that and it is entirely possible that it may
have been that he was made the scapegoat for the peculations of someone

else; a sister [Mary] Violet, was music director, I think it was, in the schools in Muskogee and died there – one reason Allyn's mother, a most commanding woman, disliked me so much, was her identifying me with Oklahoma where she had lost her eldest son and a talented daughter and there was a scandal about another son, and then I was so young, of course, too; then there was Grace [Edlice] who was an angel straight from heaven, tall, dark-haired, blue-eyed, kind, generous, loving – she was married to a man named [Lester] Ellingwood (the family thought beneath her, I gathered) nice man and was living in South Stillwater when I was there in 1912 but had moved to St. Paul with her family (2 sons and a daughter, in 1912 perhaps 6, 4 and 2) in 1913 – she died a number of years ago and I believe that after some time her husband re-married, I think he did well and I seem to feel that the family was on goodish terms with him in 1926; then [Maude] Irene was two years older than Allyn, the spoiled baby of the family, would now be 69 – she was married to a man named Ed[ward F.] Kelley and in 1912–13 he was Western Union manager in Duluth, at that time they had a boy [Robert] of 7 or 8, I should think. Unless I have a real block, one child [Ann Maude] must have died young, as that is 8, and your father makes 9 and he was the youngest. Allyn's mother [Mary] was born in Canada, spoke with a real brogue although I believe only her father was Irish, name was Kanar, I think, from County Cork, Catholic – I can't remember exactly when she died, perhaps along in 1916 or '17? Allyn's father came from a very good New England family, went into service in the Civil War from Minnesota (this is my recollection) and added the Jefferson to his name when he re-enlisted after being discharged as disabled from wounds – took up land in the western part of the state after peace and it was family tradition that (or so I recall it) he and the other settlers gave it up because of Indian troubles there – he went into lumbering and was woods boss and no doubt superintendent of logging operations for lumber outfits or perhaps only the one (I think I remember the St. Croix Lumber Co.?), would save up money and go out for himself and that year the snow wouldn't fall or thaw too soon or late, or whatever – and then he'd go back to the company. He was a wonderful figure of an old man when I knew him: tall, enormous square shoulders (you have his shoulders), stooped somewhat, dried flesh holding a big bonerack together, quiet, silent, interesting – I thought even then, through the dazzle of my childishness and make-believe maturity and status of wife and bride and discomfort at Mother Smith's obvious dislike how much I would like to know him, but there was no communication possible then and after 1913 I never saw him again; my recollection is that he died in 1915 [1916] or so, not too long after he had finally gone into the Catholic Church. Mother Smith was a tall, handsome woman, strong, dominating, stubborn, illogical, tenacious, no longer interested in troubling to be kind – very fine sense of humor and a pretty wit. She fascinated me, just as Father Smith interested me, and even then I was aware that I could be devoted to her if she would allow it but this she would not ever put up with.

I hope this is what you want. If anything is not clear, let me know, and if I can, I'll clarify it.

It is a pity, but you left no gloves here; there are several shelves of books, your dress clothes including shoes, a summer suit, a canvas jacket and a cord one, with a couple of pairs of summer slacks, and some papers and small things in a drawer – that's all. By the way, I have a bill from the cleaner for $7 for the two pairs of slacks dyed – were they all right?

Here there is no news, work and hope tells the story. I have had a considerable virus thing for several weeks but seem to be on the fringes now thank heaven – seem to have developed anemia in the passage of the age and the moment which must account for my slowness in throwing off viruses (virii?) etc. Up to my ears in pills of all sizes.

Lovingly,
your devoted mother,
Jill Berryman

2509 Humboldt Av. S.
[Minneapolis]

Dearest Mother,   Wednesday night [20 October 1954]

I like this country; I'm delighted with it. How suddenly all the leaves have come down. I drove w the Tates Sunday before last thro Stillwater up the St Croix [River] but we didn't stop; I'll go over one day by myself – many thanks for your account (also for mail; and how funny abt the gloves, I wonder where I stupidly put them all) – and see what I can turn up if anything there or in Bayport. Last Sunday we drove, taking a priest (who brought a superb ham & a bottle of Scotch), up to St Cloud to see Jim [J.F.] Powers & his wife who live there. The residents of the diocese are 80% Catholic. I don't know whether you know his stuff, he's one of the best story-writers in the country, a friend of Cal's, writes mostly about priests. Father [George G.] Garrelts whom we took was in college with him. Priests for a long time now have made me nervous; I used to get drunk every time I met Father [William F.] Lynch, whom I like & admire very much; but I'm very easy w Fr Garrelts and drank practically nothing (as I'm doing in general). I have been making lately what might be called a spiritual examination of unfaith and am thinking of sending it to Fr Lynch. (He's a Jesuit, editor of their review, *Thought*, and a remarkable critic of literature-&-ideas, particularly Manicheeism, and as an old Manichean now very much against it I feel strongly in league with him – as of the Bradstreet poem, say, and his recent work – a parallel he'd remarked also. I mean Manicheeism in contemporary Christian writers like Eliot & Grahame Greene.

I don't know how long it's been since I lived so quietly & pleasantly. I have met a great many people of course, but on weekends, when the Tates and Lees [Edwy and Marie-Lorraine] take me out. Otherwise, except for dinner occasionally w Allen & Caroline, or when I go over w Allen to the University for books as I did today, I see nobody. I've not had a phone put in, and for four days last week I didn't speak with a soul; it was delightful. I am clearing up short pieces long on deck, alternating stories and critical / scholarly things; accumulating momentum. I eat mostly here, have two burners & a refrigerator – also a big worktable, a desk, a good reading chair & various others, two other tables, many shelves, a bureau, a big closet, a private bath, seven windows, four lamps, and so on. Warm and utterly quiet. I am helping Allen with an anthology, and write a good many letters; otherwise just study and write. My courses begin right after Christmas. My health is fair. I try to round the lake [Lake of the Isles] every day or walk two miles over to the [Minneapolis] Art Institute, which has some gorgeous pictures, & back. I hope your virus has absolutely cleared up. Caroline is *caterinato*, that is, wrapt up in S Catherine of Siena, and from what she says of the life in [Edmund G.] Gardiner's biography [*Saint Catherine of Siena, a Study in the Religion, Literature and History of the Fourteenth Century in Italy*] I gather you would probably like it immensely if your library has it.

I've got work to do. Bless you. Give my love to Bob.

love
John

[P.S.] We went to Stillwater by Route 36, my lucky number as I think you know

[P.P.S.] Jim's book is *[The] Prince of Darkness*, J.F. Powers.

[Fr. George G. Garrelts was the Director of the Newman Foundation at the University of Minnesota.

The anthology JB had begun to help Allen Tate (and Ralph Ross) on is *The Arts of Reading* (1960).

Edwy and Marie-Lorraine Lee were a young married couple who were students at the University of Minnesota and friends of the Tates and JB.]

Hotel Chelsea, New York

Dearest John,   Friday 22 October 1954

"Happy Birthday" from me to you on this, your fortieth anniversary, is much more than an iteration of the conventional cliché. Indeed, there has never been any such feeling in the heart-meant hope for happiness for you that informs my days and nights. With the years and such understanding as they have permitted or enforced upon me, the meaning of happiness has changed in many ways, but at all times I have wished that you might experience and live in the atmosphere of not mine but your happiness for such periods as it could be born or could endure. In this wish I persist – so for happiness, read your best good as you see it, and know that is one of the few basic meanings and intents of my life.

My birthday, this year, was exceedingly important to me in ways new and somewhat strange. It is likely that this birthday, for you, may be rather like that to you. Nothing could sound more foolish than to say that, at sixty, I felt the need to put aside childish things, but so it was. I say this now so that if you feel, in yourself, ways in which your ways (my use of words is atrocious, please look through to the meaning, if you can keep your teeth off-edge) are less mature than your enormous abilities and learning, know that it is my fault for passing them on; if you do not feel such things, then your maturity in all things is achieved and this *is* my kind of happiness, at least.

Since money is few although adequate here, the bill is no larger; since it may be few there, I would so much rather you got something you really want, even if it is a steak or a film, than to send you something not inspired by knowledge or intuition. I am not an idea person, right now, so please please me by doing what Barba Villim [Mikulicic] always called out to anyone "please yourself".

Now for your real present, which actually is one from you to me. At present, I see no practical hope of being able to pay off the most onerous debt I have, that of your father's insurance to you and to Jeff. Please, John, look at this with me, with my eyes, not with yours. Since I was here and he was not, such care and schooling as I could give was mine to give – I borrowed the money to use when it was needed, as you and Jeff would have been most willing for me to do, I know, but borrowed it was. I can not cheat your father of what he meant for you, and it is for this reason that the debt lies so heavily on me and the more so that when I might have done something about repaying it I didn't but frittered away the small payments that could have been made, since I could not do it in one large grand lump sum. We are kin enough, I believe, for me to feel that your money obligation to me lies heavily on you, too – such debts as mine to you and yours to me can color a relationship abominably. So I ask you to do me the favor, since my debt to you is larger than yours to me and I ask you to forego the balance in your favor, to remove from me that burden, and to let what moneys you have had of me serve as payment in full of your father's gift to you. I ask to do this in whole not in part, so that we may both feel free. Since I do not now think it likely that the trip to Florida this fall will materialize, I shall ask Jeff to make me the same gift of his share of the money. I need this ease of heart and mind, this surcease, do not deny it to me, my son. Let me go free of the only debt I can pay to Allyn.

With all my love,
your devoted mother,
Jill Berryman

[Minneapolis]
25 October 1954

Dearest Mother,

I think this is the first adult birthday anniversary I can remember when I've not been depressed. I look at it thus. If I take 1938, thinking of the dreadful party Malcolm Cowley and Red [Alexander] Calder gave together to deplore their 40th birthdays, I was nearly 24 and that was 16 years ago. I had done nothing up to then. In the 16 years since I've done very little, but something. I can imagine 16 years ahead, that is, to the age of 56, or just a year past where Allen is now (it was with Caroline I went to that party); and I can hardly fear doing less in the next 16 years than I did in the last. So why be depressed? Allen is respected, active, courteous, sober all but one night a week, writes verse beautifully in the very small amount of the year that he writes. I confess ruefully that this by no means satisfies even the present stage of my ambition, but it is far from contemptible. Also I have outlived my father and can hardly compete with him any longer. I am willing to some extent to regard myself as his representative, but chiefly I am my own representative and custodian. I feel very happy in fact. My character is still far from being a desirable entity (you mustn't imagine that I am willing to let you persuade me that such defects come from anyone but myself); if I can become busy enough this needn't much matter, and anyway I learn as I get on. My experiences during the last two years have been invaluable – considering that I am still around to profit.

Many thanks for the five-dollar bill which I like better than you can imagine: because I am putting it in my passport, ever to be there as a reserve or to be immediately replaced. I hate being without cash. Also there is a firstrate bookshop here, over near the University, and when I go over later this week I'll pick out something I want very much to read and give it to myself from you; probably a delightful edition of Pope's poems I saw, but I'll tell you if I find something I want even more.

About the debt: I could argue that of course you *did* actually deal with my schooling, and therefore there is no debt: but I understand exactly how you feel, since I feel exactly the same way about my debt to you: and so THANK YOU DARLING. It is a fantastic relief, which will take some getting used to the feeling of. I like to think how pleased Daddy would be about it, and about the money's having preserved me at the period of my worst trouble, at the same age when he had his worst trouble. I can't possibly begin to tell you how grateful I am, first and repeatedly for all the generous and saving help, and now for this.

It is queer how everything happens here to remind me of him. Louis MacNeice (who as I think I've told you much resembles him) and his wife turned up last week lecturing, and luckily – esp. since Allen was feuding with them and wdn't see them – I was able to look after them well enough to reduce my sense of obligation for their goodness to me last summer in London. I'd been very worried that I wouldn't be, both nervously and as of money, and then of the feud. I don't blame Allen (or them): it was one of the elaborate misunderstandings that makes relations so difficult between gifted & wellknown people. I'm fond of them all. I cdn't reconcile them but I was with the MacNeices continually and took the smart 9 / 10s off. I also telephoned the Camerons ([J. Alister and Elizabeth], who will look after them now in Cincinnati. If my mental health were less good I wd have been tortured, or overset, by the quarrel, because for many years Allen tho only 15 yrs older has stood more or less as a father to me, not to speak of his present succour (of which I'll tell you more in months to come); but I am pretty well and though I felt deeply sorry I didn't turn a hair.

I must stop and get to work. I wish you may be very well, darling: one or two notes in your letters are a little disquieting: how are you? My work is going fairly. I am trying to get one whole thing, story or article, finished (or substantially so) a week; two or three more weeks will tell me better. At any rate I am getting my hand in. Again all my thanks and love,

John

[New York]

Dearest John,   Friday 29 October 1954

The illumination and illimitableness (what dreadful monsters I coin, or use) that comes with good news from one you love is so vast and deep and full and rich, the things that the word "satisfying" was made to express, that I wonder at (knowing this) my not putting all energies to that effect that those who love me may reveal in this *raison-d'être* completion. If I could only live each day as if it were all – it is, of course, but realization is too difficult of achievement for most of us, and habit and hope too strong.

Your letter written on your birthday gave me something I no longer expected, or even thought of: pure happiness. To have found your way, and through what seemed insuperable difficulties, when even the greatest for the most part fail in this finding, perhaps through inability more than refusal to search – and, if you will forgive me, so young in years. Please, I do not mean to foreshadow, but it is human to backslide and for custom to overrule: it is easier to give way than to resist: the deepest sin of the soul is not denial, but despair – I think perhaps because denial is blindness while despair is negation of the light seen and acknowledged? When I fall short, as happens daily, hourly, I think on Discipline: "For my heart's desire unto Thine is bent. I aspire to a full consent . . . Though I fail, I weep. Though I halt in pace, Yet I creep To the throne of grace". Long before the grace of faith was granted me, I tried to live by this, for "the throne of grace" substituting the best good I could conceive. I try, too, to think as often as I may on St. Ambrose's loving admonition: God promises us forgiveness but He does not promise us tomorrow in which to repent.

I hope you don't find this too tedious, or boring; I know you will not mistake it for proselyting. There is no one else to whom I can think on such matters.

These three letters, the first at-one news, mean more than I can ever express. It is very good, too, that they come from your father's state and so near where he was born and spent his boyhood and youth. It is, I suppose, bromidic, to say that one must be on terms with others before coming to terms with oneself in life, and it seems to me that you are on endurable terms with your parents now, neither too much nor too little. Never feel anything but free to speak of Allyn as you like to me, never think that I disliked or misrespected him – it was only that I did not love him and have long felt wretchedly guilty because of what came of us to him. This guilt I no longer feel, believing that then I could have done no other, more than he, but pain for the unnecessary loss and the suffering will be with me ever. As for me, I am glad that for both of us there seems now no need for you to sever our ties, but keep the offer, truly and surely made, for use if the rains should come.

I can not help being especially thankful about your birthday – mothers always take an overweening interest in birthdays, it does preen their importance as gateways, and this is, perhaps, the curious subterranean resentment one feels toward them at such times? Looking back, I can see the flashes of it in myself but in emotions and insight, as in time, looking backward is possible and often seems to bear no relation to what is to come, at least, in oneself. With all my love, darling,

                                                  Your devoted mother,
                                                  Jill Berryman

[P.S.] I am glad that the money thing is as happy for you as for me – the relief is enormous – Jeff has agreed, also, I am thankful to say.

                                                                        JB

[New York]

Dearest John,   Tuesday, 30 November 1954

It is now five weeks since you last wrote me, on your birthday, or at least that is the last letter I've had. It does not seem unduly demanding to hope or even expect news more often than that, especially when things have been a little dicky so far as security goes, of late. I am not reproaching you, John, you may not have realized how much time has gone by, or been in no mood to write or even been annoyed with or put off by something in my letters. I hope not the last but with my ineptness it may be so.

It is cogent, however, that worry and concern hinder me in ways I do not have too much strength to combat. Under par, I naturally fear the worst, that matters are intolerable with you and this state must, from the tone of your last letters, seem to me to come from financial difficulties. This brings home to me my failure in such a way as to render me incapable of avoiding the sin of despair – this is not your fault but it is a fact of which there should be recognition. (This is not subject to discussion, or reassurance, John – I know my life and my heart and my sins, and their results.) I fail in all ways, as a Christian, a human being, a mother, a wage earner, as the ever present help in time of need which a parent should be – in the past, I have failed in many more ways, but here it is for now. My greatest struggle, on returning to my faith, was to forgive myself, not to hold guilt, so it is natural that, impaired as has been my vision, the sense of guilt overwhelms me at the least letting down.

With Sunday, the first of Advent and thus the beginning of the Christian year, I set up a plan which will, I pray, habituate me in such ways as to grant me again the comfort and joy of full love of God, not just my present submission, without endangering my soul through mistaking the exercises of piety for acts of faith and grace and love and contrition. I must, then, ask you to help me by writing once a month, if you will? at least while things are not too well with either of us in things of this world. Just a postcard or a note is enough.

This is all due to my vanity, in the main, and also somewhat to the over-scrupulosity of wishing not to burden you. The chief vanity lay in my preference for not hearing rather than that you should write at my behest rather than your wish. It is natural, I suppose, to want a thing done because you were thought of and the doer wanted to do it, much more than the thing itself – perhaps not more, greed wants all, the doing and the wish of the doer. I no longer hold that duty can be forgone: in return for my attempts over the years to yield up responsibility toward you, I must ask you now to take on this duty toward me, unless there is some reason you may or can not, in which case I am afraid you must tell me so. Few can subsist on the starvation diet of uncertainty and the fear which attends it, and I am so subject to my love for you that, failing to hear, worry and fear for you consume me.

If matters are such with you as to make this duty impossible, tell me and I must then manage as best I can.

with all my love,
your devoted mother,
Jill Berryman

[P.S.] I should have told you before how I've worried and couldn't sleep. It was wrong not to let you know.

[Minneapolis]

Dearest Mother,   Sunday night [5 December 1954]
    I'm just this minute through a piece of analysis that's taken since 8 this morning, and intellectually & emotionally & physically exhausted, but I want to say if very quickly how sorry I am for your worry about my not writing. It wd be unforgiveable except that there is a reason for it: I am engaged in a sort of self-analysis, which is slow and difficult, and partly dictates what I can & cannot do. But I am well, and you must not worry, darling. A bout of what I suppose was flu, some time ago, went off at once. I am on the wagon, and enjoying the physical dividends. Certainly I have been having great difficulty about money; but it is com-pletely fantastic for you to blame yourself for this – I much more ought to be supporting you, and I wish I could; besides it won't last, for my appointment is being put through, say they, for Dec 15th and so since they pay for fortnightly I'll get paid the day I begin teaching, 3 Jan. I can't even read back thro your letters right now, I must take this out to a post-box – it is really cold tonight, the city's been white for a long time but temperatures not low – and come back & get in the hot tub I've run & go to bed. But one thing: I salute the courage and Christian kindness that prompted your letter about our possible non-relation some time; but I

can't think that will ever be, not at all. Some questions: Do you recall Pina de' Fiori? was it not a bottle in Gr Neck? did I finally ever have any, w what result? This is important. And do you remember the name of the boy whose dead hand I toucht as pallbearer (*not* Billy Ross, F J Callahan)? Did Daddy do you know prefer Bob or me? What were the names of the women he was interested in, esp the redhead wasn't there? Forgive my taxing you but do please try to remember. Bless you, and I'll write later this week. Dear love,

John

[F.J. Callahan *was* the dead boy whose hand JB touched and for whom he was a pallbearer.]

[New York]

Dearest John,   Tuesday, 7 December 1954
    Your letter of Sunday night was so gratefully received this morning, and was doubly grateful in the news it brought. I don't mean to dwell on my point but it seems now to me that one can do a loved one a deal of damage by attempting to save him the trouble of obligation or duty in the only fashion that seemed possible which might well indicate less love and concern than are the case. I do love you most devotedly and concernedly, and must always do, I judge from the past, and the comet's train on this is the need to know how things are with you, even or perhaps especially in difficult times. Now none of that need be said again for on some certain stands, of which this is one, I am fixeder than the stars. It is a trouble to say, since when you do not write over a long time, more than a month, say, you may have qualms of conscience, which I had wished to spare you as indeed, regardless of good or ill outcome, I would spare you all pain, but now it is said.
    I'll answer your questions next as best I may: the cordial is, in my memory, Alpini del Fiori (Fleurs des Alpes, although we never had the French brand) and came in a Rhine wine bottle with a leafless branch carrying short twigs inside on which there were heavy sugar crystals, the cordial being straw-colored and tasting of flowers with an undertone of the spice flavor of freshly ground black pepper – I am very sorry that I cannot say definitely that you had any although it is unlikely that you should not have tasted it, as you were permitted to taste anything we were drinking – what you may be thinking of is the evening around the fire

when you were home in perhaps your Fourth form Christmas, and we were having Cointreau in the tiny cordial goblets of which I still have two or three and you asked for some and I gave you my full goblet (tiny, you know) to taste but since it looked like water you drank it off and of course found it a choking, heady shock of surprise; I have no recollection at all of the boy for whom you were pallbearer, I am sorry – the blockage on everything possible is still wrong; the only name I recall is Marjorie (Van Eaton) Thompson, in Anadarko, who was a very tall, strongish woman of about my own age, a divorcee with a daughter of 3 or 4, daughter herself of a cattleman, who received the Anadarko Gas Company, I think it was, in the divorce settlement – it was with her that Allyn, who had been to New York trying to float a bond issue for the gas company, went to Chicago on the same errand (she had not gone to N.Y.) – she was redhaired on the sandy side, not goodlooking but I should say attractive – until the Chicago trip I had always thought of her as my friend, not Allyn's, but then it is not my nature to be suspicious or jealous, probably incapable of believing in any necessity then – I must say here, in fairness, that just as my interest in the other sex, in sex itself, came wholly from my father, yours would come mostly from me.

Now the other question, if your father preferred Bob or you. Ours was not a household in which favoritism or preferences were expected or displayed – perhaps it is in households where there is strong love or hate that such choices are surest. It seemed to me natural to love you both most dearly as my sons and as persons, each with his own flavor peculiar in the whole world to him alone – to love you as my first-born, as yourself, and to enjoy and cherish the almost five years longer knowledge of you and to have an added responsibility toward you in that I had of my own will and choice given up my life to bring Bob into the world and thus was guilty of depriving you of a mother; to love Bob as my last-born, as himself, as one who would always lack five years of your life and mine, and with the responsibility of having made the sole decision of his living and so being guilty of making him my slayer (as I was told his birth would do) and of all the ills of his life. It then seemed no more or less than natural that Allyn should love you both as his sons, each for yourself. I am and was so simple that I believed that, with rare and to-be-deplored exceptions, everyone loved everyone for himself, not comparatively. I wasn't much more than a cocoon.

Your father did not show marked partiality, I know, as that would have registered. I would say that it would be more likely that Allyn leaned toward you, his older son – at this remove, it is hard to tell, and almost impossible for me to go back of [to?] Florida deeply. There were two things in Florida, but you must bear in mind, in evaluating them, the dreadful strains and pressures, that what seemed diagonal may have been only a distortion caused by the fogs of pain and unhappiness.

There was the night when, after a futile, endless talk with Allyn, we both fell into heavy sleep – we were working 15, 16 hours a day and were physically exhausted in addition to the emotional strain. I dreamed that Bob was sitting with other children his age (although he was not six, but three or four) against a brick building, clearly a school, on a bench in a concrete playground, quite large, and that when I neared him he shied away as if he had been doing wrong and might be punished and then I saw that his right hand and part of the forearm were gone and the stump all healed so that it had happened long before and I knew nothing of it and he had not had comfort, it was the worst experience of my life to that time. It woke me, and I gathered Bob up and held him sleeping the hour or so till dawn, weeping soundlessly for him, for me, for Allyn, for you, for my mother, for all mankind. And I decided to end my life in such a way that it would seem natural, as my life was so painfilled I did not think I could bear more. But Allyn, waking, and full of the thought of death of which he had been speaking (of killing himself) for some time, said "you are telling him goodbye, aren't you?" So I knew that my death would be known as suicide and I could not cause such pain, although I doubt that the intent on my part was more than a wish to be out of agony and perhaps a late justification for what amounted, according to any number of doctors, to my decision to bring Bob into the world – in the long run, though it may have been better for you and Bob if I had done, I could not have left my sons to anyone else nor could I have believed that any-one else would love them as much as I did or care for them as well. I told Allyn that I was just trying to find comfort, as indeed was true. It is possible that Allyn preferred you so deeply that he took this as an expres-sion of my equally deep preference for Bob, I don't know.

But it was Bob that he took out in the Gulf at Clearwater, meaning to drown Bob and himself. You and Bob were playing on the beach and when I came back out and asked where Bob was, you told me that your daddy had swum way out in the Gulf with him. Eventually, after eternity, they came back, walking down the beach and then Allyn told me what he had meant to do but couldn't. Allyn was not cruel, never think so: this was not to cause anguish, he had actually meant it when he did it. He may have felt that it would be right to deprive me of Bob since he was depriving himself of you, or he may have wanted someone with him and could only take someone with so little experience of the world as to mind leaving it no more than he. Or he may have regretted loving him less and so taken him with him as a token of affection. No one now can tell. But that Allyn ever meant evil to anyone, no. And in this we were at one – evil has come of my doing and not doing but wickedly to intend, no.

Having thought and cast back as well as I can, striving greatly, I believe now, seeing then as clearly as I can, that Allyn preferred you.

I hope this is what you wanted. It is a pity there is so much about me and it is no longer meant to justify but to illuminate. It is a lesson to be learned that there is no justification whether the blame be warranted or come by accident, there is forgiveness for grief and rejection of ill doing, a different thing, as conducive to humility and loving kindness as the former to a puffing up and a false righteousness.

It is encouraging that although my new rules have been in effect ten days or less, I have mostly kept to them and where not, I regret but am not cast down unduly. This time, I am up to *Matthew* 23, and beginning to be less startled at the unfamiliarity of the *Douai Bible* on the *King James* accustomed ear. I read *The Imitation [of Christ]* almost every evening, and read in the *Missal* and other devotional books. Tomorrow is the Feast of the Immaculate Conception of our Lady, a Holy Day of Obligation, and it seemed most timely somehow that in the 22nd chapter today there lay the foundation stone, where our Lord is questioned on which is the great commandment in the law and says:

> Jesus said unto him: Thou shalt love the Lord thy God with thy whole heart, and with thy whole soul, and with thy whole mind.
> This is the greatest and the first commandment.
> And the second is like to this: Thou shalt love thy neighbor as thyself.

On these two commandments dependeth the whole law and the prophets.

As I resign not only my death but my life into His hands, I begin to feel again a trickle of the overflowing love which I hope to nourish so as never to lose it anymore. I ask for nothing from our Father except what he wills me to have and that I be granted the grace to accept thankfully whatever he sends. So, not having to ask for myself, I am free to dedicate my prayers and efforts and pains for the good of others. You will, I know, rejoice to learn that my devotions in the present and future are daily offered for Allyn, not just from time to time as in the past. I try not to derive any comfort from this. It is for me to learn to love others instead of myself without despising myself, no easy task.

I have finished *Twelfth Night,* or did I tell you? and am now in the Third Act of *The Tempest.* The *Sunday Times* magazine reported Olivier to be making *Richard III* (film). Started with *Twelfth Night* as it is on up at Jan Hus Hall and said to be a good presentation, and I had thought to get to see it. A week ago Sunday I picked up Jeff at 6:40 after 6:00 at Holy Cross, and we went by for Deac [Dunn], getting there a bit after 8, and then drove up to Roxbury; left Jeff in town to renew friendships (incredible that he knew who lived in every house and remembered such detail) while Deac and I drove up to the pass between Long Mountain and Round Top, a wonderful view; then we drove to Woodchuck Lodge, where John Burroughs lived and near where he is buried in Memorial Field, and ate our picnic lunch on the porch – very nice, and herewith evidence. My constant thoughts and prayers and love,

Your devoted mother,
Jill Berryman

[P.S.] I hope your clothes are warm enough? Delighted about the appointment, and so glad have been able to keep the apt. I wish you great good from the analysis, darling – so glad you are enjoying health dividends.

[Minneapolis]
Dearest Mother,   Friday morning [10 December 1954?]
I'm exhausted intellectually and must ramble. The reason I'm free to write is that I remember no dream from last night though I had several.

I dream every day now and haven't put in a week of such intense work for two years. I think there has been a sort of breakthrough.

I am wonderfully grateful for yr effort of remembrance; I have reason to know how costly such things are. The results are likely to be very helpful to me. For instance I've always thought it was *I* whom my father wished to drown with him. Oh yes I can see that cordial bottle. It tele-scoped in a dream with the *Pinocotheca* in *Flor*ence. The principal sub-ject was sexual but liquor was a second theme. (It's a week today since I had a drink or wanted one.) In the latter stages of an analysis I sometimes half-kill myself laughing by the way: late in a dream formidably perverse, equally aggressive & fearful, occurred this touching scene: "and they said 'See who's come?' and it was Jimmy Worden [JB's Princeton friend], friendly & guiltless" – Jimmy Worden turning out to be *me*. The mind is a glory-hole only apparently: what it really does is to combine the Magi-not Line and the Strategic Air Command. And its operations! merely they dazzle me. Some of my simplest (in appearance) dreams have proved over the long hours of assoc. & analysis more complex than any poem I ever read; a great deal to say; I have almost a new idea of the mind's strength, cunning, & beauty.

Minneapolis is beautiful again. New snow has fallen on the old, which was getting a bit dusty, and the air is so gentle today that I've propped out two of my storm-windows and thrown up the windows. I never was so comfortable in my life. Pretty soon I am going to walk around the lake. Even my coffee tastes specially good. The sun is gleaming on the snow-clad shed-roofs I look out across. I like Minneapolis.

Without enthusiasm but dutifully let me say that there seems to me a great want of sense in much of your self-accusation & self-blame, dar-ling. This is matter really for a priest but consider your saying that it seemed to you "natural" to love Bob "as one who wd always lack five years of your life & mine," or "with the responsibility of . . . making him my slayer" – consider these in the light of Augustine's definition of sin. "Sin is any thought, word, or deed against the eternal law, which is the divine ordinance of reason commanding order to be observed and forbid-ding its disturbance." Besides a Christian is bound to believe not only in sin but in the remission of sin . . Human responsibility is *sharply limited*; this is one of the major consequences of dogmatics; to indulge responsi-bility, except in its proper directions, is wanton – and in fact, psycholog-ically, an overflow or distortion of something else. What that would be is, mostly, in some other way a sense that one has not been forgiven; or, more truly, that one has not merited forgiveness. But this is precisely not for the soul to say; it is why the Church exists.

For *this* purpose, the issues of the Faith (which requires one to live at peace w God) and of psychoanalysis (which requires one to live at peace w oneself) are the same.

Your comments on my father's motives in taking Bob out with him seem to me shrewd & just as well as justly charitable. The final thrashings of my father's life seem to me (tell me what you think of this) those of a rather cold & inexpressive man feeling both so guilty and so rejected that what had been all his life (unjustly) hidden from him boiled *irresponsibly* up and unmanageably up in such a way as to bring him before no tribunal known to us.

But I can't quite *see* my father; I don't *know* him. Well, who does know his father who died when he was twelve? R.I.P.

No my clothes are not warm enough: not one item is, and as soon as my salary begins I must buy others. I ain't even got a muffler.

(Thanks for Gugg. tax clip; v. doubtful if any refund, but trying.)

(Yes, if you'd look for my gloves I'd be glad – E says they're in NY – I *thought* in a drawer in the apt. – but if locker, have the key – 3 pairs it is. Thanks & thanks for all yr. trouble w. my mail. If I didn't pay cleaning bill, send it; I'll pay it Jan 3rd.)

I am begun working up my Medieval course and am extremely interested; for one thing, delighted to have *materials* (instead of trying to teach people how to write) and materials I am not steadily *at* like Shakespeare. After a bit w late Roman philosophy, I'm using the *New Testament*, a collection of *Documents [of the Christian Church*, edited by Henry Bettenson] illustrating the history of the Church, Augustine, Aquinas, Dante. Isn't that ravishing? Tate tells me he is inclined to sin through envy. In fact, this is the only course I am giving: I give it twice, once w what are called Junior College students (freshmen & sophomores) and once w Sr Coll (jrs & srs), so that I have only one preparation but at the same time plan to handle it so differently w the two groups that I don't have to repeat myself, which I *detest* doing. But both courses meet every day, five times a week, and *that* is not so good. I mean to try to take it very easy – the students are v poorly trained anyway, I am warned – as unlike my Harvard teaching this summer as possible. I begin Jan 3rd.

I am struck by this, in the Rule of S Benedict: The monk "should have nothing at all: neither a book, nor tables, nor a pen – nothing at all."

A friend of mine named Sally Appleton I have written to suggesting that she borrow any of my books that are in your apartment, and it will be a favour to me if you'll help her getting them. I'll brief you because I'll be much surprised if you don't enjoy talking w her. She was one of Joan Griscom's Vassar group in Cambridge this summer; abt 24, a poetess, works for the Catholic monthly *Jubilee* and also now for *Thought* (she's a friend of Fr. Lynch's); makes practically nothing from these jobs, of course, and needs books. She was converted several years ago and workt at Maryfarm w Dorothy Day's Catholic Worker group, then w children in the city. Both those magazines wd interest you, she sent me a *Jubilee* & I read every word nearly. She is for intelligence & sensibility & spiritual energy one of the most remarkable young women I ever knew. I scarcely talkt w her this summer, as I did w Charie [Charlotte] Hall & of course Joan, but we correspond now and I hope she will be a friend of mine the rest of my life. She is shy, by the way, but loses it.

I was worse than a Manichean: I believed *only* in the Devil – the opposite of Origen's immortal and heart-shaking heresy that interpreted apocatastasis (universal restitution at the coming of the Messiah) as including the abolition of Hell. *What* trouble it cost to get *that* counted heresy, his sanctity & prestige were so great: theologians get as heated abt it now as they did in the 3rd century, and the end is not yet. (He is carefully omitted, too, from these *Documents* Bettenson collected. I hope your health has been much better.)

Dearest love,
John

[Joan Griscom and Charlotte Hall were friends of JB's and of Sally Appleton's. JB had met Sally Appleton at Joan Griscom's house in Cambridge where he had given a reading of *Homage to Mistress Bradstreet*.]

[Minneapolis]
Dearest Mother,   26 December [1954]
Much too busy to write properly but just a word of thanks – the loan of the scarf I'm above all grateful for, and if you knew how helpful to me the $10 sharing has been you wd have some idea of – well. I am delighted about your account. Hurrah. I will be all right myself financially this

week, perhaps even tomorrow. Anyway I am too well, and my work is too well, to worry. When time serves and I don't have to ride twenty-one horses at once (21 dreams, in every stage of interpretation) I'll answer your letters, which have interested me very much and will probably be of great service. Yes Sally [Appleton] writes that she didn't like to "ring you up out of the grey", and I expect she now will or you might drop her a note, 42 First Avenue, CA 8–3573; thanks. She does look forward to borrowing the books, it appears. Douglas & Diana [Mackie] gave me the loveliest green leather pencil-well you ever saw and 48 pencils, Eileen gave me a MAGNIFICENT alpaca-lined short storm-coat, my grey sweater (I never had a grey sweater before, it is a beauty) is much admired by the very few people I've seen, I ate my head off at the Tates' where we were all in wonderful spirits and drank to everyone absent whom we love, and I wish you the happiest of New Years. Caroline Tate told me one of the most wonderful stories, on Xmas Eve, that ever I heard. She woke up abt 4 one morning in Princeton to hear her grandsons awake and the elder Peto begging little Allen to tell him a story: after much demurring Allen agreed to tell him a story abt the Virgin Mary.

– What did she do? said Peto.

(long pause) – Went to the bathroom.

– What happened then?

(long pause) – Jackie Pig bust out of her wee-wee.

– Was he tough?

(pause) Was he tough? He knockt the wee-wee off the octopus!

– What happened then?

– Then he went up to Heaven.

Love,
John

[P.S.] I am holding my breath abt Detroit

[Mrs. Berryman had been to Detroit on business.

Douglas and Diana Mackie are the children of JB's Princeton friends, Donald and Elizabeth Mackie.]

[Minneapolis]

Dearest Mother,   after 5 p.m. 2 January [1955]

Too busy to write. Yes the diary came and *many* thanks, also the pocketnotebooks and for them. By an irony I had ordered a diary (wh I

had to have) by airpost the day before but I had much rather use one fr
you and anyway this is initialled as the one coming won't be and I'll give
it to Allen [Tate] or Sally [Appleton] – I'd give it you but somehow I
don't like the idea of *back*-giving involved. Thanks for the $21 which I'll
pay you back on the 15th.

I made no resolutions. None was necessary. I am *all* resolution. Yesterday I spent fr 8:15 A.M. to 5:40 P.M. on the very difficult and terrible
Dream Nine, the evening on the next. An unusual New Year's Day for
me. New Year's Eve I just workt, on an even more difficult and terrible
dream which I more or less finisht at exactly midnight when I happened
to glance up at my electric clock and saw the second hand coming out
from under the other two at 12, and I wished you a Happy New Year. I
have various questions to ask you but they must wait. I begin teaching
tomorrow and wonder how I can spare the time but I am looking forward
to it with pleasure. I was a bit lonely from nine to ten on New Year's Eve
(it is the first in 20 years I have passed alone, and I had another even
better reason and also at that moment my work was not well coming out)
but it passed.

Love,
John

Dearest Mother,

[Minneapolis]
Sunday night [16 January 1955]

Though I've been too busy to write (I spent 50 hours on *Mark* last
week, which as the most primitive, reliable and astonishing has always
really been my favourite Gospel) I had got progressively worried about
you and was extremely glad to hear.

A thousand thanks about the cheque, which I just have to accept
then. But I'll *fix you*, presently. It is so nice not to be penniless. I bought
overshoes yesterday; they are warm! and once I got hungry & went & had
a steak. I eat practically all my meals in, still, if you can call them meals.
I have lost about ten pounds but am in very good health.

My teaching is going beautifully and I enjoy it. The *most* surprising
& magnificent things that I think I have come on so far are both in
Matthew, Christ's Ecstasy (end of ch. 11) and the Temptations (which
really summarize the whole ministry: in the refusals to take thought for

himself, to give a sign, and to seek popularity by lowering the quality of the moral demands made on his followers; it is conjectured that the third temptation, the fundamental one & political of course, was permanent thro the ministry; I imagine these were genuine psychological experiences at the beginning of the ministry, related by him probably to Peter or Matthew).

Thanks for the enclosure wh I'll get to. I'm glad Deac [Dunn] was down – my best to him.

I have to go back to work. I'll try to write every week, something. All good luck & love in everything, dear.

John

[P.S.] I gave two very good lectures for Tate, on Campion's poetry – which were widely praised – and I wrote a beautiful short poem last week.

[Minneapolis]
Dearest Jill,   Tuesday, 15 February 1955

All's well. I have two more lectures on Thomas Aquinas (largely prepared), then there's nothing but the *Inferno* & some short romances at the end, in fact my final meetings are just three weeks from day after tomorrow. I didn't realize it had been so long since I wrote and am sorry for yr worry. It's true that I have no time at all, I don't know that I've written for a month anything but two letters to Fr Lynch & two to Eileen. The weather has been brisk off & on. Last week one day the temperature dropt 44 degrees, and it's repeatedly been 15 and 20 below zero; all this is less alarming & uncomfortable than you'd think: I have hardly minded it at all. Your scarf has been a great help. As for vitamins, I take Theragran-M regularly enough. And I have been so lucky as not even to have had a cold yet. I am not out much, after all: a few minutes a day, coming & going, and even the busses are heated. One does not willingly walk about much, however, for the ears & nose tend to drop off. It is the wind that matters most, and moisture, and we have been most lucky with them.

My own work has entirely stopt. There may be men, though I doubt it, who cd do both, but not me; however, I hope to start again soon, as the course-load eases. Ross wants me to teach the continuation-courses this Spring quarter and if we agree on terms I will. In fine I will but I desire to be paid more. It is the Reformation that attracts me, especially Luther.

The vitamins I gather you were going to send & indeed sent have not come, unless they are what I have to send 3c to the P.O. for, according to a form that came today in the post w yr letter. I expect they are.

I am glad you are taking steps against weight, and good luck darling, but extremely sorry about what I take it is continued lack of money security. Do try to worry as little as you can, I am so sorry you have to. Will you tell Bob why I haven't written, and wish him all luck from me, and say I will write.

Love,
John

Minneapolis

Dearest Mother,   Sunday 1 May [1955]

I'm extremely glad you wrote to me, I was going to send the money [owed to Brooks Brothers] this weekend anyway but there was no way to know that, and it's insufferable that you shd have any *more* trouble on my account. Thanks again. I hope you will be all right yourself; if not, please *directly* let me know; I am trying to accumulate, despite debts, a little money so that I won't starve or die of anxiety this summer, and have some cash in the bank for the first time in several years. Of course I ought to send it straight off to everybody but I just can't do it. To be without five dollars is absolutely more than I can any longer bear – until next I have to. . . .

Would you pass this on to [Bob], as just an idea: There was a good murder here a few days ago, a young woman strangled here in the "exclusive" Lake of the Isles district & tossed in an alley; she was pregnant & had accused a dentist of it, so he's arrested; many of his women patients accuse him of bothering them, with drugs etc; victim's soldier-husband has now been flown back from the Far East. The newspaper coverage here has been very poor, so far as I've seen it; and I thought myself of trying to see the dentist, the woman's relatives etc, and writing a piece for a magazine – though I've no experience of such things & am too busy anyway. Maybe Bob might like to hop out here & look at it; Edwy Lee or I cd put him up, and it wd be delightful to see him. Just a vague idea, probably of no interest, but do pass it on unless you think best not. Mrs [Mary Elizabeth] Moonen, Dr [A. Arnold] Axilrod, are the names. I know a newspaperwoman here and through her he *might* be able to get a card, though it wd be best to bring one from some N Y paper or magazine. Bob's great advantages over me wd be journalistic experience & photographic. Just an idea.

I'm delighted by your idea about the letters & articles, and of course feel nothing but interest, attention, & sympathy. You must not worry about the crudeness of the titles – that is almost inevitable – for instance I saw an article last night by Bertrand Russell called "How to Enjoy Life, Love, and Work", and I expect it was a good article too, he is one of the best living manipulators of the English language for moral ideas, besides being a Nobel prizewinner (he lectured in Princeton the day the prize was announced and the ovation was very affecting). About initials & dashes I just don't know: an editor could tell you better, and I wd guess, only guess, he'd prefer a pseudonym. Like you I like the letter-idea better, but I like both and wish you all the luck in the world. *Courage* is what writing chiefly takes, when one has not the habit. Just jump in. Draft, without thought of detail or order; then fix. In ten minutes that is what I am going to being doing with the section for my Shakespeare biography on his use of the *Bible*, and by night I expect to have six pages that I didn't have before. I have been ill the last ten days or so, but today am much better (and I have a competent doctor, don't worry at all), and am also emerging from a real depression, my first in a good while. Besides you do have the habit of writing. All writing is writing, although admittedly some kinds are harder than others. But all are hard, when you think and feel and try to get things right. The two great things are to be *clear* and *short*; but rhythms matter too, and unexpectedness. You lead the reader briskly in one direction, then you spin him around, or you sing him a lullaby and then hit him on the head. Let me hear how it goes as soon as you can.

The weather has been like midsummer. All my little girl students trot around half-naked and trouble the boys and nobody listens to my lectures except my really good students although I have been very cunning on Luther, from whom I pass next week, with unconcealed horror, to Calvin. I am still reading nothing but theology and see almost nobody.

Love,
John

[JB had been sued by Brooks Brothers for an unpaid balance of $60.
JB's "Dream Song 19" refers to a mirror that belonged to Dr. Axilrod who

was convicted of murder and serving time in Stillwater Prison. JB, at the time of
writing the poem, had come into possession of the mirror.

Mrs. Berryman had written to JB about some ideas for magazine articles that
she was considering writing.]

[Minneapolis]
Dearest Jill,   Saturday afternoon [25 June 1955]
I really think I am going to die of happiness and excitement.

There's many a slip, so I've said nothing, but now the two great things
in suspense seem today to be settled.

I signed this morning with Farrar Straus for the Bradstreet poem and
the Shakespeare biography. They are taking over my Viking obligation,
and the terms are much better, and I like them very much. [Robert]
Giroux is my editor. I am thoroughly pleased.

And this morning I learned definitely at last that I have the same job
here next year – much the same courses, and so infinitely less labour of
course – and at $5300, which is 500 better than the rate I've been work-
ing at.

And coming back just now I find my books have arrived from Iowa!!!!!!
so that I have the core of my own Sh'n collection to work with.

I had excellent reason to *think* all these things wd happen; for them
actually to happen, however, is a very different matter, and I feel indescribably freer for my fascinating work. When I come to the end of this
chapter I'll write to you properly. Dear love,

John

[JB had contracted with Viking in 1953 for the Shakespeare biography.]

[Minneapolis]
Darling,   Saturday early evening [9 July 1955]
I am dreadfully sorry you did not have a better birthday. It is bad
enough to be unwell, but to have in addition to be in such uncertainty,
and even short of money, and to have plans change: I feel so grieved by
all this that I could weep. Sometimes the burden of existence seems so
heavy that one feels less like [Edmund] Husserl on his deathbed than like
Thomas Hardy. Husserl said, "Christ has forgiven all of us", but Hardy
asked to have read to him a last time the great quatrain of the *Rubaiyat*,

O Thou, who man of baser earth didst make
And didst with Paradise devise the Snake,
For all the sin wherewith the face of man
Is blacken'd, man's forgiveness give – and take!

I hope with all my heart that you will keep courage up, and that your recovery will hasten and Wednesday go well.

Never think again of the five dollars and again many thanks. I send thirty for the end of it now and if you have to use this for anything first, just let me know. I would send it you outright if I could.

At any rate my contracts finally came back from Viking this afternoon, canceled, and so my arrangements with Farrar Straus are complete.

I had better tell you what your gift is. It is a genealogical chronological history, the Kings & Queens of England & France from Charlemagne to Elizabeth I (with Popes, Emperors, etc), heavily illustrated, and the edition is being done to order, in full blue leather, so Heaven knows how soon it will be here; besides, my Blackwell account had been inactive for a long time and there may have been delay over that.

I've been since four this morning at very hard & delicate work and am very nervous: I am going to bathe & shave & go out to a French film at the edge of the city. Your next birthday I am going to spend with you.

Dearest love,
John

[The gift book JB ordered from Blackwell's was Giusseppe Fattorusso's *Kings and Queens of England and France: A Genealogical, Chronological History.* 2 vols. Florence, 1953–54.]

Minneapolis
Dearest Mother,   Wednesday [24 August 1955?]
I'm remiss at writing because so busy and literally out of the world, dealing solely with dreams, of which I have now alas 120 since November, and seeing scarcely anyone. I am unblocking gradually, or rather in violent painful strides. The dream I did yesterday was entirely about that school in Chickasha – the name of which the dream suggests may have been St Stephen's – do you remember?

Not too good luck in one detail: in addition to the Greek course, I have to give a Modern course (Lenin, Eliot, Freud, Joyce, etc) this Fall and will be hard pressed. I am working at them already. Whether I'll be able to come East before Thanksgiving I don't know yet.

A specimen page for the Bradstreet poem has come, and it's stunning; [Peter] Beilenson, who is one of the best American designers, put on his seven-league boots when he did it. Gollancz has offered to bring it out in England, but Giroux thinks Faber ought to have a look first. Ben Shahn is doing drawings, if he & Giroux can come to terms; I'm curious to see what they'll be like.

I bought a vast window-fan, so the weather immediately improved. Also I've been on picnics twice to Wisconsin, in a deep gorge with water-fall on Apple River.

You haven't written since just before the (Cin'ti) Chamber of Horrors, and I'm anxious to hear.

I am lost in the changes of this lawyer-business. Do I still owe some money or not? I haven't cashed your cheque of the 5th for $15. Let me know. I am getting low in cash but will be all right. I hope your health & spirits haven't got down in all the rain and heat.

Dearest love,
John

[The school in Chickasha, Oklahoma, was St. Joseph's Academy.]

Minneapolis

Dearest Mother,   Sunday [18 September 1955]

Sorry not to write: except for laying out my courses, and keeping on with the dream-work, I've been indolent & tired, though in very good spirits. With this latter work I have gone about as far as I can for the present; I have done a great part of more than 150 dreams, and I doubt if anyone has ever gone deeper, and I am stale and wish to come up. My courses are going to be interesting, as usual. Also last night I began Shakespeare again.

Proofs of the Bradstreet book came yesterday and they are beautiful; but I still don't know the publication date, because Shahn & my publisher have still not come to an arrangement.

No reminder was necessary about Bob's birthday: I had it laid out.

That "Dream Song" is the first of a large number. They will help each other out.

I'm sorry: I ran out of cash, and had in the end to cash your old $15 cheque, which I meant to return. Tomorrow I'll have money & send it you. Let me know if I owe you more than fifteen.

I am distressed, dear, to hear that the Chelsea [Hotel] is lifting your rent so. Tell me at once when you decide abt moving, if you will. I haven't found a place yet, but am now, since yr letter, seriously thinking of an unfurnisht place. You say bed (is that the three-quarter one?) and the maple table, yes, and what chest of drawers is it? I have a chair in Princeton & of course library & gramophone etc. It's expensive but tempting. I'd forgotten all about the stuff at your place. Can you truly spare the things?? Be honest. I must think. I'll write again very soon. My lectures begin tomorrow week. Edwy Lee described to me your party in detail, and I was delighted. You bowled him over. He's a nice boy, not v reliable though, I wdn't tell him much, but he seems to be getting in better shape which I'm glad to see. I hope you're keeping well.

Love,
John

[Minneapolis]
Dearest Jill,   Sunday [25 September 1955]
It's a great relief, both on your account and on mine, that the [Chelsea] Hotel's been more reasonable as I take it and that you're not moving immediately. I am wild to move myself but have not found anything, and have not been able either to substantiate your excellent idea abt the part-load return haul from New York.

Here's the fifteen, & again all thanks.

I'm getting intellectual indigestion from so much preparation, and am glad my courses begin tomorrow. I *hope*, even this week, to settle down to Shakespeare daily as well. Rough year it's going to be, but I feel ready.

I hope yr New England jaunt is fun as well, and that the Government will lie down & wag its tail abt your income tax. I wish they wd toss me back the Guggenheim excess they looted me of; I'm told it may take years. Eisenhower's attack makes me sorry, gloomy, and alarmed. Idea of Nixon turns me pale. However, all this may lead to Stevenson.

Dear love,
John

1929 – 3rd St South
Minneapolis
Dearest Jill,   Columbus Day [10 October 1955]

First chance I've had to write and even now I must be short. My courses are swamping me; I underestimated them.

I at last found an excellent apartment and moved last Thursday. Big high livingroom, with range-&-sink unit in corner with refrig; big bedroom left, with big bathroom off it; the study where I'm writing, right. Modern, & pretty well furnisht. Five min walk from my office: I just cross the Mississippi in fact. With heat & utilities, air-conditioning, $80. I only this morning got it in order but I like it.

I'll have to see about the furniture, but I could certainly use the books that are at your place. Would two cartons or so hold them? I don't like you to pack or take them to the post office, but maybe Bob would, one day?

Haven't found yr last few letters yet, in the chaos of my papers. I'll write again at the weekend. I hope you're well, and busy but not too busy. Shahn & Farrar Straus have come to terms, & he's making drawings.

Love,
John

Minneapolis
Dearest Mother,   Thursday [5 January 1956]

I'm sorry abt the virus – yr letter only came today – and hope you got to New Hampshire, and, whether or not, have thrown it off altogether. I gave in the other day and bought a heavy winter coat, fur collar, sheepskin lined, long; but it cost me practically nothing – I won't even tell you what, till you see it.

A thousand thanks for the diary and the notebooks. It is wonderful how many things one does *not* have to transfer from one year's diary, addresses, etc, obligations done with, to another. . . .

I loafed a day, dodged invitations and got written almost the whole of an article I have owed *Poetry* for a whole year. It goes off tom'w or Sat, and delighted me in the writing – it has no importance, just a chronicle review, but I am so unused to sitting at the typewriter making sentences that are to be set up in type, that it filled me with bliss, and got me in practice.

I love the glasses. I now have a stunning decanter that E gave me, a very handsome cocktail pitcher that Ann [Levine] did, and these, and the two Swedish glasses (highball) that I bought myself for housewarming; and hope nobody throws any more stones at me for a bit. News very bad indeed came today: that I have to give *three* courses in the Spring quarter, each meeting every day. I thought the Univ of Minn had done to me everything in its repertory, but I was wrong. My spirit is not broken by this utterly unforeseen information, but it wd be exaggerating to say that I regard it as welcome, for it will seriously affect my work. Ah well. My lectures this quarter are much better & easier than before and my students unusual sprightly.

Let me hear how you is, darling.

Love,
John

[The article JB was working on, "The Long Way to MacDiarmid," appeared in the April 1956 issue of *Poetry*. The books reviewed were: *The Metal and the Flower* by P.K. Page, *Poets of Today* by Harry Duncan, *Samurai and Serpent Poems* by Murray Noss, *Another Animal* by May Swenson, *Birds in the Mulberry* by George Abbe, *A Character Invented* by LeRoy Smith, *Events and Signals* by F.R. Scott, *Leaves Without a Tree* by G.S. Fraser, and *Selected Poems* by Hugh MacDiarmid.

Elizabeth Ann Levine (or Ann, as many people called her) was a graduate student at the University of Minnesota and a friend of the Bellows. Berryman had begun seeing her shortly after his arrival in Minneapolis.]

1929 South 3rd St,
Minneapolis

Dearest Jill,   Sunday evening [26 February 1956]

I understand completely about Lent and am in deep sympathy with you.

I am also *very* sorry for not having written. I had nothing good to tell, and much bad, but too complicated for letters. Briefly, the attacks upon my department that we expected have been coming and are more severe than we expected, and it is still quite impossible to say what is going to happen. Anyway it looks as if my permanent appointment will certainly not be able to go through this year; and the whole department may be knocked to pieces altogether, but it is idle to anticipate this until it happens. Some weeks I have spent more hours defending my job (in endless committee meetings and so on) than I have doing it. We are all very much discouraged and weary. But the quarter ends this next week and we have a respite. Don't worry about this until I tell you more when I know more. . . .

Shahn made the drawings, nine of them, very handsome, but the book cannot come out till the Fall; which is unlucky also.

I gave a big public lecture on the *Tempest* lately, which seemed very successful (it was easily the best lecture I ever gave), as were a smaller one on Existentialism and three on Christian origins. Week after next I fly to the coldest place in the whole world (Bemidji, where the State Teachers College is) to give a Convocation address. My courses have been fair, considering the pressures, and are at any rate better than when I gave them first. Needless to say, I have not got much real work done. I think: soon. Bless you thro' Lent, darling. Dearest love,

John

[P.S.] Health pretty fair, considering.

[P.P.S.] I am going to write to Bob at the end of this week. It has been impossible. Saul [Bellow] has remarried, wh. is good.

[The Department of Interdisciplinary Studies at the University of Minnesota, which was made up of the Humanities, Social Science and Natural Science Programs, was undergoing attacks by several other departments and by individuals at faculty meetings. Despite the understandable insecurities expressed by JB in this letter and the next one, his appointment was renewed for the following academic year. Saul Bellow had married Alexandra ("Sondra") Tschacbasov.]

Minneapolis

Darling,   Wednesday night, 27 June [1956]

I am in the middle of the second act of a play and write scatteredly. The evening my lectures finished, Saul & Sondra [Bellow] turned up from Reno and stayed w me several days, then I was making up exams & ill, then I started writing, finished the first act, was ill again, now have to finish the draft by the end of next week, in order to have *one* week to prepare my [Stephen] Crane & [William Dean] Howells course which then goes for five weeks——during which I also mean to revise my play into sense. So: scatteredly.

At the end, in the last faculty mtg, they cut loose on us again; and after promise after promise, not only do I not have a permanent appointment, but neither of my two superiors has had the guts to tell me. . . .

Unbound sheets of my book came, and then [Conrad] Aiken gave them permission to quote what he wrote me three years ago and they have it on the front flap: "It seems to me to be the finest poem ever written by an American, a classic right on the doorstep." They are pleased by this.

Play is a comedy abt Washington DC right now: single set, a Georgetown garden; 8 people. Saul wanted to collaborate, but I had to go on by myself – I set it up years ago and he's two-thirds of the way thro' a novel. Arthur Miller stayed w them 6 wks, ringing up Marilyn Monroe constant. Silly world it is. (Saul is even going their marr. app.) New typewriter I finally *must* have. Some remnant grandiosity, after all this insult, got out above: read, of course, "*one* of the fin*est* poem*s*". Bloody hard work, plays.

love, John

[The play JB was revising is entitled *It's Been Real – Or – A Tree, A Tree.* It has not been published.]

Early in the summer of 1956, JB and Ann Levine had become engaged and were eager to marry. However, JB's divorce from Eileen had not yet been finalized.

[Minneapolis]

Dearest Jill,   Thursday night [11 October 1956]

After several more wild conversations, and a couple of calm ones, betw E [Eileen] and myself, my lawyer informs me today that he has received the notice-of-summons or whatever the hell it is from her, *signed*, and has filed it and the 30-day waiting period has begun. I suppose things will now go along, but one never knows. Unhappily both our lawyers are both supremely wilful; both, both. When the 30 days are up, the case can get on the docket quickly, *he says*, and it's a matter of a few minutes in court. That decree is final. BUT: there is a six months' non-remarriage business in Minnesota, as well as various other states, so we'll have to go to Iowa (ugh) or Kansas City or somewhere to get hitched legal.

We may decide to be as dark as the grave about this. I don't know. At any rate please be extremely unknowing with Blanche [Levine, Ann's

mother] and indeed everyone. When she askt me privately the other evening I just said I was switching lawyers & cdn't tell *at all* WHEN it wd
be. If you have relevant ideas I will certainly be glad to hear them, though
I don't wish to place any further burden of thought on you. We'll work it
out.

I was intensely nervous until today, except during most of the nearly
full-three days we were in the North woods – which I enjoyed as much,
almost, and so did A [Ann Levine], as Bayport. Stunning weather, the
four (Ralph [Ross] & a friend) of us got on wellnigh perfectly, nobody
else about, walking, music, pingpong, an outboard motor A & I made a
trip in, and Sunday I even went swimming – very very briefly, alone. My
courses are all right; the Greek course is taking more time than I expected,
as I now fill in my background and of course my acquaintance with the
Iliad is improving; my modern course has seventy-six in it; the attacks on
my department have begun again, but it's imposs yet to say what will
happen – with three of our best friends in the English Dept away this
year, almost anything might, and indeed there is to be a public debate
next week about whether to abolish the Dept of Gen Studies.

A deafening silence seems to be greeting AB [*Homage to Mistress
Bradstreet*], with the lone exception of a – big deal! – review in the *Chicago Sun-Times* last Sunday which is at any rate more knowledgeable
than the two first *(Balt. Sun* & *N Y Times)*. At the risk of appearing to
be in love with myself I'll quote the beginning & end: "Any man who
cares for poetry will read JB's beautiful, powerful, tender, love-committed
new poem. . . . Having sustained this ambitious piece through that discipline, Berryman shows himself unbested by any poet of his generation,
and it is impossible to imagine that his work would not win for him one
or more of the nation's poetry awards". But as usual there is no *critical*
remark, and again not a single quotation, and as for "impossible to imagine": Haha, and who ever reads or even heard of the *Chicago Sun-Times*
anyway? But Ann is pleased, & added, at the bottom of a grocery note,
"I love John Logan!" (the reviewer). Tate sent me from Cambridge before
he left a blurb to be passed on to Giroux (I did, & hear nothing): "This
poem adds a fourth to the three first-rate long poems by Americans in
this century—the others being by Pound *(Cantos)*, Eliot *(Wasteland)*,
and (Hart) Crane *(The Bridge)*".* Woof woof. End of self-love section.

---

* The parenthetical insertions in this quotation are JB's own.

A enjoyed her talk with you, and also – *mirabile dictu* – her first *real* driving lesson, yesterday; in spite of her nervousness. She thinks the instructor is excellent and he thinks she will be good.

Truth is, I am pretty well resigned to the book's nearly-complete immediate failure. If they are going to get nonentities to review me, and if the big journals are going to ignore the book (there are no signs of reviews in: *Time, The Herald-Tribune, Newsweek, The New Yorker, The Sat Review* – which last hates me in fact, as you probably remember), nothing of real interest will happen for years. However, I expect that it will then happen. But it has taken me two weeks to get resigned, after my sense of injury in having the [*New York*] *Times* put John Holmes on my book; and I still feel some disappointment, since my situation is brilliantly unsatisfactory and I had rather hoped that the book might get me commissions for writing or a job less paranoiac or something. Can't tell: maybe people will read the poem underground, or Farrar Straus will advertise it with the advance opinions, or the literary magazines will sufficiently make a point of it to cause interest. Ship foundering, not sunk. We must *wait*. It is the restlessness of three years' waiting that I am suffering, which I pretend is the fortnight.

Can't imagine who the stuttering man is [probably Edward Hoagland who had been a student of JB's at Harvard]; I pass in review those who stutter that I've known and see nobody likely.

The [package of] Rutgers books are prob for me. The book of yrs I had in mind was Plutarch [*The Lives of the Noble Grecians and Romans*], of wh I've got the first vol here now and will trade it back to you for the second.

Thanks for the cocktail napkins. I put on the postcard comprehensive thanks for all your goodness in New York, and repeat it. You helpt Ann unspeakably, and me. I'm glad the apartment is rolling on; tell me how looks. We haven't found one yet.

A joke: I've had two letters from Faulkner, whom Eisenhower is prodding – fast – to organize Amer writers to see how to improve relations betw us & foreign lands. The second is wholly serious, & methodical, but the first is only partly so and among his own suggestions are these:

"1) Anesthetize, for one year, American vocal cords.

2) Abolish, for one year, Amer passports.

3) Commandeer every Amer automobile.

Secrete Johnson grass seed in the cushions and every other available place. Fill the tanks with gasoline. Leave the switch key in the switch and push the car across the iron curtain."

His fourth sugg is more serious and his long quote fr the President is solemn indeed; but I thought these wd amuse you. I'll show you some time my reply, which is also partly clowning but chiefly serious

Keep well, darling, and very well.

Love,
John

[P.S.] Maybe better not let anyone know of this Faulkner quotation who might cite it – Only for friends – & Bob, to whom my love & tell him I *hope* to send him less Paleolithic pictures presently.

In November, Mrs. Berryman visited JB in Minneapolis and met Ann Levine. During this time, as the following letter reveals, mother and son had another of their serious quarrels—and Mrs. Berryman returned to New York a day earlier than planned.

[New York]

Dear John,   Wednesday, 21 November 1956

I recognize, now, how much I have been to blame with you for how long. Part of your anger has been, it seems to me, a resentment against unjust accusations – unjust despite conduct, since the behavior flowed from the accusing. Blame causes guilt, either in belief or in conduct that proves the accusation.

And anger brings anger in its train. And anger I felt, condemning the conduct without looking to the real. Anger I used to bolster myself to the stand of being willing to, having to yield up our association rather than to go on with irregular and (or so I thought then) unjustified outbursts. It is a thing that needs any crutch to stand with, to give up a son and the more so that I have, along with much else, that I see now, a loving heart. I have loved you too much for wisdom, or it is perhaps nearer truth to say that with love or in anger, I am not wise.

It does prove, to me at least, that I recognized the validity of Ann's understanding of you and felt rather than knew that her instinctive knowledge of you was right and true, and due. Never before, under circumstances no matter how dire, (since your senior year, and then you were not away) have I felt it possible to think of cutting myself off from you.

Somehow, somewhere in me, was the profound surety that you might need if not me someone and I might be that one. With Ann I feel that you have the one you need, and felt this or even with anger's strength and without understanding as I do now I could not have torn away so.

I do not plead my nerves or tensions as an excuse for that scene, but certainly they are what caused it. You are not without fault as indeed who is but the deep base cause is mine. For this sin I cannot atone to you and to Ann, all I can do is to pray to be forgiven the sin against love.

It is unlikely that I will grow easier to be with, wiser, more bearable – there is no blundering like that of the well-meaning obtuse person. I can not feel that my nerves will be calmer or tensions less, as business cares must increase as I age and have to fight harder to earn a living. Your marriage is the important thing, and it well may be that continuing a relationship with me may be a hindrance to your marriage's success. If this is a decision you came or come to, I accept it with all good will. I do not take it to hold any animus or ill feeling, it is just that you must protect this, the most important relationship of your life.

If you feel that we can continue a long-distance relationship with safety to you and Ann, I shall be glad, of course. But my feelings in this matter are secondary to your welfare and hers. With love, your devoted mother,

Jill Berryman

Minneapolis
Dearest Mother,   Sunday 25 November 1956

All I can say is that I love you steadily and see no point in going over what happened here, – for which I am no more willing to acknowledge your accepting a primary measure of blame than I am prepared to take it on myself. Life does not work that way. One thing I can tell you though will help explain what must have seemed mysterious as well as abominable: I had all the weekend a strong sense of impending nightmare, which made all the preparation (done as I know with every good will and in fact blazing kindness on your part) seem like tempting the gods. My sense was perfectly justified. On the Tuesday, when I rang up my lawyers to find out exactly when the 30-day waiting period ended they apologized to me for perhaps not having made it clear to me that the 30-day waiting period had not yet begun, but wd begin only after a prior 30-day waiting period. That was good. I had tried twice to hang myself the night after you left. But they required the 3 witnesses, they said, that I had previously told them I cd not possibly supply (to the desertion), *moreover*; and for days it lookt as if no divorce wd be possible. Since I am being cheated & insulted left & right (after 3 wks, I have had no answer from [Antal] Dorati to my letter) I was not surprised, although I was horrified, by this. Now the [divorce] hearing is set for Dec 20th and *may* work.

. . . A has a cold but is otherwise well, indeed blooming. I got her some Courvoisier & chocolates, which – both of which – it appears she likes. I am sorry that you told her mother whatever impelled her to address A here, but I do not blame you & it has passed I think over. We both owe you & give you one thousand thanks for all yr goodness abt the apartment & the car. Detailed thanks also abt the spread bill $6.60 for wh I enclose a cheque & for extras: I wd have paid for yr whole trip if I cd afford it.

Love,
John

[P.S.] The Greek bks go off tom'w.

[JB had agreed to translate Paul Claudel's *"Le Chemin de la Croix"* for Antal Dorati's composition, *Cantata Dramatica*. Dorati was then conductor of the Minneapolis Symphony Orchestra. The music was ultimately set to the French text, but JB's translation, "The Way of the Cross," was sung at the February 6, 1959, performance.]

[Minneapolis]
Monday [26 November 1956]

Incredible! – good news – out of the blue, *Partisan* has given me a Rockefeller fellowship in poetry for '57: $4000.

J.

Following three years of separation and numerous legal delays, JB was divorced by Eileen on December 19. He and Ann were married exactly one week later in Sioux Falls, South Dakota, and spent their honeymoon in the Black Hills.

[Minneapolis]

Dearest Mother,   Sunday [6 January 1957?]

It is shocking news abt yr back. Is this slipping-out like a disc business in one of the sacral segments just below? What are they doing about it?

I'm glad Bob is there? Will you telephone us as soon as you are up to it? I'm sorry for the pain, which must be ferocious.

Ann is well, and is enjoying the use of the car immensely. She sends sympathy & love. I took the written driver's test the other day, getting 98%, but can't practice until the permit comes – usually a matter of weeks, but I called a friend [Arthur Naftalin] who is the State Commissioner of Administration & it's being hurried through.

I've not been at all well for a long time and am now through with a complete check: nothing organic wrong anywhere. I'm in my fifth day of severe withdrawal symptoms for a simultaneous cutting-to-the-bone of cigarettes & alcohol; I hear it gets less awful later. A dentist is also ripping me up twice weekly, and in general very little in life appears to me agreeable, though I recognize that I am on the mend and my terrible cough has already begun to dissolve.

Our trip West will have to wait for verbal description. We enjoyed it, so far as people in such poor nervous condition can be said to enjoy things, and it made a change. The most dramatic thing was swinging in space in metal seats up the Terry Peak ski-lift, which has no rival betw the Rockies & the Alps (4/5 of a mile long, during wh the vertical rise is a quarter of a mile), from the top of which you see four states), and which frightened A worse than anything since she was 10 yrs old.

We are trying to move, and may have found a place. Tate tells me I was second in the voting for the Bollingen, which he won, with R Wilbur third; v surprising; don't tell this. The Bollingen is the country's chief prize. There's no real news of my book yet.

Courage & patience! love,
John

[Mrs. Berryman's back problem was later diagnosed, to her surprise, as lumbago.]

2900 James Ave South, Mpls 8

Dearest Mother,   Monday [8 April 1957]

I have a great deal to write you but a million things yet to do and I can't yet write properly. I will, next Sunday, if not before. The baby is all right. I cannot decide whether he is one continuous howl, or on the whole a very *good* baby – yesterday he was the first, today the second – but I can say plainly that there is nothing whatever wrong with him in existence or behaviour, and it wd not take much for me to regard him as perfect. He is at any rate adorably sweet and I want you to see him as soon as you feel you can. I believe you will like him. I feel sure he is as grateful for the calendar as we are. I love that calendar and we had not got this next one. Oddly: on the day it came came to me a letter from Japan (you know how A & I feel abt that country) – from Tatsuo Iwase with a fantastic address in Tokyo, only wanting permission to have an article of mine translated into Japanese, but we were amused.

Yesterday came in Marie-Lorraine Lee and her children, then in the evening Saul and the McCloskys [Herbert and Mitzi], after Morgan Blum for dinner. Far too much, both for Ann & the poupie, and it wreckt even me. These are the first people he has seen since Allen Tate brought him home, and then Ralph Ross & Alicia came in directly after – but I can't say he *saw* any of them. And Blanche; she was a great strain to A, as usual; but she does not bother me, except now & then, and she really was an immense help in the multiple labour of setting up the baby here, Ann's gaining strength, proceeding with the apartment's furnishing (it is largely now done), and my winding up my lectures. We are thinking of having a nurse in and going to a dinner & reception for the Ambassador from Japan tomorrow, but it depends on how Ann feels & of course how Paul is. Ears set close to his head, a long skull w one bump, circumcision healed & umbilicus nearly, long fingers, eyes first blue now bewilderingly grey & then brown. Must post this. Be careful well.

Love,
John

[Paul Berryman was born on March 5, 1957.
Herbert McCloskey was teaching in the Political Science Department at the University of Minnesota.
Morgan Blum was teaching in the Humanities Program at the University of Minnesota.]

2900 James Avenue South
Minneapolis

Dearest Mother,   1 June 1957
I am *very* glad you cd sublet (this is our problem too) and have relaxed, at whatever cost to work. If I relaxed just now, they cd just come & bury the parts; I am engaged in a mere survival-operation, of wh the results are not yet clear. I am glad about the car too. The baby's name is King

Pouperding the Great (alias Mr Fart-cracker, alias x & y & z), known familiarly as "Mister Poo" (to be spoken very rapidly): now the nearest thing here for a Buick is "Mister Boo"; but I think it risky to suggest names for a car. Here is $50, as of plane-fare, for whenever you can come: I'll say something of my plans in a moment.

Paul is obstinate, fiercely demanding (& slow to forgive), has strong taste-preferences (today he cast his cold eye on his first vegetable, a yellow veg; bananas he likes good), and still spends most of his waking time at visions, off somewhere, which he watches absorbedly. However: he has begun smiling – and his smiles make all of humanity's other operations look insincere – they wreathe out from behind his face through his face. Tickling his chin is one way to produce them, but only if he is in the mood; he still passes much time in mystery, abstraction, brooding. We do not know what he is thinking about, and neither do the psychologists. I think he is going to be slow-developing and am very glad about this, and meanwhile he is rather beautiful. A bad thing on his cheek has gone away, he is getting a pot, his second chin is wicked to contemplate, his skin is ravishing all over, and he smells good. He has taken to smiling sometimes *while* you change him; I cannot say more.

Tuesday, 11 June [1957]

I haven't been able to get back to this until now. My plans, after undergoing all sorts of changes, have stabilized at this: I leave for the Orient about July 1st (and will then be there for something betw two & three months), so that I take it you'll wait and come out from N.C. [North Carolina] Ann's plans are uncertain as yet – one of us will write soon. We may not go to Italy at all (thanks abt Robert [Fitzgerald's] gun – you did just right), but meet in Spain when my Indian stint is over.

There was various news. After failing to get either the National Bk Award or the Pulitzer, I was given the Harriet Monroe award, a serious business of $500 in reporting which the NYTimes described me a "young poet"; and there was another overwhelming review of the book in *The New Republic*, in some ways better than [John] Ciardi's. The English Dept here finally about-faced and asked for a joint appointment for me at tenure level, and apparently this is going through at a fairly high salary level. The Library of Congress has asked me to read there next Febr 24, at $300 to $500. Those are the chief items. My health has been very poor but I expect the next fortnight to make a profound difference; I'm through at the University except for details.

Paul's smiles increase, and he studies the cats you sent for hours at a time. You will certainly like him. I took a carbon of this to send to Bob and must get them in the mail now. All three of our loves,

John

[Mrs. Berryman had given (with payments still remaining) JB and Ann her red Ford convertible, "Rudolph," and bought a 1953 Buick for herself. She had asked JB for help – "perhaps one of Paul's favorite words" – in naming it.

JB was preparing to leave on a lecture tour of India under the auspices of the United States Information Service. The tour was to stop first in Japan, and Ann and Paul were to meet him in Italy at the conclusion of the trip.

The University of Minnesota granted JB a joint appointment with tenure, in the Humanities Program and the English Department, and promoted him to Associate Professor of Interdisciplinary Studies.]

[Japan]

Darling –   Wednesday afternoon, 10 July 1957

It doesn't seem possible that I am crossing Japan (or Honshu, or most of it) on a train, but I am. Weird heights terraced, are left just now. Mostly we have been going along the coast – it is nine hours altogether, on this express, from Tokyo to Kyoto – with the open sea visible on the left and hills on the right – hills not with trees but clothed in them. Paddy-fields both sides, peasants in them planting or whatever. Till Yokohama & below it, the ride was as interesting as Trenton, New Jersey; since then it's been wonderful – except for the large advertising character-signs set in the landscape, of wh. I counted 37 in the last 100 yards before a river and 10 in the first 50 yds after it. They have mostly disappeared now, nature makes the most of its space, so to speak, here. Slopes are scalloped.

Kyoto, Saturday evening

At the above point an auto-salesman educated in the U.S. askt to join me – and since I got here I have been studying gardens, in a daze of unhappiness & attention. This afternoon I went thro' the celebrated tea ceremony at the house of the greatest living authority – historical & aesthetic alike – on both it *and* Japanese gardens (on wh. he's written a shelf of books, one of wh. is the *reason* I'm in Japan), Mirei Shigemori, whom by a series of coincidences I met – and a Zen priest was there, and a man named Suzuki who was interpreting for me – and last night I was reading the famous D.T. Suzuki's essays on Zen Buddhism in an Anchor bk [*Zen Buddhism, Selected Writings*] I brought fr. Mpls. Life is odd, odd. I was rather dead fr. travel on arrival but my garden at my inn (& my rooms, unlike anything I ever saw) brought me at once to life – & *peace*. I rose at 7 & wandered – shopped: I hope you will like your Tokyo dolls (with nothing fun for years) but I sent you something more serious from here (the metal top lifts *out*), along w. a very different doll. Yesterday I studied my garden fr. 7 to 11:30, then went to Nijo Castle, & then Ryoan-ji, where the waterless garden (the most famous in the world, of abt 1500) was the object of my stop over in Japan. I'll *tell* you abt it. I have elaborate notes on both "my" garden & it, wh. will form (lead to) part of the prelude to my book. Today I kept thinking, then went thro Nishi Hongan-ji, regularly thought of as the hottest surviving example of Buddhist architecture anywhere, then put the diplomatic people here to work & wound up w. Shigemori's. One thing I especially wanted to see at Nishi Hongan-ji, paintings of the Thirty-Six Famous Poets, was or were destroyed by a typhoon *last year* (1956) – *were* 1600 or so. The tea ceremony lasted four hours, by the way, in fair imitation, as to length, for Indian socializing, I'm warned. But in India most of the people I'll be dealing with will speak English – *nobody* here does, much as the books kid you.

I have wished repeatedly that you were with me, & in fact conducted w. you on the train a sort of dialogue – wh. I was preluding w. description, when interrupted. It is all in my head but must wait: I've written only one letter to Ann & must get another off before I go back to Tokyo (& so straight to India) tomorrow night. I promist Ralph a letter at once too – ain't writ it yet; this is my (lousy) second. My strength has been going to recovering – massages nightly, eating – & surviving the alternating *rain* – *heat* that was supposed to end here yesterday and hasn't – & discovering – the results I think will appear

love,
John

[JB spent four days in Kyoto studying the gardens and the great Zen temples there, especially Ryoan-ji and Daisen-in.

Between July 22 and September 3, JB gave twenty-six lectures at fourteen universities and colleges in Poona, Bombay, Cuttack, Patna, Calcutta, Serampore and Ahmedabad, sharing the platform with Howard Munford, Professor of American Literature at Middlebury College, Vermont.

Claridge's Hotel
New Delhi, India

Dearest Jill–   11 September 1957

I flew down here this morning to see the Taj, before going out to Karachi & Athens tom'w afternoon, & am glad I did, because photos give you no idea of its qualities – it is not white but thousand-hued, and all this inlaid – you have to *feel* the marble before standing off to look – it is far more sumptuous than I expected even, but also austere in the highest degree – and in certain lights it seems to float on its great platform – the strategy straight-on view does it no sort of justice – and the feeling inside, by the ceremonial caskets & then the actual ones below, is indescribably solemn, pathetic, & grand. – A virus I pickt up in Calcutta 3 wks ago made the 2nd half of the tour a nightmare, tho' I missed only one lecture. I am glad to be done, & anxious to see Ann & the Poo. But I saw much less of India than I hoped – I missed Elephanta, Konarak! Ajanta! Jaipur – a heavy list – not to speak of the whole South. Perhaps I may come back some day, *not!* in the summer. I lost 10 lbs but am otherwise recovering (I actually collapsed in Ahmedabad). – I am v. pleased you liked the Japanese stuff, and very sorry the Phelpses are not working out. – We spent two wonderful days in Benares, and a Calcutta banker instructed me a little in Yoga. I achieved the free-lotus position at the 1st try.

Love,
John

[P.S.] I believe the tour is regarded by the Dept. [of State] as a decided success. They caress me – and are reading my own report with awe.

[JB's essay "Thursday Out" provides a vivid record of his visit to the Taj Mahal.

Mrs. Berryman had worked a short time for Phelps Industries in Skyland, North Carolina.]

Levanto

Dearest Jill ⊤   Thursday 19 September [1957]

I'm out of Asia, & fine except that I have no energy – it's taken since last Saturday when I got here (after 15 hours' sleep in Rome) to put this pen to this paper as I now do. I haven't even unpacked, but I just emptied *one* bag & found the letter I wrote you in Agra, which I'll send along with. I think another week or ten days will see me very well. My spirits are excellent, I swim a little, & loaf, and talk Ann's ear a bit off, and admire the Poo. They are both perfect. I never saw Ann look or feel better, and Mr Poo is the happiest, healthiest, most adorable little baby person in existence. We have long confabs & airplane games. He insists on standing much of the time – I just balance him, not support him; or he springs up, pulverizing my groin, & back down, & up, & down, & up . . He is so grown that for a second I hardly knew him, but he is entirely himself, and I must say that in various ways he does now look exactly like me. He is a perfect anthology of expressions, shy, gay, crowing, brooding (a lot of this), observing – & he reaches for everything, but so far mostly with his knuckles in. This place is beautiful, a beach in a basin of high hills. At first everyone seemed impossibly *white* & *big* & prosperous & energetic, but I [am] getting used to it. My flight out was v. tiring, & I didn't stop at Athens. We have no plans yet. Either we'll stay here a while, I think, or move to the Costa Brava (W. Spain). Now mail can go safely & fast, please write more news & ask Bob if he won't too.

love, dear –
John

Madrid
9 November 1957

Darling,

I am sitting in an icy room, late Sunday afternoon, at the far end of our hotel from our room where the Poozer & Ann are, feeling very gay, as they are too, and drinking Tio Pepe which warms everything but my feet. I am going to make a swing, Segovia-Valladolid-Salamanca-Avila, prob not including Burgos which is a little too far north for my time, and then we are moving south, to Seville. Life here was in many ways hell until we solved it lately by getting an extra room and taking the Poo in turns, so that the responsible one doesn't suffer for the other too when he howls at night, and both A & I have now had some sleep for the first time in weeks. Poo is the most adorable thing you ever saw, for hours, especially during the day, and then WOW WOW WOW. He is brilliantly healthy – he had some diarrhea (who doesn't?) but an excellent doctor fixed that and says he is perfect. The problems are 1) teething – he now has *two* teeth, each of wh cost our heart's blood; 2) us in the same room, and traffic-noise, and imperfect bed & playing-place etc; 3) A's nerves as they react inevitably on his – I was with him night before last and all day yesterday while Ann went to Toledo, and he slept through last night (that is, woke but never cried) for the first time in I don't know when – of course I am a marvellous change for him, a whole new system of play & talk, and then I have not lately been ill for three weeks as Ann has. She picked up in Barcelona a ganglionitis wh is epidemic there but which the fool we consulted did not recognize, so it went untreated for 3 weeks; it's now gone. I felt out of order myself and had a thorough going-over at the Brit-Amer Hospital here and proved fine, just exhausted. Travelling w a baby, even a Poo (of wh, as you know, there is only one), is IT.

Poo is as strong as a horse, spends every second he can standing, makes long speeches when he feels particularly good and windmills with *joie de vivre* (to windmill is the same as to rooster flap up the wings), has pulled off my nose & out both my eyes and is a great reader – he has destroyed parts of every book he has reached, and his reach is good, for he can now crawl practically anywhere, given the incentive. I introduced him at three o'clock morning before last to his first serious literature: "Hickory dickory dock": which I say to him very solemnly, as he never saw anything said before, and with great emphasis, and no cue to him. He gets so interested he doesn't know what to do. Most of course of what we do is to make him laugh which he does freely. His other favourite recent thing from me is, said v softly, "Tippi-tippi-Tim, Tippi-Tim": he gurgles all over when he hears this. He *is* unusually beautiful by the way; there never I think was a hansomer baby than Mr Poozer-doo, and we likes him very well, as you can see; notwithstanding his merciless, wilful, & well-timed attacks upon our mental & physical well-being, resulting in my sleeping only from five to six-thirty night before last. Mister Baby (which we also call him), it was a privilege. His great mercy to us so far, apart from his beauty & joyfulness, is that his particularized will has as yet no stamina: he does not resent things being taken from him or kept from him that he can't have. *That* will be the day. *Dies Irae*; for he is going to be as stubborn as the grasp of Hell on silly man, if I read him correctly. I am very glad of it, and my defences are prepared in depth. He will win, fortunately. How could he lose anyway? For, besides being himself, who is probably far superior to me, he has me to go on: he Studies me, Ann says, like a creature hypnotized.

As for me, I am a character better than I used to be, darling. My responsibilities & labours & anxieties in recent months (to give these things their true heavy names, which rightly make us uneasy), along with my great happiness in Kyoto & Benares & Toledo, have changed me for the better, besides making me quiet, which I never was. Your good, or your wonderful, letter on my birthday was a great help lately. But I'll write again shortly about myself & you & these travels & so on.

Love,
John

Salamanca

Darling   16 November [1957]

I just came in – it's 10:30 or nearly time for (Spanish) dinner & I'm hungry – I'm having a beer in a splendid leathery place, behind glass, because it's chilly, in the Plaza Mayor – imagine a plaza say half the size of a football field, a bit longer than wide, w. one unbroken 4-storied bldg going round it, all 4 sides arcades & hundreds of people chattering & milling – and brightly lit! perh. the only place in Spain that is. This is thought the finest plaza in the country, of its non-Madrid, non-Barcelona kind (i.e., not *vast*), & it's v. gay & handsome. I liked the little Plaza Todo cover in Toledo, but it has no architectural pretensions; & besides one cd then still sit out. I must go eat but I wanted to write *something*. A city a day isn't conducive to, etc, but *what*, – I admit, – in *my* experience, is?? The crowd's thinning – if one dare use the word "crowd" of Spaniards, every one of whom is in his estimation absolutely alone in a universe that does not even have any other Spaniards in it, much less anyone or anything else. What a race. What an interesting race. Even in India I never saw men's faces so absorbing, and *all* the most beautiful women in the world are Spaniards. The thing is that they have completely caught on, that the world is a crummy place, but they cdn't personally care less – they are entirely indifferent to comfort, for instance; and they have *not* caught on to what troubles everyone else, that man is not so good either. In fact it's never occured to them. It's due, must be, to their great complexity – they are all Iberian, Roman, Berber, Arab, Jewish, & a dozen other things of course, but mostly these; as if *only*

certain parts of these origins cd join, i.e. makeout in combination; so
that you get not doubt or elaboration (tho' verbally you get the 2nd) but
certainly – simplicity – a self-ignorance so massive as to look like, & *feel*
like, theological truth. But I must go eat. I am going to like Salamanca –
I greatly did Segovia, Valladolid not so well. Before sitting down here I
did what I always do, after finding a hotel & checking in – walkt thro'
the narrow streets to look at the Cathedral – here, Cathedrals – in the
darkness.

Dinner was splendid: a cold consommé, one of these unbelievably
good dishes they make w. eggs & asparagus, red peppers, peas, meat, I
don't know what – "A *la Flamenco*" this one was called; I had even better
one at lunch in Valladolid (a red wine, strong – "*fuerte!*"), and just by the
name of the restaurant, a steak & potatoes, & one of their enormous
sweets (flan, 2 kinds of ice cream, custards, cherries). This was 50 *pesetas*,
or a dollar. My room, in a good clean hotel but not really posh, is 55,
directly on the Plaza Mayor – which I'll describe to you more particularly
in the morning. I'm reading St Teresa's autobiography [*The Life of Saint
Teresa of Avila*, tr. by J.M. Cohen]. I expect you've read it – I never had
except bits of course; this is a first-class translation publ'd this year by
Penguin (I bought it in India, wisely, for Engl. bks are v. hard to get
here). It is wonderful, & purely Spanish. "I began to understand the truth
wh. I had heard as a child, that all is nothing . . I set such store by my
word that I shd never, I believe, on any account have turned back, once
I had announced my intention."

Sunday 12:30 p.m.

I wish just one shop were open, so I cd buy a beret, I just saw one for
17 *Pts*, and it's raw. But the fog has mostly lifted. No bus today, but I
have a train at 3 – alas – I wish I cd stay here a week. I *love* this city, just
as I knew I would. – The Plaza is thus:

[A small drawing by JB of the plaza appears here.]

It's 18th century & the large & splendid town-hall built into the N
side is by [Jose de] Churriguera – My window was directly against it, W.,
on the 2nd floor (Eur. 2nd floor). I just checkt out of my hotel. I must
look at some other things & get some food – I can't post this till tom'w
in Avila anyway. The great University here was to me wildly exciting, &
the "new" cathedral (1509 +).

Avila, Monday 2 p.m.

This is a lovely city – I just walked round the 11th century walls wh. entirely enclose it – but the *mental* effort of taking in the history & vision of a new city everyday is beginning to dissolve me. I'll be glad to get to Seville & sit quiet. Poo by the way is *perfect* again – he's been healthy all thro' but he sleeps all night, A. says (I called her last night), he is entirely well disposed as he hasn't been since Levanto. I hope so, for the hotel there is expensive (mine here is 30 again – 60 cents – but then I only have water in my tap fr. 8 to 11 in the morning – I don't mean hot water, tho' it is not then, I mean *any* water). I am going to bring you a thing from here if I can find it when the shops open at 4. I was in the chapel built on the site of the room in her fa's house – that good man – where the saint was born, but searcht in vain for the crucifix that she held when she died. Her book is entrancing – shrewd, candid, vain, cajoling, domineering, piercingly wise, & vivid, & obsessed, & practical. She was clearly very beautiful also. I think she must have been much like you, esp. in her energy. I pray things will go better for you, darling.

Love,

John

[P.S.] I can't *tell* you how incredibly useful to me on this trip have been the leather notebooks – I'd be lost without them. I use whichever one I'm in twenty times a day, or so.

JB, Ann and Paul sailed from Spain on the Diaz de Solis, *docking in New York in the latter part of December.*

Upon their return, Mrs. Berryman again visited them in Minneapolis. Before departing on a bus for New York, she wrote JB an extremely long despairing letter—dated midnight, January 9—in which she declared that, having exhausted all of her possibilities, bankruptcy seemed inevitable. She spoke of an "unbearable guilt for everything that has ever gone wrong in your life or Jeff's," and that with no one else to turn to for financial help she had thought of him. "I was so deep in this collapse so unexpected and coming after such relief that I couldn't see how hard it would be for you if you had to say no. After I arrived and saw how naturally absorbed you are in your work, I couldn't trouble you. It was like expecting a stream to flow backward to ask help when I should be able to give it."

The next day, on the back of her letter, JB wrote in despair:

"God forgive me. Her all these days in the apartment . . afraid to ask this

bastard son for a loan – & frantic – & not even telling me: BUT taking the finish off the table, helping plan the apt., (while I won't listen) cooking, talking (per- ishing of loneliness & fear) too much, *reading my Indian & Sp. books – desper- ate – & thinking 1) of suicide 2) of 'shaming' me by bankruptcy (& her staying on, agonized).*

"I don't deserve to live.

"And suppose I'd quarrelled w. her!! my heart shakes – she wdn't have told me at all!! & Gods knows *her feelings & what wd have happened."*

He wrote the following letter the same day:

[Minneapolis]

Darling   Friday [10 January 1958]

I want you to telephone me (collect) the second you get this. (I am going to have Bob telephone you every hour from the time I expect you in – I haven't been able to reach him yet – to tell you to call me at once.) I feel absolutely terrible that you did not talk to me. I should have known, but I was so tired (I slept 13 hours last night) that I didn't. Your letter is the most heartbreaking thing I ever read.

We can do something, and at once. *That's certain.*

Do not despair. We will do something at once. We must see that you reach the Sacony business all right, if that is the best thing, and it seems to me that it is. Do not imagine Ann & I are without resources, because *we are not.*

Call me at once. I don't write more, though I have a great deal to say, because I want this in the mail at once, to be there when you arrive – as I pray you will do safely. Just one thing: you *must not* feel that even financial failure is *shaming,* because it is *not.* But I hope, pray, and believe that no such thing will have to happen.

Call me!

my dearest, dearest love

John

[P.S.] You shd have talkt to me; you have nearly broken my heart.

[P.P.S.] Dear love, Taylor 5-9634, *right now.*

[JB subsequently sent Mrs. Berryman 800 dollars to ease her immediate financial difficulties. In a January 24 diary entry, JB concluded a self-inventory thus: ". . . Two of my sharpest, longest problems – liquor and women – are in abeyance. I am lucky for the moment. My being able to help Mother is a great point."]

[Minneapolis]

Dearest Jill,   Wednesday morning 22 January 1958

Everything held up with a heavy cold. I was in bed Friday-Sat-Sun but taught Mon & yesterday and today am somewhat better. Heavens, how cd you imagine I blamed *you* for the answering service's negligence: I'm just sorry you didn't get the money sooner. I shd have wired, I expect, and thought of it but simply didn't have the time until late that afternoon when I scribbled the note & stopt by downtown to post it. An unfortunate series, but I wdn't be superstitious about it, it's not bad luck continuing but just accident.

The rug came last night and is marvellous, it covers the floor almost wall to wall. The place does not look unfinished for the first time since we moved in. How much is it, and who do we pay, and when?

I like the tray immensely too, and am very glad of the Japanese book which I'm not sure I ever read and certainly now will.

Turning over old letters, I find you once askt me about the soft lead pencils (which in fact I learnt of from you). Eberhard Faber, 6325, Ebony, Jet black, extra smooth.

Indian interviewers quizzed me constantly abt my ancestors and it's humiliating how little I knew. Could you draw up some time a rough sheet of the families on both sides so far back as you know them? I ought to be able to tell Paul about this too.

You must try not to worry about the Sacony thing. Rest and don't worry.

I don't want ever to be paid back.

I'll telephone later in the week to see how you are. Ann's sinus is definitely better, and I think the Poo must have his tooth, he is in high spirits today and slept all night. I am getting gradually back into Shakespearean work and like it very much, and also tinkering with an old play-draft of my own. I have bought a new file-cabinet which is a great help, my old one having been stored in Princeton all these years. Tell Bob I'm glad Liza's out and hope his job lets up soon. You rest.

dear love,
John

Dearest Jill

Mr Waffle is radiant lately and will be very happy to see you on his first anniversary – as we will be too – if you can come. Allen [Tate] is reading his poetry that night, also, here in Minneapolis, that's after Son Poo goes to bed, so we can all go (getting a sitter). I can't tell you how welcome you'll be. – I was very glad you could come to the Washington thing – Ann was sorry not to, but the expense seemed too great: I did not enjoy it much; but the money is useful. I still cherish hopes of *soon* getting my library out of storage in Princeton: I need it. I think I can, unless taxes kill me.

We took him yesterday for photographs (He behaved excellently.) – done however by an old fool & I don't know whether any will be all right. We get proofs on Tuesday. Ann did a head of me that's not bad – & not good either. Of course she is just starting. My reputation has reacht my own college, which I can't say I expected it to do in my lifetime: Columbia sent me this week a thing somebody put together when irritated by claims made for Harvard's living writers – listing 39 Columbia writers, of whom I make one. Most of them, naturally, are not writers at all but *things* – things like Bennett Cerf, Oscar Hammerstein II, etc – & what I am doing there I puzzle. I am giving a reading here in April, probably, and have accepted an invitation to talk to some college deans in the Adirondacks in May, so I'll be in NY for a bit early in the summer. My department is probably going to be voted out of existence on the 10*th* of this month and I'll go gradually over into the English dept., where what life will be like I don't know.

Many thanks from Poo for the check. He has more money, with less demands on it, than anyone I know. – The [marriage] license & certificate are strange to see. They come from another world, don't they? A world nearly as different as the baffling records I've lately been studying again – of Shakespeare's marriage in 1582. I'll keep them very carefully, for the Poo of course.

I don't ask abt business, darling, because I know if you want to tell me you will – but no day passes that I don't think of you & hope all's better & well, or will be.

dearest love
John

[P.S.] My love to Bob when you speak with him

[JB had given a reading of his own work at the Library of Congress on February 24. The reading, sponsored by the Gertrude Clarke Whittall Poetry and Literature Fund, was recorded.

Mrs. Berryman had sent JB her own and John Allyn Smith's marriage license and certificate from 1912.]

[Minneapolis]
Darling   Wednesday a.m. [12 March 1958]

Television came all safe yesterday and works perfectly. We are more grateful – to the Poo – that I can tell you. There freq'y are programs I really am sorry to miss; yet there is nothing tryannical about this set – it's so small it can be ignored except when one wants it. And what a clear image! *Thank you!!*

Mr Chunky-Bulky Waffle-Fidget continues perfect. Ann is thinking v. seriously of coming to New York in a few days, for a short time, to see her mother, and will bring him of course; so you can judge for yourself.

Weather's turned marvellous. One of my big gorgeous blondes wore shorts to my lecture yesterday. After tom'w I have two weeks free. Fly to Chicago Wed morning; I've workt out a stunning programme for there – it's at a Catholic univ., Loyola.

The faculty voted to disestablish our department. Now we'll see what happens. I am in excellent spirits – good energy – brain & heart full of expectation & endeavour – I am writing prose regularly, pretty well.

dear love
John

[P.S.] May Spring see everything improve for you.
[P.P.S.] Enclose 2 L.C. [Library of Congress] programmes if Bob wd like one & perh. Deac [Dunn] or whoever you like

[Mrs. Berryman had sent JB and Ann the television as Paul's "first birthday gift to you."

Although the Department of Interdisciplinary studies was disestablished on March 10, 1958, the Humanities Program, of which JB was a member, continued as an independent program.]

[Minneapolis]
Dearest Jill   Good Friday [4 April 1958]

I'm very glad abt Shelby [Williams]'s marriage and of course I'll send them AB – but it will take a little time because I don't have one. I'll write to my publisher, & also to Shelby, tomorrow or Sunday. There's nothing wrong but I am in hospital at the moment. Exhaustion. I only had two weeks betw. quarters, and the first week was Chicago and the second week I wrote 5 new poems besides doing other things, and I began on Sunday to feel as if I were going to die shortly. I started my courses on Monday, and on Tuesday my doctor got me a private room in the Abbott [Hospital], where I am writing this. I am still very badly underweight but feel considerably better and am going out tomorrow. Nothing to worry about. For some time to come I will be under a heavy drug for part of the day (the teaching part, afternoon, after my own work is done) and he thinks I will get in shape fast. I've been suffering alternately from unmanageable irritability and a circulatory disturbance leading to partial syncope. I've written a new poem in hospital but now will be doing only prose for months.

So much has happened that I forget wh. I wr. you abt Chicago. I was never better, or, perh., as good; it bore no relation to Wash. Ann was nervous as a cat but survived. Then The Newberry Library gave me an apartment and I workt on two old stories, besides seeing Saul, & came back on Sunday. I wrote a stunning poem in Chicago too. – I never had much sense of the city before, by the way, and I don't like it much, but it *is* a city. *This* place is *not*.

An honour has turned up fr. Columbia. I've been askt to become an Associate (= member) of the Columbia Univ. Seminar on Amer. Civilization. "Seminar" is misleading – Institute wd be better – no students, just 30 or so senior Col. faculty in *all* relevant fields and a few "Associates" elsewhere; it's a Trustees' appointment, & permanent. Doesn't mean much at the moment; but may do. I have accepted. Ralph [Ross] by the way has had much more important news; he's under consideration for Dean of Gen. Studies at Columbia, with wide powers, an open field (the whole university is transforming itself), and $20,000. (There is no money at present attacht to my Col. appointment.)

It wd take too long to explain my situation here. (I have a *tenure joint* app't in Hum. & Engl.) I *cannot* be fired; but whether I will want to stay is another question.

I've written too much. Next week. I'm very tired.

Happy Easter, darling
John

[P.S.] Your sense of Judas' mind is worthy of Origen – fr. whom I'll quote you when I can the passage of infinite mercy I'm thinking of. – Truth is, I don't think we can know just how he felt, with only Mt 27 3–5.

[On March 30, Mrs. Berryman had written: "I wonder if the ills of life, the unexpectedness and the unendurable happenings were easier to bear in a world full of gods whose rulings were often at odds with each other's, where to obey one god was to fall foul of another, a world in which there was no thought of justice and so no shock at its lack."

Shelby Williams was a cousin of Mrs. Berryman.]

[Minneapolis]

Dearest Jill   25 April 1958

The [Walker Art Center, in Minneapolis] reading went well. I was better even than in Chicago, and it probably is true, as Ralph said afterward, that nobody in the room had ever heard anything like it. I see it's exactly 22 years today since I gave my first reading in this country – that Boar's Head [Poetry Society, at Columbia] thing in the new library when Richard Blackmur came. These enclosed sheets I didn't let be distributed till *afterwards*; nobody listens if they're trying to follow.

When am I coming to NY? I guess Thursday evening. I'll telephone you from Idlewild. I expect to be in the city till Sunday when we go to Sagamore. Ralph [Ross] & I are travelling together. (The *Viscount* disaster made Ralph nervous, so we're coming by *Stratocruiser*; myself I like *Viscounts*.) Ann's plans still uncertain.

I am under heavy drugs still. I'll be glad when the quarter ends. Ann & the *growing* Poo are both splendidly well & happy. – My 3 years' Federal & *State* income tax are done, anyway. But what a winter!

Yes, the Columbia appointment is an honour. I am happy that Pound is going free at last; I'm writing Frost to thank him. Thanks for clips – I see nothing but *Time* magazine.

Do try to lose some weight, yes. Ann is dieting. I am trying hard to gain – so far, vainly. I have been writing brilliantly. I'll show you next weekend. I have a style now pared straight to the bone and can make the reader's nerves jump by moving my little finger.

love
John

[JB had given a reading at Walker Art Center on April 23. It had included poems by Blake, Shakespeare, Robert Lowell, Yeats and Wordsworth, as well as a selection of his own work, ending with *Homage to Mistress Bradstreet*.

The *Vicker's Viscount*, the world's first turbine propeller airliner, had recently experienced a series of incidents that spread concern there might be problems with the plane's landing gear.]

Minneapolis

Dearest Jill   Wednesday 17 [18] June 1958

I took today a holiday and spent most of it outdoors – sun-bathing by the Lake of the Isles, and picnic there – Mr Poo explored boldly & alone along the strand – then a swim – I hadn't been in since Levanto – in [Lake] Calhoun. I feel splendid & so are we all. I'm doing Shak. 10–15 hrs a day.

All my thanks to you & the Poo for the handkerchiefs (that is, I haven't heard but I suspect they were for Father's Day so-called, no?) – Ann likes the [birthday gifts] and says grateful. Bob's pictures delighted us and I am going to write him when less busy. Here are some new ones Ann took; I like the fourth; I have to snip top & bottom to get them in the Japanese envelope.

How are you just now? It seems to me I've not heard for weeks, though it can't *be* that. I dosed liberally today from the Bronztan you gave me that I took straight round the world without using – I swam only in a club pool in Calcutta, and unexpectedly in the Bay of Bengal (at Puri) when I hadn't it with me, and by the time I got to Italy the reason was too far gone to need it.

Mr Poo has a magnificent – *chair!* – (I'll take a picture for you) bamboo w. iron legs – made in Hong Kong – which Ralph & Alicia [Ross] brought him back yesterday from the *Wisconsin Dells*. He still declines to say one word in English but is the happiest healthiest thing alive & seems to be particularly fond of *me*

love,

John

[Minneapolis]

Dearest Jill   Sunday [6 July 1958]

I just wrote various news to Bob which I'm too busy to repeat except that I finished & sent off the ms to Faber [and Faber, Limited] – I am dedicating the book to him – and *The New Yorker* is printing the poem abt the Poo shortly. Your letter to Mr Poo was splendid but write to me will you? I was sorry to miss talking with you the other day. The news abt Bob is good I think: I wrote to him at once.

My work is racing, and must, because alas I begin teaching again in a fortnight. The University have lifted my salary again for next year but I'm still much in debt. We're having a very quiet & good summer, we go swimming every day or so – the Poo loves beaches, and is generally adorable & refuses to speak one word, which is all right with me, tho' I am eager to hear what he thinks of it all. I hope you're well & taking care of yrself & cheerful

love

John

[P.S.] Four new "Dream Songs" in the last 3 weeks, at intervals of Shakespeare.

[*Homage to Mistress Bradstreet and Other Poems* was published by Faber and Faber on April 24, 1959. It carried no dedication, however.

"A Sympathy, A Welcome" was published in the August 16, 1958, issue of *The New Yorker*.]

                                                          [Minneapolis]
Dearest Mother   Friday [11 July 1958]
I just remembered yr birthday this morning – when I wrote last Sunday I expected to write again on Monday, but a combination of things (I'm sorry) knockt it out of my head – Ann went to our doctor on Mon. and found out she had, or was having, German measles – the baby has been extremely uneasy – and Tues-Wed-Th I was v. nervous, tired & depressed myself, perhaps I had a touch tho' it doesn't matter. So *Happy Birthday* tardily. I don't feel well & can't write much. I am having to give up regular Shak'n work in order to try to earn some money; after 20 yrs of success in two professions I have workt up to what an unsuccessful plumber or copywriter makes, and I thought I cd live on it but I can't. I don't begin teaching for ten days, so I have ten days.

                                                            Afternoon

I see by yr letter that Bob doesn't make any more than I do; nor does Helen. I hope they can see their way to keeping alive. I am very displeased that my brother not only did not write to me but has not answ'd either of my letters. I am very displeased.

Ann's mother is worse again.

Truth is, I don't readily see a way thro' the current difficulties, and do not at all feel prepared to start teaching again, and cannot construct an anniversary letter. I'll write when I feel less ill –

love

John

New York

Dear, dear John,   Monday, 4 August 1958

It may rest you a little to know that when I lie down to rest I dedicate to you the good of the rest that the cream may go to you to be a stay and a help, that when I labor I pray that the burden may be heavier for me and so lighten yours. I gird at myself that I cannot do more.

This is what it is to be a parent, to suffer inconsolably in the anguish or travail of the child (and that perhaps is the taproot of the difficulties between the generations, that to the parent that which she bore or which was ripped from her is still and always her child – this dream is the mist separating her from what the years and himself have made of the child, a substance he must fight against to be what he is and will become), with a pang greater than but not otherwise different from that endured when, an infant, he lay in high fever on a pillow across her arms. Not for one instant since I knew you were to come to this earth have I been me, alone, myself. A mother can only be the sum of herself and her child. The best good that can come of the relationship is that she cherish what is within her of this and release him to his proper place, alone and with his own.

You may not be in mind for a serious letter, John. At this distance it is not possible to know what is best or even good, toward you now, in your exhaustion. Perhaps it is not needful to tell you that for long I have lived toward you in the dream, knowing it for such and doing what I might to behold you and hold you for the living man you are. Perhaps the time may come when I can see you clearly as you are with the mist of generation drunk up and gone, and you see me plainly for whatever I have made of me. Then all will be ease for with the mist will go my guilts toward you and you will have freedom from any regrets toward me. This is a hope that buoys me, that some day we need not walk delicately, or remorsefully, one with the other.

You have nothing with which to reproach yourself, toward me, and I strive to offer wholeheartedly my guilts toward you for your good, just as I offer what sufferings have been in my life not for my sins which are many and grave but for your peace in life.

It has never been other with me than that, blindly in the past and confused with a shared good and now with clarity for you yourself, I wished for you more than all. My dear son.

With all my love, your devoted mother,

Jill Berryman

[Minneapolis]

Sunday [17 August 1958]

Darling

Just a note: I'm v. busy & v. tired. Ann & Poo flew to Pa. yesterday – A's mother very ill. I have only four more days of lecture & may perhaps come to NY on Monday next or so. Mr Poo is in the *New Yorker* this week. Another compensation check (for my tour) came from the wretched gov't just now, and my new [Thomas Y.] Crowell [Company] contract is working out, so I'm easier. I pray you may be. They talkt my bloody ears off at that conference in the north; Ann however enjoyed it. Silence & the sea will do me very well for a while. Maybe I'll go to the West Indies w. Saul; *maybe*. À *bien tôt*,

love,

John

[The Thomas Y. Crowell Company contract was for *The Arts of Reading* (1960).

JB had participated in a conference in Grand Marais, Minnesota, August 6–10.]

In the final months of 1958, JB and Ann's marriage was "in difficulties." As the following letter suggests, JB believed that Mrs. Berryman had contributed to their problems—and he had, for a time, broken off communication with her.

[Minneapolis]

13 January 1959

Dear Mother,

Heavy insomnia. Various serious problems have prevented my writing since I got back two weeks ago and found yr letter; I'm sorry. Ann &

I are very grateful for your generous gifts. I seldom use the diary or note-books without thinking of you.

Perhaps I ought to say that neither Ann nor I would ever dream of limiting your access to the Pou. I didn't write because I had an impression that you tried to break up my marriage, which was in difficulties, and in addition to my physical and nervous exhaustion and other things, I did not think it a good idea for me to take this any more. I am not now reproaching or blaming you for this, only explaining. I feel as you do, that people are v. unhappy & driven and that most of them wish to do as well as they can but need love and that some are highly ambivalent.

The baby is splendid but *will not talk* and bit his best friend's hand yesterday – Adam Bellow – until blood came. Ann has been v. unwell. Her mother died! I almost was put in hospital for the 3rd time last year in November but avoided it. I have been v. busy writing.

I'm v. glad to hear you are probably leaving New York. What do you plan? Please, if you go, do send the Pouker's books; and if you think of selling everything I wish you wd let me know. But about the car – a thousand thanks – but we are in the course of buying Ralph [Ross]'s car, who is going abroad shortly and has bought a Jaguar to use there & bring back; it's cheap (his car – a 6-yr-old Chrysler) and in good shape. Rudolph is okay but needs so much money put into him that it isn't sensible.

I'll have copies of my little American book [*His Thought Made Pockets & The Plane Buckt*] soon and send one. I askt Bob to show you the British page-proofs – his better eyes than mine found some more errors, of which I'm letting Faber know. I've done 50 pp. of the collaborative textbook with Ross & Tate and will be done in a week or so; just a job, tho' an interesting one; R. [Ross] thinks it will make money. I am skeptical. My lecture schedule is better than the murderous one I had all Fall.

I'm writing Deac [Dunn].

Love, and a happiest New Year,
John

[*His Thought Made Pockets & The Plane Buckt*, a collection of thirteen poems, was published on December 15, 1958, in a limited edition by C. Fredericks, a small publisher in Pawlet, Virginia. It was dedicated to Ann.]

Glenwood Hills Hospital
3901 Golden Valley Road
Minneapolis
Dear Mother,   23 February 1959

I've been here ten days, trying to avoid a complete breakdown. Both my doctors (psychiatric & medical) think I am improving rapidly, and I went over to the University today – it's miles – and gave my lecture, but clearly I will be here a good while yet. I am under continuous heavy sedatives and feel considerably less [?] than I have been doing for some weeks, months rather. I finisht the textbook (Tate wrote only 12 pages altogether in the end) and threw it to New York where they are copy-editing but I still have about 30 pp to fill in & no nerves to do it with. Hence, hospital.

Thanks from Paul for his cheque. As for the diary and notebooks, which I use everyday, I continue to think of them as gifts, since you *thought* of them. I don't see that it matters who pays for things.

But the point of this letter is to say that I have been under orders for weeks not to attempt to deal with any personal relations with anyone, even Ann, and so I have not opened yet your letter of February 7*th* and will not be able to do so for some time. As soon as I am told or feel I safely can, I will, and will write again. *All* my personal relations are & must be in abeyance until I am more nearly well.

John

[JB and Ann had separated prior to his hospitalization. They were divorced on April 28, 1959.]

New York
My dear son,   26 March 1959

Since you wrote me of your illness, I have done more concentrated thought than ever before, and for me I see what the problem has been. And I think I see it for you.

I have studied all that I could find on men of talent and men of genius and I see now that what was proper humility in placement if directed toward myself was blind stupidity toward you.

A man of talent is disciplined and trained, and indeed you are so, in your work. But the talented man's faculty for effective dealing with existing material does not begin to describe what you do. In you, original creative power works through the imagination, it is intuitive and inspired; supremely endowed, your gift, like that of all geniuses, is inexplicable and not to be analyzed.

I know that I have thought of you as greatly gifted but not until I realized that the man of talent works by rule and reason nor can he work any other way did I face up to the fact that you are a genius. Your brother knew this long ago, when he said that you suffered from an affliction he and I were not called on to bear: genius.

A greater part of your difficulties with those who are closest to you in blood or love is that you have regarded yourself and have tried to operate as a man of talent, who differs from ordinary men only in degree not in kind.

But a man of genius differs in kind, that is what I have not understood. Some men of genius, when their work is done and they come out of that world of creation which is their real world and are exiled into the world of ordinary, of other, men, are on such terms with their daimonium that once the pain of shrinking to ordinary size is past they can at least imitate the ordinary men in the life which is home to all except a genius.

Your daimonium is bitterly antagonistic to the ordinary world and is dragged with or by you into that world, whose problems can not be solved by the gifts that produce your work. Every genius stands on a peak, alone and supreme in what he creates. I am not sure that a genius can ever be what his daimonium demands, that he regard himself as equally supreme when not alone and in a world not his.

I suppose daimonium has many meanings: the one I have taken is that of an indwelling power or spirit, originality in genius. If you can ever, and you well may when you recover the health you have squandered over the years, come to such terms with your daimonium that he rests in the world which is yours and his while you restore yourself in peace and love in this world which your humanity demands you live in for all ordinary (I use that word as opposite to the extra-ordinary of genius) purposes, then indeed will all be well with you and with those you love who love you.

There have been times, John, when your daimonium by whom you were possessed seemed more an evil daemon. Having seen that, I recognize the anguish of exile that tore you, and that spirit.

For myself, my son, I accept fully what is perhaps most difficult of all to see and accept, your difference. Never again will I think of what you do in terms of what a non-genius would do.

I am happy that now I need not believe as I have done for months, that you did not love me and had not done, most likely, since you were a child. It is a comfort I had not looked to have, and I am grateful.

Towards me, you need never again feel any compulsion to write or see unless you want to do so, even if it is after months or years. You need not fear that I shall be hurt or grieved by silence or absence. I have found the shadow of a rock in this weary land, and I pray for you to find it.

Perhaps if you could be alone while in the throes of creativity, you would not be as torn and irritated and anguished and angered while working, and in turn less apt to be immured in the habits of working when the work is done?

When you recover your strength, and you will, for you have a constitution of steel or it could never have borne for so long the insuperable burdens you have placed on your "ordinary" body for indeed all bodies are ordinary, then you can rest and be at peace after the work is finished. It is not you who hates and resents and cannot endure people, particularly those who are nearest to you: it is your daimonium striking through you at all in the ordinary world in which he has no part and which takes and keeps you from him. Oh if I could only say rightly what I feel and know.

I have asked our Heavenly Father to let me offer up any good I have ever done or helped to bring about, for your easement, and to allow me to take on myself up until the time you read this letter any sin or evil or pain or suffering you may have caused. I have prayed with all that I am that God will permit me to make these offerings for you, my dear son.

> With unfailing love, your devoted mother,
> Jill Berryman

PART SIX

Last Years

1959-1972

T HE LAST DOZEN YEARS of JB's life now moved, by fits and starts, toward artistic triumph and personal tragedy. Upon leaving Glenwood Hills Hospital in March 1959—the first of many such alcohol-related hospitalizations he would undergo in the years ahead—and alone again, he resumed his pattern of destructive drinking and compulsive womanizing, while habitually thrusting himself into a punishing regime of writing and teaching.

He continued obsessively to write Dream Songs—some of which began to appear in periodicals and in his poetry readings, creating a stir—and completed his work on The Arts of Reading (1960). His teaching, even when done between trips to and from his hospital bed, was conducted with his usual relentless intensity and dazzling effectiveness. In 1961 he married Kathleen (Kate) Donahue, then twenty-two, whom he described as "a raving beauty, tall, black-haired . . . and elegant beyond praising." Together, they would have two daughters—Martha, in 1962, and Sarah, in 1971. Anchored by the sorely-needed domestic stability provided by this third marriage, he was no doubt able to keep going longer than he could have managed to do on his own.

In May 1964, JB published 77 Dream Songs which won him the Pulitzer Prize. Later that year, with Kate, he bought the first and only house he would ever own at 33 Arthur Avenue, S.E., in the Prospect Park area of Minneapolis. With the help of a Guggenheim Fellowship, the Berrymans spent the 1966–67 academic year in Dublin, where JB worked on a second and concluding volume *of* The Dream Songs. His Toy, His Dream, His Rest, *for which he received the National Book Award and the Bollingen Prize, was published in 1968.*

These years of hard-earned honors and growing public recognition—the latter aided by a long and attractive feature article about him in Life *(July 21, 1967) by Jane Howard—together with his flamboyant and spellbinding platform style, made JB much in demand for poetry readings and lectures. Other books appeared, as well, to further establish his reputation as one of the major poets of his time:* Berryman's Sonnets *(1967),* Short Poems *(1967), and* Love & Fame *(1970). During his last years JB also worked on another volume of poems,* Delusions, Etc. *(1972), on a novel,* Recovery *(1973), and on a collection of essays,* The Freedom of the Poet *(1976), all of which were published posthumously.*

Public success, however, was accompanied by mounting personal problems. After repeated hospitalizations for chronic alcoholism, JB joined Alcoholics Anonymous and throughout 1971 battled to remain sober. But with his health now seriously impaired, his marriage in difficulty, and convinced that, without drinking, he was no longer able to write or teach well, he became increasingly depressed and withdrawn. Ultimately, on January 7, 1972, he ended his life by leaping to his death from a high bridge over the Mississippi River to the frozen embankment below.

In her March 26, 1959, letter, at the end of the previous section, Mrs. Berryman's arrival at a view of her son as a man of genius whose "daimonium is bitterly antagonistic to the ordinary world" was insightful. At the same time, it enabled her to dismiss many of the differences between them and thus to preserve a relationship which, for JB in particular, had become increasingly intolerable. Yet, despite her vow to never again "think of what you do in terms of what a non-genius would do," the meetings between them over the ensuing years, though fewer in number, were often more agonizing than ever.

Still, their correspondence, even though more sporadic, never ceased for long. Both JB's letters and the several from Mrs. Berryman included in this section, also increasingly reveal one aspect of their relationship that was undergoing a radical change. As recognition and reward began to accumulate for JB, Mrs. Berryman's worsening financial situation and ill health caused her to more frequently turn to him for help—until eventually he and Kate became her chief means of support. Finally, in May 1971, they moved her to Minneapolis where she could be close to them. In these last months of his life, JB attempted, with some success, to re-establish better relations with his demanding and devoted mother.

This section opens with JB back in Minneapolis, following two weeks he spent teaching at the University of Utah's Writer's Workshop in the latter part of June 1959.

[Minneapolis]

Dearest Mother,   Tuesday [7 July 1959]

It is hot as lower hell and my BBC recording is in 50 minutes – I hope the studio is airconditioned – so this is just a note to wish you happy birthday and say I will be thinking of you with love and will try to get you on the phone tom'w. The combination of the altitude and a heat wave in Utah gave me the worst stretch of insomnia I've had I think in ten years, otherwise it was rather interesting and at any rate a change. The mountains are wonderful, and one day I went swimming in a lake, completely enclosed, at 10,000 feet, near the top of Guardsman's Pass. My stomach has been bothering me again since I got back ten days ago but mercifully it's been cool till today and I must have slept a hundred hours. How has your health been? – it seems too long since I heard – I hope the improvement has continued and nothing bad new has turned up – and that in other ways things have been better. What heat.

Love,

John

[JB's recording, with introductory remarks, of *Homage to Mistress Bradstreet*, was for the BBC Third Programme. The reading took place in the studio of KUOM, a public radio station affiliated with the University of Minnesota.]

1917 – 4th St South

Minneapolis

Dearest Mother,   Tuesday night [11 August 1959]

The simultaneous shock and relief of your letter were very great. I knew of course you were very unwell but I did not know *how* unwell. My God. It is a good thing that your vitality is one of America's major achievements. I do hope with my heart that you *will* now be better. Especially the calm is good to hear of; life is really intolerable without that.

Bob called yesterday morning but I was just off to lecture and we cdn't talk; he says he will write. I have never really known Helen [Wells] well enough to have an opinion of the marriage, I just wish them luck.

I ran into a heat wave in Utah and that & the altitude produced the worst insomnia in years, meanwhile I was working v hard. The first fortnight back I spent in bed, which gave me no time to work up my Henry James course, which therefore I'm giving from scratch, and it takes ten hours a day, in terrible heat & humidity. My Modern course meets at 9, with 70 bodies in it, and then the James at 10, supposed to be a seminar, with 50 bodies in it, including two priests, one a Jesuit from Jamaica (West Indies). I am in the middle of the 3rd wk, with two more to go: half-through. I suppose I will make it, though I hardly sleep or eat, and am tortured moreover by phone calls from 2 publishers in NY whose deadlines I have gone through. Ross however is back, which may be some help. Good news has come from Ann, she & Paul are very happy at Tivoli with the Bellows and she is relaxing. Your news and hers – I can't evaluate Bob's till I hear properly – are the only bright spots anywhere. May you keep better, and write now & then now.

Love,

John

[Mrs. Berryman had written that she had undergone treatment for what she described as "extreme hypertension" and exploratory surgery which discovered a "malignant" cyst.

Robert Jefferson married his fourth wife, Helen Loving Wells, on July 23, 1959.]

After teaching fall quarter at the University of Minnesota, JB began early in February 1960 a semester as a visiting professor in the Department of Speech at the University of California at Berkeley. During this time he also travelled to New York where, as the exchange in the following two letters makes clear, he and Mrs. Berryman had still another brief but "excruciating" visit, followed by a period of non-communication between them.

Berkeley, [CA]

Dearest Mother,   Sunday [15 May 1960?]

I have been very ill for weeks with the same prostrating business I had in India and am not better today, so this letter will be scrappy, but I think it's time to ignore that excruciating hour or so in New York. I don't know who was mostly responsible and I don't think it matters. When we meet so seldom, the emotional pressure is naturally great, and of course I took in that you were furious about my not having got in touch with you. But of course the reason I had not got in touch with you is that I was afraid of: precisely what happened, – which I was in no condition to take. I had had a savage month or so, socially, in Berkeley (for reasons it wd take me 20 pp to explain, *no* society) after a whole year of being out of the world;

and then it was far from agreeable to me to accept an award [the Brandeis University Creative Arts Award], in particular so publicly, as "promising". *Promising*. I did so, with many misgivings and much gall and a bitter smile, because I had to have the money.

Well, but this is not the fundamental trouble either. No matter what my condition, I am far from sure that I will ever again with equanimity, and undamaged affection, be able to allow myself to be smothered with talk in the way that you permit yourself to do. Thirty times I tried to make a conversation out of it. On you rushed. – I do not *blame* you, it is not for me to blame you, but I am obliged to consider what I can stand; this is from the standpoint of self-preservation. And from the standpoint of what is just and fair and reasonable, I am forced to see that such uncontrollable swarming is intensely neurotic and aggressive, and *cannot* be responded to in any way that is satisfactory. It is only to be endured, if one can safely endure it, or avoided. To meet it with anger, as I did, is certainly wrong.

Two things remain to be said. You are not aware that I almost never quarrel with anyone any more. I have had arguments, in three months here, meeting hundreds of people, with two men only, both notorious (I learned later in each case) for arrogance and effrontery, both of whom, immediately we were introduced, attacked my work, *at length*; even these I bore with in patience for some time, as in the past I wd never have done. I tell you this, not at all to dream of fixing on you a chief responsibility for our difficulty, but to explain how very unusual – for me now – and how wounding therefore – was that evening in New York.

Second, I must emphatically dissent from your position of All-or-Nothing. You have been giving me this for many years. In 1960, as in 1953, as in 1935, when I can no longer, on some occasion, bear to be crushed and obliterated under your stopless talking, you cry out that I never want to hear you say *anything*, and so you never will again. Bear in mind that I am 45 years old as I now tell you that in my opinion this is nonsense, paranoid nonsense. The fact that a man is unwilling to be driven crazy says absolutely nothing to the absurdity of supposing that he is anxious or willing to relinquish his oldest and one of his closest ties of love. Life is not black or white; it consists of getting along.

I am very sorry to write so bluntly, but it is better to be blunt than to put up with Nothingness. I must be blunter still: do you know that at 45

I am already trying very hard, during the last two years (and yesterday at lunch), *not*, when I am with young people, to talk too much? Everyone wants and needs to be heard, not smothered. Swift has written instructions to himself, for age. It is my duty and pleasure to respect you, my delight to admire you, and my lifelong practice and wish to love you; but I am long since grown a man, Mother, and must be treated with the forbearance which I myself try to extend to my son & others.

Love,

John

P.S. I hope you are well and wd love to hear in detail what is happening.

New York

Monday, 23 May 1960

Dearest John,

The news of your illness of weeks past was most distressing, and I hope that you are recovered or at least greatly improved in health now. You have, unfailingly, my love and prayers.

My reply is addressed to your love and the longing we share for peace and ease and secure abidingness between us. These are not pronouncements but a setting out of my thinking and hopes.

Our primary problem, I believe, is the extreme nervous tension which haunts and wrecks our meetings and communications.

This nervous tension has swollen to frightful proportions, nourished on pain and fear and guilt. In a tie and relationship as close and long as ours, each has been sadly at fault, each sorely injured, through blindness or intent, in anger or resentment. The anguish that one always feels at injuring the loved one lives on in painful or fearful or guilty memories. These memories surge up when one attacks and the other defends or counter-attacks, increasing nervous tension unbearably. There can be only defeat for both in a duel where the more deeply one wounds the other, the deeper is one's own injury.

These memories that nourish this nervous tension were created by other people, John. I am not that that I was twenty years ago or even two months, and neither are you. If we can cut free from the ugly memories, then the nervous tension will die out for lack of nourishment, and we will be free to be ourselves in amity and peace and love.

Let me say, then, that I have given the pain you have caused me and the pain I have caused you, the fear I have felt toward you and the guilt we have felt toward each other to God, asking Him for forgiveness and His gift of loving kindness and charitableness toward you and myself. I hold you, and myself, to be loving human beings – you a greatly valuable one, I an ordinary one, but both loving and free of blame for each other or what is love?

I have no wish to run or thought of attempting to run your life – no more than I wish to end our relationship: I thought that you had been trying for years to get free and offered freedom to save you the burden of casting me off. I accept, now, that you do not wish our relationship to end, so happily; and you must accept that I have no interest in running anyone's life but my own.

You will be glad to know that I am back from severe surgery, which it is hoped will be the last go at it. Hypnosis was used massively, and my blood pressure for the first time in more than 5 years is down to within 5 points of normal, while my calmness is a miracle to me and, I am sure, a relief to everyone else. I shall be having boosters on this new post-operative hyper-tension technique until I can manage on my own, and already I can go longer between treatments. I have known since the end of the year that surgery was inevitable and that probably didn't help reduce the hyper-tension which has ravaged and savaged me for so long.

With all my love, your devoted mother,

Jill Berryman

[P.S.] I will be glad to hear from you and of you, always.

[Mrs. Berryman had undergone surgery on the malignant spinal tumor diagnosed earlier.]

JB returned to Minneapolis from Berkeley at the beginning of the summer and was soon hospitalized for exhaustion. He taught at the University of Minnesota for the 1960–61 academic year, and in the spring of 1961 met Kathleen (Kate) Donahue, who would become his third and last wife.

His relations with his mother remained cool during this period and, although she wrote an occasional letter, it appears he did not. They did, however, meet in Mrs. Berryman's apartment in New York on Christmas Day. Fueled by too much liquor, hostilities again broke out between them, which she ended by asking him to leave. Four days later she wrote that, despite everything, "I believe in our love, John." Six weeks later she wrote the following letter:

[New York]

Dearest John   Monday, 13 February 1961

No good news is the reason for not writing, on my part, and I hope not, on yours. I know you would have written if you could, but when you can, please do, I had looked forward to your letter and was childish enough to be sorely disappointed. I do understand that it must be very difficult to find what to say to anyone in my position, but just ignore anything about illness here and tell me about you, what you are doing, and anything you like.

I, always proud of never descending to loneliness, am increasingly conscious of being alone. I don't feel durable, John. I pray God that if it be His will I die, to let it be now, now, before perhaps I get beyond acceptance and can not say, not my will but Thine. It doesn't seem likely (this is I mean this accepting is like drowning, when you are far gone it is easier to go on out than to fight one's way or try to fight back to living) but one of the things that pain and total insecurity brings is fear, of the known and the unknown, the likely and the can't be – to me, at least. . . .

The trouble is that the serum stopped working, and the new Swiss serum that was brought back by one of my surgeons is too costly for me now. I have been taking shots when the pain was unbearable and it has stopped growth and even decreased it and it may be that I can bring myself to scrape up some money if there looks an even possible chance that this stuff might bring about a miracle and that the radiation and freezing therapy or technique or whatever it is might so reinforce it that I could feel up to taking up the burden of life again. If one could just wither into the truth what a fine thing it would be.

I have had a good life and, truly, a happy one. There are no two people in the world I would rather have had for sons than you and Jeff, or for grandchildren than Shelby and Paul. And it was given to me to love greatly, and to have friends, and to exercise my skills and abilities – yes, a good life. Remember this of me, John, and, too, that I know with the marrow of my being that my sons love me and that knowledge has been the crown on my life. My dear son.

Most lovingly, your devoted mother,
Jill Berryman

[P.S.] This really sounds, sounds as if I were taking leave of life. Not yet, nor so easily, it will no doubt be a long and for me messy business, one [of?] an intolerable strain on those who love me. I don't expect to endure it with grace but at least with such vestiges of dignity as can be summoned, and no wish or will to linger.

[Minneapolis]
Darling Mother,   Sunday night, [11] June [1961]
     . . . I am ashamed of not writing. If you knew the stupid agonies I've been undergoing you wd forgive me, but I am ashamed. Not ever again will so long a time pass, and I'll try to write regularly. – To tell the truth, I've found letters almost impossible, except to the girl I love in California; I haven't written to Ann for months (I've written but not sent), I've *never* written to Eileen abt her marriage, I owe Saul Bellow *four* letters, & Cal [Robert Lowell], and so on & on. I only lecture, & suffer, & work on my poem – wrote a whole new Song tonight, or drafted it.

Wednesday, [14] June [1961]
     I don't know how long ago I wrote this "Sun. nt." page and left the letter unfinished. Really I am impossible. It is true I've been madly busy. Thank heaven you are gaining strength. Good for the beaches – a girl took me for a picnic on Monday, but I haven't seen a beach this year, and the quarry where people swim near the place I'm going in Indiana is so hot, they say, they take ice out fr. town to put in it. I'll be at The School of Letters, Indiana Univ'y, Bloomington, Ind. My plane leaves in 4 hours and I wonder whether I will be on it, with what there is to do. I moved, by the way, and my address here is as on the envelope – but I'll be in Bloomington six weeks. I pray for you, dear. I'm taking with me your beautiful letter of February. Rest, rest!

Love,
John

[In 1960 Eileen had married Robert Simpson, a former assistant dean at Princeton University and subsequently a U.S. diplomat and vice president in the international division of the Chemical Bank.]

Titusville, Florida
Dearest John,   22 June 1961
     It is, for a change, a gloomy day, heavy, grey, grey, grey, and yet in a flash the sun can and no doubt will come out and all will be golden and alive.

I feel as if old deep callouses had been sloughed off, leaving not tenderness but awareness of sensitivity and non-thickness, as a ship must feel when de-barnacled, fresh and new and yet with all that has been there only not pressing or hurting or meaning to hurt. It is so good a feeling that I must speak of it, and so calming. Perhaps I'll not be frenetic again, how I hope not.

John, I mean to be, insofar as I have strength and purpose, to be myself, my best self, as long as there is breath in me. "Know thyself": I am endeavoring to see clearly. Distance has aided me: the distance from life into what was so nearly death, distance in weakness, distance from New York, from business — maybe for me at least perspective is all.

What I know about myself in my relations with others is two-fold: I have a loving heart and am perhaps the most confirmed of optimists. And again and again I have betrayed love by being pained or grieved or resentful or angry or suspicious of pain to come, and optimism by that suspicion or even expectation. It is not only that one should be careful what he wants he may get it, one must be careful what one fears for he will almost surely get it by bringing it on.

So from here on, I shall endeavor with all that I am to give no cause of offence to anyone, and to believe that those who love me mean well and kindly by me and all others have no will to hurt me or even thought of it. It is not for me to judge, even momentarily. I pray God never again to be hurt or angered, or to hurt or anger any one of His creatures. If I keep clearly before me love and hope, I can never forget that to judge is not my duty, need, function or privilege. And so, please God, I shall be happy and make others so.

All this is prelude to feeling free to ask what I like, holding that the one asked will feel free to say no without feeling (as I have feared) that any direct question might seem an intrusion. If I can sit at ease in my skin with the sinner I am, surely no one else can be ill at ease with me? When one distorts the essential nature, the falsity even though unconscious brings unease to others. So I shall be myself and hope and think well and love — already it overjoys me to think of how simple and good my life can be if I am so.

What I want to ask is about the poem [*The Dream Songs*], of course. If you feel you can tell me about it, or let me see any rough drafts of songs or lines, I would be so glad. If not, just say so, darling. . . .

One of the most cherished memories I have, John, is your coming to stay the night, while you were writing the Bradstreet poem, and reading what you had written and talking about it, each time. It seems to me unlikely that what happened then could be repeated, a kind of identity not of creation but of understanding that marked a high point, perhaps the high point, of my life. I understood all that you read, and said, as a blind man understands, by feeling – the texture of the poem is part of the deepest knowledge in me.

Your writing means far more to me, my son, than I could ever explain. It is true that I feel the natural pride of a mother in the greatness of a son's work and a joy for you, and grief for the anguish and pain and long torment. But there is more, and none of it possessive. There is thankfulness, and awe, and wellnigh worship. I love you as a human being as well as for your sonship and I revere you as an artist. My dear son.

I have now written two long letters in as many days, maybe others will be shorter and not so pellmell on top of each other, stumbling in their haste. But I can't promise anything except that I will do as the spirit moves me.

With so much love overflowing, darling,

your devoted mother,

[P.S.] Tuesday was your grandmother's birth date, God rest her soul.

JB taught a summer-session course entitled "Minor and Major Form in Poetry" at Indiana University's School of Letters (June 17 – July 29).

Bloomington, Indiana

Darling–   Friday [7 July 1961?]

Two words (I'm madly busy) to congratulate you & wish you a happy birthday and to wish I could be there and to bless you for the two marvellous letters. – No gifts in this (But I'm going to be working on the poem as soon as I have any time, even here, & will send you on copies) little town: rain-cheque till Mpls, in 3 *weeks* hurrah! unless I've money (v. unlikely) to go to NY to see Paul – & possibly you? Plans? Say to Bob I've tried, in the dreadful heat and working *hard* (w. the best students I ever had: 15 of them – 2 beards, a nun, & a Lebanese professor) and with a horrible demanding official social life that destroys our evenings, to form a note properly to [Louis] Harris but failed: this weekend, after my

2-hr. session *tom'w* a.m. (after another long party tonight) I will. The enclosed will tell you what I'm doing. This place, new to me, is very beautiful; I'm in a corner room, 7th floor, in a tower, gorgeous views, sweltering, but better than usual. My 'phone here is Indiana Memorial Union, & my name; or I'll try you at the [Jean and Milt] Mersels' or Bob's. Say more exactly how you are physically,—I hope still improving.

Love & love, dear

John

[Robert Jefferson Berryman was working as a study director for the public opinion analysts Louis Harris and Associates.]

415 Erie St., S.E.

[Minneapolis]

Dearest Mother   Thursday [10 August 1961?] 8 p.m.

For the first time since I got back here ten days ago I felt some energy today – eating breakfast at noon (I have been most of the time in bed), *unpacking*, separating thousands of papers in dozens of folders (& out of them) – even the part of the Dream Songs I took to Indiana is 6 inches thick, & it's on my (kitchen) table so at this moment – well, I also did (in machines) laundry, *telephoned* two friends – & am not only willing but *anxious* to get up tom'w. To get up, exhausted, to face *only* un-faceable problems – no. I have been reading Jane Austen, drinking, hiding (answer no 'phone or door, except whim or signal – one little problem is that 3 young women have come to see me unbidden, one of whom wants me to *marry* her, another of whom I have sort of proposed to and wd like to spend the rest of my life with – but why don't we become unattractive as we get old??) – You see my misery. I came back ruined. It's worse here than anywhere [ends here].

[The original of this unfinished—probably never sent—letter was found among JB's papers.]

On September 1, 1961, JB and Kate Donahue were married, with a few friends in attendance, at the Court House in Minneapolis.

Minneapolis

Dearest Mother,   Wednesday night, 15 November [1961]

I have been in a continuous agony of indecision since your letter: I couldn't *not* give you the 300 (*if* I cd get anyone to lend it me) and at the same time I cd not form an opinion abt whether I had a right to. My good old ex-wife Ann rang up two days after your letter came – it was the weekend – explaining that I owed her $600 – I can't find the court decree so I don't know – including $400 from the summer when during my two salaryless months *I* thought I had to pay her nothing; and she not only threatened but is now actually taking me to court – the hearing is Monday morning, and I am changing lawyers because I couldn't tell the diff. betw her lawyer and mine: they mean to put me in jail, I gather . . Then I owed – owe – 500 (to live thro' Sept) to my own bank, and 200 of this is due Dec 4th and of course I don't have it and I haven't the faintest idea where I can get it. I have *no* savings, and yesterday had 12.50 in my checking acc't, and no insurance even for Kate as yet (I have 20,000 for Paul and believe me it kills me). I also owe 160 taxes, 244 medical, 244 prof'l, 225 other, 266 personal, *etc*. That's only over one thousand, no problem if you're Sinatra. I am sort of obliged to *save* money for two purposes: the Univ'y owes me a sabbatical next year, the first I ever (non) had, they only pay one-half, so I can't take it and without it *The Dream Songs* will never be done. Simple. (A poet named [Waclaw] Iwaniuk has just spent a year translating the Bradstr. poem into Polish.) Then most of my library [ends thus].

Friday, 24th

I've been madly busy, enmeshed in legal difficulties (my new lawyer got a continuance, after one or two of the most nerve-racking hours in the Courthouse I ever spent) and I'm racing against a [Bush] Foundation deadline. I have 65 more pages to write before next Friday, and in short I never finished the letter of last week or even got to the main point – my intense happiness, and Kate's too, about *your cheque's coming through!!!*

Now I pray that Civil Service will act properly.

What's with my brother, I never hear – but I owe him a letter, like everybody else. However I am getting slowly, though with more and more momentum (I wrote 7 pp yesterday. Thanksgiving – the oven wdn't light and the caretaker was away, so we had the scratchest dinner ever seen, no matter), into order; and will be corresponding from now on, for the first time in years.

I had a small indication also of better fortune to come. The NY people, Meridian, who are doing my Crane biog. in paperback, rang up to say its deadline is mid-Dec. and want a new preface, for which they'll pay 1000. (Oh wish-fulfilment in those accumulating zeros: it's a hundred not a thousand – but 100 unexpected looks like heaven.)

The book I'm doing is called *The Freedom of the Poet* – five essays, on *The Tempest*, Anne Frank's *Diary*, "Heart of Darkness", *Job*, and *Don Quixote* – all the thought and work long ago done, just a rapid matter of writing out: a little foundation [The Bush Foundation] in St Paul offers 1000 for an award in The Essay, and I *hope*, if I can get the thing drafted (100 pp is their length, roughly) for their Dec 1st deadline, that nobody in Minn. (one has to be a resident – so at last maybe something will accrue from this exile) will seem to have written better essays this year. Of course the real point is that I shd have written out these things years ago – individually they will be worth money, and then maybe somebody in NY or London will do the book for me.

I am also on the verge of putting the Ms. of *The Dream Songs* in order, and firing them in all directions, esp *The New Yorker* where any single one taken wd be worth *fifty dollars*, can you believe it? Of course it's pure gamble but I am sending them – even this weekend, I hope, if I can lift a few hours out of my fast critical drafting, I am only in the middle of the essay on Anne Frank – thirteen Songs; and then I am going to pray. But I've requests also, accumulated over years, from various American and British publications, and mean at last to satisfy them with Songs, quick. Then I plan to see if Faber will do 75 of them as a book – a trial run – I may try Farrar Straus with the same proposal. There are too many of them, hundreds, it's gone on too long without any public notice, I'm lost – though an American poet tells me that his friend Donald Hall, also an American poet (neither, frankly, is any good), who spent last year in London, says the mere five I published in *TLS* have had an extraordinary effect on young English poets. The gift I spoke of for you long ago now was to be copies of the Songs as I put them in order, and this will not be now long in coming.

Whilst Ann is crudifying me, I sent Pou a *Nat'l Geog* article on seahorses, with big pictures in colour, and she says he took it to school (Mrs Fraser's) and had the big boys read him the *whole article*. Today goes off to him the REAL seahorse I got years ago on the Bay of Bengal, at Puri, along with a big red Swiss rooster and other things; I was preparing him.

I cd write you fifty pages about Kate. Here is a snap of her; treasure it. She is adorable and even likes me. She says – she is located to my southwest eight feet off – she was very pleased to talk with you on the

phone and sends you her love. What is certain, whether we get East
before or not, we'll be in Vermont in July (Bread Loaf has offered me an
excellent job which I accepted, and Frost told Kate that my beloved friend
Howard Munford – whom I was in India with, remember? – lives 12
miles away) which means NY and I hope you and of course Pouker. Your
letter, and three handkerchiefs from Kate (you see how we live), were my
whole birthday, and I cannot describe my gratitude or love,

John

[Mrs. Berryman had applied for a job in the Department of Commerce. She
had written asking JB to lend her $300 to clear up past income taxes, but, as this
letter indicates, a small check from another source had made the loan unnecessary.

Waclaw Iwaniuk's Polish translation of *Homage to Mistress Bradstreet* appeared
in the winter 1962 issue of the journal *Tematy*.

JB's "Preface to the Meridian Edition" and "Additional Bibliography (1962)"
appeared in the paperback edition of *Stephen Crane*, published in February 1962.]

[Minneapolis]

Dearest Mother,   Saturday 2 December [1961]
    A rushed note to say that I can't possibly thank you enough for the
diary. I always feel truly lost without them, and yet they are such a posh
item that I never even if I have the money feel up to treating myself to
one, and I am not exaggerating in the least when I say that 1962 looks
infinitely better and more conceivable and even desirable to me when I
look at the diary. You should *certainly*, in your circumstances, not have
gotten them. Kate is delighted with hers too, but one has to use one to
know what a godsend they are. She wore the lovely earrings yest'y on her
wild rush to The [Bush] Foundation in St Paul to deliver my ms., or
two-thirds of it. They agreed (I didn't think they would) to accept it, to
consider it, that is, and let me turn in the rest on Monday. This is going
to be another insane weekend, 35 pp to turn out. But we have a foot in
the door, and a great deal of hard thinking that has been hanging around
for years undrafted is now peacefully in typescript.
    Your letter is a joy too. Back to *Don Quixote*, and page 80 (only 15
pp back inside there don't exist yet: tomorrow for them: my numbering
was purely optimistic and fraudulent – though I hope to make it good). I

have a heavy Tuesday and then one week to bring my *Crane* into paperback shape.

Blessings, gratefully, love,

John

[JB did not win the Bush Foundation prize, but the essays he had written for it formed the nucleus of the volume *The Freedom of the Poet*, published by Farrar, Straus & Giroux in 1976, four years after his death.]

[Minneapolis]

Dearest Mother   Friday [22 December 1961]

I'm sick, & have been – not out all week. My Xmas is therefore reduced to the "Alphabet," which I hope you will like, and such Dream Songs as during the next two/or three hrs I can scrape together. Kate (my messenger in sickness, to P.O.) is sending some insignificant but loving jewelry, I think. – Your card *delighted!* me & us. I drew Pou a *map of the world* with Peekskill – Mpls – Bread Loaf – seahorse in Bay of Bengal, nibble in Pacific – Adam in Chicago, you in Alexandria – his lousy cousins in Hartsdale – etc. We are worried abt the new tests. Please tell. We tho't Kate was preg. but apparently not. Soon as we have a little girl, we going to call her *Martha!* – I hope with your benediction. – We are going to get with your sweet bill a goose! which we long longing for. I wish we cd be with you. *Please!* plan on coming to visit us at Bread Loaf this summer – either when Pouk is there (I invited Ann too) or not. You know that country far better than me. A very close friend [Howard Munford], Frost tell us, is 12 mi. off. My pal in India. I want to drive to Ticonderoga. Let's bait Frost, who talk so good you forgive his megalomania.

Now, beloved Mother, I love you – and this is only a signal to say so.

Merry Christmas,

John

The "Alphabet," referred to at the beginning of this letter, is here published for the first time:

Mr. Pou & the Alphabet –
which he do not like

A is for *awful*, which things are;
B is for *bear* them, well as we can.

C is for *can* we? D is for *dare:*
E is for *each* dares, being a man.
(What does a man do? bears and dares;
and how does a little boy fare? He fares.)
F is for *floor* we stamp wif our foot,
G is for *grimy* we getting from play,
H is for *Hell* wherein they do put
the bad guys, maybe. Oh, and I is for 'Ay'
(And this will puzzle the Little Pou,
but his mommy can explain it. Do.)
J is for *Jackknife* which later will come,
when Poukie is bigger, K is for *key.*
L is for the *Little* Pou, M is for some
men who have definite reason to be.
And N is for *now*, the best time of all,
And O is for *ouch* when it hurts – quite so.
P is for *Poukie*, of *Paul* and *piano*,
and Q is for *quiet*, while Mommy tells Paul.
R is for *rudiments* Poukie now learn.
S is for *sea-horse*, erect fish, weird,
T is for *Turks* whom we take by the beard.
U is for *utter*-don't-know-where-to turn.
V is for *vowels* the Pou is to learn.
(So vivid splendid subjects hide ahead,
the stars, the grasses, asses and wisemen, letters and the word.)

W's for *why*, which ask and ask;
X is for *Xmas*, where I cannot be.
Y is for *yes* (do his Daddy love he?)
Z is for *zig-zag* – a part of our task.
(Straight's better, but few can.
My Xmas hope: boy head for man.)

Mrs. Berryman was then living in Alexandria, Virginia. On March 6, she had written to JB asking to borrow ten dollars. She added that, having applied for a "good Government job," she had twice failed to pass unofficial physicals—owing to recurring evidence of her malignancy—but hoped to pass a third physical "as soon as the final nucleus is dissolved."

Minneapolis

Dearest Mother,   Friday afternoon [9 March 1962]

I am heartsore to think of your difficulties. God knows mine are grievous but I deserve mine – yours are hopelessly unjust & monstrous. I'll
write properly over the weekend: this is only two words to accompany the
cheque that I want to get in the mail instantly – your letter just came. I
am sending 25 and I wish it were 2500. My affairs are in a very bad way,
but thank God you askt me. You must let me *know* when things are this
bad. Please write back quickly. I am utterly ashamed of myself, for not
writing regularly and I will do. There are undoubtedly things worse than
being absolutely without money, as I have often been myself – esp. in
'53 when you so marvellously relieved me & kept me alive; but it is hard
to know what they are. Please accept this lousy $25 as a Lenten gift, and
let me *hear*. I love you and I feel terrible for the pressures on you.

Kate is well (not pregnant yet, we have no idea why) and if she were
not napping at the instant wd send you her love and both our gratefulness
for your recipes which we *adore* and she is doing well with. I am anxious.
I do not know what to do. I am still riddled with ambitions – *still!!* –
and, worse, contradictory ambitions. Art, letters, scholarship? I don't
know. We have got to move (lease up, and the place is *so* small we can't
stay) and I don't know where: apt. or house (no money for house) – but I
must get my library & papers out here fr. Princeton – it's nine years now
of mere deadweight storage & professional & personal privation. I gave
my last (two-hour) lecture for winter quarter yesterday and after a few
days of chores will have a week clear, I hope. I sent 14 Dream Songs to
The New Yorker some weeks ago and have not heard. I haven't paid the
2nd half of my '60 Minnesota taxes, with HELL coming, Federal &
State, esp. State. But we have just had a great stroke of luck. There's a
thing here called single-quarter-leaves: no teaching, at full pay, for research:
and they've given me one for the Fall. I don't think I'm going to be able
to take the Sabbatical due me, bec. it's only half pay (*unless*, as I don't
expect, the Guggenheim people come through); but this is some relief.

Our snow banks are higher than my head. It was 34 below the other
day. Worst winter of all time.

My deepest prayer is for your cheque to come –

dear love,
John

[Minneapolis]

Dearest Mother,   16 June [1962]

I am very sorry and so is Kate for not writing. She has been gravidly unwell, all the moving (we are now in the *fourth* place we have stayed this month) has frazzled us further, and I am still up to my ears in business and arrangements – I just finished my income tax for instance yesterday – having secured (medical) extensions. I have days more too: we can't hope to get off before Tuesday, if then. I begin in Vermont the following Thursday, and our capacity for travel is going to be very limited, K so uncertain and never having made such a trip, and my own irritability intense, with a savage six weeks facing me at Bread Loaf. We still have to stop and find a place to live in Providence too. I've urgent business in New York (and still hope to see Paul) but we have to go thro' there anyway. I'm intensely sorry to have to say that I still can't tell whether we're going to be able to come to Washington or not. I'll let you know as soon as I can. If not before Bread Loaf, in this breakneck operation, of course we will be free after. "Free" – I sometimes lately wonder what that word refers to; three separate lawyers, besides the State gov't. have been after me lately. Even in September, come to think of it, I have to have the [hemorrhoid] operation I've been postponing for two years; hell broke loose a few days ago but I simply haven't the three weeks now, or even one week. It won't wait till Christmas, the specialist says – without crippling agony, that is; so trivial, yet incapacitating. I ran one 2½-hour seminar before I cd get to him, and – brother!

Your own serious condition I don't understand now; about the tests; you mean you'll be under constant observation? good, but how do you feel – I mean physically – apart from "frail", as you put it? I hope to God money will go better for you.

My only proper news is that last week my friends here were joined by the administration and overcame my enemies to make me a full professor. It doesn't matter, except that it may rechannel my paranoia, but they also got me out of the English Dept, and that does matter: no more double chores & insolent nagging. Everybody is delighted, except my enemies.

Love,

John

[P.S.] The Gov't have askt me to read in Washington at the Nat'l Poetry Festival, late Oct. [22–24]

[P.P.S.] In the note I just wrote to Bob I forget to mention the professor-ship: how harried can you get?

[On March 27, Mrs. Berryman had written that since she was to discontinue the "holding shots" she had been taking for her malignancy and begin a new treatment, she would be tested weekly for six months to a year to make sure the condition was under control.]

The Berrymans took up residence at the Bread Loaf School of English on June 27. JB taught two courses: "Henry James and Stephen Crane" and "Deep Form in Minor and Major Poetry." In addition, he continued to work on the Dream Songs. The poet William Meredith was also there and he and JB became friends. While at Bread Loaf, JB made some visits to Robert Frost at the Homer Noble Farm near the campus.

They next moved on to Providence, Rhode Island, where JB had contracted to teach at Brown University for the following academic year. He took over classes for Edwin Honig whose wife, Charlotte, was dying of cancer.

24 Congdon St
[Providence, R.I.]
Dearest Mother,   Sunday 25 November [1962]
I hope prayerfully yr interview on Fri. went well. Please let me hear. – The baby is postponed two weeks. K. is tired of vastness (164 lb.) but well. – Forgive pencil, can't find either pen. – Banks & lawyers are killing me. – My Harvard reading went well, v. well, people said & wrote. I was cool, & read 18 Songs or so – it was Henry's real unveiling. My old chair-man Ted Morrison! introduced me, & afterward we had drinks at Ben Brown's (my best Amer. friend at Cambridge my second year & I hadn't seen him in 24 years) who rang up fr. this Camb. the nt. before, & then were dinnered by the Committee at the Athens Olympia where Delmore & I used to go whenever we (fancied we) cd afford it. The violent emo-tional pressure of all these old associations has almost put me in hospi-tal – I rang up [Dr. James] Shea to make an appointment but then I was too nervous for the trip & cancelled it. Whatever the cause – this, or Henry's formidable success at Washington & Harvard, or baby-waiting – I've written out *14* new songs in the last week, and moreover have made a breakthrough: I'm now doing lower-keyed, *narrative & necessary* archi-tecture, as well as flashing units as usual. Henry also had himself a ball

on Mon. at a place called the Univ'y of Rhode Island 30 mi. fr. here (where I read better than at Harvard). I cannot despair of Henry. Good letters fr. Saul & Cal, who's okay. Kate fell in love w. Boston.

Excuse chat – *tired* –

Love,
John

[Mrs. Berryman was interviewed for a job as a "consultant" in the Department of Commerce, which she later wrote had fallen through because she was "caught in the middle of a presidential appointment."

In both the Harvard and Brown readings—as well as that at the National Poetry Festival—JB's unveiling of the Dream Songs was received with considerable excitement and enthusiasm.]

Providence, R.I.
2 December 1962

JILL BERRYMAN
2500 QUE ST NOW WASHDC
MARTHA WEIGHS SEVEN POUNDS FOUR OUNCES FRISKY MUCH BLACK HAIR
KATE RADIANT LUCK AND LOVE JOHN

Providence, [R.I.]
Dearest Mother   Saturday 8 December [1962]

I can't imagine why I didn't *call* instead of wiring – hectic day – I had only gone out of a mental hospital [McLean Hospital] in Boston the day before (3 new Songs) (put there for prostration after writing 14 songs during Thanksgiving week) (=18 in 3 wks) and that night I broke my ankle in a taxi accident and was marooned on the 2nd floor here for 24 hours, unable to get downstairs to let anybody in – I only got out of hosp. (one superb Song) here for *that* yesterday and will be in this cast or & these crutches for a month. Lovely sequence of luck, eh? Ankle hell. – Please come whenever you can (come stay.) – We can put you up, remember. – Readings at Harvard & elsewhere went splendidly, I'm told & written.

Love,
John

[P.S.] Be glad to autogr. program when I can look for it. Please wr. abt Govt Post.

24 Congdon St

Providence, [R.I.]

Dearest Mother,   1 January 1963

Here at last is your Xmas gift, dear. It tortures me to copy my own poetry – I don't know that I ever did it before except when Dwight & Nancy Macdonald many years ago wanted me to write out "Winter Landscape" for them – they had been v. good to me and I loved them – so I did – they had it framed, the holograph I mean; I wonder who has it now – Dwight who lives mostly in London w. his lousy new wife, or Nancy who lives still at their old place in the Village or did when I last saw her. I hear from old friends all the time. Kate & the baby are well. The baby pushes out her lower lip in pathos as you say I did. Your letter depresses me: no news is bad news. I *pray* this year will be better for you, & us all

Love,

John

[The poems JB copied for Mrs. Berryman included Dream Songs 1, 5, 23 and 27. About the latter he wrote on the page: "this is I think the *best* one for a long time."]

[Providence, R.I.

Dearest Mother,   Sunday [3 March 1963]

How are you, please send a word, I worry that no news is bad news since you would certainly let me know if all (as it never is) were well. Kate and the baby are fine. I am not. My leg is bad still – I'm now having whirlpool treatment twice a week at hospital – and in general I am just crawling to June. I still write every weekend and that is a great mistake. The Songs have been coming out all over. My public performances have been all right so far. I gave a Senior convocation here last week, about 700 people, I wore academic robe & hood for the first time since England. We went to Amherst for the memorial service for Mr Frost and talked with many old friends, including Mark. He read one of Frost's poems, "The Telephone", brilliantly, and altogether the occasion was much less dreary than I feared. I went because we are fond of the Morrisons [Theodore and Kathleen Johnston] & Gentrys [Anne Morrison and Chisholm], the people Frost lived with ever since I was an instructor at Harvard. My 3 Songs abt him were printed in the formidable first number of a *N Y Review [of Books]* scraped together by all of us, the attempt being to damn by comparison the damned *N Y Times Bk Rev* – which people are finding they can do without; no capital, though, and a second number in doubt, the first ran 100,000, none of us being paid. Have I told you Frost tried to cost me my job in Vermont [at Bread Loaf] last year, with a slander, and then months later invited Kate & me privately to his cabin and after an hour's amazing conversation *apologized* – three times – he was not a man who apologized – he said to me "I'm touchy, I'm very touchy" – some of his stories abt himself proving it I'll tell you some time. I got fond of him, having loved him all my life. It was [William] Meredith who made peace between us. His death hit me, esp after Hemingway's defection, & Faulkner's. (I enclose you the Songs – but I've sent also to England – may I have these back?) I wrote to Edmund Wilson yesterday, to my mind the most remarkable American man of letters surviving, and ill, in Cambridge, "The Devil has come of late and took off our top". Besides, Frost's going puts – as you wouldn't think it would – a problem to me. I have never wanted to be king; do you remember how I kept [Durand] Echeverria (who is now a nothing Professor of French here at Brown) between me and head-of-school at SKS? I've been comfortable since 1946 with the feeling that Lowell is far my superior (not to mention other, I mean others surviving both in life and in the advance of their work). But now somebody has sent me *The Observer's* article on Frost, by Philip Toynbee (critic novelist son of the historian), which winds up thus: "the public is undoubtedly right: Frost *was* the greatest American poet alive, even in an age that had produced Robert Lowell and John Berryman." I don't like this. And a day or so later came from the Coast a letter from a well-known editor saying that over a long conversation with a well-known young poet [James] (Dickey) they agreed that I was the "greatest" Amer. poet. You allow for hyperbole; but how much can you allow, from people whom I don't even know and who have nothing to gain from such extravagance? Two heavy votes *have* come in for *The Dream Songs* lately, though: Wilson's & [W.D.] Snodgrass's. And another Coast magazine, a big new Catholic jazz called *Ramparts*, have given fifteen sections their first prize, of $700; which may help us from starving through the summer. I can't tell what the story is. And we will never know. And who cares?

I tell you all this nonsense by way of introduction to something. What is my invisible brother up to? Reading *The Rothschilds* [: A *Family Portrait*, by Frederic Morton] – the five brothers fanned out from a ghetto into the great capitals, supporting fr country to country each other – I mourned how little Bob & I have ever done for each other. But then I thought: without *your* SKS & Columbia, and then 1938–9, and 1953 Fall, none of this (nothing) wd, prob'y, have happened.

Love,

John

[P.S.] Did you throw [Myer] Rashish "The Lay of Ike" ["Dream Song 23"] & did he acknowledge it?

[The memorial service for Robert Frost was held in Johnson Chapel, Amherst College, on February 17, 1963.

Myer Rashish was a student at Harvard when JB was teaching there. Mrs. Berryman met him while living in Washington. He held a position in the Executive Offices at the White House.]

The Bellevue

15 E Street, N.W.

Washington, D.C.

Dearest John,   Thursday, 7 March 1963

Thank you with all my heart for your wonderful letter of Sunday, and the enclosure of the Songs which are magnificent – literally, John, the hair prickled on my nape as you read them to me, sitting in Deac [Dunn]'s snowbound livingroom and yet with you, there, as you read. I return them and, since you may find them useful, two copies of which I have kept another for myself.

This letter will be broken into parts, as it must cover many subjects.

First, of course, my delight at the acclamation for the Songs, particularly Edmund Wilson's, and my relief for your summer as well as pleasure at the recognition of the award from *Ramparts*. Parenthetically, all this delay in my appointment had disappointed one of my fondest hopes: that it would come in time for me to have the worst off my hands and to have a place this summer where you and Kate, and Martha of course and perhaps most, could stay as long as you liked – I'd be away during the day all week and there to baby-sit in the evenings, and over the weekends, too, so that you and Kate could explore this wonderfully beautiful as well as historic countryside. It is barely possible still, but more of that later.

It must be, to anyone but an umbilical-fixed egoist, terrifying to be pressed to the top, and not only exposed but made a cynosure, and this must be a thousand-times true for an artist, most of all, I should think, for a poet. And particularly when the top was a peak of greatness, natural humility warring with natural knowledge of the worth of any work in one's own area including one's own whose greatness must be so difficult to accept. The burden of living to greatness can not but be of inhuman weight. You wrote, at the end, of the past, so I speak of it now: was it not more a shrinking from that intolerable light and burden that made you unwilling to accept the possibility, even, of greatness, of genius, so long ago when you refused to allow any credence to my belief in what you would do? I thank God for you, my greatly loved son, that you have had time, no matter how grievous events and the years have been, in which to bring yourself to accept what you are and will be ever more known for.

Your roof is gone, in Frost, that is clear. It will be painful to stretch to full height but pain is only a way of telling one that growth is at work, and the knowledge of what is to be makes the pain not only endurable but welcome, when accepted.

Forgive me for writing you about matters in which I have no part, except love, but that love keeps what I write from being the impertinence it else would be. God bless you, and the Songs to your good and to His . . . .

I have always in mind the money I have owed you so long, which you sent me so gladly, I shall never think of it without my heart warming at your anxiety for me and your care. I figure with interest I owe you better than $1,000 – the exact figures are with my things in storage, but it is futile to worry about exactitude till I can begin to repay you. If Commerce had come through, in December, all would have been well, but it is no use to dwell on that. The thing I feel really horrible about is the $25, I feel as if I had robbed you and Kate of it, darling. And I have never been sure enough of anything since to return it, I do feel such a leech. One of my heaviest burdens has been living against a basic principle: I hold that a parent's duty, once a child is educated, is to provide for his, the parent's, future so that he shall not be a burden financially or any other way to the child in adulthood and possibly endanger the education and nurture of his grandchildren. Love, it seems to me, between a man and his wife flows back and forth like the tides of the sea, while love between a parent and a child is like a river, flowing always on but in a curious way, with the child downstream after he comes of age as if he had gone past, and with his regard fixed ahead on his wife and children, yet perhaps if they are lucky in understand[ing], he is warmed by the conscious but not demanding love of the parent who remembers when the child was small and he was the downstreamer but only by a little, to stay close and comforting to the child learning life. I say it badly, it comes to timing, as many things do: there is a time for sheltering and a time for struggling and a time for peace which is another word for acceptance, in this sense? I am at peace, darling, in my heart and mind and will, with you and with Jeff in that I have no wish to interfere, no right to interfere, or to expect, I think that is it, to accept whatevercomes; and to believe in love given and returned . . . .

> All my love, darling,
> JB

24 Congdon St
Providence, R.I.

Dearest Mother,   9 April 1963

I'm *very* sorry not to have written sooner. I've been unwell. – Here's a miserable $10 for the telephone call. My account is low, low, my taxes unknown (but my debts less than usual, Kate says), or I'd send you money. Now: *Kate suggested* the other day that we ask you to come & stay here – STAY – until we leave, about two months hence. Old Baby (She smiles good.) would love to see you (& you her), and I wd, & Kate would. Weather improving, the top floor will be habitable now. PLEASE come. You say you'll be there 'till the 22*nd: Ramparts* say they'll hand me the $700 (hurrah for back-taxes) around the 15*th,* so if you need it – I *can* send you travel-expenses then. At present I have abt *$100 in* the bank (I owe $100 or so), K. says, & – as ever – *no* savings. Where we are going for the summer, and what is to happen next year, God knows. The U. of Minn. & I crossed wires abt summer job – just as well, – I cdn't do it: I am sick 3 days out of 4. *Next* year is complicated & doubtful. Everything depends – as always on money; is there anything else? But a friend – [William] Meredith – has nominated me for a Ford Fellowship, and my God if *that* came true I'd be all right the whole year. But it won't, & so . .

This baby is delicious – come away –
Blessings, meanwhile, & come,

John

[P.S.] I have a non-*Dr. Song* poem at abt 80 ll. now, in my one week free. It's called "The Other Chicago" and is mostly drafted out. I am trying to make money.

[P.P.S.] You could see Shelby & her baby too. I haven't myself, which is weird. Bob & I are well. Do you know I askt him to come & live here with us; & got no word. But I am weirder than him I confess.

[P.P.P.S.] Thanks for the [J. Robert] Oppenheimer stuff. His comment was so reserved & dignified I cd have cried. They are *animals*. [Lewis Lichtenstein] Strauss, [Edward] Teller, & the fool Eisenhower.

[P.P.P.P.S.] We've had disasters of which I say nothing. Were you & Dad weird, or is it just us?

["The Other Chicago" has not been published.

In December 1963, Oppenheimer had been given the Atomic Energy Commission's highest honor, the $50,000 Fermi Award. It was significant both for its recognition of Oppenheimer's contributions to theoretical physics and, most importantly, as a symbol of the U.S. government's desire to clear his name, after he had been declared a security risk in 1954.]

On June 10th, JB, Kate and Martha moved into a two-hundred-year-old Gristmill in rural Rhode Island, near Chepatchet, where they stayed most of the summer.

                                          [Chepatchet, Rhode Island]
Dearest Mother   Monday [24 June 1963]]

I'm *very* happy abt the job, esp. w. mornings free – I wish it were better but *any* job is heavenly if one hasn't got one. We're delighted you're coming too: either Fri. or Sat. is fine: let us know & we'll get you in Providence. Here's $25 (*not* to be repaid – *nor* is any of the other). I wish it were more but I'm very low. Of course you must stay *at least* thro' yr birthday – we'll have the O'Briens [Shelby and Bruce] over & Martha will coo and (bring a bathing suit) we'll all get in the waterfall – also that day, I learn in the other letter today, is William's (Meredith, this is) deadline for his new book, we'll try to lure him up fr. New London –

                                                              Love,
                                                              John

[P.S.] Martha *crawls*. It's horrible!

[Mrs. Berryman had recently found a part-time job in Washington, D.C., with an economic consultants' firm, Jesse J. Friedman and Associates. She visited JB, Kate and Martha at the Gristmill during the second week of July, and again in September.

Robert Jefferson's daughter, Shelby, had, in 1961, married a young engineer named Bruce O'Brien.]

[Chepatchet, Rhode Island]

Dearest Mother,   26 July [1963]

A great day for the baby. She stood up. For days now she sits up at ease for long periods of time and stands at her cribside dancing and yesterday she dropped the pacifier at her feet and retrieved it and recovered her position. But this evening she heaved herself up from nothing with the netting for the first time. She also likes water. We took her to Killingly and she can all but float.

I wish I could almost float. How my work is going I don't know. Every now and then I tear up something. But with 40 changes I took a piece of junk the other day and almost made it viable. Mark [Van Doren] has just sent me a letter so extravagant about one I sent him that I won't quote it. Yesterday, with a thud, came the word from [The] Ford [Foundation]: no. I am not really disappointed, having been aware for some time that the Garden of Eden has been abolished; but Kate was. Two other remote chances for grants have emerged, however.

One of K best friends comes tomorrow & will be here for her birthday.

[Conrad] Aiken's new Mod Libr anthol [*Twentieth-Century American Poetry*] with the whole Bradstr poem came yesterday. It is the longest damn poem in the book and looks odd there. Next is Wallace Stevens's "Comedian as the Letter C" and next is parts of Hart Crane's *The Bridge*.

I'm very sorry the job isn't better in every respect. The world is ridiculous. Dec seems far too for Soc. Sec. Better luck!!

Love,
John

[P.S.] K. writing.
[P.P.S.] City-plan article fascinating; sending to two friends.

[Chepatchet, Rhode Island]

Dearest Mother   1 August 1963

Kate just wrote. I have no news exc. the American poetess Sylvia Plath killed herself – The *Observer* just sent me her final poems and w. extreme reluctance I wrote a Song for her. – I sent 9 Songs to *Poetry* day before yest'y, & yest'y 4 to a Patricia Haward in London for Ital. translation. Here is Mark's letter. I am *very* glad matters are looking up. My mail is the maddest thing you ever Saw.

Love,

John

[The nine songs sent to *Poetry* appeared in the October–November 1963 issue.

Translations of the four songs sent to Patricia Howard were not published since the prospective annual (and later quarterly) in which they were to appear never materialized.]

[Chepatchet, Rhode Island]

Dearest Mother,   12 August 1963

All thanks for the obituary of Roethke, which came on Wednesday and helped in the final revision of my Song for him. My first word was the bare fact in a business letter from California on Monday – from a man I would trust two feet with a fact – so though I felt slugged I hoped it was wrong; that night I tried to get [Henry] Rago on the phone but he was out. Tuesday *Time* confirmed. Sometimes life does not seem worthwhile. I wrote to B. Here's the Song, which keep.

Thanks too for the pb's. I have only so far read Stewart's. It is very badly written but interested me enough to read it all, and I liked the hammer-part. He knows ecology and other natural process in a way most novelists don't. Queer case of an English professor who turned himself into a bestselling almost-novelist.

Mark's enormous *Coll. Poems* just came. I clip the blurb I wrote – but I've no copy so may I have it back? The Song for him has gone to Rago for their special October number, with some eight others, and I've no copy; I'll have that sent you next month.

Chilly here. I did not sleep at all last night and feel empty. The baby had roseola briefly and was uncomfortable and is now perfect again. She was so happy yesterday she sang practically all day, and till midnight too. I'm glad the man you're working for interests you. Shelby sent a note but says nothing of her job.

Kate's & my love,
John

["A Strut for Roethke" (Dream Song 18) first appeared in the *Times Literary Supplement*, August 23, 1963, and was reprinted in the *New York Review of Books*, October 17, 1963.

Henry Rago was editor of *Poetry*.

Throughout their lives, JB and Mrs. Berryman shared an enthusiasm for mysteries and she often supplied him with new titles. The Stewart referred to in this letter is probably Alfred Walter Stewart (whose pseudonym is J. J. Connington).]

[Chepatchet, Rhode Island]
Dearest Mother   4 September 1963

Yes of course come for as long as you can as soon as you can. We gave Martha – now known to me as "Twiss Twingle" (w. variations) & to Kate as "Buzzie" – bangs last night. She has many tricks & victory cries, and will please you.

I have just sent 72 *Dream Songs* to Giroux. I finished the apparatus last night. So easy: – only 8 years' work. That's abt. ⅓ of the present ms.

Yes – wedd. anniv'y, the 1st: I took Kate to Cape Cod (or *she* drove *me*) to see old friends – my first time there in 12 yrs or so – and we got woofed into a party of 100 or so at Gilbert Geldes' – everywhere I saw people who were either my acquaintances *or* their now-grown children. I did not at all forget Bob's birthday but did neglect to call him. Will do.

Still no plans. 3 deadlines. Read all clip's: thanks.

Love,
John

The University of Minnesota had granted JB a sabbatical leave for the next academic year. Having applied to various foundations for support to work on his critical biography of Shakespeare, he was awarded $4,000 by the Ingram Merrill Foundation. After six weeks in New York at the Chelsea Hotel, JB, Kate and Martha moved into a two-floor apartment, which Mrs. Berryman had helped them find, at 103 Second Street, N.E., in Washington, D.C. Mrs. Berryman, who greeted them at the door with a giant pitcher of martinis, occupied the first floor, JB and Kate the second floor. Here they stayed several months. The move

55 Lansdowne Park
Ballsbridge, Dublin
15 Dec 66

Dearest Mother
BBC television cabled the other day to want to send a man fr. London to talk abt my making a film for them. I said to let him come: shall I do this?

Strokes of luck have hit me here: a cable fr. Lowell abt Bk IV 'a tremendous & living triumph', the London Times did rev. of them — a whole page, wh. they've never done before, the other 4 in The NY Review; the Chancellors of the Academy of Amer. Poets voted me $5,000, wh. means I won't have to teach in the Summer for 4 or 5 yrs. I can hardly bear to do that any more. I must work.

Kate says love & merry Xmas & more pictures of Martha are coming soon.

I finisht my poem some 5 days ago, w. a spurt of H's Crisis's two others & then a terror 'H's Guilt.' I still have the terrible editorial & administrative labour of making Bks V & VI of the 300 but I can't write any more, at least until I am thro' w. the second volume & open the great yellow folder I brought fr. mpls, w. fragments, better than many of the finisht songs. But I feel remote & lost without my poem, & gave hell to an editor of the Irish Times the other evening, why I don't know.

We sent you some handsome mohair & Paul a gorgeous sweater & 75 Irish stamps, plus the 7s.5. I admire & love you.
merry Christmas   John

In this letter, written in Dublin, JB notes the completion of *His Toy, His Dream, His Rest*, the second volume of *The Dream Songs*.

ON FACING PAGE: Above, JB and Kathleen (Kate) Donahue, March 25, 1961, at the Waikiki Room in Minneapolis. This was their first date and an ill JB had left the hospital for an evening to keep it.

Below, JB and Kate Berryman at the Bread Loaf School of English at Middlebury College, Vermont, summer 1962.

Kate and Martha Berryman.

JB receiving the Russell Loines Award for Poetry from Robert Lowell, May 20, 1964.

Below, memorial reading for Randall Jarrell at Yale University, February 28, 1966. Left to right, seated: JB, Adrienne Rich, Mary Jarrell, and Peter Taylor. Standing: Stanley Kunitz, Richard Eberhart, Robert Lowell, Richard Wilbur, John Hollander, William Meredith, and Robert Penn Warren. *The Bettmann Archive*

JB and Kate Berryman in front of the house they lived in while in Ballsbridge, Ireland (1966–1967). *Terence Spencer, Life Magazine © Time Inc.*

JB in characteristic pose, writing *Dream Songs*, at Ryan's Bar in Dublin. *Terence Spencer, Life Magazine © Time Inc.*

JB at home in Minneapolis, in 1971.

Last photo of JB—New Years Eve, 1971.

Mrs. Berryman, on the day of JB's funeral. *Photo by Jones Dovedenas*

once again placed mother and son in close proximity which this time they passed with comparative equanimity—probably helped by the discussion Mrs. Berryman describes in the following letter:

[Washington, D.C.]

Dear, dear John   23 December 1963

I do thank you, wholeheartedly, for being so frank and open with me, and for pointing out the way we should go. This will provide a good foundation for peaceful co-existence for all of us. It will not only give you and Kate the complete freedom you require and deserve, but it will allow me to live my own retired and retiring life.

For my part, I promise:

not to offer advice or services or directions or whatever unless asked, in which case I'll be happy to respond with any information or aid possible

not to intrude into your affairs or to subject you or Kate or the baby to any interference whatever

You see, John, I was carried away by being able, after so long a time of taking, by the fact that I could do any giving at all and especially to you and Kate and the baby. This may have been intensified by exhaustion and the two falls but that is not certain, at all – the fact is that it must have been intolerable and I am so grateful to you for putting matters to me so clearly. It was a difficult chore and I regret deeply that my behavior forced it upon you, darling.

Now I can retire peacefully into my own pattern, leaving you and yours to your pattern of living. Grateful beyond words as I am that you were here Friday night and armed as I was and am by your loving care, I am become a solitary and in attempting anything else become tedious and false-seeming because of uncertainty in a different behavior.

So I shall have my usual early breakfast, a hearty lunch, and something light, generally cereal or some such, when I am hungry for it, probably around my bedtime. I am not accustomed to eating a real dinner and this will work out very well, as it leaves you and Kate free to eat dinner when you like, without having to wait on anyone else.

I accept fully your decisions about rent et al. Perhaps, because I would have them anyway, if you think you should pay two-thirds of the rent, you would let me pick up on the 'phone and paper bills? it costs only

75c, I think it is, to have your name listed at information, so the costs are properly mine, please. I will put whatever you decide is my share into the food 'kitty', and I do think I should pay for any household things, like mop or dishes, as they will be left here and I will continue to use them. But whatever you say is all right with me, darling.

All my love, your devoted mother,
JB

Early in 1964, JB left Washington, D.C., for a reading tour. He continued to drink heavily and, during the tour, collapsed and was hospitalized at Riverside Community Hospital in Los Angeles. This was the first of several hospitalizations he would face in the next year alone, and thereafter his health never fully recovered. Near the end of April, 77 Dream Songs *was published by Farrar, Straus and Company. On May 20, he received the Russell Loines Award from the National Institute of Arts and Letters in New York. In September JB and Kate bought a house in Minneapolis at 33 Arthur Avenue, S.E., within a mile of the University. In May 1965,* 77 Dream Songs *was awarded the Pulitzer Prize for Poetry.*

Abbott Hospital
[Minneapolis]
Dearest Mother   6 July [1965?]
Desperately nervous – just a note to wish you happy birthday & send love. Both my doctor & I think I am improving and I'll write properly soon – This is the first "letter" I have written since I wrote to Paul for Xmas. Thank you for his letter, which I loved – I hope you keep better & well

Love,
John

33 Arthur
Minneapolis
Dearest Mother   Friday [17 September 1965]
Just an interim note to say love & dreadfully sorry abt dog-injury – I hope it's healing well. Ann's damned suit is put off till Oct 25. I got out of hospital a week ago and was better until I lunched a Yugoslavian poet [Ivan V. Lalic] who wanted to meet (& translate) me and had to spend Wed in bed. Writing, though – 3 new songs – and preparing my course

(again my Programme has relieved me of one of my two courses). Invitation fr. Dean of Columbia [David B. Truman] to read – accepting,
prob'y for Dec [December 6] – San Francisco Nov. 9th.

Love,

John

[P.S.] We paid back taxes finally, with medical testimony.
[P.P.S.] Animal book came today: Martha loves it.

[Mrs. Berryman had been bitten on the face by a friend's German shepherd.
  Ivan V. Lalic, Serbian poet, translator and critic, was visiting the U.S. as a
participant in the State Department's Foreign Leaders Program. From 1961 to
1964, he had been Secretary General of the Yugoslav Writer's Union. Serbo-
Croatian translations of four of JB's poems, "Conversation," "The Ball Poem,"
"The Song of the Tortured Girl" and "The Moon and the Night and the Men,"
appeared in Lalic's 1972 *Anthology of Modern American Poetry*.]

*JB passed the 1965–66 academic year teaching at the University of Minne-
sota. He continued to write Dream Songs, buoyed by having been awarded a
Guggenheim Fellowship and 9,500 dollars for the next academic year, during
which he planned to live in Dublin. Mrs. Berryman lost her job at Jesse J.
Friedman and Associates the day after Thanksgiving 1965, but remained in
Washington, D.C. By the following May, she had begun working at the Catholic University of America, at first in the Department of Interdepartmental Communication, and later as an administrative assistant to the acting head of the
Department of Biology and Botany.*

<table>
<tr><td></td><td align="right">[Minneapolis]</td></tr>
<tr><td>Dearest Mother</td><td align="right">[8 July 1966?]</td></tr>
</table>

Congratulations on your birthday – I wish you cd spend it here [illeg-
ible words] cool for the moment – we hope to see you before we sail from
Montreal Aug 26*th*. Still have no house in Dublin but many leads. I
have no idea what gift you may want, on your restricted budget, so please
forgive & use the enclosed cheque – I earned the money by a critical
reading of mss. for a desperate poet here. Kate wishes you a happy birthday too. We took Martha to a birthday party and she behaved perfectly
for hours till she fell on an iron bar and electrified all that part of the
Twin Cities.

I did an immense job last month of making my poem ready to take,
registering 259 whole songs (13 brand new) of which only ten have been
published. German and Italian translations [of *Homage to Mistress Brad-*

street] are in progress. I had an abscessed tooth pulled & am exhausted & insomniac but otherwise fairly well.

The books came – thanks – and I read most of them during the final weeks of lecturing – I begin again in 10 days for 5 weeks. I am very happy that you like the job, it sounds infinitely preferable to Friedman.

Hurriedly, love,
John

[Gertrude S. Schwebell's translation, *Huldigung Für Mistress Bradstreet*, was published in Hamburg by Hoffman and Campe in 1967.

Sergio Perosa's translation, *Omàggio A Mistress Bradstreet*, was published in Torino by Giulio Einaudi in 1969.]

After sailing from Montreal on August 26, the Berrymans spent a week at the Majestic Hotel in Dublin, and then moved into a house at 55 Landsdowne Park in the suburb of Ballsbridge. There, JB continued to write more songs and to organize those which would make up His Toy, His Dream, His Rest.]

Ballsbridge, Dublin
Dearest Mother   15 December 1966
BBC television cabled the other day to want to send a man fr. London to talk abt my making a film for them. I said to let him come: shall I do this?

Strokes of luck have hit me here: a cable fr. Lowell abt Bk IV "a tremendous & living triumph", the London *Times* did nine of them – a whole page, wh. they've never done before, the other 4 in *The NY Review* [*of Books*]: the Chancellors of the Academy of Amer. Poets voted me $5000, wh. means I won't have to teach in the Summer for 4 or 5 yrs. I can hardly bear to do that anymore. I must work.

Kate says love & merry Xmas & more pictures of Martha are coming soon.

I finisht my poem some 5 days ago, w. a spurt of "H's Crisis" [*DS* 367] & two others & then a terror "H's Guilt" [*DS* 371]. I still have the terrible editorial & administrative labour of making Bks V & VI of the 300 but I – can't *write* any more, at least until I am thro' w. the second volume & open the great yellow folder I brought fr. Mpls, w. fragments, better than many of the finisht songs. But I feel remote & lost without my poem, & gave *hell* to an editor of *The Irish Times* the other evening, why I don't know.

We sent you some handsome mohair & Paul a gorgeous sweater & 75 Irish stamps, plus the *TLS*. I admire & love you.

Merry Christmas
John

[The first three "Books" or sections of *The Dream Songs* had appeared in the 1964 volume *77 Dream Songs*. Books IV through VI, referred to above—and an additional VIIth—would make up the 1968 volume *His Toy, His Dream, His Rest*.]

Dublin

Dearest Mother,   2 January 1967

Yr accident sounds horrible – I am glad you got out alive & w. so little comparatively to pay. I am also v. sorry abt yr knee – what did they say at the clinic? I am also disturbed by yr leaving yr job, which I thought you liked, demanding tho' it was: Academic department heads in our country are mostly jerks – it makes them into it, and it attracts the original jerks. I hope one or the other of the other jobs comes thro' at once. Let us know.

I had a fall last night – Thorazine, one of my drugs, has a side-effect on equilibrium – and damaged my right side. K tho't my back broken. Heavy pains all day, and can't write long, though I did my new stint tonight: 5 Songs examined & judged a day, – to get me into my NY deadline two months from now. For two cents I'd resign from apt & go to Greece – the Royal Government invited me there as their guest several yrs ago. But I must stay & work. Twissy & Kate take the taxi to the shore (Sandymount) & collect shells. I haven't been well enough to go yet. I *am* doing the BBC TV film: but probably in London – I'm tired of Dublin; no genius here. No genius in England either, but friends. Exc. Louis MacNeice, dead. It's very hard, older, to make friends. Greece in the Spring maybe where we do have friends in Athens.

Love,
John

[Mrs. Berryman had been in an automobile accident.

The Greek government had invited JB to be their official guest during either the 1965 Epidaurus Festival or the 1965 Athens Festival.

The BBC TV film was made at Ryan's Bar, JB's favorite bar in Dublin. The twenty minute film, *John Berryman Reads from the Dream Songs*, included an interview with A. Alvarez.]

Dublin

My dearest Mother   4 February 1967

I was horrified by yr accident. And glad you came out alive.

Should you be driving, dear, at your age, honey?

I finisht Bk V this week and *Life* mag. rang up fr. London to want to do a story abt me. They are so stupid & uncertain that – etc.

100 caricatures by James Gillray [*Fashionable Contracts*, London: Phaidon, 1966] came fr. Oxford this week, the raving genius. My new plan for my next book is the Chinese poem – the Gillray poem, *if* I live long enough.

We want to see you. As soon as I finish Bk VI, fly over and we'll take you on a tour of Ireland, hiring a car. *Come.* Of course I'll send you a cheque for a dim reply to your great good to me, expenses, all those years ago. The baby is waiting to see you, excited. Come.

Love,

John Berryman

[James Gillray, the eminent English caricaturist and illustrator, was born in 1757 and died in 1815. He is best known for his caricatures of the court of George III. The planned "Gillray poem" was never written.

"Scholars at the Orchid Pavillion," part of the "Chinese poem" JB planned, was published in *Delusions, Etc.* (1972).]

In response to JB's February 4 letter, Mrs. Berryman wrote that her "heart had not been so touched in years, John, as by your amazing marvellous wanting me to come and explore Ireland with you and Kate and Martha," but declined because, having left Catholic University of America, she had to find another job as soon as possible. In lieu of the gift of the trip, she later wrote asking to borrow 275 dollars, which she proposed to repay in monthly installments.

In late April, JB flew to New York to receive another award: a 5,000 dollar prize from the Academy of American Poets. While there he also gave a reading, which Mrs. Berryman attended, at the Guggenheim Museum. Soon JB returned to Dublin with Jane Howard, who with photographer Terence Spencer, had been assigned by Life *magazine to do a lengthy article on him. "Whiskey and Ink, Whiskey and Ink," appeared in the July 21, 1967, issue and added considerably to JB's growing public recognition.*

On April 24, 1967, Berryman's Sonnets, until then a well-kept secret, appeared. Written in 1947, during the course of an intense affair with a woman he calls Lise, this sequence of 115 love sonnets was published with some minor alterations and the addition of a few new sonnets. Learning about the existence of the sonnet-sequence, only upon their appearance, clearly displeased Mrs. Berryman. Another falling off in her son's letters and her inability to repay any of the money she had borrowed no doubt further rankled her.

3169 18th Street N.W.

Washington, D.C. 20010

4 July 1967

Dear John,

Thank you very much for the *[Berryman's] Sonnets*, which arrived about ten days ago, although your dedication is dated in early May. It was an astonishment to me to learn that there was such a book and that it had been published as I had heard nothing of it and had assumed from your references to the various books under weigh that you were working on the second of the Dream Songs volumes. I have read them with great interest and, again that word, astonishment. How little any of us know of another, much less of oneself. They must have been enormously private for you never to have mentioned them during the years of and after their writing when you did still speak of your work to me – I remember the hours of the nights when you would call late, too late to go to Princeton, and then sit, there at the Chelsea, and read me what you had written that day or since the last time, of the Bradstreet poem. Such recollections are treasures, especially when like my friend the owl I am acold and without even the protection of his feathers so it should be naked and acold.

I have what well may seem to you a totally inadequate apology to make you and a promise that should lift an intolerable burden from you, John.

First, the apology. The anguish that the breaking of my word is to me concerns only me, and you must judge me as you must. I can not make the repayals monthly as I had said I would do. You are due an explanation: I worked only 8 months in 1966, for a total take-home pay of $2,418.16 and was not able to go to work and to get a job till April first this year, with a take-home of $354.12. Unfortunately the operation turned out to be two; with the help of a friend I was able to make a bank loan in addition to the lifesaver you sent me, but now I have to pay off the bank loan which was not expected, and I am still taking the costly shots again and, to put it simply, there is no health in me. I should not have squandered the money on the trip to New York but, just as when you and Kate came to the Poetry Week here and of course I longed to know her, but I needed to see you as, I suppose, an affirmation of life. All I can say now is that I will pay it when I can. I didn't ask you because of the $5,000 grant which is none of my affair, but because you had offered me the trip to Ireland which was the most heartwarming gesture, and because, since I could not accept, I thought you would be willing to spend the trip money as a loan to keep me alive. In any event, all I can say now is that I will repay you when I can; right now I can't even make token payments.

Now, the promise, which is the greatest gift I have ever been able to make anyone. I give you what you so sorely need, freedom of me. I give it freely, gladly, proudly, my only regret that I could not have had the vision and wisdom to free you long ago.

This is really a two-fold gift. The practical side lifts from you a seemingly inevitable burden in the years to come. To be clear, I shall never under any circumstances ask or accept a penny from you, much less your care or responsibility for me in any way. I am not your problem, John, nor that of anyone except myself. I am a devout and practical Catholic but I would kill myself, trusting in God's goodness and wisdom, before I would lay any burden on anyone and particularly on you who were God's gift to me. I owe you and your brother such a debt as can never be paid off, the gift of sharing in the generations of man, and I owe God most of all for the gift of loving you both. I always felt doubly responsible to my mother because she did not love me, it was a grace and joy she did not have, no fault of hers or even mine since love is not a reasoned thing, one loves whom one can, or must, as your brother once said bitterly. I was overjoyed at the prospect of you, grieve still for the lost child between and then was lifted into happiness with your brother's birth. I tried to be all to you both that my mother was not to me – I was young and foolish but never so foolish as to think of you as *my* sons, but always of myself as *your* mother – yours was the gift to me, not me to you, ever. I have never felt that you or your brother owed me anything, the debt lay the other way. Whatever I was ever able to do for you, John, was not done to make up for your loss of a father but in joy and happiness that I could do something for you who had fulfilled my life for me, you and your brother.

Now the other side of this coin. This should free you of the ambivalence that has agonized you. You are free to think, even believe, what you like, John, with no feeling of treachery toward your father's memory or the latent fear that you have misjudged me. For the last time, for the record, John, I did not kill your father or drive or lead him to his death.

If you do not know in your blood and bone that I am incapable of assuming the burden of another's death, nothing I can say would make sense to you. I tell you now, however, before God who is my refuge and my strength, that I, who fear a knife only less than a snake, could not, with a gun in my hand, shoot anyone coming at me with a knife – this refusal to accept certain responsibilities is a weakness in me, but it is one from which I shall never be well. Think of me as dead, John, for your own sake remember any good that you can, and so ease your life and living. It is my daily prayer that you be given the grace to come out of the fantasy you have so long clutched to yourself, and be free. For the truth, accepted, shall set you free.

And do not mourn for me, John. This sets me free, too, so accept freely the offering, given freely, with the hope that you may find freedom and joy and the knowledge that I shall have peace in my time.

Your devoted mother,
Jill Berryman

[P.S.] This letter requires no answer, John.

[P.P.S.] I meant to say what a remarkable photograph that is, on the back of the jacket, I shall treasure it. It has been so painful to me, to see you looking like your own great-grandfather behind that Hemingwayan beard – this portrait is wonderful. Did you know that your brother and I discovered, by accident, some years ago, that we who throw out dustjackets instanter, keep the jackets on your books? But now I shall protect the photograph by cutting it out and putting it inside the *Sonnets*.

In November 1967, JB was again hospitalized, in Abbott Hospital in Minneapolis, for alcoholism and nervous exhaustion. His subsequent attempt to quit drinking elicited this paragraph from an Ash Wednesday, 1968, letter of Mrs. Berryman's:

"I was made so happy by your saying that you were not drinking, to hope that your years may be long is now real. My pain for you was always agony because I knew that you could stop any time you wanted to do so – you have a whim of iron and a will of chilled steel, and John, you forged these yourself, they were not a natural inheritance or a gift, you did not have them as a child or boy – over the long, dreadfully difficult years, you made them and it is wonderful to me to know that you yourself can save yourself. Please do not be offended by my writing of this, I thank God for your saving yourself with every breath I draw."

Throughout this time he continued to write new Songs and to organize His

Toy, His Dream, His Rest *(the second and concluding volume of* The Dream Songs*). On December 1, 1967, his collection* Short Poems *was published by Farrar, Straus and Giroux.*

During the first half of 1968, Mrs. Berryman continued to suffer with back problems and with mounting financial difficulties. In June she wrote enclosing a copy of her financial statements that showed her in need of 1,165 dollars. JB and Kate immediately sent the money to her. Mrs. Berryman later attempted to repay some of what had been sent her.

[Minneapolis]

Dearest Mother   24 August 1968

I am not cashing your cheques and don't wish to be repaid. It is the extra burdens that distress me – the storage and the car. It seems to me that you ought to disembarrass yourself of these. For yourself I wd expect to find some money monthly.

I hope you have been well. I have not, but survive – I'll write properly when I'm better. Paul is coming for a visit, which I preview with trepidation.

Love,
John

His Toy, His Dream, His Rest was published by Farrar, Straus and Giroux on October 25, 1968, and critical acclaim and several prizes were quickly forthcoming. The first award JB received was a 10,000 dollar prize from the National Endowment for the Arts. In January 1969, he and Karl Shapiro shared the Bollingen Prize for Poetry, which brought JB another 5,000 dollars for His Toy, His Dream, His Rest. *And soon thereafter the volume was voted the National Book Award, for which JB gave his acceptance speech on March 12, 1969.*

This was a heady period. Despite persistent drinking and poor health, JB continued to teach and—increasingly in demand as a public performer—to maintain a heavy schedule of poetry readings throughout the country. Following a muscle spasm which caused a painfully pinched greater occipital nerve, he was in and out of the hospital again for weeks. Mrs. Berryman visited Minneapolis during this time and helped JB with proofing the complete version of The Dream Songs *(1969). She also assisted in the compilation of the "Index of First Lines" and "Index of Titles" which conclude the volume.*

On October 2, 1969, the University of Minnesota awarded JB its highest honor by appointing him Regents' Professor of Humanities for "outstanding contributions to the teaching profession, the University, and to the public good."

The appointment carried with it an additional 5,000 dollars a year. In Novem-
ber, after an excess of drugs and alcohol, JB fell in the bathroom, spraining his
ankle and brusing his right ribs and right big toe. He was then admitted to Hazel-
den, the Minneapolis alcoholic rehabilitation center, where he remained for five
weeks of treatment.

[Minneapolis]
Dearest Mother   Thursday [18 December 1969?]

Merry Xmas & a happier New York. I was delighted w. yr news (medical) – I came yesterday out of hospital after almost a month, and know
w. gratefulness [what it is] to feel fairly well. Unfortunately my doctors
do not agree abt my drinking, and many other problems remain unsolved.

We are very sorry you are not coming but understand. Later, then. I
did some shopping from hospital and I hope dearly [you like] what you
will find for you from India – it's an old time present. The elephant(s)
stand for Patience & Perseverence – both of wh. we need. This is my 3rd
letter in 8 months. I also enclose $100, wh. use as you like: necessary or
frivolous. Kate & Twissy join in my love,

John

[Minneapolis]
Dearest Mother,   Friday, 26 December [1969]

Your lovely letter came yesterday morning as we were opening gifts
around the tree. I gave the baby a xylophone, on which she can already
bang out tunes, and to K. a beige cashmere sweater which cost me $36
to my amazement – I thought they were $15 or $18. Kate gave me a
Japanese kimono & sandals, the ones I bought in Kyoto having long since
worn out. Thanks for the list of mysteries: I've crossed out those I've read.
M. gave me a hideous turtle, modelled, baked & painted by herself.
Kate's lousy & worthless brothers, with her sad grandmother, came in for
three hours in the afternoon; thank God this only happens once a year –
I could have used half a dozen drinks but stuck to coffee.

The Hazelden programme is strenuous: 3 lectures a day, group therapy Tu. & Th., interviews w. your counsellor, your unit manager, a
psychologist, reading (books on AA [e.g., *Twelve Steps and Twelve Tra-*
ditions], [William] Glasser's reality-therapy [*Reality Therapy: A New*

Approach to Psychiatry], etc.), a daily job (mine was vacuuming the TV room and a small lounge – I hated it and it wasn't until the end of the second week that I could do it quickly, efficiently & without strain), policing your room. I was in bad shape when admitted to Hazelden and was kept in the intensive care unit for a whole week before being assigned to a unit (Thieboult Hall, 22 men) & beginning treatment. Even so, the first 4 days were pure hell: I was sweating & shaking very badly, w. great physical weakness, couldn't sleep or eat, tortured by remorse, brooding over my whole life, depressed about my lecture-course at the University, afraid of the programme – which I caught on to very quickly from the lecturing and am talking to the other men on the unit – it seemed hard & ridiculous to expect to reform one's character, morally & spiritually, in just 3 weeks' time (the usual length of treatment). If it hadn't been for 8 or 10 friends I made my first day on the unit, I might not have survived (you are free to leave at any time, though of course they argue w. you and there's no refund from the $500 you pay at the outset for 3 weeks' stay). But on the fifth day, a Saturday, I began to improve – greatly cheered by a letter that morning from my chairman, Bob Ames, saying he had got two younger men to take my final lectures, on Montaigne & Pascal (my three weeks on *Don Quixote* were taken by an instructor in the Spanish Dept., whom I'll pay); and by the end of the end of the second week I was feeling better in every way than I'd felt for many years, and continued so. Kate & the baby came every Sunday afternoon. The lectures are mostly excellent, by the staff – all of whom, except the clergymen, are themselves recovered alcoholics – and outside experts; I learnt a great deal from them: for instance, from a psychologist named Joe Lazzaro, to stop completely comparing myself to other people. My counsellor, Jim Jensen, helped me correct my thinking on various topics, particularly humility & self-sufficiency. Your treatment concludes with a "4th step", which you write out (giving specific instances of selfishness, alibis, dishonest thinking, pride, resentment & anger, intolerance, impatience, envy, phonyness, procrastination, self pity, oversensitivity, fear, etc) and use as a basis for the "fifth step" ("we admitted to God, to ourselves, and to one other human being, the exact nature of our wrongs"), an interview with a clergyman. Mine was w. a priest, young & very able, named Fr. [Hector] La Chapelle, and took five hours. It's a wonderful programme.

I'm having a wonderful time working up my proseminar on *Hamlet* which I'm giving for the Eng. Dept. this winter.

I hope you gain strength steadily, darling.

Love,

John

[On May 2, 1970, following another period of excessive drinking, JB entered the Intensive Alcohol Treatment Center at St. Mary's Hospital in Minneapolis. Robert Ames was, at this time, Director of the Humanities Program at the University of Minnesota.]

[St. Mary's Hospital]

[Minneapolis]

Dearest Mother,   Sunday 7 June [1970]

Thanks for the clippings, esp. of the student strikes – which hit me hard: only a third of my 70 kids showed up for the midquarter exam, and only about ⅔ are taking the final or writing a paper (the option I gave them). I haven't decided whether to give the rest Incompletes or F.

Hazelden last winter was good for me, but it failed in the essential point or I failed it: I took my first drink at a New Year's Eve party, and drank lightly then for several months, working v. hard & well on the 3rd or final version of my Shak. biography, to halfway thro' Ch. III. But suddenly at that point I wrote a lyric, almost my first short poem in 20 years. I wrote a second, similar in theme, in the same new & strange form & style, also first-class; and I was off in the most violent outburst since early 1953 when I wrote the Bradstr. poem. I did some 50 lyrics in 5 or 6 weeks drinking more & more heavily, until I was through with the book & up to a quart of bourbon a day, near nervous & physical prostration. Kate & my psychiatrist [Dr. Clifford O. Erickson] got me in here, the alcoholic rehabilitation ward of St Mary's Hospital, and I've been here 5 weeks. The treatment programme resembles Hazelden in some respects but is far more radical & painful – I underwent a sort of religious conversion on Tuesday of my second wk. (I'll describe this to you sometime) & am greatly improved in other ways, though the medical director thinks it will be a year before my nervous health is restored. I had a seizure after 3 wks of withdrawal, wh. is v. unusual & threatening; maybe I wdn't survive another such period. But I have good hopes that none will ever come. Pray for me.

The book (Giroux thinks it "far & away yr best book" – wh. I don't agree with but am glad to hear) is called *Love & Fame* & it will make a sensation this Fall: though it may also (Mark thinks) be "feared & hated". It's highly personal, a third about my Columbia years, a third about my first term at Cambridge (ending with a masterpiece to B.), then impressions – mostly on the same two themes – from later years, winding up w. half a dozen terrible poems on insanity & suicide, to which I've now added the eleven religious poems I've written here during the last fortnight. The London *Times* have taken all the six I sent them, *The Atlantic* two, *The New Yorker* a "Death Ballad"; these are all I've sent out.

We were coming to see you next week for a few days, but now I'm not sure I'll be fit to travel. We may also have to postpone the month in Mexico I planned for August (taking Paul), to which I have been looking forward.

I wish you were stronger, darling, & pray daily that you will be. Do you feel well enough to fly out here for a visit? If you should, the change wd certainly be good for you: and the baby wd love to see you. Here are two lines abt her in one of the new poems:

> Cross am I sometimes w. my little daughter;
> fill her eyes w. tears. Forgive me, Lord.
> ["Eleven Addresses to the Lord," No. 3]

Two passages abt. Hell:

> The damned are said to say,
> 'We never thought we wd come into this place.'
> ["Eleven Addresses to the Lord," No. 5]

and

> I don't think there's that place
> ordained for inappropriate & evil man.
> Surely they fall dull, & forget.
> ["Eleven Addresses to the Lord," No. 5]

I am in the second volume of a splendid recent history of the first two Christian centuries [*The Early Christian Church*], by the Archbishop of Quebec [Philip Carrington], one of my favorite living *New Testament* critics, original & a master esp. of *Mark*.

Love,
John

[P.S.] What is Bob's address? What d'you hear fr. him?

[In the published version of the final quotation from "Eleven Addresses to the Lord," No. 5, the first of the quoted line reads: "I'm fairly clear, my Friend, there's no such place."

Robert Jefferson had married Rose Burrell following the death of his fourth wife, Helen, from cancer. He was then working as senior analyst and vice president of Oliver Quayle and Company.]

[Minneapolis]

Dearest Mother   Monday a.m. [6 July 1970]

Happy birthday – I hope you will be feeling unusually vigorous Wednesday & can undertake a jaunt to a park or a visit to Vi [Sutton] or something inspiriting. I have Saul's new novel *Mr. Sammler's Plant* for you – the wisest artwork of my generation so far – but I don't post it because

Why don't you fly out here one day next week? We wd all love to see you & the change wd be good for you. I enclose a cheque which includes somewhat for taxis etc. Let us know, by letter or 'phone, when to meet you, eh?

I'm better physically & busy w. many things – esp.: new poems every few days (my *next* bk – 1972? – is a quarter done already) and a vast gorgeous anthology to render all existing ones superfluous & evil –

Love,

John

[JB had completed the "Opus Dei" section of *Delusions, Etc.*, which was published in April 1972.

JB was planning to edit an anthology of modern poetry with the working title *The Blue Book of Poetry*. It was never completed.]

[Minneapolis]

Dearest Mother–   Saturday 15 August [1970]

Loyola College in Montreal offers me a fantastic $19,500 for 3 months' teaching this Fall, and I've reassigned my seminars here & am going. Kate & M. stay here. I've friends there, luckily, and anyway plan to travel a lot. I'll probably come to Wash. at some point. She's not coming to Mexico either, damn her; Paul & I leave in 10 days. She has no job yet.

I finished revising the galleys [of *Love & Fame*] yesterday & returned them to NY, but I'm still making changes. My editor in London has cabled congratulations: Faber [and Faber, Ltd.] are bringing the book out next Spring, along with (I think) a new *Selected Poems* I hope to get done with this afternoon. The *Sat. Review* are doing the first five of the religious poems. I've written 3 new political poems in the past week and have included them to replace 3 poems I've killed. The book is now as wide-ranging as it is powerful.

Your coming out here to live wd only be delightful. But stay there till you're better. I'm sorry about the insomnia. Mine is hell too. We just gave Martha a bicycle and she is even more scared than she is proud. We all send love,

John

[JB and Kate and Martha (but not Paul) spent a week in Mexico, staying in Mexico City and making side trips to Taxco and to the Toltec ruins at Teotihuacan.

JB and Kate had for some time encouraged Mrs. Berryman to come and live in Minneapolis.]

St. Mary's Hospital
[Minneapolis]

Dearest Mother–   Monday noon, [November 1970]

This is a matter of unique & urgent importance: *Have you kept my letters fr. South Kent?* If so, I want them as fast as poss., air, *registered.* They may help in the present crisis of my (going on the whole *very* well, utterly different fr. last Spring's) treatment.

Also: think back carefully & be absolutely candid abt these questions:
1) Did I *hear* Daddy threaten to swim out w. me (or Bob?) & drown us both? or did you tell me later? *when?*
2) When did I first learn that he'd killed himself?
3) How did I *seem to take* his death when first told? Before the drive back to Tampa that morning? How did I *act* in the car? Back in Tampa? at the funeral parlour? in the graveyard in Holdenville [Oklahoma]? in Miami? Gloucester? thro' the 8th grade? *during the summer before I went to SKS??* (in Wash DC? – where I tho't I recognized him on the street one day – crushed?) Please tell me everything you can remember abt me that summer! (*I* can't even recall wh we were still in Jackson Hts or moved to Burbury Lane.)
4) I cannot recall *any* intellectual life in me during my 4 yrs at SKS.

Can you, in me? What did I *read?* (I recall not *one bk* – tho' I read, often, after lights out, w. a flashlight under the covers or in my closet.)

5) Can you pinpoint, or make any suggestions about, the beginning of my *return to normalcy* and the busy, effective, committed life I had as a freshman?

Many thanks. I hope yr energy & spirits are good.

Love,
John

[Washington, D.C.]
Thanksgiving, 1970

Dearest John,

Please, John, it has taken a lot of doing, to go down under layer and layer, to depths I never thought of exploring, again. It was years after Allyn's death before I freed myself from the return again and again to events done and over with – I used to wake up, sitting bolt upright in bed, saying to myself, "if I say this" or "if I do this" or "if we had only" . . hopelessly, agonizingly. It must have been very hard for John Angus to endure, I realize now. But all that time I did not nor do I now believe that Allyn knew the gun was loaded when he pulled the trigger – to carry it around, empty, still, so the doctors said, it might be the thing that made him feel strong and powerful and all agreed that it should not be taken from him, it was an assertion of self and was an affirmation of strength and even responsibility that he, alone of the men around, had a gun. I buried the bullets way down the beach, and when Allyn asked about them I said what the doctors told me to say: that they (the bullets) were old and probably no good, and that when we went to Tampa again we could get some if he wanted them; that the gun was enough to frighten any thieves or rascals away, and that was all he wanted it for, wasn't it? and he agreed. He always kept the gun on an empty bullet space, for safety, and it is possible that he, in clicking the trigger, as he often did, if he had put that bullet in the gun, it would have come around to it. None of the five bullets I buried was missing and whenever I had a chance I looked to see if there was a bullet in the gun but there never was, so the only possible solution is that Allyn did put that sixth bullet in and forgot it, and when clicked often enough would bring that sixth bullet into the firing chamber. He must have hidden that bullet somewhere outside, as I searched the apartment every day, and the car, too. I did not believe then and do not now that Allyn intended to end his life. John, he did not care enough about life to take it. Nothing outside himself was anything . . . . Allyn is the only person I ever knew who was totally self-centered: he was kind in general; amiable, pleasant, courteous; no close friends: he never, as far as I knew, ever inconvenienced himself for any one – example: while very important matters were pending at the bank in Anadarko and Allyn should have been there to handle them, he went off on a fishing trip to Colorado, despite the bank's owner insisting that he stay and despite all the arguments I put up he came back to find that he was no longer at the bank, and that is why we went to Florida . . . .

On arriving in Florida, half the property was sold, and at my mother's instigation we bought a restaurant in a very good, business-wise, location . . . . The first signs of the death of the boom came in the summer, early summer, and everything went like snow in the sun:* there was a miasma, a weight beyond enduring, the city reeked of failure. Allyn was able to sell the restaurant for cash, a third of what we paid but the best thing to do. School was over and we took an apartment for the four of us, with Mother having a room across the hall, in a building John Angus owned, out on the bay. John Angus lunched at our place every day, and he and his wife were the only friends we made; he got out of the real estate business in time to keep part of his profits; his wife wanted to go back to New York and he did not, there may have been other reasons, I don't know, but he gave her the car, half his take, and his blessing, she divorced him, and left. A Baltimorean, about my mother's age, and we (she, Allyn and I) thought he was seriously interested in her, and very pleased. As it turned out, it was just John Angus' southern courtesy, and she (Granny) never forgave him. By this time, Allyn had become infected with the disease of the failing boom, so seriously affected that he finally agreed to talk to doctors. During the free time he had on his hands, he had met up with a Cuban woman who, it came out, had been his mistress and whom he wanted to marry, he said. When the doctors told me he was in very bad condition indeed, I agreed to sue him for divorce and the custody of the children and half of our joint funds. I talked first with Allyn, pointing

---

* Compare this passage with the first lines of Berryman's "Tampa Stomp," in *Delusions, Etc.*

out that he had two sons to bring up, that we were Catholics and so far as the Church was concerned it would not be a marriage for him or for the girl who, a Cuban, was also a Catholic, I assumed. He said he couldn't think of anything else he wanted to do. Then I told him that he could, of course, see his sons whenever he wanted to, but in their home; and he said that would be all right, and that of course the furniture etc. stored in Anadarko I could have (it was everything we had and when I wrote about it, Allyn had not bothered to pay the $6 a month rent and all four possessions had been sold). He was not really to blame: he had no experience except his own wish, I realize, looking back. There was no criterion for him except his own wish or desire or purpose. John, he was more to be sorrowed over than to blame, for everything. To a human being who, lifelong, has had no goals or intents except those he wants or needs for himself, there *is* no one but himself. Such a man, out of overweening self pride, if he were a leper, say, might set out to ruin the world, but not himself, never himself. In the name of God, John, it is my deepest conviction that your father did not intentionally kill himself. Allyn was not a strong enough man to destroy his universe and that was what he was, to himself.

It has taken two days to write this, John, and I think it best to send it now. It will be another day or so before I can go back to this again, but you may be sure that I will answer your questions as soon as I can, and as fully. I hope to get them, the answers, to you in this coming week. The spirit is willing, no, anxious, but the body – heart, soul – are weak. I hope that the answers can be full enough to serve your purpose but you must keep in mind that I may, only from not being able to dig out, be unable to give you the full answers you need. I am comfortable by the knowledge that you will recognize that I do my best.

It is with such joy that I congratulate you and Kate on the forthcoming Robert and/or Sarah: the Robert is, I assume, the same namesake as your brother's, your great grandfather's, Robert Glenn Shaver? but perhaps a little for your brother, too? It would interest me greatly to know why you chose Sarah?

You do know, I hope, that nothing but physical inabilities have delayed my writing you. I have torn up more paper than ever before on any enterprise, and eventually realized that I could not answer your questions immediately, that it would not be fair or just to Allyn or to you, for it is only by understanding him that he can be seen in his own light, and surely we are all entitled to that? Clearly all his life had been self-centered, perhaps because no one really welcomed him and instead of being, as many youngest of a large family is loved and delighted in, he was not . . . . In his presence, at the full dinner table, his mother said that for an unwelcome child, the third unwelcome child, he had done very well. Perhaps if it had been a brother not a sister just older his whole life might have been different. But he became, in self defence, his own world, poor man. I had always held against him his forcing me to marry him but now I realize that being himself, the self he had made, he could do no other. I pray for him and have done so, for most of the years since his death. (I prayed dutifully for so long, but *now* in loving kindness.)

With dearest love,
Mother

[St. Mary's Hospital]
[Minneapolis]

Dearest Mother   Sunday night [29 November 1970]
    I'm dreadfully sorry that – even in my urgent then-state – I laid such a burden on you. Please just *forget it*. I finally decided, or rather was guided to a realization, that I had *gone as far as I could* with that enquiry (abt Daddy & SKS); and I *gave it up* for a day; this turned out, after a few hours, to feel so satisfactory to me, that I further decided to give it up permanently. I've done so, and I reckon it (the surrender) as one of the major advances made in this treatment. It simply is *not* God's will that I shd at present – or possibly ever – find out any more abt those mysterious subjects.
    So give it no more thought, dear.
    I wish you had more strength, tho conserve it. Let me know if you need anything.
    I've written a riotous poem to the Twiss wh. unfortunately I can't show her till she's abt seventeen. I'll send you a carbon when I type it. Seven or eight other poems also, besides much sketching. I'm going to make a book out of my 100,000 pages quotes on my treatment; I think I can do it rapidly (3 or 4 months) and it will be a service. – Home tomorrow.

Love,
John

[P.S.] No copies of *Love & Fame* yet – perh. this next wk. The *Nation* damn them jumped the gun with a *very* long *very* hostile review.

[The "Twiss" poem, which has not been published, is entitled "Daddy to Martha B."

The book that JB proposed to write on his treatment became the novel *Recovery*, published posthumously in 1973.

Love & Fame was published December 14, 1970, by Farrar, Straus & Giroux. The *Nation* review, by Hayden Carruth, appeared in the November 2, 1970, issue. JB responded with a letter which appeared in the November 30 issue of the magazine.]

[Minneapolis]

Dearest Mother –   Wednesday noon [30 December 1970?]

I took a carbon of my letter to Bob, as news to you too. We are all okay here and I hope you are.

I've changed the title of this prayer-poem ["Somber Prayer"] you want me to write out, and altered some rhythms. It's not bad now, I think.

Your *Love & Fame* will be along as soon as they come fr. NY –

Happy New Year!

Love,
John

[P.S.] Kate & Twiss send love

[Washington, D.C.]

Dearest John,   Sunday [3 January 1971?]

This is a full-of-thanks letter, for all the gifts – for the *Two Poems* and "Year's End, 1970", and for the hand-written "Somber Prayer", especially, and, of course, "A Prayer After All". When Dr. Schmidt asked, recently, if I would take regularly twice a day a tonic, I told him I had one, and he said "what is this '*you have one*', is my English so bad I do not understand, what do you mean 'have', are you taking something prescribed by your internist?" and I said, no, that my son's letters were all I needed . . and he patted me on the shoulder twice, a great gesture from that austere man, and said "so, so, I am content", and went away, beaming.

This year bids fair to be the happiest of my life, John, thanks to you, and indeed in all the conscious years never have I had cause for such happiness, never. The only other such total happiness was when you, and then your brother, were laid in my arms in the first hours of your lives. To have a loving heart and to be unloved so that your love went underground, and then to be given two sons whom I could love freely and hope for their love; for the first time I had a warm world in which to live, and give, and to know that my sons should never suffer as unwanted or unloved – I went about my ways praising God for his goodness to me, all my days. But always there was the shadow, now lifted thanks to you, that I had not earned my happiness. No one ever had easier carriage of a child, I was never sick or in pain, just full of happiness and joy, but I carried you too high and that brought on the uremic poisoning, so that a Caesarian operation was necessary, and since the surgeon had never done one before he made a low incision, and so your brother was a Caesarian birth, too . . so I felt that I had been guilty of some sin or fault that I could not bear my sons in agony, and by that agony have earned them, that they were gifts to which I was not entitled. But now, John, during that long time when you were not yourself, I did suffer, so now I no longer feel guilty, or that you and your brother were unearned. I wish I could have said this better, John. Rejoice with me, darling, in my living to be freed of guilt toward my sons, who are again truly brothers, as they were all through their childhood and well into maturity. God has been so good to me, to let me live to see this. With Tiny Tim (*not* that wretched TV horror), I, too, say "God bless us all" . . . .

This year, I sent a Christmas card to Saul Bellow, and had, recently, such a pleasant note of thanks from him, saying, too, that you would be in Chicago later this month and that day would be a red-letter one for him. It is curious, to me, that of all your friends, having seen him briefly twice, once at the hospital and once when you brought him and someone else to the Chelsea for drinks, and yet I feel that I know him – I can see his face clearly, and of course yours, at the big center table in that fine, huge room, and the other chap is a blank. People is odd and curious, thank high heaven: what could be duller than lacking the unusual and unexpected and the movement of mind and/or heart in unexpected ways and times?

With love abounding, always
Mother

[*Two Poems* was a privately printed eight page keepsake with the following at the bottom of the title page: "Season's Greetings, 1970 / from / Martha and Kate and John / and Bob Giroux." It included JB's "In Memorium (1914–1953)" and "Another New Year's Eve" which was reprinted as "Year's End, 1970" in the January 1, 1971, issue of the *New York Times*. JB had sent such holiday keepsakes of his poems to family and friends at various times throughout his life. "In Memorium (1914–1953)," "Somber Prayer," and "A Prayer After All" later appeared in *Delusions, Etc.*]

[Minneapolis]

Dearest Mother–   Sunday, 28 February 1971

I've got horribly behind w. letters, working at a poem on the Divine Office – also: mislaid half my lecture notes, so up to my neck in Dante + three public lectures (last one next Wed, D.G. [*Deo gratius*, thanks be to God]) and three readings (Chicago, Moorhead, Kansas City) etc. etc. Sorry. I finally read yr acc't of the last weeks in Florida, amazed by some of it; we'll talk when you come. Bought M. & K. rings yesterday – M. a little turquoise, Christmas "Patsy", & K. a 5-ruby (v. small) gold one, handsome. I am collecting Christian literature almost as fiercely as artbooks – Walter Lowrie's fine *Art in the Early Church* on Fri. met both greeds. Saul's new novel [*Mr. Sammler's Planet*] racing: gorgeous. Paul acc'd at [the Phillips Academy in] Andover but prob'y can't go to Holland w. Martha & me in time – we'll come earlier.

Hurriedly – Love!
John

[JB had been invited by the Rotterdam Arts Foundation to read some of his poems for "Poetry International 1971" the first week in June—and had planned on bringing Martha and Paul along. He ultimately decided against the longer trip and, instead, the three of them took a brief trip to Colorado.]

Throughout 1971 JB fought, with occasional brief slips, to retain his sobriety. He regularly attended his Alcoholics Anonymous group meetings, strove to rebuild his marriage with Kate, who was expecting their second child, and attempted to develop closer relations with his son Paul and with Mrs. Berryman. He continued to teach and to work both on new poems that would complete his 1972 volume Delusions, Etc., *and on his novel,* Recovery, *which was inspired by his experiences while undergoing treatment at St. Mary's Hospital. His religious feelings intensified, as reflected in "Eleven Addresses to the Lord" in* Love & Fame *and in many of the poems in* Delusions, Etc. *While in the hospital he considered converting to Judaism, but ultimately, for the first time since his youth, became a professed Catholic.*

Early in the year, plans were finalized for Mrs. Berryman to come and live in Minneapolis. JB and Kate had grown increasingly concerned about her dete- riorating health—three doctors had reportedly given her six months to live—and they were, at the same time, providing much of her financial support. Eventu- ally, they arranged to move Mrs. Berryman and her possessions from Washing- ton, D.C., into an apartment at 26 Arthur Avenue, S.E., just down the block from their house. On July 13, 1971—the same day JB and Kate's second daugh- ter, Sarah Rebecca, was born—Mrs. Berryman arrived in Minneapolis.

In the ensuing months, JB made an earnest effort (and to some extent suc- ceeded) in redressing his often mutually damaging relationship with Mrs. Ber- ryman. There were pleasant dinners at both households and JB would sometimes stop to see Mrs. Berryman while on his way to the university. They managed to avoid the terrible quarrels that had for so long plagued their meetings, owing in part to the absence of alcohol, to Mrs. Berryman's more frail health, and to a more withdrawn attitude on JB's part. Mrs. Berryman still tended to overstep reasonable boundaries, attending ALANON meetings with Kate and occasion- ally irritating both JB and Kate with her unasked for suggestions. At times she also expressed a dissatisfaction with her domestic arrangement, which caused JB to resent her "icy ingratitude." But, given the responsibility JB and Kate had assumed for taking care of her, they found it preferable having her near them, rather than in Washington, D.C.

As the year wore on JB's depression deepened. On December 13, he recorded in his diary continually fighting off thoughts of suicide. Heavily marked and underscored in his copy of A New Catechism: Catholic Faith for Adults, which he read during this time, is the passage: "As regards suicide, this is sometimes the result of complete hyper-tension or depressions and we cannot pass judg- ment." He was ill, twenty pounds underweight, suffering from insomnia. He felt unable to make Kate happy, was assaulted by old guilts, obsessed with his father's grave. His teaching, he feared, was going badly—and, bitterly disappointed, he had given up on his novel, Recovery.

Over the next three weeks the crisis continued. Then, at about nine o'clock in the morning on January 7, 1972, he took a bus to the university and walked across the Washington Avenue Bridge, which connects the east and west banks of the campus. Climbing over the railing near the west end, he reportedly waved, and leapt to his death on the embankment of the Mississippi River more than a hundred feet below. He was fifty-seven, but owing to the physical and psycho- logical punishment he had often courted, looked older. JB was given a Catholic funeral and is buried in Resurrection Cemetery, Mendota Heights, St. Paul.

Mrs. Berryman remained in Minneapolis, cared for by Kate, outliving her celebrated son by nearly five years. In the spring of 1972, Kate bought a duplex at 50 Arthur S.E., across the street from her own house, and Mrs. Berryman occupied the upstairs. Angry and quiet in her last years, she grew increasingly afflicted with Alzheimer's disease. After breaking a hip in a fall, she spent her final months in the Prospect Park Health Care Center in Minneapolis. She died, at eighty-two, of cardiac arrest, caused by arteriosclerotic heart disease, on September 10, 1976. Mrs. Berryman's body was cremated and her ashes were placed in JB's grave.

Index

Abbe, George, 295
Abbey Experimental Theatre, 97
Abbey Players, 96
Abbey Theatre, 100
Abbott Hospital, 318, 369
Academy of American Poets Award, 12, 364, 366
Adams, Franklin P., 219
Adams, Henry, 148, 214
Adams, J. Q., 192
Addison, Joseph, 62
Agra, 309
Ahmedabad, 308
Aiken, Conrad, 257, 297, 358
ALANON, 384
Alarm Among Clerks (Wall), 97
Alcoholics Anonymous, 332, 371–72, 383–84
Alexandria, Va., 346, 347
Alfred Hodder Fellowship (Princeton), 200, 235, 241
Algonquin Hotel, 218
Allen, Frederick Lewis, 30
Allen, Robert S., 162
Alpini del Fiori, 277
Alvarez, A., 365
Amateur Dramatic Company (A.D.C.) (Cambridge), 96, 102
Amazing Stories, 19, 29
Ambleside, 123
Ambrose, Saint, 274
America (Kafka), 120
American, The (James), 75

American Academy of Arts and Letters, 234–35
American Language (Mencken), 75
American Men of Letters Series, The, 223
American Society for the Prevention of Cruelty to Animals, 16
Ames, Dick, 36
Ames, Elizabeth, 239, 240, 241
Ames, Robert, 372–83
Ames, Van Meter, 239, 240, 241
Amherst College, 352, 354
"Among School Children" (Yeats), 73, 74
Anadarko, Okla., 15, 167, 278, 378
Anadarko Gas Company, 278
"Ancestor" (Berryman), 139, 140
Anderson, Hedli, 118
Anderson, Maxwell, 62
"Anglo"-Irish Revival, 97
"Animal Trainer (1), The" (Berryman), 141–42
"Animal Trainer (2), The" (Berryman), 141–42
Another Animal (Swenson), 295
"Another New Year's Eve" (Berryman), 383
Anthology of Modern American Poetry (ed. Lalic), 363
Antony and Cleopatra (Shakespeare), 50
"Apparition, The" (Berryman), 114
Apple River, 292
Appleton, Sally, 284–85, 286
"Apple-Tree, The" (Galsworthy), 27
Aragon, Louis, 202
Architect, The (Berryman), 81–83
Argosy, 19
Aristotle, 171

Arlen, Michael, 27
Army Specialized Training (AST) Reservists, 204
Arnold, Matthew, 52, 254
Arrowsmith (Lewis), 29
Art in the Early Church (Lowrie), 383
Arts of Reading, The, 11, 264, 269–70, 323, 324, 325, 331
Arts Theatre, 96, 120
Ascent of F6, The (Auden and Isherwood), 52, 67
Asiatics, The (Prokosch), 84–85
Aspern Papers, The (James), 75
Associated Manufacturers, Inc., 177
As You Like It (Shakespeare), 96
"At Chinese Checkers" (Berryman), 137
Athens, 308, 365
Athens Festival (1965), 365
Athens Olympia, 350
Atherton, Jane, 73
Atlantic Monthly, 374
Atomic Energy Commission, 357
"At the Hawk's Well" (Yeats), 90
"At the Year's End" (Berryman), 114–15
"At Your Age" (Fitzgerald), 27
Auden, W. H., 43, 52, 67, 94–95, 115, 118, 138, 139, 141
Augustine, Saint, 282, 283
Austen, Jane, 342
Autobiographies (Yeats), 67, 71, 90
Avila, 309, 312–13
"Away" (Berryman), 46
Axel's Castle (Wilson), 91
Axilrod, A. Arnold, 288, 289–90
Aylward, Stephen, 96, 218–19

B. (fiancée), xvi, 5, 10, 44, 102, 107, 147, 374
   JB's relationship with, 105–6, 109–13, 115, 119, 121, 125, 130, 132–35, 145, 149–51, 155, 157, 160, 162, 173
Babington's Tea Rooms, 256
Bacon, Francis, 28–29
Bagley, Bill, 19
Bagster-Collins, Robert Denzil ("Bobo"), 24, 27
Baker, Howard, 156
Bales, Peter, 211
Ballet Theatre, 173–74
"Ball Poem, The" (Berryman), 187, 227, 363
Baltimore Sun, 298
Balzac, Honoré de, 75
Barcelona, 310
Barnard College, 32
Bartlett, Samuel, 16, 23, 24
Barzun, Jacques, 218
Bateman, John, 119, 122–24
Baudelaire, Pierre Charles, 68

Baur, Harry, 46, 53, 55
Baxter, Warner, 58
Bay of Bengal, 320, 344, 346
Bayport, Minn., 265–66, 268, 298
BBC Radio, 250, 333
BBC Television, 364–65
Becket, Thomas á, Saint, 62
Beeching, Henry Charles, 60
Beilenson, Peter, 292
Bellow, Adam, 324, 346
Bellow, Alexandra ("Sondra") Tschacbasov, 295, 296–97
Bellow, Saul, 264, 295–97, 304, 318, 323, 334, 339, 351, 375, 382, 383
Bellport, N.Y., 169
Bemidji, Minn., 296
Bemidji State Teachers College, 296
Benares, 308, 311
"Bench of Desolation, The" (James), 200–201
Benet, William Rose, 230
Bennett, Jean, 32, 43, 49, 67, 72–73, 76, 81, 86, 87, 97, 101, 102–6, 109, 159, 170
Bennington College, 206, 207
Bergner, Elizabeth, 96
Beri, Boniface, 15
Berkeley, Cal., 334
"Berkeley, on His Return" (Berryman), 137
Berkeley Square (James), 76
Bernini, Pietro, 256
Berryman, Barbara Suter, 155–57, 160, 163–64, 170, 173, 177, 202, 208, 210
Berryman, Charles Peter McAlpin, 173, 210
Berryman, Eileen, *see* Simpson, Eileen Patricia Mulligan Berryman
Berryman, Elizabeth Ann Levine ("Ann") (second wife):
   divorce of, 11, 264, 325
   engagement and marriage of, 11, 264, 297–98, 302
   JB and, 11, 264, 295, 297–311, 313, 316–17, 319–25, 334, 339, 343, 347
   Mrs. Berryman and, 300–301
Berryman, Elizabeth Weston ("Liza"), 231, 245, 315
Berryman, Enid Klauber ("Nicky"), 215
Berryman, Helen Loving Wells, 321, 333–34, 375
Berryman, John:
   accidents of, 251–52, 351, 365, 371
   alcoholism of, 1, 7, 11, 200, 250, 260, 269, 282, 303, 314, 331–32, 362, 369–73, 383–84
   appearance of, 109, 121, 369
   artistic reputation of, 8–9, 316, 332, 353, 366
   birth of, 3, 10, 15
   Catholic background of, 15, 267–68

chess playing of, 115, 117, 121
childhood of, 1, 15–32, 277–280
critical works by, 2, 11, 103–5, 110–11, 136, 143, 151, 199, 226, 228, 230–33
death feared by, 255
diaries of, xvi, 6, 17, 44, 111, 285–86, 384
divorces of, 11, 264, 297, 301–2, 325
dream analysis of, 263, 276–77, 281–82, 285, 291, 292
dreams of, 17–18, 122, 165, 282, 291
early publication by, 33, 43
earnings of, 135, 144–45, 152, 154, 178, 193, 258, 288, 321, 332, 371
eczema condition of, 162
education of, *see* Cambridge University; Columbia University; South Kent School
effects of father's suicide on, 1, 6, 376–77, 384
engagements of, xvi, 5, 10, 44, 102
on English and American accents, 68, 75
English and American literary traditions compared by, 61–63
"epilepsy, *petit mal*" of, 147–48
family background of, 15, 265–68, 315
fatherhood of, 303–6, 309–11, 313, 331, 346, 351, 358, 359–60
fiction writing of, 6, 8, 11, 167, 200, 220–23, 226, 228–29
financial difficulties of, 145, 176, 178, 286, 343, 348
funeral of, 384
on greatness in poets, 353
guilt feelings of, 6, 17–18, 87, 313–14
handwriting of, xv, 63, 65, 87, 96
health of, 36, 38, 129–30, 147–49, 151–53, 160, 208–9, 231, 244–45, 258, 286, 318, 325, 332, 334, 346, 369, 373, 384
honors awarded, 2, 8, 10–12, 33, 35–36, 112–13, 199–200, 208, 220, 229–31, 234–35, 241–42, 264, 302, 305, 318, 332, 335, 370–71
Indian lecture tour of, 11, 264, 305–8
interviews with, 5, 315
Japanese gardens and temples studied by, 306–7
Japanese poetry studied by, 255
languages studied by, 19, 107, 193, 217, 252
lectures of, 2–3, 89–90, 178–90, 240–41, 259, 263, 287, 289, 295, 296, 308, 332
on letter writing, 63, 85–86, 95
on "literary personality," 63, 115
loneliness of, 44, 78, 84, 106, 108, 168, 213, 255, 286
marriages of, *see* Berryman, Elizabeth Ann Levine; Berryman, Kathleen Donahue; Simpson, Eileen Patricia Mulligan Berryman

personal library of, xvi, 2, 44, 52, 54–55, 58, 157–58
pessimism of, 122, 129–30, 139, 150
petit mal epilepsy diagnosed in, 147–49
Phi Beta Kappa election of, 10, 35
as playwright, 43–44, 62, 81–83, 88, 101–3, 149, 296–97
poetic style of, 2, 137, 263–64, 319
poetry readings of, 1, 89–90, 130, 178–90, 284, 319, 320, 332, 333, 350–51, 362, 365, 370, 383
posthumous publications of, 12, 332, 381
on preparatory school education, 116–17
reading taste of, 26–30, 43, 44, 100–101, 120, 121–22, 132, 148, 161, 171, 254–55, 360, 374, 375, 377, 383
recordings of works by, 317, 333
religious and theological studies of, 20, 204, 263, 269, 282–83, 284, 286–87, 289, 374
religious conversion of, 373, 383
religious poems of, 374–75, 381
reviews of, 228–30, 298–99, 305, 381
self-destructiveness of, 5, 17, 250, 302, 331–32, 371, 384
self-knowledge of, 6, 93, 112, 116, 272, 372
as Shakespeare scholar, 11, 43, 49, 98, 99–101, 102–5, 110–11, 199, 208–9, 211, 240–41, 250, 283, 289–90, 292–93, 315
student achievements of, 16–18, 20–21, 28, 35, 49
suffering courted by, 5, 78–79
suicide of, 12, 332, 384
syphilis, tested for, 44, 59, 61
teachers' influence on, 33, 43, 65, 71, 88
teaching of, 1–3, 10–12, 135, 140–41, 144–48, 150, 152–56, 158, 161, 169, 194–95, 199–200, 225, 233, 238–39, 250, 253, 260, 263, 269, 283–84, 286–87, 289, 290, 295–98, 306, 316–19, 331, 332–34, 341, 349–50, 352–53, 363, 370, 372, 373, 375, 383, 384
tennis playing of, 25, 27, 31, 36, 37, 68
translations by, 302
translations of works by, 221–22, 226, 304, 343, 359, 362–63
travels of, 11, 43–46, 79–87, 106–7, 121–24, 245–50, 264, 305–13, 364–66, 376
unpublished work of, 33–35, 57–58, 64, 70–71, 94, 97–98, 132, 133, 137, 167, 172–73, 212–13, 297, 357, 381
womanizing of, 6, 200, 242–43, 250, 314, 331, 342
on writers and writing, 1, 54, 55–56, 60, 61–63, 69–74, 90–94, 289
youthful essays of, 16–17, 21–22, 24, 28–29

Berryman, John Angus McAlpin ("Uncle Jack") (stepfather), 22, 26, 39, 60, 76, 77
  business career of, 3, 16, 32, 106
  death of, 227
  JB and, 10, 16, 25, 49, 121, 135, 139–40, 187
  Mrs. Berryman and, 3, 6, 10, 16, 135, 164
Berryman, Kathleen Donahue ("Kate") (third wife):
  JB and, xvi, 11, 331, 337, 342, 344–45, 346, 348–65, 371–76, 379, 381–84
  Mrs. Berryman and, 8, 332, 356, 367, 384
Berryman, Martha ("Twissy") (daughter), 352, 354, 357–61, 363–66, 371–72, 374–76
  birth of, 11, 331, 351
  JB's poem about, 374, 380–81
Berryman, Martha Shaver Little ("Jill Angel") (mother):
  ambitions for JB of, 5, 18, 33, 111, 340–41
  appearance of, 6, 159
  birth of, 3
  business career of, xvi, 3, 74, 76, 98, 104, 106, 107–8, 129, 131, 141, 149, 163–64, 177, 200, 213, 214, 216, 226–27, 242, 301, 308, 345, 358, 363, 367
  childbirth recalled by, 278–79, 382
  childhood of, 3
  compulsive talking of, 7, 335–36
  death of, xvi, 385
  dreams of, 279
  drinking habits of, 7, 277–78, 337, 360
  education of, 3
  financial problems of, 8, 288, 313–14, 332, 333, 345, 347, 365, 367–68, 370
  handwriting of, 67–68
  health of, 6, 8, 149, 165, 201, 251, 302–3, 332, 337–38, 349–50, 370, 383–85
  interference in JB's life by, 7, 302, 324, 384
  on JB, 8, 277–80, 325–27, 332, 355
  JB advised and criticized by, 5, 44, 77–79, 99, 109–10, 273–75
  JB's dependency on, 8, 44, 54, 103, 129, 130, 148, 153, 249–50, 268, 283, 286
  JB's empathy for, 172–73, 209, 312
  JB's fictional treatment of, 6
  JB's image of, 7, 18, 159
  JB's poems to, 9, 33–35, 172–73, 190, 229
  JB's quarrels with, 200, 235–38, 300–301, 332, 336–37
  JB's relationships with women feared by, 5, 134
  JB's support of, 8, 314–15, 332, 355, 383–84
  letters to JB from, xv–xvi, 18, 44, 77–79, 220–21, 235–37, 270–71, 275–76, 277–81, 300–301, 322–23, 325–27, 336–41, 361–62, 367–69, 377–80, 381–82

  literary aspirations of, 3–5, 8, 40, 96, 289–90
  marriages of, 3, 6, 10, 16, 200, 216–17, 263
  possessiveness of, 5–8, 275–77, 313–14
  pride in JB of, 8, 273–74
  religious life of, 275, 280–81, 368–69
  as restauranteur, 16
  self-analysis of, 275, 278–79, 281
  suicide contemplated by, 279
Berryman, Paul ("Poo") (son), 315–17, 320, 321, 323–25, 334, 343, 346, 365
  birth of, 11, 304
  JB and, 303–6, 309–11, 313, 370, 374–76, 383
  JB's poems to, 321, 323, 346–47
Berryman, Robert Jefferson ("Bob"; "Jeff") (brother), 66, 72, 78, 208–10, 249
  birth of, 3, 10, 15, 278–79
  career of, 196, 201–2, 203, 210–12, 213, 215, 288–89, 342, 375
  early years of, 17, 26, 31, 32, 49, 156, 169, 278–80
  on JB, 7, 8–9
  JB and, 15, 17, 36, 52, 99, 111, 116–17, 120–21, 132–33, 143–44, 152, 154–57, 164, 174–78, 187, 196, 210–12, 228, 245, 246, 277–80, 288–89, 320–21, 333–34, 343, 354, 357
  JB's poems to, 132–33, 156–57
  marriages of, see Berryman, Barbara Suter; Berryman, Elizabeth Weston; Berryman, Enid Klauber; Berryman, Helen Loving Wells; Berryman, Rose Burrell
  parents' relationship with, 277–82
  roadside accident of, 144–46
Berryman, Rose Burrell, 375
Berryman, Sarah Rebecca (daughter), 12, 331, 384
Berryman, Shelby, see O'Brien, Shelby Berryman
Berryman and O'Leary, 227
Berryman's Sonnets (Berryman), xvi, 11, 12, 200, 332, 366–67, 369
Best, Marshall A., 239
Best American Short Stories, The (ed. O'Brien), 223, 226
Best Poems of 1943, The (ed. Moult), 215
Bettenson, Henry, 283–84
Bible, 20, 98, 280–81, 289
  see also Gospels; New Testament; Old Testament
Biographia Literaria (Coleridge), 186
Bird, Ethel Berryman, 135–37, 139, 164, 227
Birds in the Mulberry (Abbe), 295
Birss, John Howard, 115
Bishop, Elizabeth, 141, 147, 253
Bishop, John Peale, 131, 132

Bishop, Margaret, 132
Bixby, Henry D., Jr., 23
Black Hills, 302
Blackmur, Helen, 206–7
Blackmur, Richard P., 59, 61, 63, 71, 91, 181,
    199, 203, 204, 206–7, 213, 223, 238, 319
Blackwell's, 291
Blaeser, Gustave, 186
Blake, William, 49, 52, 54, 60, 67, 88, 113,
    211, 320
Bloomington, Ind., 339–41
Blue Angel, The, 243
Blue Book of Poetry, The (proposed title) (Berry-
    man), 375
Blum, Morgan, 304
Blume, Peter, 131
Boar's Head Poetry Society, 319
Boehm, George, 210–11
Boggs, Tom, 142–43
Bollingen Prize in Poetry, 12, 231–33, 303,
    332, 370
Bombay, 308
Boston, Mass., 156–93, 351
"Boston Common" (Berryman), 164, 171, 175,
    188–89, 203
Boston University, 154–55
Botteghe Oscure, 250
Botticelli, Sandro, 86
Bowers, David, 206
Bowes & Bowes, 44, 52, 59, 61
Boyd, Julian, 205, 206
Boydell, Brian, 90, 101
Braden, James, 23
Bradley, A. C., 67
Bradstreet, Ann, 172
Brahms, Johannes, 165
Brandeis University, 11, 335
Brandow, Streaky, 36
Brattleboro, Vt., 176, 177, 178, 191, 193, 194
Braybrooke, Richard, Lord, 96
Breadloaf School of English (Middlebury), 345,
    346, 349, 350, 353
Brentano's, 30, 139
Breughel, Pieter, 186
Briarcliff College, 208
Bridge, The (Crane), 298, 358
Brigham, Mrs., 165
Bright, Timothy, 211
Briston, Mr. and Mrs., 251–52
Britannic, 43, 45–46, 47, 53
British-American Hospital, 310
Britten, Benjamin, 118
Broch, Hermann, 199
Brooks, Cleanth, 143
Brooks Brothers, 288–89
Brown, Ben, 119, 121, 350
Brown, Hobson, II, 26

Brown, Slater, 210
Brown University, 11, 350, 353
Buchanan, Scott, 124, 125, 129, 219
Burckhardt, Jacob, 246–47
Burnet Wood, 241
Burroughs, Edgar Rice, 96
Burroughs, John, 36, 281
"Burrow, The" (Kafka), 120
Bush Foundation, 343–46
Buson, Yosa, 255
Butler, Ingreet, 137

Caetani, Marguerite, Princess, 250
Calcutta, 308, 320
Calder, Alexander ("Sandy"; "Red"), 130–31,
    271
Callahan, F. J., 277
Calvin, John, 289
Cambridge, Mass., 152–56, 160, 168, 284
Cambridge University, xvi, 2, 5, 6, 36, 50–76,
    87–125, 157, 179, 263, 374
    see also specific colleges
Cameron, Elizabeth, 239, 245, 273
Cameron, J. Alister, 239, 245–46, 273
Campbell, Bhain, 130, 140, 143–47, 151–54
Campbell, Florence, *see* Miller, Florence
    Campbell
Campion, Thomas, 287
Cam River, 50
Canada, 267, 363, 364, 375
Cantata Dramatica (Dorati), 302
"Canto Amor" (Berryman), 227
Cantos (Pound), 62, 298
Carrington, Philip, 374
Carruth, Hayden, 381
Castle, The (Kafka), 120
Cather, Willa, 27, 29
Catherine of Siena, Saint, 269
Catholic University of America, 363, 366
CBS Radio, 135, 187
"Ceremony and Vision" (Berryman), 138
Cerf, Bennett, 316
Chamberlain, John, 131
Chambers, E. K., 136, 213
Chaplin, Charlie, 256
*Characterie: An Arte of Shorte, Swifte and
    Secret Writing by Character* (Bright), 211
Character Invented, A (Smith), 295
Charley's Aunt (Thomas), 39
Charterhouse of Parma, The (Stendhal), 214
Chasseurs dans la neige (Breughel), 186
Chateau du Girard le Diable, 108
Chaucer, Geoffrey, 60, 76
Chekhov, Anton, 220
Chelsea Hotel, 251, 258–59, 293, 360, 367,
    382
Chemical Bank, 339

Chemin de la Croix, Le (Claudel), 302
Chepatchet, R.I., 356–60
Chess-Player's Handbook, The (Staunton), 115
Chiappe, Andrew, 51, 53, 54, 59, 61, 85, 89, 196, 219
Chicago, Ill., 317–18, 383
Chicago Sun-Times, 298
Chickasha, Okla., 15, 291–92
Childs, Marquis William, 217
Christian College, 3
Chumley's, 218
Church of the Transfiguration (The Little Church Around the Corner), 16
Churriguera, Jose de, 312
Ciardi, John, 305
Cincinnati, Ohio, 238–43, 254, 273
Civilian Public Service (CPS) camps, 203–4
Civilization of the Renaissance in Italy, The (Burckhardt), 247
Civil War, U.S., 267
Clare College (Cambridge), 10, 43, 52–53, 58–61, 166, 220
Clark, Bobby, 35
Clark, William, 239
Clarke, George Herbert, 176, 204
Claudel, Paul, 302
Clearwater Isle, Fla., 16, 279–80
Cleopatra: A Meditation (Berryman), 101–3
Clough, Arthur Hugh, 254
Clucas, Lowell M., Jr., 26
Coates, Bob, 131
Cocteau, Jean, 46, 121
Codman, William C., 165, 168
Cohen, J. M., 312
Colebrook, Joan, 210, 223–24
Coleridge, Samuel Taylor, 54, 135, 142, 185–86, 189
Collected Poems (Van Doren), 359
Collected Poems (Yeats), 92
Collected Poems of Thomas Hardy, 142
Colorado, 378, 383
Columbia, Mo., 3
Columbia Poetry, 33
Columbia Review, 33
Columbia University, 88, 119, 122, 124, 150, 155–56, 169, 263, 316
   JB appointed Associate of Seminar on American Civilization at, 318, 319
   JB as assistant in English at, 135, 137, 140, 144–45
   JB as undergraduate at, 10, 32–33, 35–36, 88, 116, 354, 374
   library of, 103, 319
"Comedian as the Letter C" (Stevens), 358
Commerce Department, U.S., 345, 351
Complete Poetry and Selected Prose (Donne), 60

Cone, Edward, 248
Congreve, William, 200
Connecticut, 10, 130–31
Connecticut Yankee in King Arthur's Court, A (Twain), 27
Connington, J. J., 360
"Conversation" (Berryman), 363
"Coole Park" (Yeats), 70
Cooperative Bureau for Teachers, 248–49
Corbière, Édouard Joachim, 151
Cornell University, 205
Corwin, Norman, 187
Cosi Fan Tutte (Mozart), 174–75
Costa Brava, 309
Côte d'Azur, 245
Country Wife, The (Wycherly), 120
County Cork, 267
Coward, Noel, 88
Cowley, Abraham, 54, 67
Cowley, Malcolm, 131–32, 138, 271
Cowley, Muriel, 131–32
Crane, Hart, 1, 115, 210, 298, 358
Crane, Stephen, 2, 222–23, 238, 250, 296
   see also Stephen Crane
Crawshaw, Richard, 93
Creative Arts Award (Brandeis University), 11, 335
Crève-coeur, Le (Aragon), 202
Crime and Punishment (Dostoievsky), 161
Criterion, 115, 225–26
Critic, The (Sheridan), 96
Crucifixion (El Greco), 87
Cummings, E. E., 210
"Curse, The" (Berryman), 138
Cuttack, 308
Cymbeline (Shakespeare), 101

"Daddy to Martha B." (Berryman), 380–81
Daiches, David, 238
Daisen-in, 307
Dante Alighieri, 60, 88, 215, 216, 264, 283, 383
"darkfield microscopy," 59, 61
Davenport, Russell W., 215
Davidson, John, 225
Davie, Donald, 9
Davis, Emerson F., 173
Dawbarn, H. Dunlop, 21, 23
Day, Dorothy, 284
"Death Ballad" (Berryman), 374
Defoe, Daniel, 75
Deirdre of the Sorrows (Synge), 99
Dekker, Thomas, 82
Delusions, Etc. (Berryman), 12, 332, 366, 375, 381, 383
Derbyshire, Dr., 147
"Desires of Men and Women" (Berryman), 137

Detroit, 140, 145–54
Devlin, Denis, 246–47
Dewey, Thomas Edmund, 214
Dial, 143, 180
Diary of Anne Frank, 344
Diary of Samuel Pepys, The, 96
Diaz de Solis, 313
Dickey, James, 353
Dickinson, Emily, 62
Dilettante Society (Clare College), 43, 89
Dirty Hands (Blackmur), 59
"Disciple, The" (Berryman), 188
Dispossessed, The (Berryman), 11, 140, 142,
   161, 178, 199, 228–31
Dobbs, Howard W., 222
"Doctor Sapp" (Berryman), 137
Documents of the Christian Church (ed. Bet-
   tenson), 283–84
D'Olier, Franklin, 203
Donahue, Kathleen, *see* Berryman, Kathleen
   Donahue
Donga, Pierre ("Pedro"), 45–46, 53, 55, 84, 85
Don Giovanni (Mozart), 174
Donne, John, 49, 50, 54, 56, 60, 61, 67, 171
Don Quixote (Cervantes), 344, 345, 372
Dorati, Antal, 302
Dostoievsky, Feodor Mikhailovich, 75
Douai Bible, 280
Doubleday, 226
Downing, George, 96
Dramatist, The: Or Stop Him Who Can (Rey-
   nolds), 88
Draper, Paul, 35
"Dream Song 1" (Berryman), 352
"Dream Song 5" (Berryman), 352
"Dream Song 7" (Berryman), 58
"Dream Song 19" (Berryman), 289–90
"Dream Song 23" (Berryman), 352, 354
"Dream Song 27" (Berryman), 352
"Dream Song 100" (Berryman), 9
"Dream Song 166" (Berryman), 7
"Dream Song 270" (Berryman), 7–8
"Dream Song 283" (Berryman), 46
"Dream Song 371" (Berryman), 364
Dream Songs, The (Berryman), 2, 263–64,
   292, 332, 340, 342–44, 348, 350–54,
   359, 360, 365, 370
   *see also His Toy, His Dream, His Rest; 77
   Dream Songs*
Dryden, John, 52, 56, 59, 69
Dublin, 12, 97–98, 331, 363–66
Duke University, 196
Dulon, Clara Christiane, 18
Duncan, Harry, 295
Dunn, H. L. ("Deac"), 207, 281, 287, 317,
   324, 354
Dutcher, Richard, 167

Early Christian Church, The (Carrington), 374
Eberhardt, Richard, 230
Echeverria, Durand, 21, 26, 353
Einstein, Albert, 199
Eisenhower, Dwight D., 293, 299–300, 357
"Elegy for Freud" (Berryman), 146
"Eleven Addresses to the Lord" (Berryman),
   383
   No. 3, 374
   No. 5, 374–75
   see also Love & Fame
Eliot, T. S., 50, 60, 62, 115, 180, 185, 230,
   242, 269, 292, 298
Ellingwood, Grace Edlice Smith, 267
Ellingwood, Lester, 267
Elliston Professorship of Poetry (University of
   Cincinnati), 11, 200, 238, 250
Elvin, Herbert Lionel, 120
Emerson, Ralph Waldo, 62
Emperor Jones, The (O'Neill), 30
Empson, William, 52, 250
Encyclopedia Britannica, 254
English Poems of John Milton, The (Beeching),
   60
Enormous Room, The (Cummings), 210
Epidaurus Festival (1965), 365
"Epilogue" (Berryman), 154
Erich Kahler, 222
Erickson, Clifford O., 373
"Essay upon Love" (Berryman), 57–58
Euretta J. Kellett Fellowship, 10, 36, 53
Euripides, 88
Events and Signals (Scott), 295
Existentialism, 296

Faber and Faber, Limited, 292, 320, 321, 324,
   344
Fadiman, Clifton, 218–19
Fadiman, Pauline, 219
Fanning, Mary Ruth, 36–37
Far Eastern Fabrics, Inc., 256
Farrar, Straus and Company, 290–91, 294,
   299, 344, 346, 362, 370, 381
Far Sawrey, 122–23
Fashionable Contracts (Gillray), 366
Fathers, The (Tate), 132
Fattorusso, Giusseppe, 291
Faulkner, William, 299–300, 353
Femme Villa, frescoes of (Botticelli), 86
Fermi Award, 357
Ferris, Walton, 192
Fielding, Henry, 75
Films in Review, 171
Finer Grain, The (James), 200–201
"First Night at Sea" (Berryman), 46
"Fisherman, The" (Yeats), 74
Fitzgerald, F. Scott, 27, 210

Fitzgerald, Robert, 253, 257, 305
Fitzsimmons, J. A., 148
Five Young American Poets, 10, 118, 130, 137, 144, 147, 148, 182
Florence, 245, 253, 282
Flowering Judas (Porter), 157
Folger Shakespeare Library, 192
Fontana della Barcaccia (Bernini), 256
Ford Foundation Fellowship, 356, 358
Forester, Frank, 21, 23
"For Ingreet Butler" (Berryman), 137
Fraser, Gordon, 44, 59, 61, 77, 85, 111, 119, 151
Frazer, James G., 202
Fredericks, C., 324
Freedom of the Poet, The (Berryman), 2, 12, 332, 344–46
Freud, Sigmund, 214, 292
Frost, Robert, 319, 345, 346, 350, 353, 355
   JB's poem about, 352–53
   memorial service for, 352–54
Fulgens and Lucres (Medwall), 214
Full Moon in March, A (Yeats), 52

Galsworthy, John, 27
Gardiner, Edmund G., 269
Garrelts, George G., 269–70
Gassner, John, 219
Gauss, Christian, 199, 222
Geldes, Gilbert, 360
Gendel, Milton, 248–49
General Refractories Company, 32
Generals Die in Bed (Harrison), 26–27
Genesis (Schwartz), 159, 162
Genesis, Book of, 259
"Gentleman from America, The" (Arlen), 27
Gentry, Anne Morrison, 352
Gentry, Chisholm, 352
George Saintsbury: The Memorial Volume (ed. Oliver and Muir), 143
George III, King of England, 366
Gerould, Gerald Hall, 205
Gertrude Clarke Whittall Poetry and Literature Fund, 317
Gillray, James, 366
Giraudoux, Jean, 46
Giroux, Robert, 33, 49, 63, 151, 170, 173, 187, 218–19, 290, 292, 298, 360, 374, 383
Glasser, William, 371–72
Glenwood Hills Hospital, 325, 331
Godfrey, Maude Penney, 266
Godfrey, Ted, 266
Godwin, Tony, 151
Golden Bough, The (Frazer), 202
Goldsmith, Oliver, 97
Gollancz, 292

Goodbye to All That (Graves), 27
Gordon Fraser's, 44, 59
Gospels, 96, 204, 280
Gotham Book Mart, 230
Grand Marais, Mich., 141–43
Grand Marais, Minn., 323
Grasmere, 123
Graves, Robert, 27
Great Modern Short Stories (ed. Overton), 27
Great Short Stories of Henry James, The (ed. Rahv), 216
Greco, El, 87
Greece, 365
Greene, Graham, 269
Greenhead Ghyll, 123
Greg, W. W., 222
Gregg, John Robert, 211
Gregg Institute, 211
Gregory, Lady Augusta, 92
Grierson, J. C., 60
Grinnell College, 254, 257
Griscom, Joan, 284
Guarantors Prize *(Poetry)*, 11, 199, 229–30
Guerry, Alexander, 222
Giulio Einaudi, 364
Guggenheim Fellowship, 11, 12, 204, 241–42, 293, 331, 348
Guggenheim Museum, 366
Gulf of Mexico, 279–80
Gustafsson, Karl, 218
Gustafsson, Nils O., 200, 216–17, 219
Guy Fawkes' Day, 74–75

Haffenden, John, 12
Haggin, B. H., 158, 165, 166, 218–19
haiku, 255
Hall, Charlotte ("Charie"), 284
Hall, Donald, 344
Halliday, Ernest Milton ("Milt"), 32, 43*n*, 45, 49, 63, 81, 84, 86, 87, 95, 118
Hals, Franz, 87
Hamlet (Shakespeare), 67, 87, 373
Hammerstein, Oscar, II, 316
Hanson, Lawrence, 143
Harcourt, Brace & Co., 151
Hardwick, Elizabeth, 254
Hardy, Thomas, 142, 157, 290–91
Harmonium (Stevens), 234
Harper's, 142
Harriet Monroe Poetry Prize, 11, 264, 305
Harrison, Charles Yale, 26–27
Harriss, R. P., 206
Harvard University, 2, 10, 130, 150, 152, 161, 169, 176–90, 192, 258–59, 316
   JB's poetry readings at, 178–90, 350–51
Haward, Patricia, 359

Hawkes, Herbert E., 86, 112, 119
Hawkshead, 123–24
Hawthorne, Nathaniel, 148
Hayward, John, 60
Hazelden alcoholic rehabilitation center, 371–73
"Heart of Darkness" (Conrad), 344
Heath, Geoffrey, 117, 151
Heffers, 44, 52, 55
Heidelberg, 106–7
Hemingway, Ernest, 27, 238, 353, 369
Henn, T. R., 54
Henry IV (Shakespeare), 98, 100, 103
Henry V (Shakespeare), 100
Henry Holt and Company, 223, 226
"Henry James" (Berryman), 216
Henry James: The Major Phase (Matthiessen), 216
"Henry's Crisis" (Dream Song 367) (Berryman), 364
Henry's Fate & Other Poems, 1967–1972 (Berryman), 12
"Henry's Guilt" (Dream Song 371) (Berryman), 364
Henzell, A. Willoughby, 27
Hepburn, Audrey, 256
Herodotus, 254–55
"Herodotus" (Berryman), 132
Herrick, Robert, 120
Hillberry, Clarence B., 140, 147
Hillyer, Robert, 180, 181, 188–89, 232
His Thoughts Made Pockets & The Plane Buckt (Berryman), 11, 264, 324
His Toy, His Dream, His Rest (Berryman), 12, 332, 363–65, 366, 369–70
  see also *Dream Songs, The; 77 Dream Songs*
Hitler, Adolf, 151
Hoagland, Edward, 299
Hoffman and Campe, 364
Hogarth Press, 48
Holdenville, Okla., 266–67, 376
Holland, 383
Holmes, John, 299
Holy Cross, 281
Holy Family Church, 15
"Homage to Film" (Berryman), 56, 58, 113, 150
Homage to Mistress Bradstreet (Berryman), xii–xiii, 11, 172, 199, 228, 242, 244, 246, 247, 250, 264, 284, 290–92, 320, 333, 341, 343, 345, 358
Homage to Mistress Bradstreet and Other Poems (Berryman), 321
"Homage to Sextus Propertius" (Pound), 55–56
Homer Noble Farm, 350
Honig, Charlotte, 350
Honig, Edwin, 350

Hopwood Awards (University of Michigan), 148–49, 150
Horace Rackham School for Graduate Studies (University of Michigan), 145
Houghton Mifflin, 177, 203
Howard, Jane, 332, 366
Howells, William Dean, 296
"How to Enjoy Life, Love, and Work" (Russell), 289
Hubbell, Lindley Williams, 137
Hudson Review, 250
Huldigung Für Mistress Bradstreet (tr. Schwebell), 364
"Humane Practices" (Berryman), 16
Humboldt, Alexander von, 186
Hunter College, 32, 159
Husserl, Edmund, 290
Hutchins, Robert Maynard, 218

"Ideal Way of Living, The" (Berryman), 17
Ideas of Order (Stevens), 54
Idylls of the King (Tennyson), 27
Ile de France, 125
Iliad (Homer), 298
"Imaginary Jew, The" (Berryman), 11, 167, 200, 220–23, 226, 228–29
Imitation of Christ, The (Thomas à Kempis), 280
Immaculate Conception, Feast of, 280
India, 11, 264, 305–8, 311, 312, 344–45, 346
Indiana University School of Letters, 339, 341–42
In Dreams Begin Responsibilities (Schwartz), 136
Inferno (Dante), 88, 287
Ingram Merrill Foundation, 360
"In Here" (Berryman), 253, 255
"In Memorium (1914–1953)" (Berryman), 383
"In Memory of Major Robert Gregory" (Yeats), 74
Institute for Advanced Study (Princeton), 201
Intensive Alcohol Treatment Center (St. Mary's Hospital), 373, 383
Introduction to Bibliography (McKerrow), 157
Iona Preparatory High School, 194–95, 196
Iowa City, Iowa, 250–60, 265
Iowa State University, 228
Irish Times, 364
"Irony" (Saintsbury), 143
Irony: An Historical Introduction (Thomson), 52, 143
Isherwood, Christopher, 52, 67
Italy, 305–6, 320
It's Been Real-Or-A Tree, A Tree (Berryman), 297
Ivory Tower, The (James), 75

Iwaniuk, Waclaw, 343, 345
Iwase, Tatsuo, 304

Jackson Heights, N.Y., 10, 16, 376
Jacobs, Michael, 188
James, Henry, 75–76, 200–201, 215–16, 333–34
James, William, 171, 214
Jan Hus Hall, 281
Japan, 264, 304, 306–7
Jarrell, Randall, 147, 199, 230
Jefferson, Thomas, 204–5, 214
Jensen, Jim, 372
Jesse J. Friedman and Associates, 358, 363, 364
Jesus Boat Club (Cambridge), 117
Jesus Christ, 286–87
Jesus College (Cambridge), 88
Jeunesse, La, 86
Job, Book of, 118, 344
John, Gospel According to, 96
John Berryman Reads from the Dream Songs, 365
John Dryden (Van Doren), 59
John Simon Guggenheim Memorial Foundation, 242
Johnson, Annette, 141
Johnson, Norman, 138
Johnson, Samuel, 52, 54, 62, 96, 200
Johnson, Thomas H., 152
Johnson Chapel, 354
Jones, Lewis W., 206–7
Jones, Theodore F., II ("Stump"), 23, 28
Jooss Ballet, 158
Josephson, Matthew, 131
Joshi, 255
Joyce, James, 292
Juan-les-Pins, 245
Jubilee, 284
Judaism, 383
Judas Iscariot, 319
Juno and the Paycock (O'Casey), 96

Kafka, Franz, 116, 120, 122
Kahler, Erich, 199, 221–22, 226
Kakinomoto-no-Hitomaro, 255
Kanar (great-grandfather), 267
Kansas City, Mo., 383
Karachi, 308
Keats, John, 44, 50, 52, 54, 63, 245
Kelley, Edward F., 267
Kelley, Maude Irene Smith, 267
Kelley, Robert, 267
Kemmis, Jasper, 17, 23
Kenyon Review, 132, 133, 136, 137, 138–39, 142, 150, 151, 152, 171, 203, 220–21
Kenyon Review-Doubleday Doran Award, 11, 200, 220

Kerr, Robert S., 191
Kettle, Arnold, 112
Kierkegaard, Søren, 122, 202, 222
King James Bible, 280
King Lear (Shakespeare), 11, 64, 82, 98, 101, 108, 111, 120, 199, 205, 209, 213, 216, 221–22, 226, 250, 254
Kings and Queens of England and France: A Genealogical, Chronological History (Fattorusso), 291
Kipling, Rudyard, 49
Kitchin, Geoffrey, 90
Klauber, Enid, see Berryman, Enid Klauber
kokoro-no-furusato, 255
Krutch, Joseph Wood, 218
KUOM Radio, 333
Kyoto, 306–7, 311

La Chapelle, Hector, 372
Lake Calhoun, 320
"Lake Isle of Innisfree, The" (Yeats), 92
Lake of the Isles, 269, 288, 320
Lalic, Ivan V., 362–63
Landon, Alfred, 38, 40
Langley, Thomas F., 59, 61
"Last Days of the City" (Berryman), 97–98, 99, 113
Laughlin, James, IV, 125, 132, 138, 142, 147, 149, 151, 160
Lawrence, D. H., 27, 157
"Lay of Ike, The" (Dream Song 23) (Berryman), 354
Lazzaro, Joe, 372
League of American Authors, 204
Leaves Without a Tree (Fraser), 295
Lee, Edwy, 269–70, 288, 293
Lee, Marie-Lorraine, 269–70, 304
Leir, 221
Lemon, Jack, 176, 177, 179, 193
Lenin, Nikolai, 292
Le Roy, Hal, 35
Lester Harrison, Inc., 226
"Letter, The" (Maugham), 27
Letters of Keats, The, 44, 50, 52, 63, 245
"Letter to His Brother" (Berryman), 132–33, 139
"Let There Be Law" (Van Doren), 219
Levanto, 308, 313, 320
Levin, Harry, 155
Levine, Blanche, 297–98, 302, 304, 317, 322–24
Levine, Elizabeth Ann, see Berryman, Elizabeth Ann Levine
Levinson Prize (Poetry), 11, 200
Lewis, Sinclair, 29, 38
Liberty Mutual Insurance Company, 175
Library of Congress, 192, 203–5, 217–18, 305, 317

Lichtenstein, Lewis, 357
Life, 229–30, 332, 366
Life of Saint Teresa of Avila, The (tr. Cohen), 312–13
Life of Samuel Taylor Coleridge, The (Hanson), 143
Limelight, 243
"Lise," xvi, 11, 200, 366
Little, Alvin Horton (grandfather), 3
Little, Martha May Shaver (grandmother), 3, 15–16, 168, 215, 378
    death of, 228
    JB's relationship with, 25, 26, 36–37, 49, 66, 76, 139, 164, 174, 175, 176, 209, 212
Little, Martha Shaver, *see* Berryman, Martha Shaver Little
"Little Useful," 165
Lives of Noble Grecians and Romans, The (Plutarch), 299
Lives of the Poets (Johnson), 52
Living Thoughts of St. Paul, The (Maritain), 256
Locke, Mahlon William, 38–39
Logan, John, 298
London, 46–49, 272
"London" (Berryman), 46
London, Kurt, 135, 136
London Mercury, 93
"Long Way to MacDiarmid, The" (Berryman), 295
Look, Stranger! (Auden), 67, 95
Louis Harris and Associates, 341–42
Louisiana State University, 119
Louvre Museum, 86–87
Love & Fame (Berryman), xvi, 12, 43n, 45, 46, 102, 177, 332, 374–76, 381, 383
"Lovers, The" (Berryman), 220–23
Love's Labour's Lost (Shakespeare), 106
Lowell, Robert ("Cal"), 199, 223–24, 250, 253, 254, 257–58, 259, 269, 320, 339, 351, 353, 364
Lowrie, Walter, 383
Lowry, Malcolm, 225–26
Loyola College (Montreal), 375
Loyola University (Chicago), 317
Luke, Gospel According to, 96
Luther, Martin, 287, 289
Lutz, Deke, 36
Lutz, Edna, 36
Lynch, William F., 269, 284, 287
Lyrical Ballads (Wordsworth), 184
Lyric Moderns, 143

Mabry, Jim, 196
Mabry, Marie, 174, 175, 176, 191, 193, 234, 246
Mabry, Tom, 254–55
McAlester, Okla., 3, 10, 15, 167

Macbeth (Shakespeare), 104
McCloskey, Herbert, 304
McCloskey, Mitzi, 304
McCullough, Paul, 35
MacDiarmid, Hugh, 295
MacDonald, Dwight, 210, 224, 352
MacDonald, Nancy, 352
McKenna, Rollie, 240
McKerrow, Ronald Brunless, 157
Mackey, Jeanne, 167
Mackie, Diana, 285
Mackie, Donald, 233, 238, 285
Mackie, Douglas, 285
Mackie, Elizabeth ("Betty"), 233, 238, 285
Mackin, Jack, 223–24
Mackin, Nela, *see* Walcott, Nela
McLean Hospital, 351
MacLeish, Archibald, 62, 183, 185, 192, 205, 218
MacNeice, Hedli, 249, 272–73
MacNeice, Louis, 52, 199, 249, 272–73, 365
McQuiggan, Dr., 147
McRae, Caroline Genevieve Smith ("Cad"), 266
McRae, Ranald J., 266
Madrid, 309–10
Magdalene College (Cambridge), 44, 53, 102
Magic Mountain, The (Mann), 39
Maine, 223–24
Makinson, George, 23
Malraux, André, 46
Manicheeism, 269
Manifold, John, 88
Mann, Thomas, 139, 199
Mansfield, Katherine, 27
Man with a Glove (Titian), 86
"Maria Concepcion" (Porter), 158
Mariana Griswold Van Rensselar Prize, 33
Maritain, Jacques, 256
Mark, Gospel According to, 96, 286, 374
Marshall, Margaret, 135, 136
Marvell, Andrew, 60, 67, 101
Maryfarm, 284
Matthew, Gospel According to, 96, 204, 280, 286–87
Matthew's (The Turk's Head), 59
Matthiessen, F. O., 216
Maugham, William Somerset, 27, 239
Mauriac, François, 46
Maxwell, Baldwin, 256
Mayo Clinic, 258
Measure for Measure (Shakespeare), 103, 110
"Meditation" (Berryman), 113, 150
"Meditation II" (Berryman), 132
Medwall, Henry, 214
"Meeting" (Berryman), 102
Melville, Herman, 62, 75
Mena, Ark., 215, 228

Mena, Arturo, 46
Mencken, H. L., 75, 234
Mendelson, Edward, 118
"'Mental Traveller, The" (Blake), 211
Merchant of Venice, The (Shakespeare), 101
Meredith, William, 350, 353, 356, 357
Meridian, 343, 345
Meriwether, Marion, 131
Merrill, Pete, 19
Mersel, Jean, 342
Mersel, Milt, 342
Merton, Thomas, 218
Metal and the Flower, The (Page), 295
Metropolitan Opera House, 173–74
Mexico, 166, 374–76
Mexico City, 376
Miami, Fla., 376
"Michael" (Wordsworth), 123
"Michael Robartes and the Dancer" (Yeats), 72
Middlebury College, 308
Mikulicic, Banba Villim, 227, 270
Miller, Arthur, 297
Miller, Florence Campbell, 141, 143–44,
     146–47, 151
Milton (Tillyard), 67
Milton, John, 49, 54, 60
Minneapolis, Minn., 1, 8, 12, 263–73, 276–
     77, 281–306, 313–25, 331–34, 337–39,
     342–50, 362–64, 370–77, 380, 383–85
Minneapolis Art Institute, 269
Minneapolis Symphony Orchestra, 302
Missal, 280
"Miss Brill" (Mansfield), 27
Mississippi River, 332, 384
Mizener, Arthur, 203
Mizzen, Mrs., 51, 58, 59, 72, 108
Modern American Poetry (ed. Untermeyer), 227
Modern Library, 27, 30, 75, 203, 254, 358
Moe, Henry Allen, 241–42
Mona Lisa (da Vinci), 86
"Monocle de Mon Oncle, Le" (Stevens), 234
Monroe, Marilyn, 297
Montaigne, Michel Eyquem de, 67, 68, 372
Montreal, 363, 364, 375
"Moon and the Night and the Men, The"
     (Berryman), 176, 188, 204, 363
Moonen, Mary Elizabeth, 288
Morris Gray Foundation, 179, 189
Morris Gray Poetry Reading (Harvard), 130,
     178–90
Morrison, Kathleen Johnston, 352
Morrison, Theodore, 152–53, 154–56, 166,
     177, 180–82, 350, 352
Morton, Frederic, 354
Moses, W. R., 138, 141, 147
"Mother & Son" (Berryman), 172–73
Moult, Thomas, 215

Mountain Lion, The (Stafford), 225
Mourning Becomes Electra (O'Neill), 30, 115
Mourning Bride (Congreve), 200
Mozart, Wolfgang Amadeus, 174–75
"Mr. Pou & the Alphabet" (Berryman), 346–47
Mr. Sammler's Planet (Bellow), 375, 383
Mrs. Dalloway (Woolf), 55
Muir, Augustus, 143
Muir, Edwin, 120
Mulligan, Agnes, 192, 193
Mulligan, Eileen, *see* Simpson, Eileen Patricia
     Mulligan Berryman
Munford, Howard, 308, 345, 346
Murder in the Cathedral (Eliot), 62
Murray, Gilbert, 48
Murray, J. Harold, 35
Museum of Modern Art, 254
My Antonia (Cather), 29, 30
My Country (Davenport), 215
"Mysteries, The" (Berryman), 222

Naftalin, Arthur, 303
Naples, 248
Nashe Society (St. John's College), 43
Nation, 233, 381
     JB as poetry editor of, 10, 130, 135–36,
          139–43, 145, 146, 151
     JB published by, 33, 143, 205
National Book Award, 12, 305, 332, 370
National Endowment for the Arts Award, 12,
     370
National Endowment for the Humanities, 12
National Geographic, 344
National Institute of Arts and Letters, 11, 362
National Poetry Festival, 349, 351
National Service Board for Religious Objectors,
     204
Nazis, 106
Neaves (Head porter, Memorial Court, Cam-
     bridge University), 58
"Nervous Songs, The" (Berryman), 178–79
     see also Dispossessed, The
Neue Rundschau, Die, 221–22
Neva-Wet Corporation, 74, 76, 98
Newberry Library, 318
Newby Bridge, 123
New Catechism, A: Catholic Faith for Adults,
     384
New Delhi, 308
New Directions, 10, 130, 164, 170, 182, 183,
     226, 230
New Directions in Prose and Poetry, 121, 125,
     138, 222
Newman Foundation, 270
Newnham College (Cambridge), 44, 102, 112
*New Poems/1943, An Anthology of British and
     American Verse* (ed. Williams), 175

New Republic, 139, 140, 161, 187, 305
Newsweek, 299
New Testament, 96, 283, 374
  see also Bible; Gospels
New Treasury of War Poets, The, 177, 204
New York, N.Y., 3, 10, 11, 16, 32–36, 43, 129, 193–96, 250–51, and *passim*
New Yorker, 259, 299, 321, 323, 344, 348, 374
New York Herald-Tribune, 136, 142, 299
New York Review of Books, 353, 360, 364
New York Times, 215, 240, 281, 298–99, 305, 383
New York Times Book Review, 215, 353
New York University, 227
New York World-Telegram, 187
"Night and the City" (Berryman), 114
Nijo Castle, 307
Niké of Samothrace, 86
Nishi Honganji, 307
Nixon, Richard M., 293
Nobel Prize, 230, 289
North, Thomas, 254
Noss, Murray, 295
"Note for a Historian" (Berryman), 113, 114
"Note on E. A. Robinson" (Berryman), 33
"Note on Poetry, A" (Berryman), 182
Nozze di Figaro, Le (Mozart), 174
Nurske, Ragnar, 201

Oates, Virginia, 248
Oates, Whitney Jennings, 248–49
O'Brien, Bruce, 357–58
O'Brien, Edward J., 223
O'Brien, Shelby Berryman, 156, 170, 338, 357–58, 360
Observer (London), 353, 359
"Ode to the Confederate Dead" (Tate), 65
O'Donnell, George Marion, 49, 63, 144, 147
Odyssey (Homer), 256
Oedipus Rex (Sophocles), 48, 121
"Of Gamatan's Transaction" (Campbell), 143, 146
Oglethorpe University, 204–5
O. Henry Memorial Award Prize Stories of 1946, 223, 226
Oldham, Charles, 102
Oldham Shakespeare Scholarship, 6, 10, 43, 53, 102–3, 104–5, 108–9, 112–13, 115, 119
Old Man of Coniston, 124
Old Testament, 118
Old Vic Theatre, 87, 101, 250
O'Leary, Miss, 227
Oliver, John W., 143
Oliver Quayle and Company, 375
Olivier, Laurence, 87, 222, 281
Omaggio A Mistress Bradstreet (tr. Perosa), 364

"On a Portrait in Dublin" (Berryman), 138
Ondine (Giraudoux), 256
O'Neill, Eugene, 30, 44
"1 September 1939" (Berryman), 176, 204
"On First Reading Genesis" (Wilson), 259
Only Yesterday (Allen), 30
"On the London Train" (Berryman), 136, 139, 182–83
Open Air Theatre (Regents Park), 108
Oppenheimer, J. Robert, 357
"Opus Dei" (Berryman), 375
  see also Delusions, Etc.
Orange Blossom, 15–16
Oregon, 266
Origen, 284, 319
Othello (Shakespeare), 103
"Other Chicago, The" (Berryman), 357
Overstreet, Harry Allen, 182–85
Overton, Grant, 27
Oxford Book of French Verse, XIIIth Century-XXth Century, The, 67
Oxford Book of Sixteenth Century Verse, The, 213
Oxford Book of Seventeenth Century Verse, The, 52
Oxford English Dictionary, 91–92
Oxford University, 366

Pacific Mills, 141, 164
Page, P. K., 295
Panic (MacLeish), 62
Paris, 79–87, 121–22, 245, 246, 249–50
Paris Exposition, 85
Paris Review, 5
Parnell, Charles Stewart, 92, 99
"Parnell's Funeral" (Yeats), 74, 92
"Parting as Descent" (Berryman), 138, 227
Partisan Review, 11, 135–36, 139, 142, 199, 216, 226, 230, 246–47, 250, 264, 302
Pascal, Blaise, 372
Patna, 308
Patterson, Albion, 17, 28–29
"Paul's Case" (Cather), 27
Pawlet, Va., 324
Peacock Theatre, 97, 98
Pearson, Drew, 162
Peattie, Donald Culross, 68
Peck, Gregory, 256
Penguin, 312
Pepys, Samuel, 96
Per Amica Silentia Lunae (Yeats), 71
Perne, Andrew, 92
Perosa, Sergio, 364
Perry, Jack Leslie, 161
Persons, Dorothy, 206–7, 251
Persons, Stow, 206, 251
Peter, Saint, 287

Peterhouse College (Cambridge), 92
Phelps Industries, 308
Philadelphia Orchestra, 219
Phillips, Anita Maximilian, 253
Phillips Academy, 383
Phoenix (Lawrence), 157
Piazza del Popolo, 256
Piazza di Spagna, 256
Pigtail, 17, 21–22
Pillar of Fire (Tudor), 174, 196
Pisan Cantos (Pound), 232
Pius XII, Pope, 247
Plath, Sylvia, 359
Plato, 254–55
Playboy of the Western World (Synge), 96, 100
Plays (Synge), 100
Plaza Mayor, 311, 312
Plaza Todo, 311
Pleiades, 253
Plutarch, 254–55, 299
"Poem for Bhain, A" (Berryman), 154
"Poem in May" (Berryman), 113
Poems (Berryman), 10, 130, 137, 154, 170, 203
Poems (Dryden), 52
Poems of John Donne, The (ed. Grierson), 60
Poems on Several Occasions (Prior), 58
Poetical Works of Edward Taylor, The (ed. Johnson), 152
Poetry, 11, 199, 229–30, 294–95, 359, 360
"Poetry International 1971," 383
"Poetry of Ezra Pound, The" (Berryman), 230–31
Poetry Society (Cambridge), 120
Poetry Society of America, 11
Poets of Today (Duncan), 295
"Point of Age, A" (Berryman), 171
Politics, 215, 226
Pollexfen, George, 92
Poona, 308
Pope, Alexander, 60, 272
"Pornography and Obscenity" (Lawrence), 157
Porter, Katherine Anne, 157, 158
Portrait of a Lady (James), 75
Postgate, John Percival, 254
Pound, Ezra, 55–56, 62, 91, 94, 230–33, 298, 319
Powers, J. F. ("Jim"), 268, 270
"Prague" (Berryman), 121, 138
"Prayer After All, A" (Berryman), 381, 383
"Prayer for Old Age, A" (Yeats), 73
Prickett, Maude, 174
Pride and Prejudice (Austen), 37
Prince of Darkness, The (Powers), 270
Princeton Library, 246
Princeton, N.J., 199–223, 225–33, 243–45
Princeton University, 2, 11, 194–95, 199–200, 202, 203, 222, 235, 237, 254, 289

Prior, Matthew, 55, 58
Prisoner of Shark Island, The, 54
" 'Prisoner of Shark Island, The', with Paul Muni" (Berryman), 58
Prokosch, Frederic, 84–85
Prophetic Books (Blake), 52
Prospect Park Health Care Center, 385
Proust, Marcel, 1
Provence, 245
Providence, R.I., 349, 350–54
"Prussian Officer, The" (Lawrence), 27
Psychical Research Society, 90
Public School 69, 10, 16
Pulitzer Prize, 12, 231, 305, 331, 332, 362
Puri, 320, 344
Putnam, Phelps, 132, 133, 138
Putnam, Ruth, 132, 133

Queen Mary, 77
Quentin Durward (Scott), 24

Rabelais, François, 120
"Race, The" (Berryman), 24
Rago, Henry, 359–60
Rahv, Phillip, 216
Rain (Maugham), 239
Ramparts, 353, 354
Ramsey, Arthur S., 51, 53, 54, 59, 61, 63, 66, 68, 75, 95–96
Ransom, John Crowe, 115, 120, 133, 138, 144, 171, 257–58
Rapallo, 245, 253
Rashish, Myer, 354
Rawlinson, George, 254
Reality Therapy: A New Approach to Psychiatry (Glasser), 371–72
"Recovery" (Berryman), 43n
Recovery (Berryman), 6, 8, 12, 250, 332, 381, 383, 384
Redman, Ben Ray, 224–25
Redpath, Theodore, 112
Reed, Gallagher ("Gringo"), 36
Reformation, 287
Reid, Forrest, 91
Reilly, Charles Phillips, 170–71, 196, 219
Reinhardt, Max, 48
Reisterstown, Md., 99, 135–40, 227
"Relic, The" (Donne), 50
Rembrandt van Rijn, 54, 87
Resor Mansion, 239
Responsibilities (Yeats), 93
Resurrection Cemetery, 384–85
Reynolds, Frederick, 88
Rice, Philip B., 135–36, 138, 142
Richards, I. A., 50, 52
Richard III (Shakespeare), 259, 281
Riders to the Sea (Synge), 28

Rilke, Rainer Maria, 184–85
Rimbaud, Arthur, 68, 122
Rindlaub, Jean, 130, 131, 132
"Ritual at Arlington" (Berryman), 48, 55, 58, 60, 65, 69, 81
Riverside Community Hospital, 362
Robinson, E. A., 33, 183, 185
Rockefeller Foundation Poetry Fellowship, 11, 199, 264, 302
Rockefeller Foundation Research Fellowship, 11, 199, 204–5, 208, 209
Roethke, Theodore, 359–60
Rogers, Will, 27
Roman Catholic Church, 15, 268, 283, 379
Roman Holiday, 253, 256
Rome, 245–48, 256
Roosevelt, Franklin D., 40, 214, 219
Rosenthal, Henry, 218–19
Ross, Alicia, 304, 320
Ross, Billy, 277
Ross, Ralph, 263, 264, 270, 287, 298, 304, 307, 318, 319, 320, 324
Rothschilds, The; A Family Portrait (Morton), 354
Rotterdam Arts Foundation, 383
"Round of Visits, A" (James), 201
Rowley, George, 246–47, 248
Roxbury, N.Y., 36–38
Royal Opera House, Covent Garden, 48
Rubaiyat (Khayyam), 290–91
Rubens, Peter Paul, 86
"Rudolph" (car), 257, 306, 324
Ruggles, Charles, 39
Rule of Saint Benedict, 284
Rummel, Walter Morse, 46
Russell, Bertrand, 289
Russell Loines Award, 11, 362
Ryan's Bar, 365
Rylands, George, 43, 51, 53–54, 55, 60–61, 65, 71, 88, 120
Ryoan-ji, 307

Sagamore, 319
"Sailing to Byzantium" (Yeats), 74
Saint Catherine of Siena, a Study in the Religion, Literature and History of the Fourteenth Century in Italy (Gardiner), 269
St. Croix Lumber Co., 267
St. Croix River, 268
St. Elizabeth's Hospital, 231
St. John's College (Annapolis), 124, 125, 129, 150, 152
St. John's College (Cambridge), 43, 53, 59
St. Joseph's Academy, 15, 291–92
St. Louis, Mo., 3
St. Patrick's (Dublin), 92

St. Patrick's (N.Y.), 173
St. Paul, Minn., 384–85
St. Peter's Basilica, 246–47
Saintsbury, George, 143
Saintsbury Miscellany, A: Selections From His Essays and Scrapbooks, 143
St. Tropez, 245, 246
St. Vincent's Hospital, 251
Salamanca, 309, 311–12
Samuel Taylor Coleridge: A Biographical Study (Chambers), 136
Samurai and Serpent Poems (Noss), 295
Sasakwa, Okla., 3
Satterthwaite, James Buckley, 112
Saturday Review of Literature, 232–33, 299
Schmidt, Dr., 381
"Scholars at the Orchid Pavillion" (Berryman), 366
Schorer, Mark, 155
Schwartz, Delmore, 130, 135–38, 141, 142, 150, 155, 159–60, 162, 170, 176, 179–80, 183, 188–89, 192, 196, 207, 218, 223, 229, 350
Schwartz, Gertrude, 155, 179, 181, 188–89, 226–27
Schwebell, Gertrude S., 364
Scott, F. R., 295
Scott, Walter, 24
Scott gramophone, 165–66
Seattle, Wash., 233–34
"Second Cactus, The" (Berryman), 138
"Second Coming, The" (Yeats), 74
"Second Letter to His Brother" (Berryman), 156–57
Segovia, 309, 312
Selden, John, 259
Selected Poems (MacDiarmid), 295
Selected Poems (Pound), 230
Sense of the Past, The (James), 75–76
Serampore, 308
Seven Types of Ambiguity (Empson), 52
77 Dream Songs (Berryman), 11–12, 331, 362, 365
  see also Dream Songs, The; 77 Dream Songs
Seville, 309, 313
Sewanee Review, 140, 205, 216, 222–23
Sewanee University of the South, 222
Shafarman, Eugene M., 148, 153
Shafer, Bob, 36
Shafer, Sunny, 36
Shahn, Ben, 292, 294, 296
Shakespeare (Van Doren), 132, 140
Shakespeare, William, 51, 55, 254, 316, 320
  JB's lifelong study of, 37, 43, 49, 98, 99–101, 102, 103–5, 110–11, 119, 208–9, 211, 240–41, 283, 292–93, 315
  JB's textual and biographical work on, 2, 11,

Shakespeare, William (*continued*)
    103–5, 110–11, 243–44, 250, 289, 290,
    360
  works of, 11, 37, 50, 64, 67, 82, 96, 98,
    100–101, 103–4, 110–11, 177
Shakespearean Tragedy (Bradley), 67
"Shakespeare at Thirty" (Berryman), 250
Shakespeare Memorial Theatre, 101
Shapiro, Karl, 231, 370
Shaver, Robert Glenn (great grandfather), 140,
    379
Shaw, Robert Gould, 188
Shea, James, 235, 350
Shelley, Percy Bysshe, 54, 60, 91
Shelley Memorial Award (Poetry Society of
    America), 11, 199–200, 231
Sheridan, Richard Brinsley, 96
Shields, Arthur, 100
Shigemori, Mirei, 306–7
Shorter Oxford English Dictionary, 54
Short Poems (Berryman), 12, 332, 370
Sickness Unto Death, The (Kierkegaard), 202
Simpson, Eileen Patricia Mulligan Berryman
    ("Rusty") (first wife):
  JB's relationship with, 130, 162–63, 170–71,
    176, 180–81, 186, 188–96, 203, 216–25,
    227–28, 234, 238–40, 246–47, 254, 256–
    58, 260, 285, 287, 295
  JB's separation and divorce from, 11, 200,
    250, 264, 297, 302
  jobs of, 175, 178, 192, 194, 201–2, 226
  marriages of, 10, 130, 173–74, 339
Simpson, Robert, 339
Sioux Falls, S. Dak., 302
Sitwell family, 229–30
"Six Poems" (Berryman), 138
Sky Grew Dark, The (proposed title) (Berry-
    man), 37
Skyland, N.C., 308
Sloane, William, 219
Smith, Allan, 266
Smith, Amy Penney, 266
Smith, Ann Maude, 267
Smith, Cora ("Code"), 266
Smith, Edith Marjorie, 266
Smith, Ernest Bramah, 200
Smith, George Ernest ("Ern"), 266
Smith, John Allyn (father), 257
  attempted suicide of, 279–80, 283, 377
  birth of, 263, 265
  early life of, 263, 265–67, 274, 380
  extra-marital affairs of, 276, 278, 378–79
  family background of, 263, 265–68
  JB's relationship with, 3, 15–16, 277–80,
    283, 376, 384
  life insurance of, 271–72
  marriage of, 3, 263, 317

Mrs. Berryman's relationship with, 3, 15–
    16, 263, 274, 278–80, 377–80
  suicide of, 1, 3, 6, 10, 16, 263, 266, 376–79
Smith, Leonard Jefferson (grandfather), 265–68
Smith, Leroy, 295
Smith, Martha Little, *see* Berryman, Martha
    Shaver Little
Smith, Mary Kanar (grandmother), 267–68,
    380
Smith, Mary Violet, 267
Smith, Robert Hall, 266
Smith, Robert Paul, 196
Smith, Thomas Leroy, 266
Smith, William James ("Will"), 266–67
Smith College, 32, 206
Snodgrass, W. D., 353
"Somber Prayer" (Berryman), 381, 383
"Song from Cleopatra" (Berryman), 150
Song of Myself (Whitman), 241
"Song of the Idiot, The" (Rilke), 185
"Song of the Tortured Girl, The" (Berryman),
    363
Songs of Carthage (Wharton), 49
Sonnets (Shakespeare), 37
Soule, George, 131
Southern Review, 43, 58, 65, 69, 114, 115,
    137, 142, 143, 148, 149, 150, 163, 171
Southern Review Poetry Prize, 58
South Kent School, xv, xvi, 1, 6, 10, 16–32,
    49, 116–17, 353, 354, 376
South Stillwater, Minn., 265–67
Spain, 305, 308–13
Spanish Civil War, 94
Spencer, Terence, 366
Spencer, Theodore, 179–81, 189
Spengler, Oswald, 99
Spenser, Edmund, 91
Spooner, Edward Tenney Casswell, 84
Sportswear Stylist, 200, 213, 214, 216, 217
Stackpole, Paul, 39
Stafford, Jean, 199, 223, 225
Stalky & Co. (Kipling), 49
State Department, U.S., 177, 191, 192–93,
    264, 308
  Foreign Leaders Program of, 363
  Foreign Service Personnel Division of, 292–
    93
Stationers' Register, 221
"Statue, The" (Berryman), 136, 139, 186–87
Staunton, Howard, 115
Steeves, Harrison R., 135, 150, 219
Stegner, Wallace, 155
Stephen Crane (Berryman), 11, 199, 226, 228,
    230–33, 343, 345–46
Stevens, Wallace, 54, 66, 120, 138, 141, 207,
    234, 358
Stevenson, Adlai, 293

Stewart, Alfred Walter, 359–60
Stewart, Walter, 206–7
Stillwater Prison, 290
Stories and Artists (James), 216
Stout, Rex, 218
Stratford-upon-Avon, 101, 110
Strauss, Lichtenstein Lewis, 357
Strauss, Richard, 158
Straw, The (O'Neill), 30
"Strut for Roethke, A" (Dream Song 18) (Berryman), 360
"Sunday Morning" (Stevens), 234
"Survivor" (Berryman), 132, 133–34
Suzuki, D. T., 307
Sweden—Ancient and Modern, 217
Sweden: The Middle Way (Childs), 217
"Sweeney Among the Nightingales" (Eliot), 50
Swenson, May, 295
Swift, Jonathan, 62, 74, 79, 92, 99, 103, 336
Swinburne, Algernon Charles, 54
"Symbol" (Berryman), 64, 71
"Sympathy, A Welcome, A" (Berryman), 321
Synge, John Millington, 28, 88, 96, 97, 99, 100

Table Talk (Selden), 259
Taj Mahal, 308
Tampa, Fla., 3, 10, 15–16, 376
Tate, Allen, 43, 55, 58, 63, 65, 115, 129–33, 136, 138, 142, 144, 147, 192, 203, 205, 215, 218, 223, 254, 263, 268–73, 283, 285–86, 287, 298, 303
  as father figure, 263, 273
  JB's collaboration with, 264, 269–70, 324, 325
Tate, Caroline, 129–32, 254, 268–69, 271, 285
Tate, Nancy, 131, 132
Taxco, 376
Taylor, Edward, 151–52
Taylor, John F., 92
tea ceremony, Japanese, 307
Teachers Credit Union, 145
"Telephone, The" (Frost), 352
Telfer, William, 51, 53
Teller, Edward, 357
Tempest, The (Shakespeare), 242, 281, 296, 344
Tennyson, Alfred, Lord, 27, 52
Teotihuacan, 376
Teresa of Avila, Saint, 7, 312–13
"Testament" (Berryman), 253, 255
"Textual Criticism" (Postgate), 254
Thackeray, William Makepeace, 1
"That the Night Come" (Yeats), 93
Thirkill, Henry, 51, 53, 59
"Thirty Bob a Week" (Davidson), 225

Thirty-Six Famous Poets, 307
Thirty-Six Poems (Warren), 140
Thomas, Dylan, 43, 151, 251
Thomas Aquinas, Saint, 202, 283, 287
Thomas Y. Crowell Company, 323
Thomson, J. A. K., 52, 143
Thoreau, Henry David, 203
Thorp, Willard, 206–7
Thought, 269, 284
"Three-Day Blow, The" (Hemingway), 27
Thumbs Up, 35
Thunder Over Mexico, 96
Thurber, James, 218–19
"Thursday Out" (Berryman), 308
Tillyard, E. M. W., 54, 60, 61, 67
Time, 202, 203, 210, 299, 319, 359
Times (London), 112, 228, 364, 374
Titian, 86
Titusville, Fla., 257
Tokyo, 304, 306, 307
Toledo, 310–11
"Toward Statement" (Berryman), 114
Toynbee, Arnold, 220
Toynbee, Philip, 353
"Trial, The" (Berryman), 114, 117–18, 132
Trial, The (Kafka), 120
Trilling, Lionel, 218
Trinity College (Cambridge), 52, 112
Trinity Hall, 120
Troilus and Cressida (Shakespeare), 247–48
Trollope, Anthony, 132
Truman, David B., 363
Truro, Mass., 210, 224
Tudor, Anthony, 196
Tully, Charles, 176
"Turk's Head, The" (Matthew's), 59
Turn of the Screw, The (James), 75
Twain, Mark, 27, 62
Twelfth Night (Shakespeare), 177, 281
Twelve Steps and Twelve Traditions, 371
Twentieth Century (proposed quarterly), 226
Twentieth-Century American Poetry, 358
Twentieth Century Verse, 118, 132
Twenty-Five Poems (Berryman), 149
"Twenty Poems" (Berryman), 10, 130, 132
Two Poems (Berryman), 381–83

Ulysses (Joyce), 226
Under the Volcano (Lowry), 225
Unicorn Press, 215
"Union Square" (Berryman), 167
United States Information Service, 11, 306
University of California at Berkeley, 334
University of Chicago, 11, 264
University of Cincinnati, 11, 200, 238–42, 250
University of Iowa, 250–59
  JB's dismissal from, 11, 260, 263, 264

University of Iowa Writers' Workshop, 250, 256
University of Michigan, 145, 148–49
University of Minnesota:
   English Department at, 298, 305–6, 316, 318, 349, 373
   Humanities Program at, 2–3, 11, 12, 264, 296, 304, 305–6, 317, 318
   Interdisciplinary Studies Department at, 296, 298, 306, 316–17
   JB as Regents' Professor of Humanities at, 2, 12, 370–71
   JB as teacher at, 2, 11, 12, 263–64, 269, 283–84, 286–87, 290, 291–92, 293, 306, 316–17, 325, 333–34, 337, 372–73, 383, 384
   JB's sabbatical leave from, 360
   Library of, xvi
   Political Science Department at, 304
   radio station of, 333
University of North Carolina Press, 144
University of Rhode Island, 351
University of Salamanca, 312
University of Utah, 332–33
University of Vermont, 237
University of Washington, 233–34
Untermeyer, Louis, 227, 232
Use of Poetry, The (Eliot), 60
Utah, 333

Valladolid, 309, 312
Van Doren, Carl, 136, 218–19
Van Doren, Charles, 219
Van Doren, Dorothy, 131, 219
Van Doren, Irita, 135, 136, 142
Van Doren, John, 219
Van Doren, Mark, 33, 43, 45, 51, 55, 58, 59, 63, 65, 75, 86, 103, 115, 135, 140, 234, 352
   JB's correspondence with, 49, 65, 79, 95, 113, 116, 124, 138, 358–59
   JB's relationship with, 33, 43, 65, 81, 129, 131–33, 136, 173, 174, 195–96, 207, 218–19, 374
   literary party honoring, 218–19
Van Eyck, Jan, 108
Variations (Brahms), 165
Vaughan, Henry, 74, 79
Vecello, 87
Velasquez, Diego, 87
"Velvet Glove, The" (James), 200
Verlaine, Paul, 122
Vicker's Viscount, 319, 320
Viking, 239, 243–44, 290–91
Vinci, Leonardo da, 86–87
Vision, A (Yeats), 52

Vittorini, Elio, 229
Vogel, Arthur, 106, 107

Wagner, Charles, 219
waka, 255
Walcott, John, 224
Walcott, Nela, 207, 223–24
Walden (Thoreau), 203
Walker, William R., 59
Walker Art Center, 319, 320
Wall, Mervyn, 97
Walpole, Horace, 62
Walters, Raymond, 242
Walton, William, 158
Wanning, Andrews, 102, 108, 155
Ward, John, 19, 21, 28, 109
War Poets, The (ed. Williams), 207
Waren House, 168, 181
Warren, Robert Penn, 43, 65, 69, 95, 113, 138, 140, 142, 217–18
Washington, D.C., 218, 316–17, 349, 354, 358, 360–62, 363, 376
Washington Avenue Bridge, 332, 384
Wasserman test, 59, 61
Wasteland, The (Eliot), 298
Waves, The (Woolf), 37
Wayne State University, 2, 10, 130, 140–41, 144–48, 150, 242
Way of the Cross, The (tr. Berryman), 302
Way of the World, The (Congreve), 200
W. B. Yeats: A Critical Study (Reid), 91
"Weather, The" (Berryman), 21–22
Weaver, Raymond, 219
Webster, Jean, *see* Bennett, Jean
Weird Tales, 19
Welsford, Enid, 112
Weltner, Phillip, 205
West, Frank, 22
Weston, Elizabeth, *see* Berryman, Elizabeth Weston
Wharton, Lewis, 49
Where Did You Go? Out. What Did You Do? Nothing. (Smith), 196
"Whiskey and Ink, Whiskey and Ink" (Howard), 366
"White Feather (After a News Item)" (Berryman), 161
"White Feather, The" (Berryman), 160–61, 188
Whitman, Walt, 37, 62, 240–41, 250, 253
Who's Who in America, 257–58
Wilbur, Richard, 303
Williams, Oscar, 175, 207
Williams, Shelby, 317–18, 319
Williams, Tennessee, 44
Williamsburg, Ont., 38–40
William Sloan Associates, 223, 233

Willis, John, 211
Wilson, Edmund, 91, 132, 133, 199, 210, 259, 353, 354
Wilson, F. P., 112
Windermere Lake, 123
"Winter Landscape" (Berryman), 187, 227
Winterset (Anderson), 62
Winter's Tale, The (Shakespeare), 67, 100–101, 108
"Winter Tryst" (Van Doren), 218
Wolfe, Thomas, 1
Woman's College (Greensboro, N.C.), 206
Wood, Anthony, 96
Woodin, William J., 23
Woodward, Samuel A., 17, 24
Woolf, Leonard, 48
Woolf, Virginia, 37, 48, 55
Worden, James, 238, 282
Words and Poetry (Rylands), 51
"Words for Music Perhaps" (Yeats), 74
Wordsworth, William, 54, 61, 120, 123–24, 184–85, 320
World I Breathe, The (Thomas), 152
"World-Telegram" (Berryman), 138, 140, 187–88

Wray Castle, 123
Writer's Workshop (University of Utah), 332–33
Wycherley, William, 96, 120

Yale University, 205
"Year's End, 1970" (Berryman), 381, 383
Yeats, Anne, 98
Yeats, William Butler, 37, 49, 52, 54, 88, 97, 132, 179–80, 320
    description of, 100
    JB on, 62, 69–74, 90–94, 98–100, 230
    JB's correspondence with, 69–70
    JB's meeting with, 43, 99–100
    JB's talks on, 43, 88, 89–90
    literary influences on, 91, 92
    symbology of, 60, 92
    works of, 52, 67, 70, 71, 73–74, 90, 92–93
Young, Mrs., 108
Yugoslav Writer's Union, 363

Zen Buddhism, 307
Zen Buddhism, Selected Writings, 307